The Political Thought

of Woodrow Wilson

THE AMERICAN HERITAGE SERIES

Oskar Piest, *Founder*

THE

American Heritage

Series

UNDER THE GENERAL EDITORSHIP OF

LEONARD W. LEVY AND ALFRED YOUNG

ʬ

The Political Thought

of Woodrow Wilson

EDITED BY

E. DAVID CRONON

The University of Wisconsin

THE BOBBS-MERRILL COMPANY, INC.
A Subsidiary of Howard W. Sams & Co., Inc.
PUBLISHERS • INDIANAPOLIS • NEW YORK • KANSAS CITY

The Political Thought

of Woodrow Wilson

Foreword

There should be no question for this generation as to the importance of Woodrow Wilson, whose presidency witnessed both the culmination of the progressive movement of the early twentieth century and the emergence of the United States as a world power in World War I. There is perhaps a need to justify a new anthology of his writings. His major speeches and state papers are hardly unknown and not difficult to locate. Some of his "classic" books and essays have been reprinted. Yet it is remarkable that no anthology has come to grips with the special problem that confronts the serious student of Wilson.

Early in his career as political scientist and historian Wilson wrote books and essays that presented a developed system of political thought. Throughout his active public career as campaigner, Governor of New Jersey, and President, he presented his opinions frequently in addresses and messages that to this day are models of eloquent rhetoric. Yet to claim that these formal expressions of "Wilsonian idealism" are the sum of the man's thought would be misleading. Wilson was a man of action as well as thought. He was also a man who would modify his position, sometimes drastically. What does one select to represent the "real" Woodrow Wilson?

Professor Cronon's solution to this problem has been to focus on Wilson's response to specific historic issues. He presents Wilson's opinions topically and, within each topic, in chronological sequence. Secondly, he matches Wilson's public pronouncements with his private letters. This, together with headnotes that demonstrate a sure grasp of the historic context, enables the reader to examine Wilson's thought in its specific setting and as it evolved.

With such an arrangement, Professor Cronon has also been able to illustrate the thesis about Wilson that he develops in his introductory analysis. While others have pondered whether Wilson in his domestic policy was a "conservative or a progressive," Professor Cronon sees him as "both, but in different proportions at various stages of his career." In the field of foreign policy the author sees him as "a curious blend of morality and practicality." And as a political leader, he reveals him as a man who thought much about the functioning of American political institutions yet failed to master them to achieve his goals.

This book is one of a series the aim of which is to provide the essential primary sources of the American experience, especially of American thought. The series, when completed, will constitute a documentary library of American history, filling a need long felt among scholars, students, libraries, and general readers for authoritative collections of original materials. Some volumes will illuminate the thought of significant individuals; some will deal with movements, and others will be organized around special themes. Many volumes will deal with the large number of subjects traditionally studied in American history and for which, surprisingly, there are no documentary anthologies; others will introduce contemporary subjects of increasing importance to scholars. The series aspires to maintain the high standards demanded of contemporary editing, providing authentic texts, intelligently and unobtrusively edited. It will have also the distinction of presenting pieces of substantial length that give the full character and flavor of the original. The series will be the most comprehensive and authoritative of its kind.

Alfred Young
Leonard W. Levy

Contents

PART I

WOODROW WILSON: A SELF-PORTRAIT

DOCUMENT 1

"The Profession I Chose Was Politics. . . ."

(Letter to Ellen Louise Axson, October 30, 1883)

1

DOCUMENT 6

"No Leaders, No Principles; No Principles, No Parties"

("Cabinet Government in the United States," 1879)

29

DOCUMENT 7

"Making Parties Responsible"

("Committee or Cabinet Government?" 1884)

53

The Nature of the Presidency

DOCUMENT 8

"The Unifying Force in Our Complex System,
the Leader Both of His Party and of the Nation"

(Constitutional Government in the United States, 1908)

61

DOCUMENT 9

The Length of Presidential Tenure

(Letter to A. Mitchell Palmer, February 5, 1913)

78

DOCUMENT 10

The Danger of an Interregnum

(Letter to Robert Lansing, November 5, 1916)

84

Administration: Theoretical and Practical
The Student of Administration

PART IV

THE NEW FREEDOM ENUNCIATED

PART V

THE NEW FREEDOM ENACTED

Immigration

Woman Suffrage

Economy in Government

The New Freedom Appraised

PART X

THE POLITICS OF PEACEMAKING

Introduction

I

Thomas Woodrow Wilson (he abandoned the first name after graduation from college) was born on December 28, 1856, in a Presbyterian manse at Staunton, Virginia. The birthplace was appropriate, for on both sides he came from Scottish stock that had deep roots in the Calvinist faith. His father, the Reverend Joseph Ruggles Wilson, was the son of an Ohio newspaper editor, and had been but seven years in his Staunton pulpit when Thomas Woodrow Wilson was born. The child's mother, Jessie Woodrow, came from a family that had produced a distinguished line of Presbyterian ministers and scholars. Both parents were deeply religious, and they raised their four children on a stern Calvinist fare of daily prayers, hymn singing, and Scripture study. The young Wilson grew up never doubting the existence of a personal God or the ultimate triumph of His will through the operation of an inflexible moral law.

Wilson's youth was spent in a succession of Presbyterian manses in the deep South during the harsh years of the Civil War and Reconstruction. Although Northern born and bred and the son of an abolitionist, the Reverend Dr. Wilson kept slaves. He agreed with his parishioners on the justice of secession, and served for a time as a chaplain in the Confederate Army. The family's commitment to the Lost Cause was something less than total, nevertheless. Both the Woodrows and the Wilsons were divided in spirit and place by the sectional conflict, and two of Dr. Wilson's

brothers were Union officers. Consequently young Tommie
Wilson grew up very much aware of the horrors of war but
without fully sharing the bitterness of defeat that afflicted
so many Southerners of his generation. As a young man he
could even tell a Virginia audience that the death of the
Confederacy had been as good for the South as for the
nation. In most respects, however, his outlook remained
distinctively Southern. He shared the upper-class Southerner's fierce loyalty to family, chivalrous view of women,
and paternalistic and condescending attitude toward the
Negro (See the present volume, Document 49). In later life
Wilson confessed that the only place in the world where
nothing had to be explained to him was the South.

Both Jessie and Joseph Wilson were well educated and
took an active interest in the intellectual development of
their children. Dr. Wilson liked to read aloud to the family
— Dickens, Scott, and other nineteenth-century authors —
and to raise current questions for stimulating table discussion. He insisted on precision in thought and expression,
often requiring young Tommie to put his ideas on paper so
that his logic and exposition could be ruthlessly dissected.
The father doubtless did much to develop the lean yet mov-
ingly expressive prose style that distinguished Woodrow
Wilson's writing and speaking in later years. Both parents
hoped their eldest son would follow his father into the
ministry. With this in mind they sent him first for a year at
Davidson College, a struggling Presbyterian school near
Charlotte, North Carolina, and then in 1875 sent him to
the more prominent Presbyterian College of New Jersey at
Princeton.

The four years as a Princeton undergraduate did much to
stimulate and shape Wilson's thought, although not in the
direction of the ministry. He was popular with his fellow
students and active in a variety of extracurricular affairs,
ranging from debate and journalism to athletics, and also

stood high in his class scholastically. He developed a keen interest in government and public affairs, and read *The Federalist* and such British political theorists as Burke, Bright, Macaulay, and — especially — Bagehot. He was fascinated by the leadership qualities of great men, publishing an article on Bismarck as a sophomore and another on Pitt in his senior year. He eagerly followed accounts of British parliamentary proceedings, and drew up a constitution for the Liberal Debating Club which was modeled on the parliamentary system. In his senior year he achieved a great triumph by publishing a long article, "Cabinet Government in the United States," in the *International Review*. In it the young scholar soberly analyzed the defects of Congress, noted the great power wielded by its often irresponsible committees and proposed that the executive branch be strengthened by giving cabinet members seats in Congress and the right to initiate legislation and take part in debate (See Document 6). This admiration for parliamentary government, and the desire to adapt some of its features to the American system, remained a lifelong characteristic of Wilson's thought.

After his graduation from Princeton in 1879 Wilson sought to pursue his interest in public affairs by means of a traditional legal career. Some months of study at the University of Virginia Law School, and even more a winter of unrewarding practice in Atlanta in 1882, convinced him that his talents and interests lay outside the practice of law. Reluctantly, for the move would probably mean the end of any hope for an active political career, Wilson decided to prepare himself for a life of teaching and scholarship. He would have to content himself with the study rather than the practice of politics; if he would influence men it must be through his pen or his lectures rather than on the stump or in legislative debate (See Documents 1 and 2). In the fall of 1883, therefore, at the rather advanced age of twenty-six, Wilson enrolled in the new but already prestigious Johns Hopkins University at Baltimore for graduate work in history and political science.

Johns Hopkins marked another important turning-point in Wilson's life. He persuaded his major professor, the eminent historian Herbert Baxter Adams, to let him study contemporary American government rather than what Wilson regarded as Adams' dull excursions into the ancient roots of political institutions. The result was a brilliant and widely acclaimed doctoral dissertation that was published as a book, *Congressional Government,* in 1885, even before Wilson received the Ph.D. degree. The book pursued a theme Wilson had been developing since Princeton: the dangerous expansion of the power of Congress, a subject dear to the hearts of Southerners in the period of Radical Reconstruction (See Documents 6 and 7). Ironically for one who would later develop to the fullest extent the potentialities of the White House for legislative and popular leadership, Wilson in this work virtually wrote off the President as a nonentity.

In the fall of 1885 Woodrow Wilson also launched his academic career, and for the first time became financially self-supporting, as an associate professor of history at the brand-new Bryn Mawr College in Pennsylvania. The new professor found his income timely, for the previous June he had married Ellen Louise Axson, a native of Georgia and like himself the child of a Presbyterian clergyman. Ellen Wilson was a woman of beauty and intelligence, whose serene confidence in her husband would provide a necessary steadying influence on his career.

Wilson's rise up the academic ladder was swift. In 1888 he moved to a professorship at Wesleyan University in Connecticut, where he reveled in the chance to teach men instead of women, and two years later he joyously accepted a call to be professor of jurisprudence and political economy at his beloved Princeton. There his carefully polished and forensically brilliant lectures soon made him one of the most popular teachers. His large lecture hall was jammed to capacity whenever he rose to speak. To stave off a series of efforts to lure their star professor to other institutions, the Princeton trustees were soon obliged to raise his salary above that of any other faculty member and to supplement it further with a fund raised by admiring alumni. Meanwhile, Wilson's writing and his lectures around the country were bringing him a growing reputation as an informed and forceful spokesman on public affairs.

In politics Wilson was by inheritance and inclination a Jeffersonian states'-rights Democrat. He feared the concentration of power, whether in private or governmental hands, and preferred to leave authority widely dispersed among local and state governments rather than have it centralized in Washington. He heartily agreed with his party's doctrine that the protective tariff was an iniquity whose effect was to tax the great bulk of the nation for the benefit of the industrial interests of the Northeast. Indeed, as early as 1882, as a fledgling lawyer in Atlanta, he had denounced the principle of protection before the United States Tariff Commission (See Document 40). The high-tariff policy of the Republican Party, Wilson believed, stifled competition, fostered trusts, and severely limited the economic opportunities of farmers and small business-men.

But to Wilson at this time the tariff was only one example of unwise and dangerous governmental intervention in economic affairs. He agreed with Jefferson that governments ought to keep to a bare minimum their restraints upon the individual. In his first book, *Congressional Government*, Wilson quoted with approval William Graham Sumner's warning that civil institutions should "not alter the play of the economic forces."[1] Wilson, who was never much interested in economics, would only grudgingly and uncertainly move away from his early faith in the doctrine of *laissez faire.* In the nineties his conservative economic views and his reverence for law and order led him to oppose the Populists and the Democratic radicals led by William Jennings Bryan. He voted the Gold Democratic ticket in 1896, and thereafter worked to restore the party to sound leadership (See Documents 22-29).

Wilson's great popularity as a teacher, and his growing national reputation—in the dozen years after returning to Princeton he published nine books and thirty-five articles, besides speaking extensively to groups across the country—led the Princeton trustees to bestow upon him their highest honor. In 1902 they voted unanimously to make him the first lay president in Princeton's history. Wilson accepted with delight (he had chafed under the lax and indecisive leadership of outgoing president Francis L. Patton), and promptly set out to make Princeton one of the great universities of the land.

The eight years as president of Princeton brought Woodrow Wilson notable triumphs as well as humiliating failures, and revealed both his bold and imaginative leadership and his curious inability to compromise in order to stave off defeat. The new president quickly overhauled Princeton's antiquated administrative structure, launched an impressive building program, and revised the cluttered curriculum. "I am not going to propose that we compel the undergraduates to work all the time," he said, "but I am going to propose that we make the undergraduates want to work all the time."[2] Wilson's most significant reform was

---

[1] Woodrow Wilson, *Congressional Government: a Study in American Politics* (4th ed.; Boston: Houghton Mifflin Company, 1887), p. 296.

[2] Woodrow Wilson, "Princeton Ideals," December 9, 1902, in *The Public Papers of Woodrow Wilson,* ed. Ray Stannard Baker and William E. Dodd (New York: Harper & Brothers, 1925), I, 468.

the preceptorial system of instruction, under which students were taught in small groups by a carefully selected body of young scholars whom the president personally recruited. Within a remarkably brief period Wilson had made Princeton probably the most exciting of American campuses and had won a name as one of the great educational reformers of his time.

There was, unfortunately, a darker side to Wilson's presidency at Princeton. Several of his later proposals — particularly his plan to abolish the upper-class eating clubs and his desire to make the Graduate School an integral part of the university community — provoked mounting opposition from some of the faculty and trustees and a vocal segment of the alumni. Proud and strong-willed, sensitive to criticism, Wilson when faced with defeat revealed an inflexibility and Scottish stubbornness that sadly undercut his once-firm leadership. He was unable to admit that his opponents might have valid arguments and was unwilling to concede that they might also share his love for Princeton. Allowing himself to break with close friends, he attributed mean and sordid motives to them. Characteristically, he saw his own stand as a great moral crusade for democracy against the selfish forces of privilege. By 1910, when Wilson resigned to run for governor of New Jersey, his position at Princeton had become untenable, and a great many of the faculty and trustees were relieved to see him go.

Wilson's decision to enter politics at the age of fifty-three was not entirely a product of his difficulties at Princeton. He had never really abandoned his youthful dream of a political career. He still yearned to apply first-hand his ideas of government. Conditions in New Jersey, moreover, were ripe for new political leadership. For several years Wilson's national stature, his forensic talents, and especially his conservative political views had attracted the attention of some prominent old-guard Democrats.

Chief among these was Colonel George Harvey of *Harper's Weekly*, who hoped through Wilson to rout the Bryanite wing and restore the Democratic Party to sound doctrine. Wilson at this time fully shared Colonel Harvey's distaste for Bryan. In an indiscreet 1907 letter—which would come back to haunt him—Wilson had expressed the wish that Bryan might be knocked "once for all into a cocked hat" (See Document 29).

Harvey managed to persuade the somewhat dubious boss of the New Jersey Democratic organization, James Smith, Jr., that the scholarly president of Princeton would make an ideal gubernatorial candidate. Smith, who recognized the need to improve his party's tarnished image in the state, first satisfied himself that Wilson represented no threat to his control. Then he forced the nomination through a pliant convention—much to the unhappiness of the minority of Democratic reformers, who saw Wilson as simply another machine candidate. Once on the stump, however, Wilson was forced to grapple with the issues that had been agitating progressives for more than a decade. Gradually he shifted ground, until by Election Day he was campaigning as a wholehearted reformer, denouncing the very boss-system to which he owed his nomination (See Document 30). The result was an impressive 50,000-vote majority, and Wilson's election as New Jersey's first Democratic governor in a generation.

Woodrow Wilson's seemingly abrupt conversion to progressivism during the 1910 gubernatorial campaign doubtless contained elements of expediency. He was enough of a student of politics to know that he could not be elected without the votes of the independents and of the progressives of both parties. Yet expediency alone is too simple an explanation. There had always been several strands to Wilson's political thought, all reinforced by his iron Calvinist morality. His study of constitutional history had led him to respect the law and the orderly development of society and to distrust radical change. At the same time, he revered democracy and believed passionately in the worth and dignity of the individual. Except for his early interest in tariff policy, he had always been more concerned with the political than the economic man; only belatedly had he begun to wrestle with the problem of the enormous growth and concentration of economic power in the United States since the Civil War. His early commitment to *laissez faire* economics made him fear government regulation, yet he could not deny the obvious evils that had accompanied industrialism: the ruthless destruction of competition and economic opportunity, the often brutal treatment of an oppressed working class, the flagrant disregard of public welfare and safety, and the cynical corruption of government. Forced by suspicious New Jersey progressives to take a stand on specific reforms, Wilson found himself gradually and sincerely coming to agree with them. And the way had been prepared by Wilson's recent unhappy battles at Princeton, against what he regarded as the forces of wealth and privilege.

Never one to enlist in a crusade halfway, Wilson now began to see himself as the leader of the progressive forces in New Jersey and, ultimately, the nation. He adroitly seized control of the state party from the surprised bosses, and used consummate political skill to maneuver a sweeping program of reform through a reluctant legislature. The program included a corrupt-practices law, strict regulation of railroads and public utilities, a direct primary, and an employers'-liability act (See Documents 31 and 32). Within a matter of months New Jersey had moved from one of the worst to one of the best governed states in the union, and Wilson had emerged as a leading progressive contender for the Democratic Presidential nomination in 1912 (See Documents 33 and 34). At the Baltimore nominating convention, Wilson's candidacy got off to a slow start. But with the aid of timely support from William Jennings Bryan (of whom Wilson no longer held a low opinion), the onetime scholar emerged with the coveted prize on the forty-sixth ballot. Control of the party was firmly in the hands of its progressive wing, and Wilson had managed to gain the nomination without making damaging concessions or disrupting party unity. Both points were important, for the majority Republican Party was hopelessly split between its conservative wing, led by President William Howard Taft, and an insurgent faction that had bolted to form a new Progressive Party under the leadership of former President Theodore Roosevelt.

The campaign that followed was the most significant in more than a generation. Taft, animated chiefly by a desire to frustrate Roosevelt's ambitions, kept his activity to a minimum. Roosevelt and Wilson, however, engaged in a spirited debate over the nature and future course of the progressive movement. Roosevelt was running on a platform of advanced social reform; he called his program the New Nationalism and advocated a broad expansion of federal regulatory powers. He argued frankly that big business was a fact of modern industrial life and that what was required was suitable regulation by the national government to protect the public interest. Large corporations, perhaps even some monopolies, were inevitable under industrialism, he said, and their size alone need not be feared so long as the government kept a watchful eye on their activities. Wilson, on the other hand, called for a New Freedom in economic affairs, a restoration of the competition that had been stifled by the new industrial trusts. Still wary of excessive governmental interference, he was confident that competition would have a curative value once the trusts had been smashed. Predictably, he advocated a lower tariff and stricter enforcement of the antitrust law. While he did not reject out of hand Roosevelt's proposal of

a federal trade commission, he insisted that it must not
simply put a stamp of approval upon monopolies (See
Documents 35–39, and 45).

Election Day, November 5, brought an overwhelming
mandate for progressivism, for between them Wilson and
Roosevelt received better than two-thirds of the votes cast.
Wilson won a landslide in the Electoral College—435
votes to Roosevelt's 88 and Taft's 8. His popular vote was
less impressive, however; only a little more than six million, out of nearly fifteen million, it was less than Bryan
had polled in any of his three campaigns. Clearly the Democrats were still a minority party. They did have control of
Congress, but such a tenuous control that all of Wilson's
legislative and administrative skill would be required to
accomplish his program.

Once in the White House, Wilson moved swiftly and
confidently to assert his leadership. His actual political
experience was meager—a scant but impressive two years
as governor—but he had been in training for the Presidency most of his life. He had once written off the executive in the face of irresponsible Congressional power, but
now the potential of the White House seemed virtually
limitless to him. "The President," Wilson had declared
in 1908 after observing Theodore Roosevelt in action, "is at
liberty, both in law and conscience, to be as big a man as
he can. . . . His office is anything he has the sagacity and
force to make it" (See Document 8). Characteristically, one
of his first acts was to call Congress into special session,
and when the lawmakers assembled he went dramatically
to Capitol Hill to urge an end to the high protective tariff
system. Ever since Jefferson's day Presidents had sent
their messages to be read by a clerk, but Wilson wanted to
emphasize forcibly his great interest in tariff reform as well
as his desire to establish a close working relationship with
the legislative branch (See Document 41).

The President's address to Congress was only the first of

a number of innovations designed to strengthen the executive's role in the legislative process. Ever mindful of the
unique powers of the British prime minister, Wilson
sought to establish as never before the position of the
President as leader of both his party and the nation. He
conferred repeatedly with Congressional leaders, both at
the White House and in the hitherto little-used President's
Room at the Capitol. He had a special telephone line installed so that he could reach party leaders quickly and
directly. Always he stressed the importance of the party
caucus and party loyalty; Democrats might freely differ
and debate an issue within the caucus, he said, but they
must loyally close ranks when the majority had determined the party's course (See Documents 18 and 19).
When, owing to the activities of a powerful protectionist
lobby, the tariff bill seemed in jeopardy in the Senate,
Wilson appealed to the country at large to rescue the
measure (See Document 43). In the end the combination
of Presidential eloquence, persuasion, and pressure
achieved the first significant tariff reduction since the Civil
War. And the new law included (for the purpose of making
up the lost revenue) another important progressive reform—the first graduated income tax under the recently
adopted Sixteenth Amendment.

Even before Congress had completed its work on the
tariff, Wilson called upon the lawmakers to deal with an
even knottier and more complex problem. This was the
reform of the country's banking and currency system (See
Document 44). Aside from a conviction that the chaotic
and inelastic banking structure must be reorganized, the
President at first had no firm views on the best method for
accomplishing the reform. He insisted, however, that the
federal government must have a voice in the operation of
any system of reserve banks; and in time he was persuaded that the government alone must issue currency. The

Federal Reserve Act of December 23, 1913, was by all odds the most important domestic reform of the Wilson administration, and it was largely the result of the President's skillful leadership of Congress. The measure, thoroughly in accord with Wilson's progressive thought, retained private operation of the banking system at the local level yet provided public control at the top through a government-appointed Federal Reserve Board. The act also included the first national economic stabilizers—though their significance was as yet scarcely realized—consisting of centralized control over discount rates, flexible bank reserves, and an elastic currency issued solely by the Treasury.

The third major part of Wilson's New Freedom program to restore competition to the economy was reform of the antitrust law (See Document 46). He had declared many times his faith that businessmen as a group were basically honest and needed only to be freed from the stifling evils of unfair and monopolistic competition, which stemmed, he believed, from misguided tariff policy and the concentration and misuse of banking capital. Accordingly, he favored a series of proposals, soon combined into the Clayton bill in the House, to prohibit a long list of unfair trade practices, including interlocking directorates and stock ownership. Many progressives, however, protested that this approach was too naïve and cumbersome to deal with the problem effectively, that unscrupulous businessmen and their high-priced legal advisers could always devise ways to get around the law faster than Congress could act to close the loopholes. Instead, the progressives favored a trade commission to serve as a constant watchdog over business practices, with the power to order an offender to cease any activities the commission deemed unfair or in restraint of trade. Wilson had not rejected this proposal when it was advanced by Roosevelt in the 1912 campaign, but he had insisted that such a commission must be dedicated to the maintenance of genuine competition and must not merely legalize existing monopolies (See Document 45). Now he wavered, under the pressure of criticism of the Clayton bill by progressives whom he respected. Encouraged by his expert adviser on the subject, Louis D. Brandeis, Wilson finally threw his influence behind a bill to establish a strong federal trade commission, with the power to investigate business practices and to issue cease-and-desist orders against unfair or monopolistic conduct. As before, Congress responded to his leadership, and in the fall of 1914 passed both the Federal Trade Commission measure and a somewhat watered-down Clayton Act.

Wilson now considered the New Freedom virtually complete. To the surprise of some progressives, he suggested that it was time to pause and allow the new reforms to have their effect (See Document 54). The President's acceptance of government control over banking and currency, and—even more—his acceptance of a strong trade commission showed how far he had moved toward Theodore Roosevelt's New Nationalism ideas. In 1915 and 1916, prodded by more advanced progressives, he moved still farther. No doubt partly to attract the support of Roosevelt's followers in the coming Presidential campaign, but also partly because he had come sincerely to believe in the need for more reform, Wilson persuaded Congress to adopt a variety of social-justice measures. These were drawn in part from the Bull Moose platform of 1912, and included a ban on child labor (a measure subsequently nullified by the courts), an eight-hour day for railroad workers, an act improving the working conditions of American seamen, workmen's compensation for federal employees, greater self-government for the Philippines, a system of federal farm-loan banks to expand rural credit, and a tariff commission to provide expert information on tariff rates (See Document 55).

In all this Wilson revealed—as he had in 1910—a capacity to modify his ideas and enlarge his program while at the same time shrewdly undercutting his opposition. By the 1916 campaign his credentials as the leader of the progressive forces in the country were virtually unchallengeable, a fact made clear by Roosevelt's unwillingness to revive the nearly dead Bull Moose. Although the peace issue helped Wilson achieve his narrow victory over the Republican candidate, Charles Evans Hughes, his gain of nearly three million votes over 1912 showed that he had attracted a sizable number of progressive Republicans and independents who had followed Roosevelt in 1912. The realignment of the two major parties along progressive and conservative lines, foreshadowed in 1912, was now more evident. It would be an important part of the Wilsonian legacy.

But by this time the President's chief concern was with foreign rather than domestic policy. Ironically, upon entering the White House Wilson had expressed the hope that his administration might avoid foreign crises, for although he had vacationed abroad several times he had never paid much attention to foreign affairs. Even before the outbreak of the First World War in 1914, however, the President discovered that his most difficult and perplexing problems were of foreign origin. He also quickly learned, to his dismay, that his influence in this realm was far less pervasive and effective than it was in his dealings with party leaders in Congress.

Wilson and his first Secretary of State, William Jennings Bryan, were equally inexperienced and ill-informed in foreign affairs, but they shared certain convictions about the role of the United States in the world. Though not pacifists, both abhorred war and disapproved of the use of force in settling international disputes; both were suspicious of the imperialist powers and rather embarrassed by America's own colonial dependencies; both wished to civilize and uplift the world; and, as devout Presbyterians, both believed that the proper basis for American foreign policy was simple Christian morality. Wilson and Bryan were not oblivious to the utility of overseas markets and investments, or to the strategic importance of such possessions as the nearly completed Panama Canal, but from the first they sought to base their diplomacy on moral considerations. They proclaimed repeatedly that the United States sought neither additional territory nor selfish advantage in its dealings with its neighbors (See Documents 56, 59, and 60). Thus one of Wilson's first acts as President was to inform a group of American bankers that they could no longer rely on State Department support for their participation in an international loan to China, because the terms of the loan seemed unjust and clearly against the best interests of the Chinese (See Document 57). With Wilson's blessing, Bryan immediately launched a campaign to minimize the danger of war through a series of cooling-off treaties for the conciliation of disputes. Unlike the balance-of-power or dollar diplomacy of the preceding administrations, Wilsonian diplomacy had morality as its trademark. The morality was sometimes haphazardly and inconsistently applied, but it was always proclaimed with missionary fervor.

Unfortunately, Wilson's goal of a stable and peaceful world of justice and law was easier to describe than to attain, especially through unilateral American action. Nor was it always easy to sort out conflicting rights and goals. Even in the area where American power was pre-eminent—Central America and the Caribbean—the new moral diplomacy quickly ran into trouble. Determined to help the peoples of these small countries establish stable, democratic regimes, and determined to protect them from foreign dangers (and, if necessary, from themselves), Wilson intervened on an unprecedented scale (See Documents 61–64). Latin Americans, noting the proximity of the Panama Canal, were skeptical of the President's moral impulses in his repeated interference in Nicaraguan affairs and his sending of military forces to restore order in Haiti and the Dominican Republic. Mexico was a much tougher problem, and it provided a jarring awakening to the difficulty of trying to bring order out of revolutionary chaos, of seeking to lead an unwilling, alien people who suspected Wilson's motives and fiercely resented his meddling. Prodded by Americans whose interests were adversely affected by the violence and social change of the Mexican Revolution, yet resolved to look out for the needs and aspirations of the submerged Mexican masses, the President sought to influence developments he neither fully understood nor could hope to control (See Documents 65–69). His well-intentioned but disastrous interference in Mexican affairs probably helped to save the Revolution from the determined assaults of its old-regime opponents, but in the process Wilson reaped a harvest of distrust and bitterness that would plague Mexican-American relations for the next generation. The rationale of the new moral imperialism might be different, but its tools and its results seemed to be much the same as those of the older variety.

When war broke out in Europe, in August 1914, far more vexing and complicated problems loomed. From the bedside of his dying wife the distraught President drafted the proclamation of neutrality and called upon the American people to be impartial in thought as well as deed (See Document 70). He recalled wryly that the last President obliged to guard American neutral rights in a general European war had been the only other Princetonian elected to the White House, James Madison, and his effort had ended in failure and a nearly disastrous war. In this great world crisis Wilson characteristically saw a new moral role for the United States. As the most important and powerful neutral nation it must preserve neutral rights for all of the non-warring world; at the same time it must actively seek an end to the senseless carnage (See Documents 71 and 72).

Wilson called for impartiality, but at heart—like many Americans—he sympathized with the Allies, whose culture and political institutions he admired. Almost from the first the United States adopted policies that tended to aid the Allied cause. In Wilson's defense it must be noted that it was impossible for the United States to be truly impartial; given the immense American economic power, any policy, even one of complete inaction, was bound to favor one side or the other. At Secretary Bryan's urging the President discouraged loans by American bankers to the belligerents, though this was a well-established neutral right—but he reversed himself in 1915, when the Allies began to run out of cash to finance their profitable war orders. Similarly, he sought at first to prevent the export of certain weapons, notably submarines, the use of which he disapproved (See Document 73). At the same time he defended the traditional right of neutrals to trade with any and all belligerents in wartime, though in this war such trade was bound to be one-sided because British control of the seas denied the Central Powers access to the American market. Wilson was increasingly vexed over the measures taken by the Allies to tighten the economic blockade against their foes, but he could never bring himself to propose retaliation with an embargo, a weapon which had failed in Jefferson's day but which would have had real effect in Wilson's. Instead, he in effect acquiesced in the Allied violations of American rights (See Documents 74–77).

When the Germans, on the other hand, used submarines

to combat the increasing flow of American war materials to their foes, the President sternly denounced them for endangering American citizens and ships on the high seas. Curiously, he failed to recognize that if the British use of a comparable weapon, the ocean minefield, did not occasion similar losses of American lives and property it was simply because of the manner in which he had defined the issues. The United States accorded at least grudging recognition to the Allied blockade, while wholly denying the validity of the German war zone around the British Isles. The result was inevitable—a series of ominous diplomatic clashes with Berlin, beginning in 1915, in which United States' protests gained only temporary success (See Documents 78–82). When, early in 1917, the Germans concluded that their best hope of victory lay in a resumption of unrestricted submarine warfare regardless of American sensibilities, Wilson, like Madison before him, found it impossible to protect neutral rights as he had defined them short of war (See Documents 83 and 84).

While contending for neutral rights, the President also assumed the role of honest broker in seeking an end to the conflict in Europe. He believed the only hope for an enduring peace lay in securing an impartial settlement before either side won decisively. Twice he sent his trusted adviser, Colonel Edward M. House, to explore with the belligerent governments the possibility of a negotiated peace (See Document 107). But House discovered that neither side was prepared to abandon the hope of sharing in the spoils of an all-out victory. To Wilson's annoyance even the British, with whom he and Colonel House worked closely on one peace plan, never considered the time ripe to launch a peace offensive.

Shortly after his re-election, therefore, the President issued a peace appeal to the belligerents on his own initiative. Calling for a "peace without victory," he urged a

negotiated settlement between equals, with no annexations or indemnities but with reduction of armaments,
freedom of the seas, and self-determination for captive
peoples. Such a peace, he said, should be guaranteed by
all the civilized nations of the world. "I would fain believe," Wilson declared solemnly, "that I am speaking for
the silent mass of mankind everywhere" (See Document
108).

Germany's response came a few days later, with the
resumption of unrestricted submarine warfare (See Document 83). The President's position as neutral and mediator
was now untenable, though for two months he experi-
mented with an unsatisfactory armed neutrality (See Documents 89 and 90). Sadly and reluctantly, on April 2, 1917,
he went before a special session of Congress to request a
declaration of war (See Document 84). Trapped by circumstances at least partly of his own making, Wilson was quite
aware of the double irony of his position: the United States
was in effect fighting for the right to be neutral, and American entry into the war would very likely make possible
the dictated peace settlement that Wilson had hoped to
avoid.

Peace-minded himself, Wilson had only belatedly begun
to prepare the nation for war, and as a result the United
States was poorly equipped to play a major role on the
European battlefields (See Documents 85–88). Yet friend
and foe alike were amazed at the speed with which the
American nation raised, trained, equipped, and transport-
ed to France a vast army. For the most part the President
was content to leave military decisions to the professionals. He fully supported his stubborn commander in
France, General John J. Pershing, on the issue of a separate identity for the American Expeditionary Force (See
Document 104). He was impatient, however, at the failure
of the Allied navies to contain the deadly submarine menace (See Documents 105 and 106).

Granted vastly increased powers by Congress, Wilson had ample scope to develop his ideas of dynamic executive leadership. In the process, he created for future chief executives both the precedents and the tools for action in time of grave national emergency. Wilson drew heavily upon the ideology of the progressive moment in mobilizing the nation's resources for war (See Document 91). A selective-service act smoothly raised the nearly three million men required for the Army, in an operation that stressed two progressive goals: maximum efficiency in utilizing the country's skills, and the equal obligation of all citizens to serve where needed (See Document 92). Steeply graduated income, corporation, and excess-profits taxes sought to spread the war costs equitably on the basis of ability to pay. Wilson relied wherever possible on exhortation and voluntary compliance. He made drastic use of his war powers only if he considered this necessary, as when he took over the railroads or threatened to draft striking munitions workers (See Documents 93–100).

Even the ill-starred government propaganda agency, George Creel's zealous Committee on Public Information, was intended to function within the progressive tradition, informing the citizenry as to war aims and promoting security through voluntary censorship. In practice, however the Committee's distortions and oversimplifications brought a vigilante conformity rather than enlightenment. This, and the general sorry record of civil-liberties violations during the war—anticipated but not countermanded by Wilson—constitute the greatest blot on the President's otherwise impressive wartime leadership (See Documents 101–103).

While waging war Wilson also gave a great deal of thought to the coming peace settlement. He knew that the war-weary, vengeful Allies could not be trusted to draft peace terms with tolerance and impartial justice—the only approach that might achieve an enduring settlement. Under the circumstances the United States would have to provide the moral leadership to secure a stable postwar world order (See Documents 112–114). Accordingly, the President established The Inquiry, a group of scholars and experts charged (under the direction of the ubiquitous Colonel House) with exploring and collecting data on every possible question that might come before the peace conference.

Wilson meanwhile began to reveal the broad outlines of his peace program. In his famous Fourteen Points address to Congress on January 8, 1918, he laid down a series of specific and general objectives. Subsequently refined and expanded, his proposals included open diplomacy, freedom of the seas and of trade, reduction of armaments, impartial adjustment of colonial claims, self-determination for subject nationality groups—and, most important of all, a League of Nations to implement the peace settlement and to provide collective security for all nations (See Documents 115 and 116).

Wilson's Fourteen Points flew in the face of many of the secret war aims of the Allied governments, but the President was aiming his liberal peace program at the people of the world. He was confident that the program's great and immediate popularity would enable him to prevail at the peace table. When in the fall of 1918 the beaten Germans decided to end the war, it was to Wilson they turned. He then used great skill in negotiating with both the foe and his Allies, obtaining general commitments to his Fourteen Points before assenting to an ironclad armistice on November 11 (See Document 117).

Not daring to trust his peace vision to subordinates, the President determined to attend the peace conference himself (See Documents 118 and 119). His critics attributed the decision to conceit, and grumbled at this further shattering of precedent. Despite Wilson's lofty dedication, the odds against success were formidable. And the President himself was at least partly responsible for some of the obstacles. At Paris he would be only one among several prominent Allied leaders. The other Allied nations had suffered far more grievous losses than had the United States, yet until the pre-armistice negotiations Wilson had never tried very hard to commit the Allies to his generous peace aims. Wilson's stern Calvinist conscience would not permit him to bargain on peace terms when his cards were the strongest, before the United States entered the war. Later, when the Allies were desperately calling for more men and supplies, Wilson still could not bring himself to take advantage of their extremity, even for a high-minded *quid pro quo*. Characteristically he put his faith in an aroused world opinion; if that should fail, he counted on America's ability to apply some judicious postwar economic pressure.

Wilson's failure to keep in mind some elementary facts of American political life is less easily explained. Shortly before the armistice, he unwisely yielded to the pleas of worried Democrats and intervened in the off-year elections. Speaking of these elections — needlessly — in terms of a vote of confidence in his leadership, he asked the voters to strengthen his hand by returning a Democratic Congress (See Document 125). When instead the Republicans won narrow control of both houses, Wilson's highly vocal G.O.P. critics, led by the embittered Theodore Roosevelt, were able to charge that the President had been repudiated by the electorate and could no longer speak for the nation.

Another costly error was Wilson's failure to develop strong bipartisan support for his idealistic peace aims. Facing a hostile new Congress in which the Senate would be controlled by his archenemy, Henry Cabot Lodge, Wilson curiously neglected to name either a Senator or a prominent Republican to the American delegation to the peace conference, although as a long-time student of government he could scarcely have forgotten the Senate's crucial role in the treaty-making process. The President's earlier successes as legislative and party leader probably made him less mindful of the need for bipartisan statesmanship under the changed circumstances. Nor could he believe, apparently, that the American people would permit any sabotage of his noble vision of a new world order.

At Paris Wilson's austere presence dominated the peace conference. Sure of his objectives, well-informed even on obscure points, shrewdly combining lofty eloquence with a variety of unspiritual pressures, he worked tirelessly for a just, impartial settlement. Yet when the completed treaty was handed to the protesting Germans in May of 1919, it was clear that in many respects it fell far short of Wilson's bright hopes (See Documents 123 and 124). During the months of sharp conference-bargaining he had accepted a number of damaging compromises — Shantung, reparations, the war-guilt clause — that scarcely accorded with the spirit of his Fourteen Points.

There were a number of reasons for Wilson's failure to achieve all his objectives at Paris. He was, after all, only one of several major leaders at the conference, each of whom had his own ideas, national interest, and political future to pursue. Inevitably, the American President had to compromise with his colleagues on occasion. Another difficulty was that Wilson's idealistic Fourteen Points, while suitable as a general guide, were not readily applicable to some of the most perplexing problems before the conference. Some questions cut across several conflicting Points; other matters could be handled only on the basis of political decisions by the Big Four to which no amount of research by The Inquiry was relevant.

Still, it was largely Wilson's vigilance and diplomatic

skill that kept the treaty from being even more a vehicle of hatred and revenge. He was well aware of its imperfections, but he was ready to accept them in order to get his prime objective—the League of Nations. The League was central to Wilson's postwar scheme. He largely drafted the League Covenant (an appropriate Presbyterian term) and saw that it was adopted early in the conference proceedings (See Documents 120–122). At his insistence the new world organization was given a major role in executing the peace settlements. He contended that only through the League of Nations could the future peace of the world be assured. Through it, nations large and small would find security from aggression; as wartime passions cooled, moreover, it would provide the machinery to rectify any errors of the peace conference.

Back in the United States, Wilson faced the greatest test of his political career. The Republicans who controlled the Senate were determined that in the coming Presidential campaign the Democrats should not have the sole credit for making peace in Europe. They were primed to give the treaty a hostile reception. Belatedly and halfheartedly, the President had begun a campaign to attract bipartisan support for his handiwork. On a brief trip back to the United States in February he had invited Congressional leaders to confer with him about the treaty (See Document 126), though the effect of this conciliatory gesture was largely vitiated by his intemperate denunciation of his critics in a speech on the eve of his return to Paris (See Document 127). At the urging of William Howard Taft, Elihu Root, and other pro-League Republicans, he had with some difficulty effected revisions of the Covenant to recognize such special American interests as the Monroe Doctrine.

The President's address to the Senate on July 10, in which he presented the treaty for consideration, was impressive in its moving eloquence. But it failed utterly to convert the diehard Republican opposition, whose leaders were bent on attaching crippling reservations to the League Covenant (See Document 128). Privately Wilson told his lieutenants that he might accept a few interpretive reservations to the treaty, but said it would be suicidal to attach needless and mischievous substantive reservations that would reopen questions so painstakingly settled at Paris. To counteract the shrewd delaying tactics of Senator Lodge, the President invited wavering Republican lawmakers to the White House and there sought to quiet their doubts by patiently and carefully explaining the limitations on the powers of the new world organization (See Document 129). But publicity given these White House conferences tended to embarrass the Republican participants, and perhaps even to harden their partisan attitudes.

Convinced finally that he could accomplish little by his efforts to reason with the opposition, and unwilling to consider any substantial compromise, Wilson determined to take his case to the people, who had so often sustained him in the past. His worried second wife and his physician warned the President against overtaxing his frail body, but he rejected the warnings and, early in September, set out on an ambitious tour of the West. In the next three weeks he traveled eight thousand miles and delivered some thirty-seven speeches. Indifferently received at first, as the trip progressed Wilson drew ever more enthusiastic crowds (See Documents 130–133). His confidence grew; he felt that once the people understood what was at stake they would once again rally to his side against his blindly partisan foes in the Senate. "Nothing less depends upon this decision . . ." he told a cheering, overflow crowd at Pueblo, Colorado, on September 25, "nothing less than the liberation and salvation of the world. . . . We have accepted that truth and we are going to be led by it, and it is going to lead us, and through us the world, out into pastures of quietness and peace such as the world never dreamed of before" (See Document 134). This was his last major address to the American people, for that night as his train sped toward Wichita the President collapsed and his doctor ordered an immediate return to Washington. A week later at the White House Wilson was struck down by a thrombosis that left him helpless, paralyzed on the left side of his face and body. For days his very life was at stake, and for the next six months he was pitifully out of touch with affairs of state.

The President's collapse left the pro-League forces leaderless and dispirited. But the stricken prophet, isolated and out of touch with political realities, could not bring himself to believe that his great dream of American leadership in the League of Nations might actually founder on the rocks of partisanship. Twice the divided Senate voted on the peace treaty; twice Wilson sent word to his followers to stand fast against any significant compromise (See Documents 135–138). After the second adverse vote, however, even the President had to concede the demise of his peace project. "It is dead," he told his cabinet bitterly, gesturing toward the corner, "and lies over there. Every morning I put flowers on its grave."[3]

Wilson clung to the belief that the 1920 Presidential election would provide "a great and solemn referendum" on the treaty, though as a political scientist and former candidate he should have foreseen the difficulty of making any one issue central in a national campaign (See Document 139). Harding's landslide victory dashed the President's hopes. He could see now that not merely his partisan foes in Congress but also the great majority of the people had rejected his leadership. Nevertheless, he re-

---

[3]*The Cabinet Diaries of Josephus Daniels, 1913–1921*, ed. E. David Cronon (Lincoln, Neb.: University of Nebraska Press, 1963), p. 520.

mained confident that some day the nation would recognize the essential truth of his vision (See Document 140). "I am not one of those that have the least anxiety about the triumph of the principles I have stood for," he told a hushed crowd outside his Washington home, on Armistice Day of 1923, less than three months before his death on February 3, 1924. "I have seen fools resist Providence before, and I have seen their destruction, as will come upon these again, utter destruction and contempt. That we shall prevail is as sure as that God reigns."[4]

II

Few American Presidents have presented more difficult problems of interpretation than Woodrow Wilson. Like his contemporaries, Wilson's biographers have puzzled over the seeming expediency of his political shifts, have probed his eloquent but sometimes confusing rhetoric to try to determine exactly what he thought on key issues, and have wondered at the paradox of the flowering of progressive reform under the leadership of a President with strong conservative instincts. Whether to call Wilson a conservative or a progressive is a problem that has perplexed historians as much as it troubled Wilson's contemporaries. The truth is that Wilson was both—but in different proportions at various stages of his career. He was also an exceedingly complex and strong-willed personality, one whom few of his associates ever felt they knew intimately, no matter how much they admired or even revered his leadership.

Most of Wilson's early ideas and allegiances were thor-

---

[4]Edith Bolling Wilson, *My Memoir* (Indianapolis, Ind.: The Bobbs-Merrill Company, Inc., 1938), p. 356.

oughly conservative. Born in Virginia, reared in the Georgia ravished by Sherman on his march to the sea, he
shared Jefferson's fear of the vast coercive power of the
state over the lives and property of its citizens. As a Jeffersonian he was suspicious of centralized government and
stressed the equality and natural rights of the individual.
Wilson's early heroes were men like John Bright and
Richard Cobden, who sought to free British commerce
from the deadening restraints of mercantilism. Like the
Manchester liberals, Wilson had great faith in the power
of competition to insure that business and other economic interest groups would behave in socially constructive ways. His view of society was at least moderately
social-Darwinist, for his study of the past convinced him
that orderly change — the only kind he considered desirable
— came slowly, and only after popular acceptance of the
need for reform. He believed that the successful statesman
must in large part be an educator, in order to mobilize the
broad support necessary to carry out his program. At the
same time, the wise leader must remember that the pace of
change was slow, and that his success was dependent
upon his not outrunning the comprehension and approval
of his followers.

Wilson joined the progressive movement belatedly,
and at first perhaps partly out of political expediency.
Middle-class in background and outlook, he had shared the
distrust of most of his class, including such men as Theodore Roosevelt and Robert M. La Follette, for the social
unrest and agrarian radicalism of the 1890's. And he remained profoundly suspicious of governmental interference, especially at the national level, even after Roosevelt
and La Follette began to advocate progressive reforms. Yet
Wilson's conversion to progressivism, about the time of his
1910 gubernatorial campaign, did not represent so profound a shift as some observers have believed. He had

always feared the concentration of power and championed the rights of the individual. His faith in democracy never flagged throughout his life. But because he was more interested in political than in economic processes, his early concern was over the expansion of governmental power. When he awakened to the dangerous concentration of economic and political power in individual and corporate hands under the nation's accelerating industrialism, Wilson reluctantly came to favor a counterexpansion of governmental power. This expansion sought first, through tariff reform and antitrust activity, to restore competition; finally, through a variety of social justice measures, it aided those too weak or disadvantaged to protect themselves. This change in Wilson's thinking involved means more than ends, however, for his concern for the individual remained constant and paramount.

Yet Wilson's progressivism was essentially conservative and individualistic, akin more to nineteenth-century liberalism than to the burgeoning governmental activity that would characterize the next generation's New Deal. Wilson's New Freedom was in fact more backward than forward-looking; it sought to restore a presumed former freedom of opportunity that had been diminished by the growth of the trusts and giant corporations. Although Wilson's rhetoric on the subject expressed appropriate outrage, he really had no clear idea of what to do about big business. Even less than some progressives, he was not prepared to challenge the basic assumptions of the American private property capitalistic economy. And although he seemed at times to be advocating the dissolution of the trusts, his remarks on other occasions—and, even more, the record of his administration—indicate that he did not oppose bigness as such but opposed only the unfair and antisocial use of great economic power.

He wished to prevent the further growth of big business,

and to clear the path for the small entrepreneur—yet he failed to comprehend the extent to which industrialism had altered the nature of capitalism. He evoked the image of rural and small-town America—at a time when it was becoming overwhelmingly clear that the new America was to be urban and industrial. Wilson's acceptance of some of the social justice and regulatory ideas of Theodore Roosevelt's New Nationalism program suggests that by the end of his first term he had come to recognize the inadequacy of his own New Freedom approach. Reluctantly, he began to move toward the expanded governmental functions characteristic of later progressivism. The war undoubtedly forced him to go farther and faster than he preferred, and his striking development of Presidential powers to lead the nation in war influenced later progressives in a way he might well have disapproved. For Wilson was uneasy over the inevitable wartime expansion of governmental powers; after the Armistice, he proceeded to dismantle the war agencies as quickly as possible.

One powerful determinant of Wilson's political thought was his strong religious faith. A Presbyterian by inheritance and by youthful training, he remained devoutly religious throughout his life. He believed that each man was his own moral agent and would ultimately be judged by the standard of a stern and inflexible moral code. His was an intensely personal God, who was readily accessible through prayer and the revealed word. Daily Wilson sought strength and inspiration through prayer and the Scripture, and this faith in divine guidance reinforced his tendency to rely less on factual data and more on intuition in resolving difficult questions. Once he had decided on a course of action, he could easily persuade himself that the decision was dictated by obvious moral considerations and that opposition to it stemmed from base and sordid motives. He thus tended to simplify

issues other men found complex, and to moralize questions others considered secular. For Wilson, such diverse
matters as the location of the Princeton Graduate School,
the tariff schedule on wool, a loan to China, or the recognition of a new government became problems to be solved
on the basis of moral as well as practical considerations.

Wilson's foreign policy was therefore a curious blend of
morality and practicality, conditioned always by Wilson's
own middle-class values. There is no question but that he
sincerely wanted to use American power for high moral
ends, and that he wanted to give the world a noble example of disinterested leadership. In Mexico, for example, he
yearned to help the submerged masses achieve both a
voice in their government and a belated share in their
country's wealth. Yet Wilson's Anglo-Saxon and middle-
class values led him to assume that what had worked well
in America would work equally well elsewhere. When the
Mexican Revolution failed to produce a democratic government of which he could approve, when Article 27 of the
Mexican constitution of 1917 posed a serious challenge to
Anglo-Saxon concepts of private property rights, Wilson
lost much of his early sympathy for the revolutionary
movement in Mexico. He was unable to comprehend a
revolution that departed from familiar lines, nor could he
understand the aspirations of a people from a different
cultural background.

Despite the moral gloss, moreover, cynics noted that
Wilson's foreign policies — in Latin America, the Far East,
and in Europe — had for the most part the same practical
objectives, and relied on the same basic tools of power and
diplomacy, as those of previous administrations. Sometimes
used more ruthlessly, Wilson's most ambitious and imaginative undertaking, the League of Nations, was a thorough
blending of practicality and compromise, buttressed by
morality.

The League of Nations survived its founder by only twenty-two years, like Wilson, a victim of atrophied muscles and a faltering heart. Its indifferent record scarcely justified Wilson's high hopes for an international parliament through which disputes might be adjusted through reason and the pressure of world opinion rather than force. In fact, the League flatly failed its greatest test, the prevention of another world war. Whether the result might have been different had the United States followed Wilson's lead and played a major role in the new world order, no man can say. Yet Wilson's vision had captured the imagination of the world. This was shown by the determination of a later generation of statesmen to erect another world organization, the United Nations, upon the ruins of the old League. And by then only a few voices would be raised in the United States against wholehearted American participation. This demonstrated perhaps the most important element in Wilson's political legacy, for Wilson, more than any other man, had prepared the American people for leadership in the collective search for peace and security.

The passage of time has shown that Wilson greatly overestimated the power of an aroused world opinion to restrain an aggressor. Clearly moral force must still be backed by more substantial and traditional deterrents. Wilson was likewise too optimistic about the willingness of the great powers to entrust their vital interests to the doubtful impartiality of an international body. The greatest success of the League, like that of the United Nations, came in resolving disputes in which the major powers were not substantially involved. The need and effectiveness of banking potentially dangerous fires at this level, however, must not be overlooked out of disappointment over the organization's inability to settle all problems. For more critical matters, Wilson's international parliament provided what he would regard as justification enough for its existence—the machinery through which the great powers might keep open a neutral channel to negotiate their differences short of war. Basic to Wilson's plan was the assumption that the great powers would recognize the utility of such machinery and would have the wisdom to use it. If they did not—and that was the fate of the League—then there was little prospect of averting another major war in the future.

Few American Presidents have given so much thought as Woodrow Wilson gave to the functioning of American political institutions and the leadership potential of the Presidency. Wilson's interest in government began early and continued to the end of his life. As a young man he was fascinated by examples of dynamic leaders influencing the course of history, and dreamed of playing such a role himself. Even while a Princeton undergraduate, he was confident enough that he knew how to improve the inefficient and often undemocratic operation of Congress to publish a lengthy article on the subject (See Document 6).

As a Southerner, Wilson shared his section's distaste for the dominance of Congress during Reconstruction. Not surprisingly, he at first concluded that the President's opportunities for effective leadership were restricted by the intransigence and irresponsibility of the legislative branch. But the experience of Grover Cleveland—and, even more, of Theodore Roosevelt—persuaded him that he had greatly underestimated the potentialities of the Presidency. By the time of his election in 1912 Wilson had come to believe that perhaps only the British prime minister possessed a better forum from which to guide his nation.

Admiration, even reverence, for British parliamentary government remained a hallmark of Wilson's political thought even after he had revised his view of the possibilities for vigorous executive action under the American constitutional system. Many of his acts as President reflected this belief in the superiority of certain aspects of parliamentary government, and showed a desire to adapt them to American institutions. Wilson saw the President as far more than the chief administrator of the nation. He felt that the American President, like the British prime minister, should also be a legislative and party leader. Thus, Wilson constantly stressed the importance of the party caucus and the need for party loyalty in developing a legislative program. Much more than previous Presidents, he assumed an active role in all aspects of the legislative process.

Unfortunately, under the American system Wilson could not automatically count on his party's controlling the legislative branch while he held his executive office. When he lost legislative control with the elections of 1918, his once-firm mastery of Congress deteriorated, and he experienced the worst political defeat of his career. Having stressed party government for six years, he could not easily or convincingly switch to a lofty appeal for bipartisan support. And unlike a prime minister, he could not dissolve an obstructive Congress and take his case to the people in a national election based on issues of his own choosing. Yet on occasion Wilson sought to achieve a similar effect through his appeals for public support — as in his denunciation of the tariff lobby in 1913, for example (See Document 43), or his abortive speaking tour on behalf of the peace treaty in 1919 (See Documents 130 – 134).

Wilson's admiration for the quick and efficient transfer of power under the parliamentary system led him to devise a secret plan for possible use after the Presidental election of 1916. He proposed that if his Republican opponent, Charles Evans Hughes, were elected, Wilson and Vice President Marshall should resign — after appointing Hughes Secretary of State so that he might take office immediately (See

Document 10). Wilson's narrow victory rendered this imaginative scheme unnecessary, but the plan showed his interest in making American political institutions more efficient and responsive to the popular will.

Although the League of Nations was Wilson's most famous legacy, his development of the Presidential office was fully as important. Expanding on Theodore Roosevelt's vigorous example, Wilson greatly extended the powers and functions of the Presidency, leaving for his successors both the precedents and the tools for bold leadership. More than any chief executive before him, he developed the legislative powers of his office, establishing the modern pattern of the President as the leader of his party and of Congress. Even as a minority President, he managed skillfully to push through an impressive program of reform, embracing a substantial reduction of the tariff, democratization of the tax structure, the first national economic stabilizers, stronger antitrust protection, federal supervision of business practices, and a variety of social justice measures. Reluctantly leading the nation into war, he accomplished an unprecedented mobilization of men and material swiftly and without a major scandal touching his administration. A combination of moral and strategic considerations led him to meddle disastrously in Latin American affairs — but in the process he foreshadowed a later President's Good Neighbor Policy by renouncing territorial ambitions and suggesting a Pan-American organization to provide collective security and the peaceful arbitration of disputes (See Documents 60 and 109). In this as in other areas, the bright promise of Wilson's words did not always square with his actions, but his idealistic goals remain as a challenge to later generations.

A Wilson Chronology

1856   *December 28.*

Thomas Woodrow Wilson born at Staunton, Virginia, the third child and first son of Reverend Joseph Ruggles Wilson and Janet (Jessie) Woodrow Wilson.

1858   Wilson family moves to Augusta, Georgia, where Dr. Wilson serves as Presbyterian minister.

1870   Family moves to Columbia, South Carolina, where Dr. Wilson joins faculty of Columbia Theological Seminary.

1873–   Wilson enters Davidson College, North Carolina,
1874   but is forced to withdraw because of ill health.

1875   Enters College of New Jersey at Princeton, where he develops keen interest in government and public affairs.

1879   *June.*

Is graduated from Princeton.

August.

Publishes first major article, "Cabinet Government in the United States," in the *International Review.*

Fall.

Enters University of Virginia Law School.

1880   Ill health forces withdrawal from law school, but continues legal studies at home in Wilmington, North Carolina.

1882   Launches brief law partnership with Edward I.

	Renick in Atlanta, Georgia. Opposes protective tariff before U.S. Tariff Commission.
1883	Meets and becomes engaged to Ellen Louise Axson. In fall enters Johns Hopkins University for graduate study in history and political science.
1884	Publishes article, "Committee or Cabinet Government?" in *Overland Monthly*.
1885	*January.* Publishes first book, *Congressional Government.* *June 24.* Marries Ellen Louise Axson at Savannah, Georgia. *September.* Becomes associate professor of history at Bryn Mawr College.
1886	Receives Ph.D. degree from Johns Hopkins.
1888	Appointed to professorship at Wesleyan University, Middletown, Connecticut.
1889	Publishes *The State*, an ambitious textbook on government.
1890	Appointed professor of jurisprudence and political economy at Princeton.
1893	Publishes *Division and Reunion, 1829–1889,* and *An Old Master and Other Political Essays.* Speaks and writes increasingly on education and public affairs.
1902	Elected president of Princeton June 9; inaugurated October 25. Publishes *A History of the American People,* in five volumes.
1902–1905	Revises Princeton curriculum and administration; establishes preceptorial system of instruction.
1907–1910	Growing opposition to Wilson's reforms at Princeton, especially his proposal to abolish the upper-class eating clubs and his plan to make

the Graduate School a central part of the University community.

1910   *September 15.*
Nominated as Democratic candidate for governor of New Jersey.
October 20.
Resigns presidency of Princeton.
November 8.
Elected governor after campaign as progressive.

1911   *January 17.*
Inaugurated governor of New Jersey.
January–April.
Seizes control of state Democratic organization and pushes reform program through legislature.

1912   *July 2.*
Receives Democratic Presidential nomination on 46th ballot at Baltimore convention.
November 5.
Elected President of the United States.

1913   *March 4.*
Inaugurated President.
April 8.
Personally goes before special session of Congress with address requesting tariff reform.
May 26.
Denounces tariff lobby.
June 23.
Addresses Congress on banking and currency reform.
October 3.
Signs Underwood-Simmons Tariff Act.
October 27.
Renounces territorial ambitions in Latin America in speech at Mobile, Alabama.
December 23.

Signs Federal Reserve Act.

1914   *April 21–22.*

Orders U.S. naval forces to occupy Veracruz, Mexico.

August 4.

Proclaims U.S. neutrality on outbreak of World War I.

August 6.

Death of Ellen Axson Wilson.

September 26.

Signs Federal Trade Commission Act.

October 15.

Signs Clayton Anti-Trust Act.

1915   *January 2.*

Vetoes literacy test for immigrants.

February 4.

Germany establishes war zone around British Isles.

February 10.

U.S. warms Germany of "strict accountability" for any American losses through submarine activity.

March 4.

Signs La Follette Seamen's Act.

May 7.

British Passenger liner "Lusitania" is sunk, with loss of 124 Americans.

May 13, June 9, and July 21.

U.S. protests to Germany over sinking of "Lusitania." Secretary of State Bryan resigns, rather than sign second note, and is succeeded by Robert Lansing.

September 1.

Germany gives "Arabic" pledge not to sink liners without warning.

October 19.

U.S. recognizes Carranza regime in Mexico as *de facto* government.

December 18.

Marriage of Wilson and Edith Bolling Galt.

1916   *January 28.*

Nominates Louis D. Brandeis to Supreme Court; Brandeis is confirmed after hard fight in Senate on June 1.

March 15.

General Pershing leads punitive expedition into Mexico in search of Villa.

March 24.

"Sussex" is torpedoed, leading to renewed diplomatic crisis with Germany.

May 8.

Accepts German pledge on submarine warfare.

May 27.

First endorses League of Nations concept at meeting of League to Enforce Peace.

June 16.

Renominated for Presidency by Democratic Party.

July 17.

Signs Federal Farm Loan Act.

August 29.

Signs Johnson Act for greater autonomy for Philippines.

September 1.

Signs Keating-Owen Child Labor Act.

September 3.

Signs Adamson Act, providing eight-hour day for railroad workers.

September 7.

Signs Shipping Act to create U.S. Shipping Board.

November 7.

Re-elected President.

December 18.

Asks all belligerents to state their peace terms.

1917   *January 22.*

Delivers "peace without victory" address to
  Senate.

January 27.

Pershing expedition begins withdrawal from
  Mexico.

January 29.

Vetoes second literacy test for immigrants; veto
  overridden by Congress.

February 3.

Breaks diplomatic relations with Germany over
  the resumption of unrestricted submarine warfare.

February 26.

Requests authority from Congress to arm American merchant ships.

March 1.

Releases text of Zimmermann note promising
  German aid to Mexico in recovering lost American territory.

March 4.

Denounces "little group of willful men" in Senate
  for blocking armed-ship bill.

March 5.

Inaugurated for second term as President.

March 13.

U.S. extends *de jure* recognition to Carranza
  government.

April 2.

Asks Congress to declare war on Germany.

April 6.

Signs war resolution.

April 14.

Creates Committee on Public Information, headed by George Creel.

May 18.

Signs Selective Service Act.

May 19.

Appoints Herbert C. Hoover to head wartime food program.

June 5.

Nearly ten million men registered under selective service draft.

June 25.

First troops of American Expeditionary Force arrive in France.

July 28.

War Industries Board established.

December 26.

Orders railroads put under government management.

1918   *January 8.*

Makes Fourteen Points address to Congress, stating U.S. war aims.

March 4.

Appoints Bernard M. Baruch to head reorganized War Industries Board.

May 20.

Signs Overman Act, strengthening Presidential power to reorganize executive agencies.

September 30.

Urges Senate to approve Woman Suffrage amendment.

October 6–7.

Germany and Austria-Hungary ask Wilson to negotiate armistice.

October 8–29.

Wilson skillfully negotiates with both Allies and Germany and Austria-Hungary over armistice terms. Gains general commitment to Fourteen Points.

October 25.

Appeals for Democratic Congress.

November 5.

Republicans win control of Congress by margin of 1 vote in Senate and 45 votes in House of Representatives.

November 11.

Armistice proclaimed.

November 18.

Wilson announces that he will head American delegation to peace conference.

November 29.

Peace commissioners named; no Senator or prominent Republican included in delegation.

December 4.

Wilson and peace delegation sail for Europe.

December 14.

Wilson arrives in Paris. Given tumultuous welcome in France, and subsequently in Great Britain and Italy.

1919   *January 18.*

Delivers address at opening of peace conference.

January 25.

Council of Ten accepts League of Nations concept and names Wilson to head committee to draft League Covenant.

February 4.

Wilson presents draft of Covenant to peace conference.

February 15.

Sails for United States; arrives in Boston, February 24.

March 4.

Makes Metropolitan Opera House speech, denouncing League critics, on eve of return to Paris.

March 14.

Arrives back in Paris.

April 3.

Bedridden with case of influenza or possibly slight stroke.

April 7.

Orders "George Washington" readied for possible departure from peace conference.

April 28.

Presents revised Covenant to peace conference with changes to recognize Monroe Doctrine and other U.S. interests.

June 28.

Signs Versailles Treaty and departs for U.S.

July 10.

Addresses Senate, presenting Treaty for approval.

September 3.

Begins western speaking tour on behalf of Treaty.

September 26.

Collapses after Pueblo speech, returns to Washington.

October 3.

Stricken by thrombosis, paralyzed on left side.

November 19.

Senate rejects Treaty both with and without Lodge reservations.

1920   *February 28.*
        Esch-Cummins Transportation Act returns rail-
            roads to private control, but strengthens Inter-
            state Commerce Commission.
        March 19.
        Senate again rejects Treaty.
        April 14.
        Wilson resumes cabinet meetings for first time
            since stroke; advises Attorney General Palmer
            "not to let the country see red."
        June 10.
        Signs Federal Water Power Act creating Federal
            Power Commission.
        October 3.
        Issues appeal that 1920 Presidential election be
            a national referendum on League of Nations.
        November 2.
        Warren G. Harding elected President.
        December 10.
        Wilson awarded Nobel Peace Prize for work
            creating League of Nations.
1921   *March 4.*
        Wilson's second term as President expires; accom-
            panies Harding to inauguration. Moves into
            home on S Street in Washington.
1923   *November 10.*
        Makes last formal address (by radio): "The Signifi-
            cance of Armistice Day."
        November 11.
        Makes last public statement, to Armistice Day
            crowd in front of Washington home.
1924   *February 3.*
        Death of Woodrow Wilson.

Selected Bibliography

ORIGINAL SOURCES

The basic source on the life and thought of Woodrow Wilson is, of course, the voluminous Woodrow Wilson Papers in the Library of Congress. Also useful is the Ray Stannard Baker Collection at the Library of Congress, which contains Wilson correspondence and other material gathered by Baker for his authorized biography. Additional unpublished Wilson material is located at Princeton University, where Arthur S. Link and his associates are preparing the authoritative, multivolume edition of Wilson's Papers. In time the Princeton holdings will be the most complete and best organized collection of original and photocopied Wilson manuscript materials. Until the Link edition of the Wilson Papers appears, however, the best published collection of Wilson's speeches, correspondence, and shorter writings is *The Public Papers of Woodrow Wilson*, edited by Ray Stannard Baker and William E. Dodd (6 vols.; New York and London: Harper & Brothers, 1925–1927), which also contains a detailed bibliography of Wilson's publications. Additional Wilson correspondence is quoted extensively in Ray Stannard Baker's authorized biography, *Woodrow Wilson: Life and Letters*, (8 vols.; Garden City, N.Y.: Doubleday, Page & Company, 1927–1939), and in *The Priceless Gift: the Love Letters of Woodrow Wilson and Ellen Axson Wilson*, edited by Eleanor

Wilson McAdoo (New York: McGraw-Hill Book Company, 1962). Wilson's 1912 campaign speeches have been meticulously transcribed and edited from the original shorthand notes of his stenographer by John Wells Davidson in *A Crossroads of Freedom: the 1912 Campaign Speeches of Woodrow Wilson* (New Haven, Conn.: Yale University Press, 1956).

During his academic career Wilson published a large number of books and articles dealing with politics and public affairs. Many of his more significant articles were included in the Baker-Dodd edition of *The Public Papers of Woodrow Wilson* mentioned above, but the student of Wilson's thought should not overlook the articles on the following list, all of which were omitted from the Baker-Dodd collection and some of which are reproduced in part in this volume. Those titles of Wilson's books marked by an asterisk are also available in an inexpensive modern paperback edition.

Congressional Government: a Study in American Politics. Boston: Houghton, Mifflin Company, 1885. **Paperback.** New York: Meridian Books, Inc., 1956.

Constitutional Government in the United States. New York: Columbia University Press, 1908. **Paperback.** New York: Columbia University Press, 1961.

Division and Reunion, 1829–1889. New York and London: Longmans, Green & Co., 1893. **Paperback.** New York: Collier Books, 1961.

George Washington. New York and London: Harper & Brothers, 1896.

A History of the American People. 5 vols. New York and London: Harper & Brothers, 1902.

Mere Literature, and Other Essays. Boston and New York: Houghton, Mifflin Company, 1896.

The New Freedom: a Call for the Emancipation of the Generous Energies of a People. New York and Garden

City, N.Y.: Doubleday, Page & Company, 1913. **Paperback**. Englewood Cliffs, N.J.: Prentice-Hall, Inc., 1961.

An Old Master, and Other Political Essays. New York: Charles Scribner's Sons, 1893.

The State: Elements of Historical and Practical Politics. Boston: D. C. Heath & Company, 1889.

Leaders of Men. T. H. Vail Motter, ed. Princeton, N. J.: Princeton University Press, 1952.

"Character of Democracy in the United States," *Atlantic Monthly*, LXIV (November 1889), 577–588.

"Conservatism, True and False," *Princeton Alumni Weekly*, IX (December 16, 1908), 186–189.

"The English Constitution," *Chautauquan*, XII (October 1890–January 1891), 5–9, 149–154, 293–298, and 430–434.

"The Government and Business," *Princeton Alumni Weekly*, VIII (March 18, 1908), 386–389.

"Ideals of Public Life," *Princeton Alumni Weekly*, VIII (November 27, 1907), 160–162.

"On the Political Future of the South," *Princeton Alumni Weekly*, V (December 3, 1904), 160–161.

"Responsible Government under the Constitution," *Atlantic Monthly*, CVII (April 1886), 542–553.

"The Spirit of Jefferson," *Princeton Alumni Weekly*, VI (April 28, 1906), 551–554.

"Of the Study of Politics," *New Princeton Review*, III (March 1887), 188–189.

Wilson's views on foreign policy are developed and elaborated in correspondence and memoranda in Department of State, *Papers Relating to the Foreign Relations of the United States, 1913–1921* (Washington, D.C.: Government Printing Office, 1920–1936), and in the following *Foreign Relations* supplements: *The World War* (7 vols.; 1928–1932); *The Paris Peace Conference* (13 vols.;

xc *Selected Bibliography*

1942–1947); and *The Lansing Papers, 1914–1920* (2 vols.; 1939–1940). Useful on both foreign and domestic issues are *The Intimate Papers of Colonel House*, edited by Charles Seymour (4 vols.; Boston and New York: Houghton Mifflin Company, 1926–1928), and *The Cabinet Diaries of Josephus Daniels, 1913–1921*, edited by E. David Cronon (Lincoln, Neb.: University of Nebraska Press, 1963).

A convenient guide to writings by and about Wilson is *Woodrow Wilson: a Selected Bibliography of His Published Writings, Addresses, and Public Papers*, edited by Laura S. Turnbull (Princeton, N.J.: Princeton University Press, 1948). Also of great use are the bibliographies in the biographies and secondary works listed below, especially the works by Arthur S. Link.

COLLATERAL READING

The definitive biography of Woodrow Wilson is Arthur S. Link's exhaustively researched and insightful *Wilson*, of which five volumes have been published or are in press: Vol. I, *The Road to the White House*; Vol. II, *The New Freedom*; Vol. III, *The Struggle for Neutrality, 1914–1915*; Vol. IV, *Confusions and Crises, 1915–1916*; Vol. V, *Campaigns for Progressivism and Peace, 1916–1917* (Princeton, N.J.: Princeton University Press, 1947, 1956, 1960, 1964, 1965). Other helpful studies by Link include *Woodrow Wilson and the Progressive Era, 1910–1917* (New York: Harper & Brothers, 1954; paperback, New York: Harper Torchbooks, 1963), which contains an excellent essay on sources, and *Wilson the Diplomatist: a Look at His Major Foreign Policies* (Baltimore, Md.: The Johns Hopkins Press, 1957; paperback; Chicago: Quadrangle Books, 1965). Still useful are Ray Stannard Baker, *Woodrow Wilson: Life and Letters*, mentioned above, and Ray Stannard Baker, *Woodrow Wilson and World Settlement* (3 vols.; Garden City, N.Y.: Doubleday, Page & Company, 1922). Arthur C. Walworth, *Woodrow Wilson* (Vol. I, *American Prophet;* Vol. II, *World Prophet;* New York: Longmans, Green & Co. 1958), is good on Wilson's personality and private life. The best one-volume biography is Herbert C. F. Bell, *Woodrow Wilson and the People* (Garden City, N.Y.: Doubleday, Doran & Company, 1945), but other good short biographies are John M. Blum, *Woodrow Wilson and the Politics of Morality* (Boston: Little, Brown and Company, 1956), which is also available in an inexpensive paperback edition published by the same firm, and John A. Garraty, *Woodrow Wilson* (New York: Alfred A. Knopf, 1956).

There is a wealth of secondary literature dealing with Woodrow Wilson and his era, and the output shows no sign of diminishing. For the student of Wilson's thought, the following works will be particularly helpful: William Diamond, *The Economic Thought of Woodrow Wilson* (Baltimore, Md.: The Johns Hopkins Press, 1943); *The Philosophy and Policies of Woodrow Wilson*, edited by Earl Latham, (Chicago: The University of Chicago Press, 1958); and Harley Notter, *The Origins of the Foreign Policy of Woodrow Wilson* (Baltimore, Md.: The Johns Hopkins Press, 1937).

Editor's Note

Throughout his life Woodrow Wilson devoted a great deal of thought and study to problems of government and public affairs. In the process he produced a vast amount of published and unpublished writing. Consequently, one can hope to illustrate only the more important aspects of his thought in a work such as this. Limitations of space have precluded treatment of some subjects, and other subjects have had to be covered in less detail than their complexity would ideally warrant. The documentary material that makes up the bulk of this volume has been selected to show the dominant characteristics of Wilson's political thought, the range of his interests, and the development of his ideas over the course of a varied career as a scholar, administrator, and political leader. The organization is both topical and chronological, for whereas certain dominant threads run throughout Wilson's thought he also changed his ideas in response to new circumstances. His shift from academic to political pursuits, from the study to the practice of politics, naturally led him to rethink some of his earlier assumptions. There remain, nevertheless, an impressive body of political thought, and—even more—an approach to politics, that are uniquely Wilsonian. Both are amply revealed in the documentary selections.

Wherever possible, the individual documentary selections have been reproduced in their entirety. In the case of passages from Wilson's books or from some of his longer articles and speeches, it has been necessary to omit material that is repetitive or discursive. Such omissions are indicated by the standard ellipsis symbol (. . .), and by the notation that the document is an excerpt from a larger work. In such cases the reader may wish to refer to the original source for a fuller treatment of the subject. The excerpted passages faithfully reflect Wilson's thinking, however.

I wish to express my deep appreciation to a number of persons and institutions for their assistance in the preparation of this book. The staffs of the Library of Congress and the State Historical Society of Wisconsin did much to facilitate my research in their collections of published and unpublished Wilson material. No one can write about Woodrow Wilson without acknowledging a great debt to the labors and insights of Arthur S. Link, the foremost Wilson authority. I am grateful to Professor Link and his publisher, Princeton University Press, for permission to quote several Wilson documents previously published by Professor Link in Volumes II and III of his definitive biography, *Wilson: The New Freedom* (1956), and *Wilson: The Struggle for Neutrality,* 1914–1915 (1960), as well as excerpts from Wilson's essay, *Leaders of Men,* edited by T. H. Vail Motter (1952). Professor John Wells Davidson kindly permitted me to use a number of extracts from his authoritative edition of Wilson's 1912 campaign speeches, *A Crossroads of Freedom* (Yale University Press, 1956). Doubleday & Company, Inc., allowed me to quote Wilson material from Ray Stannard Baker, *Woodrow Wilson: Life and Letters* (8 vols.; 1927–1939); Ray Stannard Baker, *Woodrow Wilson and World Settlement* (3 vols.; 1922); and Joseph P. Tumulty, *Woodrow Wilson as I knew Him* (1921). The McGraw-Hill Book Company gave permission to quote from *The Priceless Gift: The Love Letters of Woodrow Wilson and Ellen Axson Wilson*, edited by Eleanor Wilson McAdoo (1962).

I am particularly indebted to William M. Tuttle, Jr., for his painstakingly careful assistance at all stages of the preparation of this volume. Lastly, I owe most of all to my wife Jean, whose apprehensive awareness of deadlines is a useful tonic, and who as always helped immeasurably to meet this one.

E. David Cronon

Madison, Wisconsin
September 1965

PART 1

Woodrow Wilson: A Self-Portrait

A. YOUTHFUL AMBITION

As a public figure Woodrow Wilson gave the impression of austerity and aloofness, but to his family and a few intimates he revealed a warmth of affection and a high-spirited humor that were quite different from the rather forbidding public image. Wilson was not ordinarily given to introspection and only occasionally shared his innermost feelings with others. One such occasion was the period of his graduate study at Johns Hopkins University, from 1883 to 1885. As a lonely young lover separated from his fiancée, Ellen Axson, Wilson sought to share with her both a frank estimate of himself and some of his ambitions for their future life together.

DOCUMENT 1

"The Profession I Chose Was Politics. . . ."

Being quite sensible of the tendency of a certain very alluring topic to engross all the spaces of my letters, if I once allow myself to enter upon it, I purpose *beginning* this one with the fulfillment of a long-standing promise. I am going to tell you something about the ways and means of "the Hopkins," as far as those ways and means concern me. And I am going to do this, not because I think the subject intrinsically a very interesting one, but because I have, heretofore, been showing you only what was in my heart, and nothing of all the schemes that are in my head. I want to share everything with you, my darling; I want your sympathy in everything.

You know I am naturally extremely reserved. It would be a sheer impossibility for me to confide anything concerning only myself—especially any secret of my intellect —to anyone of whose sympathy I could not be absolutely sure beforehand; but there can be no greater delight in my life, my love, than making you the keeper of *all* my secrets, the sharer of all my hopes, *because I am sure of your love.* I used to *try* to tell you of the objects of my ambition when I was sure only of my love for you; but I could not do it because I did not know of your love for me.

Then, too, there is something else that urges me to tell you all about myself, and that is the desire that your love should be founded upon knowledge. Of course I don't believe that a woman can love a man for anything but qualities of heart and traits of character. She can't *love* his *intellectual* qualities. But it is nevertheless true that those qualities enter largely into the make-up of his character. They cannot all be acquired. Some of them must be in the essential fibre, current in his blood and native to his constitution. I know that you love me altogether and that you are quite willing to take me on trust:—if I were not con-

Excerpt from letter to Ellen Louise Axson, October 30, 1883, pp. 29–35. From *The Priceless Gift: The Love Letters of Woodrow Wilson and Ellen Axson Wilson,* ed. Eleanor Wilson McAdoo. Copyright 1962. McGraw-Hill Book Company. Used by permission.

vinced of that, I should be miserable indeed; but in giving myself I don't want to give by halves. I want you to know just what sort of fellow you are getting.

I think that it is only very recently that I have known myself—indeed I am not altogether certain that the acquaintance is complete yet. Like everybody else I have learned chiefly by means of big mistakes. I've had to earn my own experience. It took me all my college days to learn that it was necessary and profitable to study. Having made that tardy discovery, I left college on the wrong tack. I had then, as I have still, a very earnest political creed and very pronounced political ambitions. I remember forming with Charlie Talcott (a class-mate and very intimate friend of mine) a solemn covenant that we would school all our powers and passions for the work of establishing the principles we held in common; that we would acquire knowledge that we might have power; and that we would drill ourselves in all the arts of persuasion, but especially in oratory (for he was a born orator if any man ever was), that we might have facility in leading others into our ways of thinking and enlisting them in our purposes. And we didn't do this in merely boyish enthusiasm, though we were blinded by a very boyish assurance with regard to the future and our ability to mould the world as our hands might please. It was not so long ago but that I can still feel the glow and the pulsations of the hopes and the purposes of that moment – nay, it was not so long ago but that I still retain some of the faith that then prompted me. But a man has to know the world before he can work in it to any purpose. He has to know the forces with which he must cooperate and those with which he must contend; must know how and where he can make himself felt, not reckoning according to the conditions and possibilities of past times but according to a full knowledge of the conditions of the present and the possibilities of the immediate future. He must know the times into which he has been born: and this I did *not* know when I left college and chose my profession, as I proved by my choice.

The profession I chose was politics; the profession I entered was the law. I entered the one because I thought it would lead to the other. It was once the sure road; and Congress is still full of lawyers. But this is the time of leisured classes — or, at least, that time is very near at hand — and the time of crowded professions. It is plain to see why lawyers used to be the only politicians. In a new country, in communities where every man had his bread to earn, they were the only men (except the minister and the physician) who stopped amidst the general hurry of life to get learning; and they were the only men, without exception, who were skilled in those arts of forensic contest that were calculated to fit men for entering the lists at political tilts, or for holding their own in legislative debate. They could hope, too, when a turn of parties might have come, or their own popularity might have waned, to return to their places at the bar to find a place still open for them, to find themselves not altogether and hopelessly crowded out; they could even, like Webster and Jeremiah Mason and many others of less genius, make law and statecraft live and thrive together, pleading causes in the courts even while holding seats in the Senate or leading parties in the House.

But those times are passing away. A man who has to earn a livelihood cannot nowadays turn aside from his trade for intervals of officeholding and political activity. He cannot even do two things at once. He is constrained by a minute division of labour to bend all his energies to the one thing that is nearest at hand. Even in the law men are becoming specialists. The whole field of legal knowledge, which former generations of American lawyers have superficially worked, is too big for any one man now, and practitioners are contenting themselves with cultivating small corners of it, digging deep and getting large crops out of small areas. And of course these small tenant farmers have to work much more diligently than did the great proprietors of former times. The law is more than ever before a jealous mistress. Whoever thinks, as I thought, that he can practice law successfully and study history and politics at the same time is wofully [sic] mistaken. If he is to make a living at the bar he must be a lawyer *and nothing else*. Of course he can compass a certain sort of double-calling success by dint of dishonesty. He can obtain, and betray, clients by pretending a knowledge of the law which he does not possess; and he can often gain political office by the arts of the demagogue. But he cannot be both a learned lawyer and a profound and public-spirited statesman, if he must plunge into practice and make the law a means of support.

In a word, my ambition could not be fulfilled at the bar; the studies for which I was best fitted, both by nature and by acquired habit, were not legitimate in a law office, and I was compelled in very justice to myself to seek some profession in which they would be legitimate. Evidently, however there was small latitude of choice. A professorship was the only feasible place for me, the only place that would afford leisure for reading and for original work, the only strictly literary berth with an income attached. True, professorships were scarce and hard to get, and professors could not participate actively in public affairs; but even a professorship might be gotten as soon as a competence at the bar, and the occupancy of office had never been an essential part of my political programme. Indeed I knew very well that a man without independent fortune must in any event content himself with becoming an *outside* force in politics, and I was well enough satisfied with the prospect of having whatever influence I might be able to exercise make itself felt through literary and non-partisan agencies: for my predilections, ever since I had any that were definite, have always turned very strongly towards a literary life, notwithstanding my decided taste for oratory, which is supposed to be the peculiar province of public men.

With manhood came to me an unquenchable desire to excel in two distinct and almost opposite kinds of writing: political and *imaginative*. I want to contribute to our literature what no American has ever contributed, studies in the philosophy of our institutions, not the abstract and occult, but the practical and suggestive, philosophy which is at the core of our governmental methods: their use, their meaning, "the spirit that makes them workable." I want to divest them of the theory that obscures them and present their weakness and their strength without disguise, and with such skill and such plenitude of proof that it shall be seen that I have succeeded and that I have added something to the resources of knowledge upon which statecraft must depend. But the *imaginative* writing? I don't mean that I want to write poetry. I am quite aware that at my birth no poet was born; but the imagination has other spheres besides the creations of a poetic fancy and can freshen and beautify the world without the aid of the musical cadences of verse. I believe that there's entirely too much moping and morbid thought amongst jaded human beings, that there's a great deal of joy and fun in the world that people miss for lack of time to look around; and I believe that there are inexhaustible sources of cheer, just as there are endless combinations of music, in our *language*. Now isn't it a legitimate ambition to wish to write something (!) that will freshen the energies of tired people and make the sad laugh and take heart again: some comedy full of pure humour and peopled with characters whose livers are in order, who live up to the moral that life, even with the pleasures of vice left out, is worth living: lay sermons full of laughter and a loving God: a fiction that may be suffered to live, if only because it has real people in it and no sham enthusiasm? I could wish to be the favoured correspondent of children as well as a counsellor of the powers of the earth.

But where does oratory come in? It does not generally come into the lectures of college professors; but it should. Oratory is not declamation, not swelling tones and an excited delivery, but the art of persuasion, the art of putting things so as to appeal irresistibly to an audience. And how can a teacher stimulate young men to study, how can he fill them with great ideas and worthy purposes, how can he draw them out of themselves and make them to become forces in the world without oratory? Perfunctory lecturing is of no service in the world. It's a nuisance. "The mind is not a prolix gut to be stuffed," as father used to tell his students, "but a delicate organism to be stimulated and directed."

And so I'm brought back, by association of ideas, to the point from which I set out, the University. Its chief charm for advanced students, as well as its chief *danger* perhaps, is its freedom of method. The professors act rather as guides and counsellors than as instructors. Their lectures are intended to direct our work, to point out sources of information and suggest points of view. Each man is allowed to follow his own methods of study, which he can safely and profitably do if he have matured purposes, but which allows him full opportunity to fritter away his time if he have no fixed habits of study. The temptation in my own case is to confine myself to those paths of constitutional study which have become familiar, and therefore most attractive, to me. I have a distinct dread (partly instinctive and partly instilled by my home training) of too much reading, and I am, consequently, so much averse from *scattering* my forces that I possibly limit them to too narrow a sphere.

The sessions of the *Seminary* are occupied in the reading of papers (generally by students of longest standing in the University) upon special subjects political and social, such as the Spanish settlements in Florida and the constitution and history of such socialistic communities as Brooke farm and others more obscure; and the preparation of these papers illustrates one of the best features of the University work, its *cooperative* feature. Instead of requiring all to go over the whole field in any given branch, each man is assigned a limited topic for special study upon which he is expected to make a report in class; and his knowledge of the other topics involved is gained from the papers read by his classmates.

But I must really draw this huge letter to a close. Its bulk is already alarming, and I have a dim suspcion that, after all my writing, I have told you very little that you did not know before. What I have wished to emphasize is the *object* for which I came to the University: to get a special training in historical research and an insight into the most modern literary and political thoughts and methods, in order that my ambition to become an invigorating and enlightening power in the world of political thought and a master in some of the less serious branches of literary art may be the more easy of accomplishment. To charge me with egotism and presumption in entertaining such an ambition would, I freely admit, be a just commentary on my plans; but I am conscious in my most secret heart of making not the least pretension to *genius* and of relying altogether on hard work and a capacity for being taught. I am by no means confident of reaching the heights to which I aspire, but I *am* sure of being able to climb *some* distance; and I shall never be embittered by finding myself unable to get to the top. It will be invigorating to breast the hill anyway—much more invigorating than easy walking on level ground—and all my energies are eager for the exercise. One thing at least shall not retard my influence if I can help it, and that is a lame *style* in writing. Style is not

much studied here; *ideas* are supposed to be everything—their vehicle comparatively nothing. But you and I
know that there can be no greater mistake; that, both in its
amount and its length of life, an author's influence depends upon the power and the beauty of his style, upon
the flawless perfection of the mirror he holds up to nature;
upon his facility in catching and holding, because he
pleases, the attention: and style shall be, as, under my
father's guidance, it has been, one of my chief studies. A
writer must be artful as well as strong.

You will doubtless smile at the character of this profuse
epistle, as I have done; but its composition has done me
lots of good. I've worked off any amount of stored-up steam
in writing it! . . .

DOCUMENT 2

"I Have a Strong Instinct of Leadership. . . ."

. . . Yes, darling, there is, and has long been, in my mind a
"lurking sense of disappointment and *loss,* as if I had
missed from my life something upon which both my gifts
and inclinations gave me a claim." I do feel a very real
regret that I have been shut out from my heart's *first* primary ambition and purpose, which was to take an active, if
possible, a leading, part in public life, and strike out for
myself, if I had the ability, a *statesman's* career. That is my
heart's—or rather my *mind's*—deepest secret. . . . But
don't mistake the feeling for more than it is. It is nothing
more than a regret; and the more I study the conditions of
public service in this country the less personal does the
regret become. My disappointment is in the fact that there

Excerpt from letter to Ellen Louise Axson, February 24, 1885, in *The Priceless Gift*, ed. McAdoo, pp. 118–119.

is no room for such a career in this country for *anybody*, rather than the fact that there is no chance for *me*.

Had I independent means of support, even of the most modest proportions, I should doubtless have sought an entrance into politics *anyhow*, and have tried to fight my way to predominant influence even amidst the hurly-burly and helter-skelter of Congress. I have a strong instinct of leadership, an unmistakably oratorical temperament and the keenest possible delight in affairs; and it has required very constant and stringent schooling to content me with the sober methods of the scholar and the man of letters. I have no patience for the tedious toil of what is known as "research"; I have a passion for interpreting great thoughts to the world; I should be complete if I could inspire a great movement of opinion, if I could read the experiences of the past into the practical life of the men of to-day and so communicate the thought to the minds of the great mass of the people as to impel them to great political achievements. Burke was a *very* much greater man than Cobden or Bright; but the work of Cobden and Bright is much nearer to the measure of my powers, it seems to me, than the writing of imperishable thoughts upon the greatest problems of politics which was Burke's mission. I think with you, darling, that "of all the world's workers those which take by far the highest rank are the writers of noble books." If one could choose between the two careers, *with the assurance that he had the capacity for either,* "it would seem to *me* that there would be no room for hesitation even."

But my feeling has been that such literary talents as I have are *secondary* to my equipment for other things; that my power to write was meant to be a hand maiden to my power to speak and to organize action. Of course it is quite possible that I have been all along entirely misled in this view: I am ready to accept the providential ordering of my life as conclusion on that point. Certainly I have taken the course which will, with God's favour, enable me to realize *most* of what I proposed to myself, and I do not in the least repine at the necessity which has shut me out from all other courses of life. It is for this reason that I have never made these confessions so fully before: I did not want even to *seem* to be discontented with my lot in life. I shall write with no less diligence of preparation, both moral and mental, and with no less effort to put all that is best in myself into my books because I have had to give up a cherished ambition to be an actor in the affairs about which my *pen* can now be busy. The new channels of work shall not clog my enthusiasms, and nothing shall lower my ideals or make a pause in my effort to realize them. One thing there is which I have now that I did not have when I dreamed and planned about a career as statesman and orator; one thing that I had no conception of then, and which is more to me than the strength and inspiration of *any* ambition: that one priceless, inestimable thing is *your love,* my Eileen! But continue to love me as you do now, and I shall stop short of nothing noble of which my powers are capable. I accept your judgment: the writer's career *is* the highest: and you shall help me to write truely and wor-thily, to write so that every page shall testify, by its hon-esty, by its clarity, by its unsoured temper, that I have lived in the light of your love. . . .

B. THE LONELINESS
OF THE PRESIDENCY

Wilson generally got on well with reporters, though he never quite got used to their interest in his private life. (He once angrily denounced the attention paid by the press to the social life of his three daughters, two of whom married during his tenure in the White House.) On March 20, 1914, the President gave an impromptu talk at a housewarming party at the new headquarters of the National Press Club in Washington. His remarks revealed both a wistful recognition of the loneliness of the Presidency and an awareness that the public did not always see the warmth of his inner spirit.

DOCUMENT 3

Address to the National Press Club, March 20, 1914

I was just thinking of my sense of confusion of identity, sometimes, when I read the articles about myself. I have never read an article about myself in which I have recognized myself, and I have come to have the impression that I must be some kind of a fraud, because I think a great many of these articles are written in absolute good faith. I tremble to think of the variety and falseness in the impressions I make — and it is being borne in on me so that it may change my very disposition — that I am a cold and removed person who has a thinking machine inside which he adjusts to the circumstances, which he does not allow to be moved by any winds of affection or emotion of any kind, that turns like a cold searchlight on anything that is presented to his attention and makes it work.

I am not aware of having any detachable apparatus inside of me. On the contrary, if I were to interpret myself, I would

The Public Papers of Woodrow Wilson, ed. Ray Stannard Baker and William E. Dodd (New York: Harper & Brothers, 1925–1927), III, 94–98.

say that my constant embarrassment is to restrain the emotions that are inside of me. You may not believe it, but I sometimes feel like a fire from a far from extinct volcano, and if the lava does not seem to spill over it is because you are not high enough to see the caldron boil. Because, truly, gentlemen, in the position which I now occupy there is a sort of, I do not know how else to express it than to say, passionate sense of being connected with my fellow men in a peculiar relationship of responsibility, not merely the responsibility of office, but God knows there are enough things in this world that need to be corrected.

I have mixed, first and last, with all sorts and conditions of men—there are mighty few kinds of men that have to be described to me, and there are mighty few kinds of experiences that have to be described to me—and when I think of the number of men who are looking to me as the representative of a party, with the hope for all varieties of salvage from the things they are struggling in the midst of, it makes me tremble. It makes me tremble not only with a sense of my own inadequacy and weakness, but as if I were shaken by the very things that are shaking them and, if I seem circumspect, it is because I am so diligently trying not to make any colossal blunders. If you just calculate the number of blunders a fellow can make in twenty-four hours if he is not careful and if he does not listen more than he talks, you would see something of the feeling that I have.

I was amused the other day at a remark that Senator Newlands made. I had read him the trust message that I was to deliver to Congress some ten days before I delivered it, and I never stop "doctoring" things of that kind until the day I have to deliver them. When he heard it read to Congress he said: "I think it was better than it was when you read it to me." I said: "Senator, there is one thing which I do not think you understand. I not only use all the brains I have, but all I can borrow, and I have borrowed a lot since I read it to you first."

That, I dare say, is what gives the impression of circumspectness. I am listening; I am diligently trying to collect all the brains that are borrowable in order that I will not make more blunders than it is inevitable that a man should make who has great limitations of knowledge and capacity. And the emotion of the thing is so great that I suppose I must be some kind of a mask to conceal it. I really feel sometimes as if I were masquerading when I catch a picture of myself in some printed description. In between things that I have to do as a public officer I never think of myself as the President of the United States, because I never have had any sense of being identified with that office.

I feel like a person appointed for a certain length of time to administer that office, and I feel just as much outside of it at this moment as I did before I was elected to it. I feel just as much outside of it as I still feel outside of the Government of the United States. No man could imagine himself the Government of the United States; but he could understand that some part of his fellow-citizens had told him to go and run a certain part of it the best he knew how. That would not make him the Government itself or the thing itself. It would just make him responsible for running it the best he knew how. The machine is so much greater than himself, the office is so much greater than he can ever be, and the most he can do is to look grave enough and self-possessed enough to seem to fill it.

I can hardly refrain every now and again from tipping the public the wink, as much as to say, "It is only 'me' that is inside this thing. I know perfectly well that I will have to get out presently. I know that then I will look just my own proper size, and that for the time being the proportions are somewhat refracted and misrepresented to the eye by the large thing I am inside of, from which I am tipping you this wink."

For example, take matters of this sort. I will not say

whether it is wise or unwise, simple or grave, but certain precedents have been established that in certain companies the President must leave the room first, and people must give way to him. They must not sit down if he is standing up. It is a very uncomfortable thing to have to think of all the other people every time I get up and sit down, and all that sort of thing. So that when I get guests in my own house and the public is shut out I adjourn being President and take leave to be a gentleman. If they draw back and insist upon my doing something first, I firmly decline.

There are blessed intervals when I forget by one means or another that I am President of the United States. One means by which I forget is to get a rattling good detective story, get after some imaginary offender, and chase him all over—preferably any continent but this, because the various parts of this continent are becoming painfully suggestive to me. The Post Offices, and many other things which stir reminiscence have "sicklied them o'er with a pale cast of thought." There are Post Offices to which I wouldn't think of mailing a letter, which I can't think of without trembling with the knowledge of all the heart-burnings of the struggle there was in getting somebody installed as Postmaster.

Now, if I were free I would come not infrequently up to these rooms. You know I never was in Washington but for a very few times, and for a very few hours, until I came last year, and I never expect to see the inside of the public buildings in Washington until my term is over. The minute I turn up anywhere I am personally conducted to beat the band. The Curator and the Assistant Curator and every other blooming official turns up, and they show me so much attention that I don't see the building. I would have to say "Stand aside and let me see what you are showing me."

Some day after I am through with this office I am going

to come back to Washington and see it. In the meantime I am in the same category as the National Museum, the Monument, the Smithsonian Institution, or the Congressional Library, and everything that comes down here has to be shown the President. If I only knew the appearance to assume—apparently I can assume other appearances that do not show what is going on inside—I would like to have it pointed out, so that I could practice it before the looking glass and see if I could not look like the Monument. Being regarded as a national exhibit, it will be much simpler than being shaken hands with by the whole United States.

And yet, even that is interesting to me, simply because I like human beings. It is a pretty poor crowd that does not interest you. I think they would have to be all members of that class that devotes itself to "expense regardless of pleasure" in order to be entirely uninteresting. These look so much alike—spend their time trying to look so much alike—and so relieve themselves of all responsibility of thought—that they are very monotonous, indeed, to look at; whereas, a crowd picked up off the street is just a jolly lot—a job lot of real human beings, pulsating with life, with all kinds of passions and desires.

It would be a great pleasure if, unobserved and unattended, I could be knocked around as I have been accustomed to being knocked around all my life; if I could resort to any delightful quarter, to any place in Washington that I chose. I have sometimes thought of going to some costumer's—some theatrical costumer's—and buying an assortment of beards, rouge and coloring and all the known means of disguising myself, if it were not against the law.

You see I have a scruple as President against breaking the law and disguising one's self is against the law, but if I could disguise myself and not get caught I would go out, be a free American citizen once more and have a jolly time. I might then meet some of you gentlemen and actually tell you what I really thought.

PART II

Political Processes

As a political scientist, Wilson devoted much thought and study to problems of government. He was convinced that the best form of government was a representative democracy that jealously guarded the rights of the individual. He feared the concentration of power, whether in private or governmental hands, though in time he came to recognize the need for more regulation by the national government of the increasingly complex industrialized economy. An admirer of the British parliamentary form of government since his student days at Princeton, Wilson as President sought to adapt some features of the parliamentary system to American political institutions. His efforts were not always successful, but his imaginative use of his office greatly strengthened the Presidency.

A. LEADERSHIP

From his youth on, Wilson was greatly interested in the question of leadership, both in the abstract and in specific situations involving influential historical figures. As an undergraduate he tried to discern what

Reprinted from *Leaders of Men,* ed. T. H. Vail Motter by permission of Princeton University Press. © 1952 by Princeton University Press, pp. 19–20, 25–26, 29, 39–40, 41–44, 44–45, and 49–50.

factors made for successful leadership by great men, and he published character sketches on Bismarck and Pitt in the *Nassau Literary Magazine*. Wilson concluded that a leader must not be too advanced for his times if he hoped to win a following, for society evolved slowly. Yet the true leader should not always seek compromise when a high moral principle was at stake.

DOCUMENT 4

"You Must Lead Your Own Generation, Not the Next"

Perhaps the best statement of Wilson's views on leadership, at least for the period before he had experienced high office, is to be found in a manuscript he began while a professor at Princeton in the 1890's. Never completed, the study was first published three decades after Wilson's death.

Those only are leaders of men, in the general eye, who lead in action. The title belongs, if the whole field of the world be justly viewed, no more rightfully to the men who lead in action than to those who lead in silent thought. A book is often quite as quickening a trumpet as any made of brass and sounded in the field. But it is the estimate of the world that bestows their meaning upon words: and that estimate is not often very far from the fact. The men who act stand nearer to the mass of men than do the men who write; and it is at their hands that new thought gets its translation into the crude language of deeds. The very crudity of that language of deeds exasperates the sensibilities of the author; and his exasperation proves the world's point—proves that, though he may be back of the leaders, he is not the leader. In his thought there was due and studied proportion; all limiting considerations were set in their right places as guards to ward off misapprehension. Every cadence of right utterance was made to sound in the careful phrases, in the perfect adjustments of sense. Just and measured reflection found full and fit expression. But when the thought is translated into action all its shadings disappear. It stands out a naked, lusty thing sure to rasp the sensibilities of every man of fastidious taste. Stripped for action, a thought must always shock those who cultivate the nicest fashions of literary dress, as authors do. But it is only when it thus stands forth in unabashed force that it can perform feats of strength in the arena round about which the great public sit as spectators, awarding the prizes by the suffrage of their applause.

Here, unquestionably, we come upon the heart of the perennial misunderstanding between the men who write and the men who act. The men who write love proportion, the men who act must strike out practicable lines of action and neglect proportion. This would seem sufficiently to explain the well-nigh universal repugnance felt by literary men towards democracy. The arguments which induce popular action must always be broad and obvious arguments: only a very gross substance of concrete conception can make any impression on the minds of the masses; they must get their ideas very absolutely put, and are much readier to receive a half-truth which they can understand than a whole truth which has too many sides to be seen all at once. . . .

The competent leader of men cares little for the interior niceties of other people's characters: he cares much— everything for the external uses to which they may be put. His will seeks the lines of least resistance; but the whole question with him is a question as to the application of force. There are men to be moved: how shall he move them? He supplies the power; others supply only the materials upon which that power operates. The power will fail if it be misapplied; it will be misapplied if it be not suitable both in its character and in its method to the nature of the materials upon which it is spent; but that nature is, after all, only its means. It is the power which dictates, dominates; the materials yield. Men are as clay in the hands of the consummate leader.

It often happens that the leader displays a sagacity and an insight in the handling of men in the mass which quite baffle the wits of the shrewdest analyst of individual character. Men in the mass differ from men as individuals. A man who knows, and keenly knows, every man in town may yet fail to understand a mob or a mass-meeting of his fellow-townsmen. Just as the whole tone and method suitable for a public speech are foreign to the tone and method proper in individual, face to face dealings with separate men, so is the art of leading different from the art of writing novels. . . .

Men are not led by being told what they don't know. Persuasion is a force, but not information; and persuasion is accomplished by creeping into the confidence of those you would lead. Their confidence is gained by qualities which they can recognize, by arguments which they can assimilate: by the things which find easy entrance into their minds and are easily transmitted to the palms of their hands or the ends of their walking-sticks in the shape of applause. Burke's thoughts penetrate the mind and possess the heart of the quiet student; his style of saying things fills the attention as if it were finest music; but they are not thoughts to be shouted over; it is not a style to ravish the ear of the voter at the hustings. If you would be a leader of men, you must lead your own generation, not the next.

Your playing must be good now, while the play is on the boards and the audience in the seats: it will not get you the repute of a great actor to have excellences discovered in you afterwards. Burke's genius made conservative men uneasy. How could a man be safe who had so many ideas? . . .

The whole question of leadership receives a sharp practical test in a popular legislative assembly. The revolutions which have changed the whole principle and method of government within the last hundred years have created a new kind of leadership in legislation: a leadership which is not yet, perhaps, fully understood. It used to be thought that legislation was an affair proper to be conducted only by the few who were instructed for the benefit of the many who were uninstructed: that statesmanship was a function of origination for which only trained and instructed men were fit. Those who actually conducted legislation and undertook affairs were rather whimsically chosen by Fortune to illustrate this theory, but such was the ruling thought in politics. The Sovereignty of the People, however, that great modern principle of politics, has erected a different conception — or, if so be that, in the slowness of our thought, we hang on to the old conception, has created a very different practice. When we are angry with public men nowadays we charge them with subserving instead of forming and directing public opinion. . . .

. . . Society is not a crowd, but an organism; and, like every organism, it must grow as a whole or else be deformed. The world is agreed, too, that it is an organism also in this, that it will die unless it be vital in every part. That is the only line of reasoning by which we can really establish the majority in legitimate authority. This organic whole, Society, is made up, obviously, for the most part, of the majority. It grows by the development of its aptitudes and desires, and under their guidance. The evolution of its institutions must take place by slow modification and nice all-round adjustment. And all this is but a careful and abstract way of saying that no reform may succeed for which the major thought of the nation is not prepared: that the instructed few may not be safe leaders, except in so far as they have communicated their instruction to the many, except in so far as they have transmuted their thought into a common, a popular thought.

Let us fairly distinguish, therefore, the peculiar and delicate duties of the popular leader from the not very peculiar or delicate crimes of the demagogue. Leadership, for the statesman, is interpretation. He must read the common thought: he must test and calculate very circumspectly the preparation of the nation for the next move in the progress of politics. If he fairly hit the popular thought, when we have missed it, are we to say that he is a demagogue? The nice point is to distinguish the firm and progressive popular thought from the momentary and whimsical popular mood, the transitory or mistaken popular passion. But it is fatally easy to blame or misunderstand the statesman. Our temperament is one of logic, let us say. We hold that one and one make two and we see no salvation for the people except they receive the truth. The statesman is of another opinion. One and one doubtless make two, he is ready to admit, but the people think that one and one make more than two and until they see otherwise we shall have to legislate on that supposition. This is not to talk nonsense. The Roman augurs very soon discovered that sacred fowls drank water and pecked grain with no sage intent of prophecy, but from motives quite mundane and simple. But it would have been a revolution to say so and act so in the face of a people who believed otherwise, and executive policy had to proceed on the theory of a divine method of fowl digestion. The divinity that once did hedge a king, grows—not now very high about the latest Hohenzollern—not so high but that one may see that he is a bumptious young gentleman slenderly equipped with wisdom or discretion. But who that prefers growth to revolution would propose that legislation in Germany proceed independently of this hereditary accident?

In no case may we safely hurry the organism away from its habit: for it is held together by that habit, and by it is enabled to perform its functions completely. The constituent habit of a people inheres in its thought, and to that thought legislation—even the legislation that advances and modifies habit—must keep very near. The ear of the leader must ring with the voices of the people. He cannot be of the school of the prophets; he must be of the number of those who studiously serve the slow-paced daily need.

In what, then, does political leadership consist? It is leadership in conduct, and leadership in conduct must discern and strengthen the tendencies that make for development. The legislative leader must perceive the direction of the nation's permanent forces and must feel the speed of their operation. There is initiative here, but not novelty; there are old thoughts, but a progressive application of them. . . .

. . . Practical leadership may not beckon to the slow masses of men from beyond some dim, unexplored space or some intervening chasm: it must daily feel the road that leads to the goal proposed, knowing that it is a slow, a very slow, evolution to wings, and that for the present, and for a very long future also, Society must walk, dependent upon practicable paths, incapable of scaling sudden, precipitous heights, a road-breaker, not a fowl of the air. In the words of the Master, Burke, "to follow, not to force, the public inclination—to give a direction, a form, a technical dress, and a specific sanction, to the general sense of the community, is the true end of legislation." That general sense of the community may wait to be aroused, and the statesman must arouse it; may be inchoate and vague, and the statesman must formulate and make it explicit. But he cannot, and should not, do more. The forces of the public thought may be blind: he must lend them sight; they may blunder: he must set them right. He can do something to create such forces of opinion; but it is a creation of forms, not of substance, and without such forces at his back he can do nothing effective. . . .

Nevertheless, leadership does not always wear the harness of compromise. Once and again one of those great Influences which we call a Cause arises in the midst of the nation. Men of strenuous minds and high ideals come forward with a sort of gentle majesty as champions of a political or moral principle. They wear no armour; they bestride no chargers; they only speak their thought, in season and out of season. But the attacks they sustain are more cruel than the collisions of arms. Their souls are pierced with a thousand keen arrows of obloquy. Friends desert and despise them. They stand alone: and oftentimes are made bitter by their isolation. They are doing nothing less than defy public opinion, and shall they convert it by blows? Yes, presently the forces of the popular thought hesitate, waver, seem to doubt their power to subdue a half score stubborn minds. Again a little while and they have yielded. Masses come over to the side of the reform. Resistance is left to the minority and such as will not be converted are crushed.

What has happened? Has it been given to a handful of men to revolutionize by the foolishness of preaching the whole thought of a nation and of an epoch? By no means. None but Christian doctrine was ever permitted to dig entirely new channels for human thought, and turn that thought quickly about from its old courses; and even Christianity came only "in the fullness of time" and has had a triumph as slow-paced as history itself.

No cause is born out of its time. Every successful reform movement has had as its efficient cry some principle of equity or morality already accepted well-nigh universally, but not yet universally applied in the affairs of life. Every such movement has been the awakening of a people to see a new field for old principles. These men who stood alone at the inception of the movement and whose voices then seemed as it were the voices of men crying in the wilderness, have in reality been simply the more sensitive organs of Society—the parts first awakened to consciousness of a situation. With the start and irritation of a rude and sudden summons from sleep, Society resents the disturbance of its restful unconsciousness, and for a moment racks itself with hasty passion. But, once get it completely aroused, it will sanely meet the necessities of conduct revealed by the hour of its awakening.

DOCUMENT 5

"The Indomitable Individual"

Wilson believed that a leader might compromise on the *pace* of his movement but not its *direction* if he was confident of the essential truth of his goal. Thus, leadership required both flexibility and courage to stand against the popular mood.

Excerpt from address at McCormick Theological Seminary, November 2, 1909. *Public Papers*, II, 184–185.

. . . I have often preached in my political utterances the
doctrine of expediency, and I am an unabashed disciple of
that doctrine. What I mean to say is, you cannot carry the
world forward as fast as a few select individuals think. The
individuals who have the vigour to lead must content
themselves with a slackened pace and go only so fast as
they can be followed. They must not be impracticable.
They must not be impossible. They must not insist upon
getting at once what they know they cannot get. But that is
not inconsistent with their telling the world in very plain
terms whither it is bound and what the ultimate and complete truth of the matter, as it seems to them, is. You cannot make any progress unless you know whither you are
bound. The question is not a pace. This is a matter of expediency, not of direction; that is not a matter of principle.
Where the individual should be indomitable is in the
choice of direction, saying: "I will not bow down to the
golden calf of fashion. I will not bow down to the weak
habit of pursuing everything that is popular, everything
that belongs to the society to which I belong. I will insist
on telling that society, if I think it so, that in certain fundamental principles it is wrong; but I won't be fool enough
to insist that it adopt my programme at once for putting it
right." What I do insist upon is, speaking the full truth
to it and never letting it forget the truth; speaking the truth
again and again and again with every variation of the
theme, until men will wake some morning and the theme
will sound familiar, and they will say, "Well, after all, is it
not so?" That is what I mean by the indomitable individual. Not the defiant individual, not the impracticable individual, but the individual who does try, and cannot be
ashamed, and cannot be silenced; who tries to observe
the fair manner of just speech but who will not hold his
tongue. . . .

B. THE DEFECTS
OF CONGRESSIONAL GOVERNMENT

One of Wilson's early concerns was what he regarded as the malfunctioning of the national legislative branch. Congress, he concluded, had gained too much power at the expense of the executive branch, and was neither efficiently nor democratically run. If not corrected, the situation might threaten the stability of American political institutions. His pessimistic view doubtless stemmed in part from his distaste for some Congressional actions during Radical Reconstruction, as well as from his belief in the superiority of certain aspects of British parliamentary government.

DOCUMENT 6

"No Leaders, No Principles;
No Principles, No Parties."

In his first major article, written while he was a senior at Princeton and published two months after his graduation, Wilson proposed a remedy for the imbalance of power between the legislative and executive branches. Drawing on the parliamentary system, he suggested that cabinet members be given seats in Congress and the right to take part in debate. Such a reform, he argued, would tend to improve the caliber of legislative leadership and would

Thomas W. Wilson (Woodrow Wilson), "Cabinet Government in the United States," *International Review*, VII (August 1879), 146–63.

strengthen the President by giving him command of his party in Congress.

Our patriotism seems of late to have been exchanging its wonted tone of confident hope for one of desponding solicitude. Anxiety about the future of our institutions seems to be daily becoming stronger in the minds of thoughtful Americans. A feeling of uneasiness is undoubtedly prevalent, sometimes taking the shape of a fear that grave, perhaps radical, defects in our mode of government are militating against our liberty and prosperity. A marked and alarming decline in statesmanship, a rule of levity and folly instead of wisdom and sober forethought in legislation, threaten to shake our trust not only in the men by whom our national policy is controlled, but also in the very principles upon which our Government rests. Both State and National legislatures are looked upon with nervous suspicion, and we hail an adjournment of Congress as a temporary immunity from danger. In casting about for the chief cause of the admitted evil, many persons have convinced themselves that it is to be found in the principle of universal suffrage. When Dr. Woolsey, in his admirable work on Political Science, speaks with despondency of the influence of this principle upon our political life, he simply gives clear expression to misgivings which he shares with a growing minority of his countrymen. We must, it is said, purge the' constituencies of their ignorant elements, if we would have high-minded, able, worthy representatives. We see adventurers, who in times of revolution and confusion were suffered to climb to high and responsible places, still holding positions of trust; we perceive that our institutions, when once thrown out of gear, seem to possess no power of self-readjustment, — and we hasten to cast discredit upon that principle the establishment of which has been regarded as America's greatest claim to political honor,—the right of every man to a voice in the Government under which he lives. The existence of such sentiments is in itself an instructive fact. But while it is indisputably true that universal suffrage is a constant element of weakness, and exposes us to many dangers which we might otherwise escape, its operation does not suffice alone to explain existing evils. Those who make this the scapegoat of all our national grievances have made too superficial an analysis of the abuses about which they so loudly complain.

What is the real cause of this solicitude and doubt? It is, in our opinion, to be found in the absorption of all power by a legislature which is practically irresponsible for its acts. But even this would not necessarily be harmful, were it not for the addition of a despotic principle which it is my present purpose to consider.

At its highest development, *representative* government is that form which best enables a free people to govern themselves. The main object of a representative assembly, therefore, should be the discussion of public business. They should legislate as if in the presence of the whole country, because they come under the closest scrutiny and fullest criticism of all the representatives of the country speaking in open and free debate. Only in such an assembly, only in such an atmosphere of publicity, only by means of such a vast investigating machine, can the different sections of a great country learn each other's feelings and interests. It is not enough that the general course of legislation is known to all. Unless during its progress it is subjected to a thorough, even a tediously prolonged, process of public sifting, to the free comment of friend and foe alike, to the ordeal of battle among those upon whose vote its fate depends, an act of open legislation may have its real intent and scope completely concealed by its friends and undiscovered by its enemies, and it may be as fatally mischievous as the darkest measures of an oligarchy or a despot. Nothing can be more obvious than the fact that the very life of free, popular institutions is dependent upon their breathing the bracing air of thorough, exhaustive, and open discussions, or that select Congressional committees, whose proceedings must form their very nature be secret, are, as means of legislation, dangerous and unwholesome. Parliaments are forces for freedom; for "talk is persuasion, persuasion is force, the one force which can sway freemen to deeds such as those which have made England what she is," or our English stock what it is.

Congress is a deliberative body in which there is little real deliberation; a legislature which legislates with no real discussion of its business. Our Government is practically carried on by irresponsible committees. Too few Americans take the trouble to inform themselves as to the methods of Congressional management; and, as a consequence, not many have perceived that almost *absolute* power has fallen into the hands of men whose irresponsibility prevents the regulation of their conduct by the people from whom they derive their authority. The most important, most powerful man in the government of the United States in time of peace is the Speaker of the House of Representatives. Instead of being merely an executive officer, whose principal duties are those immediately connected with the administration of the rules of order, he is a potent party chief, the only chief of any real potency,—and must of necessity be so. He must be the strongest and shrewdest member of his party in the lower House; for almost all the real business of that House is transacted by committees whose members are his nominees. Unless the rules of the House be suspended by a special two-thirds vote, every bill introduced must be referred, without debate, to the proper Standing Committee, with whom rests the privilege of embodying it, or any part of it, in their reports, or of rejecting it altogether. The House very seldom takes any direct action upon any measures introduced by individual members; its votes and discussions are almost entirely confined to committee reports and committee dictation. The whole attitude of business depends upon forty-seven Standing Committees. Even the discussions upon their directive reports are merely nominal,— liberal forms, at most. Take, as an example of the workings of the system, the functions and privileges of the Committee of Ways and Means. To it is intrusted the financial policy of the country; its chairman is, in reality, our Chancellor of the Exchequer. With the aid of his colleagues he determines the course of legislation upon finance; in English political phrase, he draws up the *budget*. All the momentous questions connected with our finance are debated in the private sessions of this committee, and there only. For, when the budget is submitted to the House for its consideration, only a very limited time is allowed for its discussion; and, besides the member of the committee to whom its introduction is intrusted, no one is permitted to speak save those to whom he through courtesy yields the floor, and who must have made arrangements beforehand with the Speaker to be recognized. Where, then, is there room for thorough discussion,—for discussion of any kind? If carried, the provisions of the budget must be put into operation by the Secretary of the Treasury, who may be directly opposed to the principles which it embodies. If lost, no one save Congress itself is responsible for the consequent embarrassment into which the nation is brought,—and Congress as a body is not readily punishable.

It must at once be evident to every thinking man that a policy thus regulated cannot be other than vacillating, uncertain, devoid of plan or consistency. This is certainly a phase of representative government peculiar to ourselves. And yet its development was most natural and apparently necessary. It is hardly possible for a body of several hundred men, without official or authoritative leaders, to determine upon any line of action without interminable wrangling and delays injurious to the interests under their care. Left to their own resources, they would be as helpless as any other mass meeting. Without leaders having authority to guide their deliberations and give a definite direction to the movement of legislation; and, moreover, with none of that sense of responsibility which constantly rests upon those whose duty it is to work out to a successful issue the policies which they themselves originate, yet with full power to dictate policies which others must carry into execution,—a recognition of the need of some sort of leadership, and of a division of labor, led to the formation of these Standing Committees, to which are intrusted the shaping of the national policy in the several departments of administration, as well as the prerogatives of the initiative in legislation and leadership in debate. When theoretically viewed, this is an ingenious and apparently harmless device, but one which, in practice, subverts that most fundamental of all the principles of a free State,—the right of the people to a potential voice in their own government. Great measures of legislation are discussed and determined, not conspicuously in public session of the people's representatives, but in the unapproachable privacy of committee rooms.

But what less imperfect means of representative government can we find without stepping beyond the bounds of a true republicanism? Certainly none other than those which were rejected by the Constitutional Convention. When the Convention of 1787, upon the submission of the report of the Committee of Detail, came to consider the respective duties and privileges of the legislative and executive departments, and the relations which these two branches of the Government should sustain towards each other, many serious questions presented themselves for solution. One of the gravest of these was, whether or not the interests of the public service would be furthered by *allowing some of the higher officers of State to occupy seats in the legislature.* The propriety and practical advantage of such a course were obviously suggested by a similar arrangement under the British Constitution, to which our political fathers often and wisely looked for useful hints. But since the spheres of the several departments were in the end defined with all the clearness, strictness, and care possible to a written instrument, the opinion prevailed among the members of the Convention that it would be unadvisable to establish any such connection between the Executive and Congress. They thought, in their own fervor of patriotism and intensity of respect for written law, that paper barriers would prove sufficient to prevent the encroachments of any one department upon the prerogatives of any other; that these vaguely broad laws — or principles of law — would be capable of securing and maintaining the harmonious and mutually helpful co-operation of the several branches; that the exhibition of these general views of government would be adequate to the stupendous task of preventing the legislature from rising to the predominance of influence, which, nevertheless, constantly lay within its reach. But, in spite of constitutional barriers, the legislature has become the imperial power of the State, as it must of necessity become under every representative system; and experience of the consequences of a complete separation of the legislative and executive branches long since led that able and sagacious commentator upon the Constitution, Chief-Justice Story, to remark that, "if it would not have been safe to trust the heads of departments, as representatives, to the choice of the people, as their constituents, it would have been at least some gain to have allowed them seats, like territorial delegates, in the House of Representatives, where they might freely debate without a title to vote." In short, the framers of the Constitution, in endeavoring to act in accordance with the principle of Montesquieu's celebrated and unquestionably just political maxim, — that the legislative, executive, and judicial departments of a free State should be *separate*, — made their separation so complete as to amount to *isolation*. To the methods of representative government which have sprung from these provisions of the Constitution, by which the Convention thought so carefully to guard and limit the powers of the legislature, we must look for an explanation, in a large measure, of the evils over which we now find ourselves lamenting.

What, then, is Cabinet government? What is the change proposed? Simply to give to the heads of the Executive departments — the members of the Cabinet — seats in Congress, with the privilege of the initiative in legislation and some part of the unbounded privileges now commanded by the Standing Committees. But the advocates of such a change — and they are now not a few — deceive themselves when they maintain that it would not necessarily involve the principle of ministerial responsiblity, — that is, the resignation of the Cabinet upon the defeat of any important part of their plans. For, if Cabinet officers sit in Congress as official representatives of the Executive, this principle of responsibility must of necessity come sooner or later to be recognized. Experience would soon demonstrate the practical impossiblity of their holding their seats, and continuing to represent the Administration, after they had found themselves unable to gain the consent of a majority to their policy. Their functions would be peculiar. They would constitute a link between the legislative and executive branches of the general Government, and, as representatives of the Executive, must hold the right of the initiative in legislation. Otherwise their position would be an anomalous one, indeed. There would be little danger and evident propriety in extending to them the first right of introducing measures relative to the administration of the several departments; and they could possess such a right without denying the fullest privileges to other members. But, whether granted this initiative or not, the head of each department would undoubtedly find it necessary to take a decided and open stand for or against every measure bearing upon the affairs of his department, by whomsoever introduced. No high-spirited man would long remain in an office in the business of which he was not permitted to pursue a policy which tallied with his own principles and convictions. If defeated by both Houses, he would naturally resign; and not many years would pass before resignation upon defeat would have become an established precedent,—and resignation upon defeat is the essence of responsible government. In arguing, therefore, for the admission of Cabinet officers into the legislature, we are logically brought to favor *responsible Cabinet government* in the United States.

But, to give to the President the right to choose whomsoever he pleases as his constitutional advisers, after having constituted Cabinet officers *ex officio* members of Congress, would be to empower him to appoint a limited number of representatives, and would thus be plainly at variance with republican principles. The highest order of responsible government could, then, be established in the United States only by laying upon the President the necessity of selecting his Cabinet from among the number of representatives already chosen by the people, or by the legislatures of the States.

Such a change in our legislative system would not be so radical as it might at first appear: it would certainly be very far from revolutionary. Under our present system we suffer all the inconveniences, are hampered by all that is defective in the machinery, of responsible government, without securing any of the many benefits which would follow upon its complete establishment. Cabinet officers are now appointed only with the consent of the Senate. Such powers as a Cabinet with responsible leadership must possess are now divided among the forty-seven Standing Committees, whose prerogatives of irresponsible leadership savor of despotism, because exercised for the most part within the secret precincts of a committee room, and not under the eyes of the whole House, and thus of the whole country. These committees, too, as has been said, rule without any of that freedom of public debate which is essential to the liberties of the people. Their measures are too often mere partisan measures, and are hurried through the forms of voting by a party majority whose interest it is that all serious opposition, all debate that might develop obstructive antagonism, should be suppressed. Under the conditions of Cabinet government, however, full and free debates are sure to take place. For what are these conditions? According as their policy stands or falls, the ministers themselves stand or fall; to the party which supports them each discussion involves a trial of strength with their opponents; upon it depends the amount of their success as a party: while to the opposition the triumph of ministerial plans means still further exclusion from office; their overthrow, accession to power. To each member of the assembly every debate offers an opportunity for placing himself, by able argument, in a position to command a place in any future Cabinet that may be formed from the ranks of his own party; each speech goes to the building up (or the tearing down) of his political fortunes. There is, therefore, an absolute certainty that every phase of every subject will be drawn carefully and vigorously, will be dwelt upon with minuteness, will be viewed from every possible standpoint. The legislative, holding full power of final decision, would find itself in immediate contact with the executive and its policy. Nor would there be room for factious government or factious opposition. Plainly, ministers must found their policies, an opposition must found its attacks, upon well-considered principles; for in this open sifting of debate, when every feature of every measure, even to the motives which prompted it, is the subject of out-spoken discussion and keen scrutiny, no chicanery, no party craft, no questionable principles can long hide themselves. Party trickery, legislative jobbery, are deprived of the very air they breathe, — the air of secrecy, of concealment. The public is still surprised whenever they find that dishonest legislation has been allowed to pass unchallenged. Why surprised? As things are, measures are determined in the interests of corporations, and the suffering people know almost nothing of them until their evil tendencies crop out in actual execution. Under lobby pressure from interested parties, they have been cunningly concocted in the closet sessions of partisan committees, and, by the all-powerful aid of party machinery, have been hurried through the stages of legislation without debate; so that even Press correspondents are often as ignorant of the real nature of such special measures as the outside public. Any searching debate of such questions would at once have brought the public eye upon them, and how could they then have stood? Lifting the lid of concealment must have been the discovery to all concerned of their unsavory character. Light would have killed them.

We are thus again brought into the presence of the cardinal fact of this discussion, — that *debate* is the essential function of a popular representative body. In the severe, distinct, and sharp enunciation of underlying principles, the unsparing examination and telling criticism of opposite positions, the careful, painstaking unravelling of all the issues involved, which are incident to the free discussion of

questions of public policy, we see the best, the only effective, means of educating public opinion. Can any one
suppose for one moment that, in the late heated and confused discussions of the Bland silver bill, the Western
papers would have had any color of justification in claiming that the Resumption Act of 1875 was passed secretly
and without the knowledge of the people, if we had then
had responsible government? Although this all-important
matter was before the country for more than a year; was
considered by two Congresses, recommended by more
than one Congressional committee; was printed and circulated for the perusal of the people; was much spoken of,
though little understood by the Press at the time—the
general mass of our population knew little or nothing
about it, for it elicited almost no statesmanlike comment
upon the floor of Congress, was exposed to none of the
analysis of earnest debate. What, however, would have
been its history under a well-ordered Cabinet government? It would have been introduced—if introduced at
all—to the House by the Secretary of the Treasury as a
part of the financial policy of the Administration, supported by the authority and sanction of the entire Cabinet. At
once it would have been critically scanned by the leaders
of the opposition; at each reading of the bill, and especially in Committee of the Whole, its weak points would have
been mercilessly assailed, and its strong features urged in
defence; attacks upon its principle by the opposition
would have been met by an unequivocal avowal of "soft
money" principles from the majority; and, defended by
men anxious to win honors in support of the ministry, it
would have been dissected by all those who were at issue
with the financial doctrines of the majority, discussed and
re-discussed until all its essential, all its accidental features, and all its remotest tendencies, had been dinned
into the public ear, so that no man in the nation could have

pretended ignorance of its meaning and object. The educational influence of such discussions is two-fold, and operates in two directions,—upon the members of the legislature themselves, and upon the people whom they represent. Thus do the merits of the two systems—Committee government and government by a responsible Cabinet—hinge upon this matter of a full and free discussion of all subjects of legislation; upon the principle stated by Mr. Bagehot, that "free government is self-government,—a government of the people by the people." It is perhaps safe to say, that the Government which secures the most thorough discussions of public interests,—whose administration most nearly conforms to the opinions of the governed,—is the freest and the best. And certainly, when judged by this principle, government by irresponsible Standing Committees can bear no comparison with government by means of a responsible ministry; for, as we have seen,—and as others besides Senator Hoar have shown,—its essential feature is a vicious suppression of debate.

Only a single glance is necessary to discover how utterly Committee government must fail to give effect to public opinion. In the first place, the exclusion of debate prevents the intelligent formation of opinion on the part of the nation at large; in the second place, public opinion, when once formed, finds it impossible to exercise any immediate control over the action of its representatives. There is no one in Congress to speak for the nation. Congress is a conglomeration of inharmonious elements; a collection of men representing each his neighborhood, each his local interest; an alarmingly large proportion of its legislation is "special;" all of it is at best only a limping compromise between the conflicting interests of the innumerable localities represented. There is no guiding or harmonizing power. Are the people in favor of a particular policy,—what means have they of forcing it upon the sovereign legislature at Washington? None but the most imperfect. If they return representatives who favor it (and this is the most they can do), these representatives being under no directing power will find a mutual agreement impracticable among so many, and will finally settle upon some policy which satisfies nobody, removes no difficulty, and makes little definite or valuable provision for the future. They must, indeed, be content with whatever measure the appropriate committee chances to introduce. Responsible ministries, on the other hand, form the policy of their parties; the strength of their party is at their command; the course of legislation turns upon the acceptance or rejection by the Houses of definite and consistent plans upon which they determine. In forming its judgment of their policy, the nation knows whereof it is judging; and, with biennial Congresses, it may soon decide whether any given policy shall stand or fall. The question would then no longer be, What representatives shall we choose to represent our chances in this haphazard game of legislation? but, What plans of national administration shall we sanction? Would not party programmes mean something then? Could they be constructed only to deceive and bewilder?

But, above and beyond all this, a responsible Cabinet constitutes a link between the executive and legislative departments of the Government which experience declares in the clearest tones to be absolutely necessary in a well-regulated, well-proportioned body politic. None can so well judge of the perfections or imperfections of a law as those who have to administer it. Look, for example, at the important matter of taxation. The only legitimate object of taxation is the support of Government; and who can so well determine the requisite revenue as those who conduct the Government? Who can so well choose feasible means of taxation, available sources of revenue, as those who have to meet the practical difficulties of tax-collection? And what surer guarantee against exorbitant estimates and unwise taxation, than the necessity of full explanation and defence before the whole House? The same principles, of course, apply to all legislation upon matters connected with any of the Executive departments.

Thus, then, not only can Cabinet ministers meet the needs of their departments more adequately and understandingly, and conduct their administration better than can irresponsible committees, but they are also less liable to misuse their powers. Responsible ministers must secure from the House and Senate an intelligent, thorough, and practical treatment of their affairs; must vindicate their principles in open battle on the floor of Congress. The public is thus enabled to exercise a direct scrutiny over the workings of the Executive departments, to keep all their operations under a constant stream of daylight. Ministers could do nothing under the shadow of darkness; committees do all in the dark. It can easily be seen how constantly ministers would be plied with questions about the conduct of public affairs, and how necessary it would be for them to satisfy their questioners if they did not wish to fall under suspicion, distrust, and obloquy.

But, while the people would thus be able to defend themselves through their representatives against malfeasance or inefficiency in the management of their business, the heads of the departments would also have every opportunity to defend their administration of the people's affairs against unjust censure or crippling legislation. Corruption in office would court concealment in vain; vicious trifling with the administration of public business by irresponsible persons would meet with a steady and effective check. The ground would be clear for a manly and candid defence of ministerial methods; wild schemes of legislation would meet with a cold repulse from ministerial authority. The salutary effect of such a change would most conspicuously appear in the increased effectiveness of our now crumbling civil, military, and naval services; for we should no longer be cursed with tardy, insufficient, and misapplied appropriations. The ministers of War, of the Navy, of the Interior, would be able to submit their estimates in person, and to procure speedy and regular appropriations; and half the abuses at present connected with appropriative legislation would necessarily disappear with the present committee system. Appropriations now, though often inadequate, are much oftener wasteful and fraudulent. Under responsible government, every appropriation asked by an Executive chief, as well as the reasons by which he backed his request, would be subjected to the same merciless sifting processes of debate as would characterize the consideration of other questions. Always having their responsible agents thus before them, the people would at once know how much they were spending, and for what it was spent.

When we come to speak of the probable influence of responsible Cabinet government upon the development of statesmanship and the renewal of the now perishing growth of statesmanlike qualities, we come upon a vital interest of the whole question. Will it bring with it worthy successors of Hamilton and Webster? Will it replace a leadership of trickery and cunning device by one of ability and moral strength? If it will not, why advocate it? If it will, how gladly and eagerly and imperatively ought we to demand it! The most despotic of Governments under the control of wise statesmen is preferable to the freest ruled by demagogues. Now, there are few more common, and perhaps few more reasonable, beliefs than that at all times, among the millions of population who constitute the body of this great nation, there is here and there to be found a man with all the genius, all the deep and strong patriotism, all the moral vigor, and all the ripeness of knowledge and variety of acquisition which gave power and lasting fame to the greater statesmen of our past history. We bewail and even wonder at the fact that these men do not find their way into public life, to claim power and leadership in the service of their country. We naturally ascribe their absence to the repugnance which superior minds must feel for the intrigues, the glaring publicity, and the air of unscrupulousness and even dishonesty which are the characteristics, or at least the environments, of political life. In our disappointment and vexation that they do not, even at the most distressing sacrifice of their personal convenience and peace, devote themselves to the study and practice of state-craft, we turn for comfort to re-read history's lesson,—that many countries find their greatest statesmen in times of extraordinary crisis or rapid transition and progress; the intervals of slow growth and uninteresting everyday administration of the government being noted only for the elevation of mediocrity, or at most of shrewd cunning, to high administrative places. We take cold consolation from the hope that times of peril—which sometimes seem close enough at hand—will not find us without strong leaders worthy of the most implicit confidence. Thus we are enabled to arrive at the comfortable and fear-quieting conclusion that it is from no fault of ours, certainly from no defects in our forms of government, that we are ruled by scheming, incompetent, political tradesmen, whose aims and ambitions are merely personal, instead of by broadminded, masterful statesmen, whose sympathies and purposes are patriotic and national.

To supply the conditions of statesmanship is, we conclude, beyond our power; for the causes of its decline and the means necessary to its development are beyond our ken. Let us take a new departure. Let us, drawing light from every source within the range of our knowledge, make a little independent analysis of the conditions of statesmanship, with a view to ascertaining whether or not it is in reality true that we cannot contribute to its development, or even perchance give it a perennial growth among us. We learn from a critical survey of the past, that, so far as political affairs are concerned, great critical epochs are the man-making epochs of history, that revolutionary influences are man-making influences. And why? If this be the law, it must have some adequate reason underlying it; and we seem to find the reason a very plain and conspicuous one. Crises give birth and a new growth to statesmanship because they are peculiarly periods of action, in which talents find the widest and the freest scope. They are periods not only of action, but also of unusual opportunity for gaining leadership and a controlling and guiding influence. It is opportunity for transcendent influence, therefore, which calls into active public life a nation's greater minds, — minds which might otherwise remain absorbed in the smaller affairs of private life. And we thus come upon the principle, — a principle which will appear the more incontrovertible the more it is looked into and tested, — that governmental forms will call to the work of administration able minds and strong hearts constantly or infrequently, according as they do or do not afford them at all times an opportunity of gaining and retaining a commanding authority and an undisputed leadership in the nation's councils. Now it certainly needs no argument to prove that government by supreme committees, whose members are appointed at the caprice of an irresponsible party chief, by seniority, because of reputation gained in entirely different fields, or because of partisan shrewdness, is not favorable to a full and strong development of statesmanship. Certain it is that statesmanship has been steadily dying out in the United

States since that stupendous crisis during which its government felt the first throbs of life. In the government of the United States there is no place found for the leadership of men of real ability. Why, then, complain that we have no leaders? The President can seldom make himself recognized as a leader; he is merely the executor of the sovereign legislative will; his Cabinet officers are little more than chief clerks, or superintendents, in the Executive departments, who advise the President as to matters in most of which he has no power of action independently of the concurrence of the Senate. The most ambitious representative can rise no higher than the chairmanship of the Committee of Ways and Means, or the Speakership of the House. The cardinal feature of Cabinet government, on the other hand, is responsible leadership, — the leadership and authority of a small body of men who have won the foremost places in their party by a display of administrative talents, by evidence of high ability upon the floor of Congress in the stormy play of debate. None but the ablest can become leaders and masters in this keen tournament in which arguments are the weapons, and the people the judges. Clearly defined, definitely directed policies arouse bold and concerted opposition; and leaders of oppositions become in time leaders of Cabinets. Such a recognized leadership it is that is necessary to the development of statesmanship under popular, republican institutions; for only such leadership can make politics seem worthy of cultivation to men of high mind and aim.

And if party success in Congress — the ruling body of the nation — depends upon power in debate, skill and prescience in policy, successful defence of or attacks upon ruling ministries, how ill can contending parties spare their men of ability from Congress! To keep men of the strongest mental and moral fibre in Congress would become a party necessity. Party triumph would then be a matter of might in debate, not of supremacy in subterfuge. The two great national parties—and upon the existence of two great parties, with clashings and mutual jealousies and watchings, depends the health of free political institutions—are dying for want of unifying and vitalizing principles. Without leaders, they are also without policies, without aims. With leaders there must be followers, there must be parties. And with leaders whose leadership was earned in an open war of principle against principle, by the triumph of one opinion over all opposing opinions, parties must from the necessities of the case have definite policies. Platforms, then, must mean something. Broken promises will then end in broken power. A Cabinet without a policy that is finding effect in progressive legislation is, in a country of frequent elections, inviting its own defeat. Or is there, on the other hand, a determined, aggressive opposition? Then the ministry have a right to ask them what they would do under similar circumstances, were the reins of government to fall to them. And if the opposition are then silent, they cannot reasonably expect the country to intrust the government to them. Witness the situation of the Liberal party in England during the late serious crisis in Eastern affairs. Not daring to propose any policy,—having indeed, because of the disintegration of the party, no policy to propose,—their numerical weakness became a moral weakness, and the nation's ear was turned away from them. Eight words contain the sum of the present degradation of our political parties: *No leaders, no principles; no principles, no parties.* Congressional leadership is divided infinitesimally; and with divided leadership there can be no great party units. Drill in debate, by giving scope to talents, invites talents; raises up a race of men habituated to the methods of public business, skilled parliamentary chiefs. And, more than this, it creates a much-to-be-desired class who early make attendance upon public affairs the business of their lives, devoting to the service of their country all their better years. Surely the management of a nation's business will, in a well-ordered society, be as properly a matter of life-long training as the conduct of private affairs.

These are but meagre and insufficient outlines of some of the results which would follow upon the establishment of responsible Cabinet government in the United States. Its establishment has not wanted more or less outspoken advocacy from others; nor, of course, have there been lacking those who are ready to urge real or imaginary objections against it, and proclaim it an exotic unfit to thrive in American soil. It has certainly, in common with all other political systems, grave difficulties and real evils connected with it. Difficulties and evils are inseparable from every human scheme of government; and, in making their choice, a people can do no more than adopt that form which affords the largest measure of real liberty, whose machinery is least imperfect, and which is most susceptible to the control of their sovereign will.

Few, however, have discovered the real defects of such a responsible government as that which I now advocate. It is said, for instance, that it would render the President a mere figure-head, with none of that stability of official tenure, or that traditional dignity, which are necessary to such figure-heads. Would the President's power be curtailed, then, if his Cabinet ministers simply took the place of the Standing Committees? Would it not rather be enlarged? He would then be in fact, and not merely in name, the head of the Government. Without the consent of the Senate, he now exercises no sovereign functions that would be taken from him by a responsible Cabinet.

The apparently necessary existence of a partisan Executive presents itself to many as a fatal objection to the establishment of the forms of responsible Cabinet govern-

ment in this country. The President must continue to
represent a political party, and must continue to be anxious to surround himself with Cabinet officers who shall
always substantially agree with him on all political questions. It must be admitted that the introduction of the
principle of ministerial responsibility might, on this account, become at times productive of mischief, unless the
tenure of the presidential office were made more permanent than it now is. Whether or not the presidential term
should, under such a change of conditions, be lengthened
would be one of several practical questions which would
attend the adoption of a system of this sort. But it must be
remembered that such a state of things as now exists, when
we find the Executive to be of one party and the majority
in Congress to be of the opposite party, is the exception,
by no means the rule. Moreover we must constantly keep
before our minds the fact that the choice now lies between
this responsible Cabinet government and the rule of irresponsible committees which actually exists. It is not hard
to believe that most presidents would find no greater inconvenience, experience no greater unpleasantness, in
being at the head of a Cabinet composed of political opponents than in presiding, as they must now occasionally do,
over a Cabinet of political friends who are compelled to
act in all matters of importance according to the dictation
of Standing Committees which are ruled by the opposite
party. In the former case, the President may, by the exercise
of whatever personal influence he possesses, affect the action of the Cabinet, and, through them, the action of the
Houses; in the latter he is absolutely helpless. Even now it
might prove practically impossible for a President to gain
from a hostile majority in the Senate a confirmation of his
appointment of a strongly partisan Cabinet drawn from his
own party. The President must now, moreover, acting

through his Cabinet, simply do the bidding of the committees in directing the business of the departments. With a responsible Cabinet—even though that Cabinet were of the opposite party—he might, if a man of ability, exercise great power over the conduct of public affairs; if not a man of ability, but a *mere* partisan, he would in any case be impotent. From these considerations it would appear that government by Cabinet ministers who represent the majority in Congress is no more incompatible with a partisan Executive than is government by committees representing such a majority. Indeed, a partisan President might well prefer legislation through a hostile body at whose deliberations he might himself be present, and whose course he might influence, to legislation through hostile committees over whom he could have no manner of control, direct or indirect. And such conditions would be exceptional.

But the encroachment of the legislative upon the executive is deemed the capital evil of our Government in its later phases; and it is asked, Would not the power of Congress be still more dangerously enlarged, and these encroachments made easier and surer, by thus making its relations with the Executive closer? By no means. The several parts of a perfect mechanism must actually interlace and be in strong union in order mutually to support and check each other. Here again permanent, dictating committees are the only alternative. On the one hand, we have committees directing policies for whose miscarriage they are not responsible; on the other, we have a ministry asking for legislation for whose results they are responsible. In both cases there is full power and authority on the part of the legislature to determine all the main lines of administration: there is no more real control of Executive acts in the one case than in the other; but there is an all-important difference in the character of the agents employed. When carrying out measures thrust upon them by committees, administrative officers can throw off all sense of responsibility; and the committees are safe from punishment, safe even from censure,whatever the issue. But in administering laws which have passed under the influence of their own open advocacy, ministers must shoulder the responsibilities and face the consequences. We should not, then, be giving Congress powers or opportunities of encroachment which it does not now possess, but should, on the contrary, be holding its powers in constant and effective check by putting over it responsible leaders. A complete separation of the executive and legislative is not in accord with the true spirit of those essentially English institutions of which our Government is a characteristic offshoot. The Executive is in constant need of legislative co-operation; the legislative must be aided by an Executive who is in a position intelligently and vigorously to execute its acts. There must needs be, therefore, as a binding link between them, some body which has no power to coerce the one and is interested in maintaining the independent effectiveness of the other. Such a link is the responsible Cabinet.

Again, it is objected that we should be cursed with that instability of government which results from a rapid succession of ministries, a frequent shifting of power from the hands of one party to the hands of another. This is not necessarily more likely to occur under the system of responsibility than now. We should be less exposed to such fluctuations of power than is the English government. The elective system which regulates the choice of United States Senators prevents more than one third of the seats becoming vacant at once, and this third only once every two years. The political complexion of the Senate can be changed only by a succession of elections.

But against such a responsible system the alarm-bell of

centralization is again sounded, and all those who dread seeing too much authority, too complete control, placed within the reach of the central Government sternly set their faces against any such change. They deceive themselves. There could be no more despotic authority wielded under the forms of free government than our national Congress now exercises. It is a despotism which uses its power with all the caprice, all the scorn for settled policy, all the wild unrestraint which mark the methods of other tyrants as hateful to freedom.

Few of us are ready to suggest a remedy for the evils all deplore. We hope that our system is self-adjusting, and will not need our corrective interference. This is a vain hope! It is no small part of wisdom to know how long an evil ought to be tolerated, to see when the time has come for the people, from whom springs all authority, to speak its doom or prescribe its remedy. If that time be allowed to slip unrecognized, our dangers may overwhelm us, our political maladies may prove incurable.

DOCUMENT 7

"Making Parties Responsible"

During his graduate study at Johns Hopkins in the 1880's, Wilson continued his study of contemporary American political institutions. In 1885 he published his doctoral dissertation and first book, *Congressional Government,* in which he developed further his analysis of the defects of Congress. A year earlier, however, he had summarized some of his conclusions and proposed remedies in a maga-

---

Excerpts from Woodrow Wilson, "Committee or Cabinet Government?" *Overland Monthly,* III (January 1884), 24–27, 33.

zine article that once again reflected the influence of the British parliamentary system upon his thought.

. . . It is only by making parties responsible for what they do and advise that they can be made safe and reliable servants. It is plain to see that this caucus on which our present party system rides is a very ugly beast, and a very unmanageable one. He cannot be driven with a chirp, nor commanded with a word. He will obey only the strong hand, and heed only the whip. To rail at him is of no good. He must be taken sternly in hand, and be harnessed, whether he will or no, in our service. Our search must be for the bit that will curb and subdue him.

In seeking an escape from the perplexity, manifestly the safest course is to content ourselves with traveling ways already trodden, and look to the precedents of our own race for guidance. Let, therefore, the leaders of parties be made responsible. Let there be set apart from the party in power certain representatives who, leading their party, and representing its policy, may be made to suffer a punishment which shall be at once personal and vicarious, when their party goes astray, or their policy either misleads or miscarries. This can be done by making the leaders of the dominant party in Congress the executive officers of the legislative will; by making them also members of the President's Cabinet, and thus at once the executive chiefs of the departments of State and the leaders of their party on the floor of Congress; in a word, by having done with the Standing Committees, and constituting the Cabinet advisers both of the President and of Congress. This would be Cabinet government.

Cabinet government is government by means of an executive ministry chosen by the chief magistrate of the nation from the ranks of the legislative majority — a ministry sitting in the legislature and acting as its executive committee; directing its business and leading its debates;

representing the same party and the same principles; "bound together by a sense of responsibility and loyalty to the party to which it belongs," and subject to removal whenever it forfeits the confidence and loses the support of the body it represents. Its establishment in the United States would involve, of course, several considerable changes in our present system. It would necessitate, in the first place, one or two alterations in the Constitution. The second clause of Section Six, Article I, of the Constitution runs thus: "No Senator or Representative shall, during the term for which he was elected, be appointed to any civil office under the authority of the United States which shall have been created, or the emoluments whereof shall have been increased, during such time; and no person holding any office under the United States shall be a member of either House during his continuance in office." Let the latter part of this clause read: "And no person holding any other than a Cabinet office under the United States shall be a member of either House during his continuance in office," and the addition of four words will have removed the chief constitutional obstacle to the erection of Cabinet government in this country. The way will have been cleared, in great part at least, for the development of a constitutional practice, which, founded upon the great charter we already possess, might grow into a governmental system at once strong, stable, and flexible. Those four words being added to the Constitution, the President might be authorized and directed to choose for his Cabinet the leaders of the ruling majority in Congress; that Cabinet might, on condition of acknowledging its tenure of office dependent on the favor of the Houses, be allowed to assume those privileges of initiative in legislation and leadership in debate which are now given, by an almost equal distribution, to the Standing Committees; and Cabinet government would have been instituted.

To insure the efficiency of the new system, however,

additional amendments of the Constitution would doubtless be necessary. Unless the President's tenure of office
were made more permanent than it now is, he could not
fairly be expected to exercise that impartiality in the
choice of ministers, his legislative advisers and executive
colleagues, which would be indispensable to good government under such a system; and no executive Cabinet
which was dependent on the will of a body subject to
biennial change—and which, because it is elected for only
two years, is the more apt to be ruled by the spirit of faction and caught by every cunningly-devised fable—could
have that sense of security without which there can be
neither steadiness of policy nor strength of statesmanship.
It must become necessary to lengthen both Presidential
and Congressional terms. If the President must expect his
authority to end within the short space of four years, he
must be excused for caprice in the choice of his Secretaries. If no faithfulness and diligence of his can extend
the period of his official authority by even so much as a
single week, it cannot be reasonable to expect him to sacrifice his will to the will of others, or to subordinate his
wishes to the public good during the short season of that
brief authority's secure enjoyment. And, if Cabinets be
vouchsafed but two years in which to mature the policies
they may undertake, they cannot justly be blamed for haste
and improvidence. They could not safely be appointed, or
safely trusted to rule after appointment, under a system of
quadrennial presidencies and biennial legislatures. Unless
both Presidential and Congressional terms were extended,
government would be both capricious and unstable. And
they could be the more easily extended, because to
lengthen them would be to change no *principle* of the
Constitution. The admission of members of Congress to
seats in the Cabinet would be the only change of principle
called for by the new order of things.

Cabinet government has in it everything to recommend it. Especially to Americans should it commend itself. It is, first of all, the simplest and most straightforward system of party government. It gives explicit authority to that party majority which in any event will exercise its implicit powers to the top of its bent; which will snatch control if control be not given it. It is a simple legalization of fact; for, as every one knows, we are not free to choose between party government and no-party government. Our choice must be between a party that rules by authority and a party that, where it has not a grant of the right to rule, will make itself supreme by stratagem. It is not parties in open and legitimate organization that are to be feared, but those that are secretly banded together, begetters of hidden schemes and ugly stratagems.

Cabinet government would, moreover, put the necessary bit in the mouth of beast caucus, and reduce him to his proper service; for it would secure open-doored government. It would not suffer legislation to skulk in committee closets and caucus conferences. Light is the only thing that can sweeten our political atmosphere — light thrown upon every detail of administration in the departments; light diffused through every passage of policy; light blazed full upon every feature of legislation; light that can penetrate every recess or corner in which any intrigue might hide; light that will open to view the innermost chambers of government, drive away all darkness from the treasury vaults, illuminate foreign correspondence, explore national dockyards, search out the obscurities of Indian affairs, display the workings of justice, exhibit the management of the army, play upon the sails of the navy, and follow the distribution of the mails — and of such light Cabinet government would be a constant and plentiful source. For, consider the conditions of its existence. Debate would be the breath of its nostrils: for the ministers' tenure of office would be dependent on the vindication of their policy. No member of a Cabinet who had identified himself with any pending measure could with self-respect continue in office after the majority, whose representative he would be, had rejected that measure by a formal and deliberate vote. If, under such circumstances, he did not at once resign, he would forfeit all claim to manly independence. For him to remain in office would be to consent to aid in administering a policy of which he was known to disapprove, and thus to lose the respect of all honorable opponents and the support of all conscientious friends. It would be sacrificing principle to an unworthy love of office; preferring mere place to integrity; openly professing willingness to do the bidding of opponents rather than forego the empty honors of conspicuous station held without conspicuous worth. A man who held an office thus would soon be shamed into retirement; or, were no place left for shame, would be driven from his authority by a scorn-laden vote.

Moreover, the members of the Cabinet would always be *united* in their responsibility. They would stand or fall together in the event of the acceptance or rejection of any measure to which they had given their joint support. Otherwise, they would be no better leaders than the present Standing Committees; the differences, the disputes, and the antagonisms of the council-board would be renewed and reheated in the debates on the floor of Congress; the country would be scandalized at seeing ministers cross swords in open contention; personal spites would flame out in public between uncongenial ministers; there would be unseemly contests for the leadership. An ununited Cabinet could offer neither effectual guidance to the Houses nor intelligible advice to the Executive. United responsibility is indispensable in Cabinet government, because, without it, such government lacks its most admirable and valuable, its quintessential feature: namely, responsible leadership. Every deliberative body should have an accepted and responsible leader, and a legislative body without such a leader must dissipate its power like an unbanked stream. And a Cabinet that leads must be itself led, and act as if with one mind; else legislation will drift as helplessly and as carelessly as it does now, under the Committees, for want of some one influence to guide it.

A ministry united in action and in responsibility for their acts, must, manifestly, rule by debate. Their power and success would depend on the ascendency of their policy, and the ascendency of their policy would depend on the suffrages of the Houses. That policy must be vindicated in the eyes of Representatives and people alike. Defeat on a measure of importance would bring the necessity of resignation, and resignation would mean the incoming of the opposition leaders to power and authority. Debate would, therefore, of course be sought by Ministry and Opposition alike—by the one, that the triumph of their party might be approved a righteous triumph; by the other, that that triumph might be changed into defeat, and they themselves snatch victory and command. What greater earnest of sincerity and fidelity could there be than such a system as this? No minister could afford to ignore his party's pledges. Abandoned party platforms would furnish fine material for stout party coffins, and the ranks of the opposition would supply hosts of eager undertakers. How could a Cabinet face the ordeal of debate, after ignoring its promises and violating its engagements? And yet, how could it escape that trial when the Opposition were demanding debate, and to decline it would be of all confessions the most craven? Always eager to assail the ministers, the champions of the Opposition would have an unquenchable zeal for the fight, and no Ministry could afford to refuse them battle. . . .

It cannot be too often repeated, that while Congress remains the supreme power of the State, it is idle to talk of steadying or cleansing our politics without in some way linking together the interests of the Executive and the Legislature. So long as these two great branches are isolated, they must be ineffective just to the extent of the isolation. Congress will always be master, and will always enforce its commands on the administration. The only wise plan, therefore, is to facilitate its direction of the government, and to make it at the same time responsible, in the persons of its leaders, for its acts of control, and for the manner in which its plans and commands are executed. The only hope of wrecking the present clumsy misrule of Congress lies in the establishment of responsible Cabinet government. Let the interests of the Legislature be indissolubly linked with the interests of the Executive. Let those who have authority to direct the course of legislation be those who have a deep personal concern in building up the executive departments in effectiveness, in strengthening law, and in unifying policies; men whose personal reputation depends upon successful administration, whose public station originates in the triumph of principles, and whose dearest ambition it is to be able to vindicate their wisdom and maintain their integrity.

Committee government is too clumsy and too clandestine a system to last. Other methods of government must sooner or later be sought, and a different economy established. First or last, Congress must be organized in conformity with what is now the prevailing legislative practice of the world. English precedent and the world's fashion must be followed in the institution of Cabinet Government in the United States.

C. THE NATURE OF THE PRESIDENCY

Wilson's early view, based on the ineffectual performance of the immediate post-Civil War chief executives, was that the Presidency offered little opportunity for vigorous leadership. But the sturdy
independence of Grover Cleveland—and even more
the strenuous activity of Theodore Roosevelt—persuaded him that he had underestimated the potentialities of the office. By the time he entered the White
House he had come to see that the powers of the Presidency were virtually limitless, and that the office
might be as big as the man who occupied it.

DOCUMENT 8

"The Unifying Force in Our Complex System,

the Leader Both of His Party and of the Nation"

Wilson's mature view of the Presidency was contained in a
series of lectures on American government which he gave
at Columbia University in 1907. The lectures were published as a book the following year.

It is difficult to describe any single part of a great governmental system without describing the whole of it. Governments are living things and operate as organic wholes.
Moreover, governments have their natural evolution and

Woodrow Wilson, *Constitutional Government in the United States* (New
York: Columbia University Press, 1908), pp. 54, 57–61, 63–64, 65–74,
and 77–81.

are one thing in one age, another in another. The makers of the Constitution constructed the federal government upon a theory of checks and balances which was meant to limit the operation of each part and allow to no single part or organ of it a dominating force; but no government can be successfully conducted upon so mechanical a theory. Leadership and control must be lodged somewhere; the whole art of statesmanship is the art of bringing the several parts of government into effective coöperation for the accomplishment of particular common objects, — and party objects at that. Our study of each part of our federal system, if we are to discover our real government as it lives, must be made to disclose to us its operative coördination as a whole: its places of leadership, its method of action, how it operates, what checks it, what gives it energy and effect. Governments are what politicians make them, and it is easier to write of the President than of the presidency. . . .

. . .. The presidency has been one thing at one time, another at another, varying with the man who occupied the office and with the circumstances that surrounded him. One account must be given of the office during the period 1789 to 1825, when the government was getting its footing both at home and abroad, struggling for its place among the nations and its full credit among its own people; when English precedents and traditions were strongest; and when the men chosen for the office were men bred to leadership in a way that attracted to them the attention and confidence of the whole country. Another account must be given of it during Jackson's time, when an imperious man, bred not in deliberative assemblies or quiet councils, but in the field and upon a rough frontier, worked his own will upon affairs, with or without formal sanction of law, sustained by a clear undoubting conscience and the love of a people who had grown deeply impatient of the régime he had supplanted. Still another account must be given of it during the years 1836 to 1861, when domestic affairs of many debatable kinds absorbed the country, when Congress necessarily exercised the chief choices of policy, and when the Presidents who followed one another in office lacked the personal force and initiative to make for themselves a leading place in counsel. After that came the Civil War and Mr. Lincoln's unique task and achievement, when the executive seemed for a little while to become by sheer stress of circumstances the whole government, Congress merely voting supplies and assenting to necessary laws, as Parliament did in the time of the Tudors. From 1865 to 1898 domestic questions, legislative matters in respect of which Congress had naturally to make the initial choice, legislative leaders the chief decisions of policy, came once more to the front, and no President except Mr. Cleveland played a leading and decisive part in the quiet drama of our national life. Even Mr. Cleveland may be said to have owed his great rôle in affairs rather to his own native force and the confused politics of the time, than to any opportunity of leadership naturally afforded him by a system which had subordinated so many Presidents before him to Congress. The war with Spain again changed the balance of parts. Foreign questions became leading questions again, as they had been in the first days of the government, and in them the President was of necessity leader. Our new place in the affairs of the world has since that year of transformation kept him at the front of our government, where our own thoughts and the attention of men everywhere is centred upon him.

Both men and circumstances have created these contrasts in the administration and influence of the office of President. We have all been disciples of Montesquieu, but we have also been practical politicians. Mr. Bagehot once remarked that it was no proof of the excellence of the

Constitution of the United States that the Americans had operated it with conspicuous success because the Americans could run any constitution successfully; and, while the compliment is altogether acceptable, it is certainly true that our practical sense is more noticeable than our theoretical consistency, and that, while we were once all constitutional lawyers, we are in these latter days apt to be very impatient of literal and dogmatic interpretations of constitutional principle.

The makers of the Constitution seem to have thought of the President as what the stricter Whig theorists wished the king to be: only the legal executive, the presiding and guiding authority in the application of law and the execution of policy. His veto upon legislation was only his "check" on Congress,—was a power of restraint, not of guidance. He was empowered to prevent bad laws, but he was not to be given an opportunity to make good ones. As a matter of fact he has become very much more. He has become the leader of his party and the guide of the nation in political purpose, and therefore in legal action. The constitutional structure of the government has hampered and limited his action in these significant rôles, but it has not prevented it. The influence of the President has varied with the men who have been Presidents and with the circumstances of their times, but the tendency has been unmistakably disclosed, and springs out of the very nature of government itself. It is merely the proof that our government is a living, organic thing, and must, like every other government, work out the close synthesis of active parts which can exist only when leadership is lodged in some one man or group of men. You cannot compound a successful government out of antagonisms. Greatly as the practice and influence of Presidents has varied, there can be no mistaking the fact that we have grown more and more inclined from generation to generation to look to the

President as the unifying force in our complex system, the leader both of his party and of the nation. To do so is not inconsistent with the actual provisions of the Constitution; it is only inconsistent with a very mechanical theory of its meaning and intention. The Constitution contains no theories. It is as practical a document as Magna Carta.

The rôle of party leader is forced upon the President by the method of his selection. The theory of the makers of the Constitution may have been that the presidential electors would exercise a real choice, but it is hard to understand how, as experienced politicians, they can have expected anything of the kind. They did not provide that the electors should meet as one body for consultation and make deliberate choice of a President and Vice-President, but that they should meet "in their respective states" and cast their ballots in separate groups, without the possibility of consulting and without the least likelihood of agreeing, unless some such means as have actually been used were employed to suggest and determine their choice beforehand. It was the practice at first to make party nominations for the presidency by congressional caucus. Since the Democratic upheaval of General Jackson's time nominating conventions have taken the place of congressional caucuses; and the choice of Presidents by party conventions has had some very interesting results. . . .

In reality there is much more method, much more definite purpose, much more deliberate choice in the extraordinary process than there seems to be. The leading spirits of the national committee of each party could give an account of the matter which would put a very different face on it and make the methods of nominating conventions seem, for all the undoubted elements of chance there are in them, on the whole very manageable. Moreover, the party that expects to win may be counted on to make a much more conservative and thoughtful selection of a candidate than the party that merely hopes to win. The haphazard selections which seem to discredit the system are generally made by conventions of the party unaccustomed to success. Success brings sober calculation and a sense of responsibility. . . .

. . . What is it that a nominating convention wants in the man it is to present to the country for its suffrages? A man who will be and who will seem to the country in some sort an embodiment of the character and purpose it wishes its government to have, — a man who understands his own day and the needs of the country, and who has the personality and the initiative to enforce his views both upon the people and upon Congress. It may seem an odd way to get such a man. It is even possible that nominating conventions and those who guide them do not realize entirely what it is that they do. But in simple fact the convention picks out a party leader from the body of the nation. Not that it expects its nominee to direct the interior government of the party and to supplant its already accredited and experienced spokesmen in Congress and in its state and national committees; but it does of necessity expect him to represent it before public opinion and to stand before the country as its representative man, as a true type of what the country may expect of the party itself in purpose and principle. It cannot but be led by him in the campaign; if he be elected, it cannot but acquiesce in his leadership of the government itself. What the country will demand of the candidate will be, not that he be an astute politician, skilled and practised in affairs, but that he be a man such as it can trust, in character, in intention, in knowledge of its needs, in perception of the best means by which those needs may be met, in capacity to prevail by reason of his own weight and integrity. Sometimes the country believes in a party, but more often it believes in a man; and conventions have often shown the instinct to perceive which it is that the country needs in a particular presidential year, a mere representative partisan, a military hero, or some one who will genuinely speak for the country itself, whatever be his training and antecedents. It is in this sense that the President has the rôle of party leader thrust upon him by the very method by which he is chosen.

As legal executive, his constitutional aspect, the President cannot be thought of alone. He cannot execute laws. Their actual daily execution must be taken care of by the several executive departments and by the now innumerable body of federal officials throughout the country. In respect of the strictly executive duties of his office the President may be said to administer the presidency in conjunction with the members of his cabinet, like the chairman of a commission. He is even of necessity much less active in the actual carrying out of the law than are his colleagues and advisers. It is therefore becoming more and more true, as the business of the government becomes more and more complex and extended, that the President is becoming more and more a political and less and less an executive officer. His executive powers are in commission, while his political powers more and more centre and accumulate upon him and are in their very nature personal and inalienable.

Only the larger sort of executive questions are brought to him. Departments which run with easy routine and whose transactions bring few questions of general policy to the surface may proceed with their business for months and even years together without demanding his attention; and no department is in any sense under his direct charge. Cabinet meetings do not discuss detail: they are concerned only with the larger matters of policy or expediency which important business is constantly disclosing. There are no more hours in the President's day than in another man's. If he is indeed the executive, he must act almost entirely by delegation, and is in the hands of his colleagues. He is likely to be praised if things go well, and blamed if they go wrong; but his only real control is of the persons to whom he deputes the performance of executive duties. It is through no fault or neglect of his that the duties apparently assigned to him by the Constitution have come to be his less conspicuous, less important duties, and that duties apparently not assigned to him at all chiefly occupy his time and energy. The one set of duties it has proved practically impossible for him to perform; the other it has proved impossible for him to escape.

He cannot escape being the leader of his party except by incapacity and lack of personal force, because he is at once the choice of the party and of the nation. He is the party nominee, and the only party nominee for whom the whole nation votes. Members of the House and Senate are representatives of localities, are voted for only by sections of voters, or by local bodies of electors like the members of the state legislatures. There is no national party choice except that of President. No one else represents the people as a whole, exercising a national choice; and inasmuch as his strictly executive duties are in fact subordinated, so far at any rate as all detail is concerned, the President represents not so much the party's governing efficiency as its controlling ideals and principles. He is not so much part of its organization as its vital link of connection with the thinking nation. He can dominate his party by being spokesman for the real sentiment and purpose of the country, by giving direction to opinion, by giving the country at once the information and the statements of policy which will enable it to form its judgments alike of parties and of men.

For he is also the political leader of the nation, or has it in his choice to be. The nation as a whole has chosen

him, and is conscious that it has no other political spokesman. His is the only national voice in affairs. Let him once
win the admiration and confidence of the country, and no
other single force can withstand him, no combination of
forces will easily overpower him. His position takes the
imagination of the country. He is the representative of no
constituency, but of the whole people. When he speaks in
his true character, he speaks for no special interest. If he
rightly interpret the national thought and boldly insist
upon it, he is irresistible; and the country never feels the
zest of action so much as when its President is of such
insight and calibre. Its instinct is for unified action, and it
craves a single leader. It is for this reason that it will often
prefer to choose a man rather than a party. A President
whom it trusts can not only lead it, but form it to his own
views.

It is the extraordinary isolation imposed upon the President by our system that makes the character and opportunity of his office so extraordinary. In him are centred both
opinion and party. He may stand, if he will, a little outside
party and insist as if it were upon the general opinion. It is
with the instinctive feeling that it is upon occasion such a
man that the country wants that nominating conventions
will often nominate men who are not their acknowledged
leaders, but only such men as the country would like to
see lead both its parties. The President may also, if he
will, stand within the party counsels and use the advantage of his power and personal force to control its actual
programs. He may be both the leader of his party and the
leader of the nation, or he may be one or the other. If he
lead the nation, his party can hardly resist him. His office
is anything he has the sagacity and force to make it.

That is the reason why it has been one thing at one time,
another at another. The Presidents who have not made
themselves leaders have lived no more truly on that ac-

count in the spirit of the Constitution than those whose force has told in the determination of law and policy. No doubt Andrew Jackson overstepped the bounds meant to be set to the authority of his office. It was certainly in direct contravention of the spirit of the Constitution that he should have refused to respect and execute decisions of the Supreme Court of the United States, and no serious student of our history can righteously condone what he did in such matters on the ground that his intentions were upright and his principles pure. But the Constitution of the United States is not a mere lawyers' document: it is a vehicle of life, and its spirit is always the spirit of the age. Its prescriptions are clear and we know what they are; a written document makes lawyers of us all, and our duty as citizens should make us conscientious lawyers, reading the text of the Constitution without subtlety or sophistication; but life is always your last and most authoritative critic.

Some of our Presidents have deliberately held themselves off from using the full power they might legitimately have used, because of conscientious scruples, because they were more theorists than statesmen. They have held the strict literary theory of the Constitution, the Whig theory, the Newtonian theory, and have acted as if they thought that Pennsylvania Avenue should have been even longer than it is; that there should be no intimate communication of any kind between the Capitol and the White House; that the President as a man was no more at liberty to lead the houses of Congress by persuasion than he was at liberty as President to dominate them by authority, — supposing that he had, what he has not, authority enough to dominate them. But the makers of the Constitution were not enacting Whig theory, they were not making laws with the expectation that, not the laws themselves, but their opinions, known by future historians to lie back of them, should govern the constitutional action of the country.

They were statesmen, not pedants, and their laws are sufficient to keep us to the paths they set us upon. The President is at liberty, both in law and conscience, to be as big a man as he can. His capacity will set the limit; and if Congress be overborne by him, it will be no fault of the makers of the Constitution,—it will be from no lack of constitutional powers on its part, but only because the President has the nation behind him, and Congress has not. He has no means of compelling Congress except through public opinion.

That I say he has no means of compelling Congress will show what I mean, and that my meaning has no touch of radicalism or iconoclasm in it. There are illegitimate means by which the President may influence the action of Congress. He may bargain with members, not only with regard to appointments, but also with regard to legislative measures. He may use his local patronage to assist members to get or retain their seats. He may interpose his powerful influence, in one covert way or another, in contests for places in the Senate. He may also overbear Congress by arbitrary acts which ignore the laws or virtually override them. He may even substitute his own orders for acts of Congress which he wants but cannot get. Such things are not only deeply immoral, they are destructive of the fundamental understandings of constitutional government and, therefore, of constitutional government itself. They are sure, moreover, in a country of free public opinion, to bring their own punishment, to destroy both the fame and the power of the man who dares to practise them. No honorable man includes such agencies in a sober exposition of the Constitution or allows himself to think of them when he speaks of the influences of "life" which govern each generation's use and interpretation of that great instrument, our sovereign guide and the object of our deepest reverence. Nothing in a system like ours can be constitutional which is immoral or which touches the good faith of those who have sworn to obey the fundamental law. The reprobation of all good men will always overwhelm such influences with shame and failure. But the personal force of the President is perfectly constitutional to any extent to which he chooses to exercise it, and it is by the clear logic of our constitutional practice that he has become alike the leader of his party and the leader of the nation.

The political powers of the President are not quite so obvious in their scope and character when we consider his relations with Congress as when we consider his relations to his party and to the nation. They need, therefore, a somewhat more critical examination. Leadership in government naturally belongs to its executive officers, who are daily in contact with practical conditions and exigencies and whose reputations alike for good judgment and for fidelity are at stake much more than are those of the members of the legislative body at every turn of the law's application. The law-making part of the government ought certainly to be very hospitable to the suggestions of the planning and acting part of it. Those Presidents who have felt themselves bound to adhere to the strict literary theory of the Constitution have scrupulously refrained from attempting to determine either the subjects or the character of legislation, except so far as they were obliged to decide for themselves, after Congress had acted, whether they should acquiesce in it or not. And yet the Constitution explicitly authorizes the President to recommend to Congress "such measures as he shall deem necessary and expedient," and it is not necessary to the integrity of even the literary theory of the Constitution to insist that such recommendations should be merely perfunctory. Certainly General Washington did not so regard them, and he stood much nearer the Whig theory than we do. A President's messages to Congress have no more weight or authority than their intrinsic reasonableness and importance give them: but that is their only constitutional limitation. The Constitution certainly does not forbid the President to back them up, as General Washington did, with such personal force and influence as he may possess. Some of our Presidents have felt the need, which unquestionably exists in our system, for some spokesman of the nation as a whole, in matters of legislation no less than in other matters, and have tried to supply Congress with the leadership of suggestion, backed by argument and by iteration and by every legitimate appeal to public opinion. Cabinet officers are shut out from Congress; the President himself has, by custom, no access to its floor; many long-established barriers of precedent, though not of law, hinder him from exercising any direct influence upon its deliberations; and yet he is undoubtedly the only spokesman of the whole people. They have again and again, as often as they were afforded the opportunity, manifested their satisfaction when he has boldly accepted the rôle of leader, to which the peculiar origin and character of his authority entitle him. The Constitution bids him speak, and times of stress and change must more and more thrust upon him the attitude of originator of policies.

His is the vital place of action in the system, whether he accept it as such or not, and the office is the measure of the man, — of his wisdom as well as of his force. His veto abundantly equips him to stay the hand of Congress when he will. It is seldom possible to pass a measure over his veto, and no President has hesitated to use the veto when his own judgment of the public good was seriously at issue with that of the houses. The veto has never been suffered to fall into even temporary disuse with us. In England it has ceased to exist, with the change in the character of the executive. There has been no veto since Anne's day, because ever since the reign of Anne the laws of England have been originated either by ministers who spoke the king's own will or by ministers whom the king did not dare gainsay; and in our own time the ministers who formulate the laws are themselves the executive of the nation; a veto would be a negative upon their own power. If bills pass of which they disapprove, they resign and give place to the leaders of those who approve them. The framers of the Constitution made in our President a more powerful, because a more isolated, king than the one they were imitating; and because the Constitution gave them their veto in such explicit terms, our Presidents have not hesitated to use it, even when it put their mere individual judgment against that of large majorities in both houses of Congress. And yet in the exercise of the power to suggest legislation, quite as explicitly conferred upon them by the Constitution, some of our Presidents have seemed to have a timid fear that they might offend some law of taste which had become a constitutional principle.

In one sense their messages to Congress have no more authority than the letters of any other citizen would have. Congress can heed or ignore them as it pleases; and there have been periods of our history when presidential messages were utterly without practical significance, perfunctory documents which few persons except the editors of newspapers took the trouble to read. But if the President has personal force and cares to exercise it, there is this tremendous difference between his messages and the views of any other citizen, either outside Congress or in it: that the whole country reads them and feels that the writer speaks with an authority and a responsibility which the people themselves have given him. . . .

One of the greatest of the President's powers I have not yet spoken of at all: his control, which is very absolute, of the foreign relations of the nation. The initiative in foreign affairs, which the President possesses without any restriction whatever, is virtually the power to control them absolutely. The President cannot conclude a treaty with a foreign power without the consent of the Senate, but he may guide every step of diplomacy, and to guide diplomacy is to determine what treaties must be made, if the faith and prestige of the government are to be maintained. He need disclose no step of negotiation until it is complete, and when in any critical matter it is completed the government is virtually committed. Whatever its disinclination, the Senate may feel itself committed also.

I have not dwelt upon this power of the President, because it has been decisively influential in determining the character and influence of the office at only two periods in our history; at the very first, when the government was young and had so to use its incipient force as to win the respect of the nations into whose family it had thrust itself, and in our own day when the results of the Spanish War, the ownership of distant possessions, and many sharp struggles for foreign trade make it necessary that we should turn our best talents to the task of dealing firmly, wisely, and justly with political and commercial rivals. The President can never again be the mere domestic figure he has been throughout so large a part of our history. The nation has risen to the first rank in power and resources. The other nations of the world look askance upon her, half in envy, half in fear, and wonder with a deep anxiety what she will do with her vast strength. They receive the frank professions of men like Mr. John Hay, whom we wholly trusted, with a grain of salt, and doubt what we were sure of, their truthfulness and sincerity, suspecting a hidden design under every utterance he makes. Our President must always, henceforth, be one of the great powers of the world, whether he act greatly and wisely or not, and the best statesmen we can produce will be needed to fill the office of Secretary of State. We have but begun to see the presidential office in this light; but it is the light which will more and more beat upon it, and more and more determine its character and its effect upon the politics of the nation. We can never hide our President again as a mere domestic officer. We can never again see him the mere executive he was in the thirties and forties. He must stand always at the front of our affairs, and the office will be as big and as influential as the man who occupies it.

How is it possible to sum up the duties and influence of such an office in such a system in comprehensive terms which will cover all its changeful aspects? In the view of the makers of the Constitution the President was to be legal executive; perhaps the leader of the nation; certainly not the leader of the party, at any rate while in office. But by the operation of forces inherent in the very nature of government he has become all three, and by inevitable consequence the most heavily burdened officer in the world. No other man's day is so full as his, so full of the responsibilities which tax mind and conscience alike and demand an inexhaustible vitality. The mere task of making appointments to office, which the Constitution imposes upon the President, has come near to breaking some of our Presidents down, because it is a never-ending task in a civil service not yet put upon a professional footing, confused with short terms of office, always forming and dissolving. And in proportion as the President ventures to use his opportunity to lead opinion and act as spokesman of the people in affairs the people stand ready to overwhelm him by running to him with every question, great and small. They are as eager to have him settle a literary question as a political; hear him as acquiescently with regard to matters of special expert knowledge as with regard to public affairs, and call upon him to quiet all troubles by his personal intervention. Men of ordinary physique and discretion cannot be Presidents and live, if the strain be not somehow relieved. We shall be obliged always to be picking our chief magistrates from among wise and prudent athletes, — a small class.

The future development of the presidency, therefore, must certainly, one would confidently predict, run along such lines as the President's later relations with his cabinet suggest. General Washington, partly out of unaffected modesty, no doubt, but also out of the sure practical instinct which he possessed in so unusual a degree, set an example which few of his successors seem to have followed in any systematic manner. He made constant and intimate use of his colleagues in every matter that he handled, seeking their assistance and advice by letter when they were at a distance and he could not obtain it in person. It is well known to all close students of our history that his greater state papers, even those which seem in some peculiar and intimate sense his personal utterances, are full of the ideas and the very phrases of the men about him whom he most trusted. His rough drafts came back to him from Mr. Hamilton and Mr. Madison in great part rephrased and rewritten, in many passages reconceived and given a new color. He thought and acted always by the light of counsel, with a will and definite choice of his own, but through the instrumentality of other minds as well as his own. The duties and responsibilities laid upon the President by the Constitution can be changed only by constitutional amendment, — a thing too difficult to attempt except upon some greater necessity than the relief of an overburdened office, even though that office be the greatest in the land; and it is to be doubted whether the deliberate opinion of the country would consent to make of the President a less powerful officer than he is. He can secure his own relief without shirking any real responsibility. Appointments, for example, he can, if he will, make more and more upon the advice and choice of his executive colleagues; every matter of detail not only, but also every minor matter of counsel or of general policy, he can more and more depend upon his chosen advisers to determine; he need reserve for himself only the larger matters of counsel and that general oversight of the business of the government and of the persons who conduct it which is not possible without intimate daily consultations, indeed, but which is possible without attempting the intolerable burden of direct control. This is, no doubt, the idea of their functions which most Presidents have entertained and which most Presidents suppose themselves to have acted on; but we have reason to believe that most of our Presidents have taken their duties too literally and have attempted the impossible. But we can safely predict that as the multitude of the President's duties increases, as it must with the growth and widening activities of the nation itself, the incumbents of the great office will more and more come to feel that they are administering it in its truest purpose and with greatest effect by regarding themselves as less and less executive officers and more and more directors of affairs and leaders of the nation, — men of counsel and of the sort of action that makes for enlightenment.

DOCUMENT 9

The Length of Presidential Tenure

Before Wilson took office Congress was considering a proposed constitutional amendment to limit a President to a

---

Letter to A. Mitchell Palmer, February 5, 1913, in *Public Papers*, III, 21 – 26.

single term. Pressed by Congressional Democrats to give
his opinion of the measure, the President-elect explained
his opposition to any such limitation and offered a succinct
summary of his views on the Presidency.

Thank you warmly for your letter of February 3. It was
characteristically considerate of you to ask my views with
regard to the joint resolution which has just come over
from the House to the Senate with regard to the presidential term.

I have not hitherto said anything about this question,
because I had not observed that there was any evidence
that the public was very much interested in it. I must have
been mistaken in this, else the Senate would hardly have
acted so promptly upon it.

It is a matter which concerns the character and conduct
of the great office upon the duties of which I am about to
enter. I feel therefore that in the present circumstances I
should not be acting consistently with my ideals with
regard to the rule of entire frankness and plain speaking
that ought to exist between public servants and the public
whom they serve if I did not speak out about it without
reserve of any kind and without thought of the personal
embarrassment.

The question is simply this: Shall our Presidents be free,
so far as the law is concerned, to seek a second term of four
years, or shall they be limited by constitutional amendment to a single term of four years or to a single term extended to six years?

I can approach the question from a perfectly impersonal
point of view, because I shall most cheerfully abide by the
judgment of my party and the public as to whether I shall
be a candidate for the Presidency again in 1916. I absolutely pledge myself to resort to nothing but public opinion to decide that question.

The President ought to be absolutely deprived of every other means of deciding it. He can be. I shall use to the utmost every proper influence within my reach to see that he is, before the term to which I have been elected is out. That side of the question need disturb no one.

And yet, if he be deprived of every other means of deciding the question, what becomes of the argument for a constitutional limitation to a single term? The argument is not that it is clearly known now just how long each President should remain in office. Four years is too long a term for a President who is not the true spokesman of the people, who is imposed upon and does not lead. It is too short a term for a President who is doing, or attempting a great work of reform, and who has not had time to finish it.

To change the term to six years would increase the likelihood of its being too long, without any assurance that it would, in happy cases, be long enough. A fixed constitutional limitation to a single term of office is highly arbitrary and unsatisfactory from every point of view.

The argument for it rests upon temporary conditions which can easily be removed by law. Presidents, it is said, are effective for one-half of their term only [,] because they devote their attention during the last two years of the term to building up the influences, and above all, the organization, by which they hope and purpose to secure a second nomination and election.

It is their illicit power, not their legitimate influence with the country, that the advocates of a constitutional change profess to be afraid of, and I heartily sympathize with them. It is intolerable that any President should be permitted to determine who should succeed him — himself or another — by patronage or coercion, or by any sort of control of the machinery by which delegates to the nominating convention are chosen.

There ought never to be another presidential nominating convention; and there need never be another. Several of the states have successfully solved that difficulty with regard to the choice of their governors, and Federal law can solve it in the same way with regard to the choice of Presidents. The nominations should be made directly by the people at the polls.

Conventions should determine nothing but party platforms and should be made up of the men who would be expected, if elected, to carry those platforms into effect. It is not necessary to attend to the people's business by constitutional amendment if you will only actually put the business into the people's own hands.

I think it may safely be assumed that that will be done within the next four years; for it can be done by statute; it need not wait for constitutional change. That being done, the question of the presidential term can be discussed on its merits.

It must be clear to everybody who has studied our political development at all that the character of the Presidency is passing through a transitional stage. We know what the office is now and what use must be made of it; but we do not know what it is going to work out into; and until we do know, we shall not know what constitutional change, if any is needed, it would be best to make.

I must speak with absolute freedom and candor in this matter, or not speak at all; and it seems to me that the present position of the Presidency in our actual system, as we use it, is quite abnormal and must lead eventually to something very different.

He is expected by the Nation to be the leader of his party as well as the Chief Executive officer of the Government, and the country will take no excuses from him. He must play the part and play it successfully or lose the country's confidence. He must be prime minister, as much concerned with the guidance of legislation as with the just and orderly execution of law, and he is the spokesman of the Nation in everything, even in the most momentous and most delicate dealings of the Government with foreign nations.

Why in such circumstances should he be responsible to no one for four long years? All the people's legislative spokesmen in the House of Representatives and one-third of their representatives in the Senate are brought to book every two years; why not the President, if he is to be the leader of the party and the spokesman of policy?

Sooner or later, it would seem, he must be made answerable to opinion in a somewhat more informal and intimate fashion—answerable, it may be, to the Houses whom he seeks to lead, either personally or through a Cabinet, as well as to the people for whom they speak. But that is a matter to be worked out—as it inevitably will be—in some natural American way which we cannot yet even predict.

The present fact is that the President is held responsible for what happens in Washington in every large matter, and so long as he is commanded to lead he is surely entitled to a certain amount of power—all the power he can get from the support and convictions and opinions of his fellow countrymen; and he ought to be suffered to use that power against his opponents until his work is done. It will be very difficult for him to abuse it. He holds it upon sufferance, at the pleasure of public opinion. Everyone else, his opponents included, has access to opinion, as he has. He must keep the confidence of the country by earning it, for he can keep it in no other way.

Put the present customary limitation of two terms into the Constitution, if you do not trust the people to take care of themselves, but make it two terms (not one, because four years is often too long), and give the President a chance to win the full service by proving himself fit for it.

If you wish to learn the result of constitutional ineligibility to re-election, ask any former governor of New Jersey, for example, what the effect is in actual experience. He will tell you how cynically and with what complacence the politicians banded against him waited for the inevitable end of his term to take their chances with his successor.

Constitutions place and can place no limitations upon their power. They may control what governors they can as long as they please and as long as they can keep their outside power and influence together. They smile at the coming and going of governors as some men in Washington have smiled at the coming and going of Presidents, as upon things ephemeral, which passed and were soon enough got rid of if you but sat tight and waited.

As things stand now the people might more likely be cheated than served by further limitations of the President's eligibility. His fighting power in their behalf would be immensely weakened. No one will fear a President except those whom he can make fear the elections.

We singularly belie our own principles by seeking to determine by fixed constitutional provision what the people shall determine for themselves and are perfectly competent to determine for themselves. We cast a doubt upon the whole theory of popular government.

I believe that we should fatally embarrass ourselves if we made the constitutional change proposed. If we want our Presidents to fight our battles for us, we should give them the means, the legitimate means, the means their opponents will always have. Strip them of everything else but the right to appeal to the people, but leave them that; suffer them to be leaders; absolutely prevent them from being bosses.

We would otherwise appear to be going in two opposite directions. We are seeking in every way to extend the power of the people, but in the matter of the Presidency we fear and distrust the people and seek to bind them hand and foot by rigid constitutional provision. My own mind is not agile enough to go both ways.

I am very well aware that my position on this question will be misconstrued, but that is a matter of perfect indifference to me. The truth is much more important than my reputation for modesty and lack of personal ambition. My reputation will take care of itself, but constitutional questions and questions of policy will not take care of themselves without frank and fearless discussion.

I am not speaking for my own re-election; I am speaking to redeem my promise that I would say what I really think on every public question and take my chances in the court of public opinion.

DOCUMENT 10

The Danger of an Interregnum

Throughout his life Wilson admired certain aspects of the parliamentary system, particularly its stress upon party responsibility, the role of the executive as a legislative leader, and the efficient transfer of power after an election. As President he sought to adapt all three of these characteristics to the American system, the first two—as we shall see—by means of vigorous Presidential leadership and the third by an imaginative proposal on the eve of the election of 1916. Wilson's victory rendered this plan unnecessary, however.

Letter to Robert Lansing, November 5, 1916, in Ray Stannard Baker, *Woodrow Wilson, Life and Letters* (8 vols.: Garden City, N.Y.: Doubleday, Doran & Company, 1927–1939), VI, 292–293. Hereafter cited as Baker, *Wilson, Life and Letters.*

MY DEAR MR. SECRETARY,

There is a matter which has occupied my thoughts throughout the campaign and which I want to lay before you before the election, while I can discuss it without any touch of feeling as to the result.

Again and again the question has arisen in my mind, What would it be my duty to do were Mr. Hughes to be elected? Four months would elapse before he could take charge of the affairs of the government, and during those four months I would be without such moral backing from the nation as would be necessary to steady and control our relations with other governments. I would be known to be the rejected, not the accredited, spokesman of the country; and yet the accredited spokesman would be without legal authority to speak for the nation. Such a situation would be fraught with the gravest dangers. The direction of the foreign policy of the government would in effect have been taken out of my hands and yet its new definition would be impossible until March.

I feel that it would be my duty to relieve the country of the perils of such a situation at once. The course I have in mind is dependent upon the consent and cooperation of the Vice President; but, if I could gain his consent to the plan, I would ask your permission to invite Mr. Hughes to become Secretary of State and would then join the Vice President in resigning, and thus open to Mr. Hughes the immediate succession to the presidency.

All my life long I have advocated some such responsible government for the United States as other constitutional systems afford as of course, and as such action on my part would inaugurate, at least by example. Responsible government means government by those whom the people trust, and trust at the time of decision and action. The whole country has long perceived, without knowing how to remedy, the extreme disadvantage of having to live for four months after a[n] election under a party whose guidance had been rejected at the polls. Here is the remedy, at any rate so far as the Executive is concerned. In ordinary times it would perhaps not be necessary to apply it. But it seems to me that in the existing circumstances it would be imperatively necessary. The choice of policy in respect of our foreign relations rests with the Executive. No such critical circumstances in regard to our foreign policy have ever before existed. It would be my duty to step aside so that there would be no doubt in any quarter how that policy was to be directed, towards what objects and by what means. I would have no right to risk the peace of the nation by remaining in office after I had lost my authority.

I hope and believe that your own judgment will run with mine in this critical matter.

Cordially and faithfully Yrs.
WOODROW WILSON

P.S. I beg that you will regard this as in the strictest sense confidential until I shall have had an opportunity to discuss it with you in person, should circumstances make it a practical problem of duty.

W.W.

D. ADMINISTRATION:

THEORETICAL AND PRACTICAL

1. The Student of Administration

Wilson's study of administration helped to prepare him for the Presidency, but like most administrators he discovered once in office that theory did not always provide answers to specific problems. Accordingly, he sometimes improvised, in a manner not contemplated

by handbooks on administrative practice but fully in
keeping with his belief in flexible and imaginative
leadership.

DOCUMENT 11

"The Field of Administration
Is a Field of Business"

Wilson developed an argument for a professional civil
service restrained by an informed and responsible public
opinion, and presented it in an early article on administration, published while he was in his first year of teaching at
Bryn Mawr.

. . . In government, as in virtue, the hardest of hard things
is to make progress. Formerly the reason for this was that
the single person who was sovereign was generally either
selfish, ignorant, timid, or a fool, — albeit there was now
and again one who was wise. Nowadays the reason is that
the many, the people, who are sovereign have no single
ear which one can approach, and are selfish, ignorant,
timid, stubborn, or foolish with the selfishnesses, the igno-
rances, the stubbornesses, the timidities, or the follies of
several thousand persons, — albeit there are hundreds who
are wise. Once the advantage of the reformer was that the
sovereign's mind had a definite locality, that it was contained in one man's head, and that consequently it could
be gotten at; though it was his disadvantage that that mind
learned only reluctantly or only in small quantities, or was

Excerpts from Woodrow Wilson, "The Study of Administration," *Political Science Quarterly,* II (June 1887), in *Public Papers, I,* 142–143,
144–145, and 148–153.

under the influence of some one who let it learn only the wrong things. Now, on the contrary, the reformer is bewildered by the fact that the sovereign's mind has no definite locality, but is contained in a voting majority of several million heads; and embarrassed by the fact that the mind of this sovereign also is under the influence of favorites, who are none the less favorites in a good old-fashioned sense of the word because they are not persons but preconceived opinions, *i.e.*, prejudices which are not to be reasoned with because they are not the children of reason.

Wherever regard for public opinion is a first principle of government, practical reform must be slow and all reform must be full of compromises. For wherever public opinion exists it must rule. This is now an axiom half the world over, and will presently come to be believed even in Russia. Whoever would effect a change in a modern constitutional government must first educate his fellow-citizens to want *some* change. That done, he must persuade them to want the particular change he wants. He must first make public opinion willing to listen and then see to it that it listen to the right things. He must stir it up to search for an opinion, and then manage to put the right opinion in its way. . . .

The field of administration is a field of business. It is removed from the hurry and strife of politics; it at most points stands apart even from the debatable ground of constitutional study. It is a part of political life only as the methods of the counting-house are a part of the life of society; only as machinery is part of the manufactured product. But it is, at the same time, raised very far above the dull level of mere technical detail by the fact that through its greater principles it is directly connected with the lasting maxims of political wisdom, the permanent truths of political progress.

The object of administrative study is to rescue executive methods from the confusion and costliness of empirical experiment and set them upon foundations laid deep in stable principle.

It is for this reason that we must regard civil service reform in its present stages as but a prelude to a fuller administrative reform. We are now rectifying methods of appointment; we must go on to adjust executive functions more fitly and to prescribe better methods of executive organization and action. Civil service reform is thus but a moral preparation for what is to follow. It is clearing the moral atmosphere of official life by establishing the sanctity of public office as a public trust, and, by making the service unpartisan, it is opening the way for making it businesslike. By sweetening its motives it is rendering it capable of improving its methods of work.

Let me expand a little what I have said of the province of administration. Most important to be observed is the truth already so much and so fortunately insisted upon by our civil service reformers; namely, that administration lies outside the proper sphere of *politics*. Administrative questions are not political questions. Although politics sets the tasks for administration, it should not be suffered to manipulate its offices. . . .

. . . The study of administration, philosophically viewed, is closely connected with the study of the proper distribution of constitutional authority. To be efficient it must discover the simplest arrangements by which responsibility can be unmistakably fixed upon officials; the best way of dividing authority without hampering it, and responsibility without obscuring it. And this question of the distribution of authority, when taken into the sphere of the higher, the originating functions of government, is obviously a central constitutional question. If administrative study can discover the best principles upon which to base such distribution, it will have done constitutional study an invaluable service. Montesquieu did not, I am convinced, say the last word on this head.

To discover the best principle for the distribution of authority is of greater importance, possibly, under a democratic system, where officials serve many masters, than under others where they serve but a few. All sovereigns are suspicious of their servants, and the sovereign people is no exception to the rule; but how is its suspicion to be allayed by *knowledge?* If that suspicion could but be clarified into wise vigilance, it would be altogether salutary; if that vigilance could be aided by the unmistakable placing of responsibility, it would be altogether beneficent. Suspicion in itself is never healthful either in the private or in the public mind. *Trust is strength* in all relations of life; and, as it is the office of the constitutional reformer to create conditions of trustfulness, so it is the office of the administrative organizer to fit administration with conditions of clear-cut responsibility which shall insure trustworthiness.

And let me say that large powers and unhampered discretion seem to me the indispensable conditions of responsibility. Public attention must be easily directed, in each case of good or bad administration, to just the man deserving of praise or blame. There is no danger in power, if only it be not irresponsible. If it be divided, dealt out in shares to many, it is obscured; and if it be obscured, it is made irresponsible. But if it be centred in heads of the service and in heads of branches of the service, it is easily watched and brought to book. If to keep his office a man must achieve open and honest success, and if at the same time he feels himself entrusted with large freedom of discretion, the greater his power the less likely is he to abuse it, the more is he nerved and sobered and elevated by it. The less his power, the more safely obscure and unnoticed does he feel his position to be, and the more readily does he relapse into remissness.

Just here we manifestly emerge upon the field of that

still larger question, — the proper relations between public opinion and administration.

To whom is official trustworthiness to be disclosed, and by whom is it to be rewarded? Is the official to look to the public for his meed of praise and his push of promotion, or only to his superior in office? Are the people to be called in to settle administrative discipline as they are called in to settle constitutional principles? These questions evidently find their root in what is undoubtedly the fundamental problem of this whole study. That problem is: What part shall public opinion take in the conduct of administration?

The right answer seems to be, that public opinion shall play the part of authoritative critic.

But the *method* by which its authority shall be made to tell? Our peculiar American difficulty in organizing administration is not the danger of losing liberty, but the danger of not being able or willing to separate its essentials from its accidents. Our success is made doubtful by that besetting error of ours, the error of trying to do too much by vote. Self-government does not consist in having a hand in everything, any more than housekeeping consists necessarily in cooking dinner with one's own hands. The cook must be trusted with a large discretion as to the management of the fires and the ovens.

In those countries in which public opinion has yet to be instructed in its privileges, yet to be accustomed to having its own way, this question as to the province of public opinion is much more readily soluble than in this country, where public opinion is wide awake and quite intent upon having its own way anyhow. It is pathetic to see a whole book written by a German professor of political science for the purpose of saying to his countrymen, "Please try to have an opinion about national affairs"; but a public which is so modest may at least be expected to be very docile and acquiescent in learning what things it has *not* a right to think and speak about imperatively. It may be sluggish, but it will not be meddlesome. It will submit to be instructed before it tries to instruct. Its political education will come before its political activity. In trying to instruct our own public opinion, we are dealing with a pupil apt to think itself quite sufficiently instructed beforehand.

The problem is to make public opinion efficient without suffering it to be meddlesome. Directly exercised, in the oversight of the daily details and in the choice of the daily means of government, public criticism is of course a clumsy nuisance, a rustic handling delicate machinery. But as superintending the greater forces of formative policy alike in politics and administration, public criticism is altogether safe and beneficent, altogether indispensable. Let administrative study find the best means for giving public criticism this control and for shutting it out from all other interference.

But is the whole duty of administrative study done when it has taught the people what sort of administration to desire and demand, and how to get what they demand? Ought it not to go on to drill candidates for the public service?

There is an admirable movement towards universal political education now afoot in this country. The time will soon come when no college of respectability can afford to do without a well-filled chair of political science. But the education thus imparted will go but a certain length. It will multiply the number of intelligent critics of government, but it will create no competent body of administrators. It will prepare the way for the development of a sure-footed understanding of the general principles of government, but it will not necessarily foster skill in conducting government. It is an education which will equip legislators, perhaps, but not executive officials. If we are to improve public opinion, which is the motive power of government, we must prepare better officials as the *apparatus* of government. If we are to put in new boilers and to mend the fires which drive our governmental machinery, we must not leave the old wheels and joints and valves and bands to creak and buzz and clatter on as the best they may at bidding of the new force. We must put in new running parts wherever there is the least lack of strength or adjustment. It will be necessary to organize democracy by sending up to the competitive examinations for the civil service men definitely prepared for standing liberal tests as to technical knowledge. A technically schooled civil service will presently have become indispensable.

I know that a corps of civil servants prepared by a special schooling and drilled, after appointment, into a perfected organization, with appropriate hierarchy and characteristic discipline, seems to a great many very thoughtful persons to contain elements which might combine to make an offensive official class,—a distinct, semi-corporate body with sympathies divorced from those of a progressive, free-spirited people, and with hearts narrowed to the meanness of a bigoted officialism. Certainly such a class would be altogether hateful and harmful in the United States. Any measures calculated to produce it would for us be measures of reaction and of folly.

But to fear the creation of a domineering, illiberal officialism as a result of the studies I am here proposing is to miss altogether the principle upon which I wish most to insist. That principle is, that administration in the United States must be at all points sensitive to public opinion. A body of thoroughly trained officials serving during good behavior we must have in any case: that is a plain business necessity. But the apprehension that such a body will be anything un-American clears away the moment it is asked, What is to constitute good behavior? For that question obviously carries its own answer on its face. Steady, hearty allegiance to the policy of the government they serve will constitute good behavior. That *policy* will have no taint of officialism about it. It will not be the creation of permanent officials, but of statesmen whose responsibility to public opinion will be direct and inevitable. Bureaucracy can exist only where the whole service of the state is removed from the common political life of the people, its chiefs as well as its rank and file. Its motives, its objects, its policy, its standards, must be bureaucratic. It would be difficult to point out any examples of impudent exclusiveness and arbitrariness on the part of officials doing service under a chief of department who really served the people, as all our chiefs of departments must be made to do. It would be easy, on the other hand, to adduce other instances like that of the influence of Stein in Prussia, where the leadership of one statesman imbued with true public spirit transformed arrogant and perfunctory bureaus into public-spirited instruments of just government.

The ideal for us is a civil service cultured and self-sufficient enough to act with sense and vigor, and yet so intimately connected with the popular thought, by means of elections and constant public counsel, as to find arbitrariness or class spirit quite out of the question.

2. Flexible Administration

DOCUMENT 12

Tapping Private Money for Public Purposes

Like most Presidents, Wilson found that he could not always attract the ablest men to public service, owing to the comparatively low scale of government salaries. This was

---

Letter to Cleveland H. Dodge, July 12, 1914, in Baker, *Wilson, Life and Letters*, IV, 33.

particularly true of the more important ambassadorships, which traditionally had been filled by men of wealth who could afford the expensive entertaining necessary to the post. To surmount this obstacle the President occasionally resorted to an ingenious, if irregular, solution. When, for example, he offered the Berlin embassy to his old colleague, Professor Henry B. Fine of Princeton, he promised an additional expense allowance that would be provided by Wilson's close friend and classmate, Cleveland H. Dodge, a wealthy financier. And when Walter Hines Page, the ambassador to Great Britain, reported in 1914 that he would have to resign because of the heavy expenses of the post, Wilson again turned to Dodge, who cheerfully offered to provide the entire subsidy of $25,000 a year and to tell no one except his wife.

Something you once, in your great generosity, offered to do for me when I wanted Harry Fine to accept the post of Ambassador to Germany, emboldens me to turn to you in a great difficulty with which I find myself brought face to face. Walter Page is obliged to spend twenty-five thousand a year more than the government allows him or he has to spend. He must come home unless I can find the money for him from some source that will put him under no obligation which will in any way touch him in the performance of his duties. He has learned his job, — learned it admirably: speaks my mind and my point of view to the ministers over there as I am sure no one else could speak them; has got a real hold, socially *and* politically; is, if I know one when I see him, for the present at any rate, an indispensable man in the right management of our foreign relations. I would not know what to do if I were obliged to part with him. My relations with him are intimate, and he has furnished me with more light on difficult foreign matters than all my other informants and advisers put together. I have, therefore, bidden him engage his present house for another year and count on me to help him.

Will you forgive me and understand me, if I turn to you? I know that you will, and that you will come to my aid if you can. I know of no other friend like you, and of no other friend to whom I could afford to turn in such a matter and with such a request. You will tell me if you cannot do it; and if you can, it will be help that I can afford, in honour and with unmeasured confidence, to accept. Thank God that it is so, and that there is room somewhere for perfect trust!

Mrs. Wilson gains slowly (ah, how slowly!) but I believe surely, and my heart grows lighter because of it even amidst this daily and hourly struggle here. She would send her warmest greetings, if she knew I was writing.

3. *The President as Discreet Lobbyist*

Although Wilson recognized the value of the independent regulatory agency in the American political structure, he was not above trying to influence its actions, as the following two letters reveal. The issue concerned a request by the railroads to the Interstate Commerce Commission to increase their rates. Higginson was a Boston financier; Daniels was a former Princeton colleague whom Wilson had appointed to the Commission.

DOCUMENT 13

"They Are as Jealous of Executive Suggestion . . ."

I have your letter of October twenty-sixth and agree with its main conclusions almost entirely. I would if I thought it

---

Letter to Henry L. Higginson, October 29, 1914, in Wilson MSS, Library of Congress.

justified make some very plain recommendations to the Interstate Commerce Commission, but they are as jealous of executive suggestion as the Supreme Court would be, and I dare say with justification. I can only hope and believe that they will see the rate case in a new light in the new circumstances.

DOCUMENT 14

"I Wonder If It Would Make Any Impression . . ."

I know how you feel and I am sure you know how I feel, but I am awaiting the decision of the Commission in the newly opened rate case with deep and serious anxiety. I believe that a concession to the railroads is absolutely necessary to steady and relieve the present extraordinary difficulties of the financial situation.

It is for this reason that I am taking the liberty of sending you this letter of Major Higginson's, which I think in the main is true. I wonder if it would make any impression on any of your colleagues to see it.

E. "A COMPACT AND FIGHTING PARTY"

1. *Partisanship, Frank and Open*

More than many Presidents, Wilson saw himself as a party leader as well as the chief executive of the

---

Letter to Winthrop M. Daniels, October 29, 1914, in Wilson MSS, Library of Congress.

nation. This meant the development of a loyal and efficient party organization in Congress, along with effective partisan campaigning to keep the party in power. Wilson strongly believed in party government and made no secret of his partisanship, as the following two letters show. Johns was the editor of the *St. Louis Post-Dispatch;* Mrs. Toy was a family friend and the wife of a Harvard professor.

DOCUMENT 15

"I Thought You Would Pardon This Word of Interest. . . ."

I know that you know me well enough and know the spirit by which I am animated well enough to make it permissible for me to say to you anything that is in my mind; and so I am going to take the liberty of saying this:

I have heard that the Post-Dispatch is not friendly to the candidacy of Mr. Collins, the Democratic candidate in the Twelfth District of Missouri. I must frankly say that I do not know Mr. Collins, but the maintenance of a large Democratic majority in the House of Representatives is so absolutely essential to the administration that I am going to ask you to be very sure of your ground before taking a positive stand against the Democratic candidate in your District.

Not that I doubt you would do so in any case, but I feel so particularly concerned that nothing should happen to break the course of what we are now trying to do that I thought you would pardon this word of interest in Mr. Collin's [*sic*] candidacy from me.

Letter to George Johns, September 19, 1914, in Wilson MSS, Library of Congress.

DOCUMENT 16

"I Cannot Fight Rottenness with Rosewater"

. . . Of course you did not like the Indianapolis speech
(that palpable lapse of taste, "Woodrow &c." was only a
silliness of the moment; was not in the notes; was produced
by the psychology of the stump, no doubt, and admits of no
excuse); I instinctively knew that you would not: any more
than you would like a real fight, or anything that wore the
aspect of partisanship. But there is a real fight on. The
Republicans are every day employing the most unscrupulous methods of partisanship and false evidence to destroy
this administration and bring back the days of private influence and selfish advantage. I would not, if I could, imitate their tactics; but it is no time for mere manners. The
barriers of taste may be overstepped in stating the truth as
to what is going on: it must be displayed naked. All that I
said was true, to my knowledge, though I did not shade it
or trace the lines of it artistically or with literary restraint.
The struggle that is on, to bring about reaction and regain
privilege is desperate and absolutely without scruple. It
cannot be met by gentle speeches or by presidential utterances which smack of no bias of party. A compact and
fighting party must be led against them. I think you cannot
know to what lengths men like Root and Lodge are going,
who I once thought had consciences but now know have
none. We must not suffer ourselves to forget or twist the
truth as they do, or use their insincere and contemptible
methods of fighting; but we must hit them and hit them
straight in the face, and not mind if the blood comes. It is a

---

Letter to Mrs. Nancy Toy, January 31, 1915, in Baker, *Wilson, Life and
Letters*, V, 126–128.

blunt business, and lacks a certain kind of refinement, but
so does all war; and this is a war to save the country from
some of the worst influences that ever debauched it. Please
do not read the speeches in which I use a bludgeon. I do
not like to offend your taste; but I cannot fight rottenness
with rosewater. Lend me your indulgence. At any rate
forgive me, if you can do nothing else.

As for the Shipping bill, it does, as you perceive, permit
us to commit blunders, fatal blunders, if we are so stupid or
so blind; but it is not a blunder in itself, and, if we use
ordinary sense and prudence, it need lead us into no dangers. The only dangers it involves have already been
created by the Ship Registry bill and the war risk insurance measure, for which the Republicans hastened to vote,
some coming back to Washington to advocate what the
shipping interests wanted who had been absent from their
seats for weeks. But the shipping interests do not want this
bill. They will do nothing themselves without a subsidy,
unless, that is, they are given government money out of
the taxes to use as they think best for themselves; if they
cannot get that, and of course they cannot, they do not
mean to let the development take place, because the control of ocean carriage and of ocean rates will pass out of
their hands. We are fighting as a matter of fact the most
formidable (covert) lobby that has stood against us yet in
anything we have attempted; and we shall see the fight to
a finish; trying, when we have won, to act like men who
know very familiarly the dangers of what they are about to
undertake. It pleases me that you should be so generously
distressed at the possibility of our doing what will lead to
disaster or even danger; but those who speak to you of
these risks have a very poor opinion of our practical sense,
and are unconsciously misled by what the press represent,
for their own purposes, as the main object of the measure
when it is not its object at all. One would suppose that this

was a bill to authorize the government to buy German ships. There would be just as stiff a fight against it, and from the same quarters, if it merely conferred the power to build ships.

The path is indeed strewn with difficulties at every turn, in this and in many other matters, and God knows I have no serene confidence in my own judgement and discretion: but of one thing I am resolved, to break the control of special interests over this government and this people. Pardon the seriousness of this letter. These are critical things in which much is wrapped up. All join me in most affectionate messages.

2. Building a Party Organization

DOCUMENT 17

Organizing the Patronage

One traditional manner in which to build an effective party organization was through judicious use of Presidential patronage. Although he often disliked—and sometimes refused to be bound by—party considerations in making appointments, Wilson recognized the importance of creating a party organization that would be loyal and sympathetic to the aims of his administration. From the first, therefore, he sought to use his patronage powers to this end.

I am going to take the liberty to make the following suggestion: When you suggest a name for appointment, will you not be kind enough to accompany the suggestion with a memorandum showing, if possible, the political affilia-

Letter to Secretary of the Navy Josephus Daniels, April 17, 1913, in Daniels MSS, Library of Congress.

tions of the person suggested, stating by whom his name was recommended, and just as many other particulars as might assist us in determining just what his temper and attitude in affairs would be?

I hope that it will not be burdensome to carry out this suggestion. It would greatly assist me.

3. Loyalty to the Caucus

Another important aspect of responsible party government, in Wilson's view, was loyalty to the party by its individual members. In Congress this meant loyalty to the party caucus, and in his dealings with Democratic legislators the President never lost an opportunity to stress this obligation, praising the faithful and gently reproving those who wavered in their support.

DOCUMENT 18

"A Sound and Statesmanlike Conception

of How a Party Must Act . . ."

That was a splendid speech you delivered in caucus. I have heard a great many speak of it and I want to say that it not only shows a great heart, but a sound and statesmanlike conception of how a party must act in order to govern a great country and really determine legislative policy.

I think you know, my dear Senator, my feeling towards you, and everything that you do serves to enhance it.

Letter to William J. Stone, January 27, 1915, in Wilson MSS, Library of Congress.

DOCUMENT 19

"Yielding to the Determination
of a Decisive Majority . . ."

You are right in thinking that differences of opinion upon public questions cannot alter my personal feeling towards men whom I respect and with whom it is a pleasure for me to work and I thank you for judging me so truly. I must in frankness say, however, that the recent situation in the Senate distressed and disturbed me not a little. I do not see how party government is possible, indeed I can form no working idea of the successful operation of popular institutions, if individuals are to exercise the privilege of defeating a decisive majority of their own party associates in framing and carrying out the policy of the party. In party conference personal convictions should have full play and should be most candidly and earnestly presented, but there does not seem to me to be any surrender either of personal dignity or of individual conviction in yielding to the determinations of a decisive majority of one's fellow workers in a great organization which must hold together if it is to be serviceable to the country as a governing agency.

This conviction on my part lies back of and supports every conclusion that I have come to in years of study not only, but in recent years of experience, with regard to the feasibility and efficiency of party government, and I beg, my dear Senator, that you will allow me to press this view upon you with the earnestness of a conviction which underlies all others.

Letter to Thomas W. Hardwick, March 15, 1915, reprinted from *Wilson: The Struggle for Neutrality, 1914–1915* by Arthur S. Link by permission of Princeton University Press, p. 160n. © 1960 by Princeton University Press.

DOCUMENT 20

An Analysis of the 1918 Democratic Defeat

Perhaps the best example of Wilson's partisanship was his unwise and—as it turned out—disastrous appeal for the election of a Democratic Congress in 1918 (See Document 125). The President took his rebuff philosophically, however, and in an address to members of the Democratic National Committee on February 28, 1919, he attributed the defeat in part to a lack of party loyalty by Congressional Democrats.

Personally, I am not in the least discouraged by the results of the last Congressional election. Any party which carries out through a long series of years a great progressive and constructive programme is sure to bring about a reaction, because while in the main the reforms that we have accomplished have been sound reforms, they have necessarily in the process of being made touched a great many definite interests in a way that distressed them, in a way that was counter to what they deemed their best and legitimate interests. So that there has been a process of adaptation in the process of change. There is nothing apparently to which the human mind is less hospitable than change, and in the business world that is particularly true because if you get in the habit of doing your business a particular way and are compelled to do it in a different way, you think that somebody in Washington does not understand business, and, therefore, there has been a perfectly natural reaction against the changes we have made in the public policies of the United States. In many instances, as in the

Joseph P. Tumulty, *Woodrow Wilson as I Knew Him* (Garden City, N.Y.: Doubleday, Page & Company, 1921), pp. 332–334.

banking and currency reform, the country is entirely satisfied with the wisdom and permanency of the change, but
even there a great many interests have been disappointed
and many of their plans have been prevented from being
consummated. So that, there is that natural explanation.
And then I do not think that we ought to conceal from
ourselves the fact that not the whole body of our partisans
are as cordial in the support of some of the things that we
have done as they ought to be.

You know that I heard a gentleman from one of the
southern States say to his Senator (this gentleman was
himself a member of the State Legislature)—he said to his
Senator: "We have the advantage over you because we
have no publication corresponding with the *Congressional
Record* and all that is recorded in our state is the vote, and
while you have always voted right we know what happened in the meantime because we read the *Congressional Record.*" Now, with regard to a great many of our fellow
partisans in Washington, the *Congressional Record* shows
what happened between the beginning of the discussion
and the final vote, and our opponents were very busy in
advertising what the *Congressional Record* disclosed. And
to be perfectly plain, there was not in the minds of the
country sufficient satisfactory evidence that we had supported some of the great things that they were interested
in any better than the other fellows. The voting record was
all right and the balance in our favour; but they can show a
great many things that discount the final record of the vote.

Now, I am in one sense an uncompromising partisan.
Either a man must stand by his party or not. Either he has
got to play the game or he has got to get out of the game,
and I have no more sufferance for such a man than the
country has. Not a bit. Some of them got exactly what was
coming to them and I haven't any bowels of compassion
for them. They did not support the things they pretended

to support. And the country knew they didn't,—the country knew that the tone of the cloakroom and the tone of the voting were different tones. Now, I am perfectly willing to say that I think it is wise to judge of party loyalty by the cloakroom, and not by the vote and the cloakroom was not satisfactory. I am not meaning to imply that there was any kind of blameworthy insincerity in this. I am not assessing individuals. That is not fair. But in assessing the cause of our defeat we ought to be perfectly frank and admit that the country was not any more sure of us than it ought to be. So that we have got to convince it that the ranks have closed up and that the men who constitute those ranks are all on the war-path and mean the things they say and that the party professes. That is the main thing.

Now, I think that can be accomplished by many processes. Unfortunately, the members of Congress have to live in Washington, and Washington is not a part of the United States. It is the most extraordinary thing I have ever known. If you stay here long enough you forget what the people of your own district are thinking about. There is one reason on the face of things. The wrong opinion is generally better organized than the right opinion. If some special interest has an impression that it wants to make on Congress it can get up thousands of letters with which to bombard its Senators and Representatives, and they get the impression that that is the opinion at home and they do not hear from the other fellow; and the consequence is that the unspoken and uninsisted-on views of the country, which are the views of the great majority, are not heard at this distance. If such an arrangement were feasible I think there ought to be a Constitutional provision that Congressmen and Senators ought to spend every other week at home and come back here and talk and vote after a fresh bath in the atmosphere of their home districts and the opinions of their home folks.

DOCUMENT 21

Relations with Congress: The Lighter Side

Although he generally impressed the public and even some
of his associates as being rather aloof and forbidding, Wilson was well aware of the importance of keeping on friendly terms with his party lieutenants in Congress, as this
exchange between the President and his private secretary,
Joseph P. Tumulty, suggests.

MEMORANDUM FOR THE PRESIDENT

SENATOR [John Sharp] Williams called today and asked
me to urge you to shake hands with Mrs. Jones and her
little daughter. I would not lay this matter before you if it
were not that the old Senator's heart seemed to be deeply
in it. He has been such a wonderful friend that I thought I
would "put it up to you."

The Secretary

Okeh, just after lunch (28th) say 2 p.m.   W.W.

Memorandum, August 27, 1919, in Wilson MSS, Library of Congress.

PART III

From Conservatism to Reform

A. THE LIMITED OBJECTS
OF GOVERNMENT

1. The Servant, Not the Master of Society

Wilson remained essentially a Jeffersonian states'-rights Democrat until he entered the White House. Indeed, his early concern was the protection of the individual from the arbitrary power of the government, and even during his first term as President he was doubtful of the wisdom and constitutionality of such measures as Prohibition and a ban on child labor. Although Wilson was never a believer in strict *laissez faire*, for many years he was suspicious of reformers who proposed expanding governmental power to accomplish this or that desirable end. Government, he argued, must be the servant and not the master of society.

DOCUMENT 22

"Nothing May Be Done by Leaps"

Wilson provided an early view of the proper objects of government in his second book, a wide-ranging textbook on the historical development of government.

... 1266. **The Extreme Views Held.** — What part shall government play in the affairs of society? — that is the question which has been the gauge of controversial battle. Stated in another way, it is the very question which I

Woodrow Wilson, *The State: Elements of Historical and Practical Politics* (Boston: D. C. Heath & Company, 1889), pp. 656–657, 659–661, 663–665, and 667.

postponed when discussing the functions of government (sec. 1231), *"What,"* namely, *"ought the functions of government to be?"* On the one hand there are extremists who cry constantly to government, "Hands off," *"laissez faire,"* *"laissez passer"!* who look upon every act of government which is not merely an act of police with jealousy, who regard government as necessary, but as a necessary evil, and who would have government hold back from everything which could by any possibility be accomplished by individual initiative and endeavor. On the other hand, there are those who, with equal extremeness of view in the opposite direction, would have society lean fondly upon government for guidance and assistance in every affair of life, who, captivated by some glimpse of public power and beneficence caught in the pages of ancient or mediaeval historian or by some dream of co-operative endeavor cunningly imagined by the great fathers of Socialism, believe that the state can be made a wise foster-mother to every member of the family politic. Between these two extremes, again, there are all grades, all shades and colors, all degrees of enmity or of partiality to state action. . . .

. . . — It is possible indeed, to understand, and even in a measure to sympathize with, the enthusiasm of those special classes of agitators whom we have dubbed with the too great name of "Socialists." The schemes of social reform and regeneration which they support with so much ardor, however mistaken they may be, — and surely most of them are mistaken enough to provoke the laughter of children, — have the right end in view: they seek to bring the individual with his special interests, personal to himself, into complete harmony with society with its general interests, common to all. Their method is always some sort of co-operation, meant to perfect mutual helpfulness. They speak, too, a revolt from selfish, misguided individualism;

and certainly modern individualism has much about it that is hateful, too hateful to last. The modern industrial organization has so distorted competition as to put it into the power of some to tyrannize over many, as to enable the rich and the strong to combine against the poor and the weak. It has given a woeful material meaning to that spiritual law that "to him that hath shall be given, and from him that hath not shall be taken away even the little that he seemeth to have."[1] It has magnified that self-interest which is grasping selfishness and has thrust out love and compassion not only, but free competition in part, as well. Surely it would be better, exclaims the Socialist, altogether to stamp out competition by making all men equally subject to the public order, to an imperative law of social co-operation! But the Socialist mistakes: it is not competition that kills, but unfair competition, the pretence and form of it where the substance and reality of it cannot exist.

1272. **A Middle Ground.** — But there is a middle ground. The schemes which Socialists have proposed society assuredly cannot accept, and no scheme which involves the complete control of the individual by government can be devised which differs from theirs very much for the better. A truer doctrine must be found, which gives wide freedom to the individual for his self-development and yet guards that freedom against the competition that kills, and reduces the antagonism between self-development and social development to a minimum. And such a doctrine can be formulated, surely, without too great vagueness.

1273. **The Objects of Society the Objects of Government.** — Government, as I have said, is the organ of society, its only potent and universal instrument: its objects must be the objects of society. What, then, are the objects of

---

[1] F. A. Walker's *Political Economy* (Advanced Course), sec. 346.

society? What *is* society? It is an organic association of individuals for mutal aid. Mutual aid to what? To self-development. The hope of society lies in an infinite individual variety, in the freest possible play of individual forces: only in that can it find that wealth of resource which constitutes civilization, with all its appliances for satisfying human wants and mitigating human sufferings, all its incitements to thought and spurs to action. It should be the end of government *to accomplish the objects of organized society:* there must be constant adjustments of governmental assistance to the needs of a changing social and industrial organization. Not license of interference on the part of government, only strength and adaptation of regulation. The regulation that I mean is not interference: it is the equalization of conditions, so far as possible, in all branches of endeavor; and the equalization of conditions is the very opposite of interference.

1274. Every rule of development is a rule of adaptation, a rule for meeting "the circumstances of the case"; but the circumstances of the case, it must be remembered, are not, so far as government is concerned, the circumstances of any individual case, but the circumstances of society's case, the general conditions of social organization. The case for society stands thus: the individual must be assured the best means, the best and fullest opportunities, for complete self-development: in no other way can society itself gain variety and strength. But one of the most indispensable conditions of opportunity for self-development government alone, society's controlling organ, can supply. All combination which necessarily creates monopoly, which necessarily puts and keeps indispensable means of industrial or social development in the hands of a few, and those few, not the few selected by society itself but the few selected by arbitrary fortune, must be under either the direct or the indirect control of society. To soci-

ety alone can the power of dominating combination belong: and society cannot suffer any of its members to enjoy
such a power for their own private gain independently of
its own strict regulation or oversight. . . .

1278. **Equalization of Competition.**—There are some
things outside the field of natural monopolies in which
individual action cannot secure equalization of the conditions of competition; and in these also, as in the regulation of monopolies, the practice of governments, of our
own as well as of others, has been decisively on the side
of governmental regulation. By forbidding child labor,
by supervising the sanitary conditions of factories, by
limiting the employment of women in occupations hurtful
to their health, by instituting official tests of the purity or
the quality of goods sold, by limiting hours of labor in
certain trades, by a hundred and one limitations of the
power of unscrupulous or heartless men to out-do the
scrupulous and merciful in trade or industry, government
has assisted equity. Those who would act in moderation
and good conscience in cases where moderation and good
conscience, to be indulged, require an increased outlay of
money, in better ventilated buildings, in greater care as to
the quality of goods, etc., cannot act upon their principles
so long as more grinding conditions for labor or more unscrupulous use of the opportunities of trade secure to the
unconscientious an unquestionable and sometimes even a
permanent advantage; they have only the choice of denying their consciences or retiring from business. In scores of
such cases government has intervened and will intervene;
but by way, not of interference, by way, rather, of making
competition equal between those who would rightfully
conduct enterprise and those who basely conduct it. It is
in this way that society protects itself against permanent
injury and deterioration, and secures healthful equality of
opportunity for self-development.

1279. **Society greater than Government.**—Society, it must always be remembered, is vastly bigger and more important than its instrument, Government. Government should serve Society, by no means rule or dominate it. Government should not be made an end in itself; it is a means only,—a means to be freely adapted to advance the best interests of the social organism. The State exists for the sake of Society, not Society for the sake of the State.

1280. **Natural Limits to State Action.**—And that there are natural and imperative limits to state action no one who seriously studies the structure of society can doubt. The limit of state functions is the limit of *necessary co-operation* on the part of Society as a whole, the limit beyond which such combination ceases to be imperative for the public good and becomes merely convenient for industrial or social enterprise. Co-operation is necessary in the sense here intended when it is indispensable to the equalization of the conditions of endeavor, indispensable to the maintenance of uniform rules of individual rights and relationships, indispensable because to omit it would inevitably be to hamper or degrade some for the advancement of others in the scale of wealth and social standing. . . .

. . . Whatever view be taken in each particular case of the rightfulness or advisability of state regulation and control, one rule there is which may not be departed from under any circumstances, and that is the rule of historical continuity. In politics nothing radically novel may safely be attempted. No result of value can ever be reached in politics except through slow and gradual development, the careful adaptations and nice modifications of growth. Nothing may be done by leaps. More than that, each people, each nation, must live upon the lines of its own experience. Nations are no more capable of borrowing experience than individuals are. The histories of other peoples may furnish us with light, but they cannot furnish us with conditions of action. Every nation must constantly keep in touch with its past: it cannot run towards its ends around sharp corners.

2. *Dangers of Governmental Interference*

While president of Princeton University Wilson spoke out frequently against federal interference in economic and business affairs. Extension of federal authority in this sphere was dangerous and ill-advised, he believed. To protect the individual against any business abuses he preferred to rely upon the courts rather than to create new regulatory commissions.

DOCUMENT 23

"But of Course It Is Socialistic"

. . . The present apparent approach of the two great parties of the nation to one another, their apparent agreement upon the chief questions now of significance, is not real, it is only apparent. At any rate it is plain that if it is in fact taking place, it does not truly represent the two great bodies of opinion that exist in the nation. There is a great and apparently growing body of opinion in the country which approves of a radical change in the character of our institutions and the objects of our law, which wishes to see government, and the federal government at that, regulate business. Some men who entertain this wish perceive that it is socialistic, some do not. But of course it is socialistic.

Excerpt from Woodrow Wilson, "Politics," *Atlantic Monthly*, C (November 1907), in *Public Papers*, II, 21–22.

Government cannot properly or intelligently regulate business without fully comprehending it in its details as well as in its larger aspects; it cannot comprehend it except through the instrumentality of expert commissions; it cannot use expert commissions long for purposes of regulation without itself by degrees undertaking actually to order and conduct what it began by regulating. We are at present on the high road to government ownership of many sorts, or to some other method of control which will in practice be as complete as actual ownership.

On the other hand, there is a great body of opinion, slow to express itself, sorely perplexed in the presence of modern business conditions, but very powerful and upon the eve of an uprising, which prefers the older and simpler methods of the law, prefers courts to commissions, and believes them, if properly used and adapted, better, more efficacious, in the end more purifying, than the new instrumentalities now being so unthinkingly elaborated. The country is still full of men who retain a deep enthusiasm for the old ideals of individual liberty, sobered and kept within bounds by the equally old definitions of personal responsibility, the ancient safeguards against license; and these men are right in believing that those older principles can be so used as to control modern business and keep government outside the pale of industrial enterprise. The law can deal with transactions instead of with methods of business, and with individuals instead of with corporations. It can reverse the process which creates corporations, and instead of compounding individuals, oblige corporations to analyze their organization and name the Individuals responsible for each class of their transactions. The law, both civil and criminal, can clearly enough characterize transactions, can clearly enough determine what their consequences shall be to the individuals who engage in them in a responsible capacity. New definitions in that field are not beyond the knowledge of modern lawyers or the skill of modern lawmakers, if they will accept the advice of disinterested lawyers. We shall never moralize society by fining or even dissolving corporations; we shall only inconvenience it. We shall moralize it only when we make up our minds as to what transactions are reprehensible, and bring those transactions home to individuals with the full penalities of the law. That is the other, the greater body of opinion; one or other of the great parties of the nation must sooner or later stand with it, while the other stands with those who burden government with the regulation of business by direct oversight.

DOCUMENT 24

"The Government and Business"

A passion for regulative legislation seems to have taken possession of the country of late; but it came upon it so suddenly, so much more like an impulse of impatence than like a deliberate purpose, that there is every indication that the careful thinking upon which it should have been founded will succeed it after it has spent its force, rather than accompany and give form and direction to it. Various abuses have sprung up in the conduct of the complex and prodigious business enterprises of the country, and the government must put an end to them by drastic regulation, is the rough and ready reasoning of the reformers. The trouble is that they have not carefully enough analyzed either the abuses or the remedy.

What is the matter with the business of the country? The abuses complained of are in fact of two kinds. The produc-

Address to the Commercial Club of Chicago, March 14, 1908, *Princeton Alumni Weekly*, VIII (March 18, 1908), 386–389.

tion of certain kinds of commodities has been concentrated in the hands of great corporations which are virtually monopolies. These monopolies have in some instances been built up by methods of competition fundamentally unrighteous and unfair and have been maintained by methods as arbitrary and as contrary to the spirit of the law as those by which they were created. The railways have in many cases assisted in the unfair competiton by granting special rates to some shippers to the exclusion of others, serving not as true common carriers but rather as the partners of particular capitalists. This is one class of abuses. Another class perhaps more far-reaching in its effects is that which is connected with the manipulation of securities and the use of trust funds. The stock of railway corporations and of many industrial stock companies has either been issued so much in excess of the real values of the forms of business or the properties represented as to be really fraudulent in character, or has been so manipulated by men in a position to influence the stock market as to be changed in value without any regard to the earning capacity of the enterprise represented, to the great profit of a few and the wholesale loss of multitudes of innocent investors. Insurance companies have used the funds accumulated in their hands not for the benefit of the policyholders but for the private benefit of their officers or for the convenience and profit of great stock jobbers. Such are the things that have gone wrong.

What remedies have been attempted? We have passed laws forbidding such combinations and such practices as would virtually constitute monopolies and have attempted to enforce them. We have forbidden discrimination in freight rates by railway companies and have tried to detect and punish them. We have gone further and tried to prescribe freight rates, and, warming to the business, have gone further still and endeavored to prescribe passenger rates as well, undertaking to look inside railway business and determine through public commissions what rates it is equitable for them to charge. We have undertaken to look inside the business of insurance companies too and to determine the character of their investments and the methods of their loans. The men who stand ouside the formal organization of the greater enterprises and manipulate their securities we have not yet undertaken to restrain or punish by any special provisions of law.

Railway corporations, it must be admitted, are specially open to regulation upon the stricter and more old-fashioned principles of government, for they are in effect our chief highways, they have been given the benefit of the State's right of eminent domain, and their lines and equipment being once created and put into use virtually give their owners a natural monopoly, so expensive would it be and so unprofitable to reproduce them. They are in some sense public instrumentalities.

But what strikes us most about all the regulation and remedial measures adopted is that they are based upon what is for us an entirely new conception of the province alike of law and of government. Our law has hitherto dealt with individuals, with specific transactions; it now undertakes to deal directly with business itself, not upon lines of exact definition such as courts of law could act upon but with a wide range of discretion which must be entrusted to commissions and cannot be assigned to judicial tribunals. Our state and federal governments are more and more undertaking through commissions to understand and analyze and regulate business, determining for example what particular corporations shall charge for their services and what they shall earn or endeavor to earn by the way of profit on their investments.

Governmental control which we are undertaking so extensively and with so light a heart sets up not a reign of law but a reign of discretion and individual judgment on the part of governmental officials in the regulation of the business of stock companies owned by innumerable private individuals and supplying the chief investments of thousands of communities. We do not content ourselves with prohibiting particular transactions, taking one transaction at a time as it clearly reveals itself in the experience of our business communities and putting the penalty for it upon those who actually engage in it; we set up public tribunals to determine how particular kinds of business shall be conducted. We seem to have made almost of a sudden and without deliberation a very radical and momentous choice of practice which is also a radical departure in principle from all that we have hitherto admitted or thought tolerable in the exercise of governmental authority. I can see no radical difference in principle between governmental ownership and governmental regulation of this discretionary kind. Advocates of governmental regulation talk of it as a necessary safeguard against socialistic programmes of reform, but it seems to me to be itself socialistic in principle. Though it goes but a little way, it does definitely move towards the entrance of government into the general field of economic enterprise. Whether government shall go further becomes a mere question of convenience or expediency and ceases to be a question of principle. Regulation by commission is not regulation by law, but control according to the discretion of governmental officials. Regulation by law is judicial, by fixed and definite rule, whereas regulation by commission is an affair of business sense, of the comprehension and thorough understanding of complex and various bodies of business. There is no logical stopping place between that and the actual conduct of business enterprises by the government.

Such methods of regulation it may be safely predicted will sooner or later be completely discredited by experience. Commissions in the future as in the past will reflect rather public opinion than business discretion. The only safe process, the only American process, the only effective process is the regulation of transactions by the definite prohibitions of law, item by item, as experience discloses their character and their effects, and the punishment of the particular individuals who engage in them.

This involves what we have in our haste so far not even attempted, namely a careful legal analysis of our present methods of business. There is law enough now to get at most of the transactions we complain of, if the courts would but read the older principles of the law in the light of new transactions; but the real difficulty is that individuals are concealed within the complex organization of modern corporations. The task of the modern judge and the modern legislator is to rediscover the individual in the organization. This is most difficult in the matter of stock manipulations and of all the subtle and complicated transactions by which so-called financiers play fast and loose with what is really private property or values of shares in legitimate and ordinarily profitable undertakings. Here we need new definitions of law. The corporation lawyer must assist us to find the men we are in search of. We know who they are, but our criminal law has not found them. If it needs new terms and definitions and prohibitions, we must supply them. It is no occult matter, but we have not seriously attempted it. It means the discrimination of real from nominal control in the management of our corporations, the discrimination of mere officials from the real masters of the greater combinations, and the fixing of responsibility upon the real masters whether they bear official titles in their organizations or not. The advice of experienced lawyers, if we will but pay for it, will easily enough enable us to accomplish our object.

The acts of corporations themselves must be checked,

not by futile and blundering attempts to dictate to each corporation how its business shall be conducted, but by bringing the officials directly to book who are responsible for forbidden or questionable transactions. The corporation itself never fails to find the really responsible official in its own processes of discipline, and it can be made to disclose to the public prosecutor the names of the men who should be proceeded against.

This old-fashioned process of seeking the individual and punishing him is much more difficult than the rough and ready process of dealing with the corporation as a whole, fining it, embarrassing its business transactions, crippling it or putting it out of business altogether, but it is the only process which will in the long run effect our purpose without putting us at a fatal disadvantage in the whole industrial development of the modern world. We must return to it and return to it soon if we would keep our place at the front of the nations who wield power and feed their millions in this eager modern day. It means on the official side, on the side of the government itself, systematic, prompt, watchful, unhesitating action in the prosecution of the individuals. It means in the field of civil law plain, easy, simple, unquestionable processes of suit such as litigants do not now have at their disposal. Above all, it means study and great discrimination on the part of the legislator.

No wise or conscientious man defends the inequitable methods of modern business. We are all in search of the same thing, of a just and effective remedy for the abuses which have brought almost all large transactions under suspicion. The present tendencies of legislation should be opposed, not because their object is a mistaken one, but simply because they are futile and will lead to utter disappointment. Governmental commissions cannot possibly understand business better than those who conduct it.

Their regulative interference with business will only complete the confusion and embarrassments into which we are so rapidly stumbling. The old processes of law are the more difficult, but the more effective. We must discover just what transactions we wish to put an end to; must devise means of discriminating and reaching the individuals who are really responsible for them; and must punish those individuals without respect of persons or consequences. We must have once more the reign of law rather than the reign of governmental officials.

DOCUMENT 25

The Ideal of Individualism

. . . We live in a very confused time. The economic developments which have embarrassed our life are of comparatively recent origin, and our chief trouble is that we do not exactly know what we are about. We have not made a thorough analysis of the facts; we are full of suspicions, but our arguments do not abound in proof. We are eager to touch the springs of action, but have not yet discovered exactly where they lie. We need nothing so much as that public thought should be instructed, purified, invigorated by plain, straightforward disinterested discussion not so much of party programmes as of facts and situations and needs. Above all things we need men who, because they are rendered independent by not seeking office or even desiring it, can hold militant ideals for which they are ready to fight in season and out of season and which they are

Excerpt from "Ideals of Public Life," address to the Chamber of Commerce, Cleveland, Ohio, November 16, 1907, *Princeton Alumni Weekly*, VIII (November 27, 1907), 161–162.

ready to expound though no man at first agree with them. If there were a large number of such men, their counsel would presently be heeded, and parties would no longer cast about for popular cries and issues. The public thought would bulk very clear to the eyes of all leaders, if formed by non-partisan processes.

I do not mean that parties can be or should be discredited. I believe that party action is the necessary process of life in a free country governed by opinion. What I mean is that the nation will not get at its real thoughts and purposes if it take counsel in public matters only of those who are party leaders and who are hampered, as party leaders must always be, by the exigencies of party contest and the necessity of always looking to the major chance at election time. Party leaders are obliged in a great degree to be opportunists. But the country cannot afford to be guided by opportunists alone. It must form its parties by very definitely forming its opinions, and opinion may dominate parties instead of merely supplying them with catch words, test candidates for office rather than merely coach them for success. Let us insist now for a little while, in this time when new thinking and new purposing is to be done, on thinking outside party formulas and class interests, as the men of our creative period did when the nation was in process of birth. Let us seek to encourage a class of public men who can make opinion, whom parties must heed and cannot use.

This is not cynical counsel based upon any pessimistic feeling that party morality is at a low ebb. On the contrary, the action of parties in our day is touched at many points with hopeful signs. Opinion everywhere prefers the process which is righteous and the man who is honest, and parties are as likely now as they ever were to serve the nation creditably and to good purpose. But they must serve the nation and not merely play a game for advantage, and they cannot serve a nation which does not definitely form and declare its thought.

Nothing is more evident in our day than that the country is confused in its thinking, and needs to look its affairs over very carefully before determining what legal and constitutional changes it will make. In our haste and eagerness to reform manifest abuses, we are inclined to enter upon courses dangerous and unprecedented, I mean unprecedented in America, and quite contrary to the spirit which has hitherto ruled in her affairs. We turn more and more with a sense of individual helplessness to the government, begging that it take care of us because we have forgotten how to take care of ourselves, begging that it will regulate our industries, scrutinize our economic undertakings, supervise our enterprizes and keep the men who conduct them within definite bounds of law and morality. We no longer know any remedy except to put things in the hands of the government. In such courses we are turning directly away from all the principles which have distinguished America and made her institutions the hope of all men who believe in liberty. Undoubtedly in our own time we must look to government to do a great many things which were once within the power of the individual and are now much beyond it, but it is none the less our duty to see that endeavor is not swallowed up in government.

We find many things done under forms of corporate organization which are clearly against the public welfare as well as against all principles of private morality, and so we strike at corporations, and, striking at corporations, embarrass the business of the country. There is no such thing as corporate morality or corporate integrity or corporate responsibility. Every transaction that is against the public welfare or right principle can be traced, if we will but take the pains to trace it, to some individual or body of individuals who are responsible for it, and those individuals should be punished without fear or favor, without checking the courses of the country's business. We must analyze our new methods of business so as to re-discover the individual in them and hold him to his personal responsibility. This, and not methods of government supervision, is the task of the enlightened lawyer and legislator, if we would bring back to America her great fame and leadership in the world of politics and law. It is difficult; it can be accomplished only by the most careful analysis of the facts; but it can be accomplished, and it will set us free alike from individual crime in the field of business and from governmental tutelage in the field of politics. Our two tasks are to break up monopolies and re-discover the individual in all matters of legal responsibility. Governmental supervision will not free us or moralize us; it will in the long run enslave us and demoralize us. But individual responsibility and an impartial enforcement of the law against those who are actually responsible will bring us alike freedom and public morals.

3. A Reverence for Old Principles

DOCUMENT 26

Conservatism: True and False

During the years before 1910, when Wilson regarded himself as a conservative, he was careful to note that he was no blind reactionary seeking to return to a long-dead past. In-

---

Excerpt from "Conservatism, True and False," address to the Southern Society, New York, December 9, 1908, *Princeton Alumni Weekly*, IX (December 16, 1908), 188–189.

stead, his conservatism demanded a constant re-examination of old principles and an effort to adapt them to new circumstances; rather than applying novel and untried remedies.

. . . The problems to be met are so great and perplexing that we have been in a temper to approach them boldly and with very radical proposals, and we have been easily rendered impatient of any who have cried a warning to us or who have tried to draw us back to slower, safer, and better-tested processes. There is a false conservatism which justifies impatience in our existing circumstances, namely that sort of conservatism which proposes a return to old measures and expedients intended for other circumstances or to old formulas now in large part emptied of their meaning. For example, the old formula "tariff for revenue only" has a barren sound to our ears in existing circumstances, because the tariff as we know it is not a system of taxation; it is, rather, a vast body of economic expedients which have been used under the guise of taxation for the purpose of building up various industries, great and small, and enriching the nation as a body of individuals rather than as a government. It would be perfectly futile to propose out of hand a tariff for revenue only, because you cannot get out of a system except by systematic effort and adjustment, and the point to determine at present is not, how may we best secure the necessary revenue for the maintenance and conduct of our government by means of duties on imports, but how shall we adjust our duties on imports to the present real circumstances of the nation and the present interests of our economic development as a whole. Let the one example serve for many. What we want is not a set of issues which will sound like echoes of circumstances which no longer exist, but a set of issues arising out of and intended for the present.

The conservatism which should be sharply distinguished from this false and bastard conservatism, which is merely reactionary, is the conservatism which seeks a return to old and well recognized principles, but a return to them in such a way as will give them a new interpretation and a new meaning for the time we live in. The true conservatism consists in re-examining old principles, seeking such a reformulation of them as will adapt them to the circumstances of a new time. There is no danger that the tested principles of government which we have derived from the long experience of our race will be discredited, if we understand their present application. They will be discredited only by applying them in some antiquated and pedantic way. The true way to keep our principles is to keep our heads, is not to be confused by new circumstances but to see how and where they square with the principles by which we are trying to be guided.

Let me take a few examples. Let my first example be drawn again from the question of the tariff, which, after all, is central to half the questions which now perplex us in regard to the reform of our economic structure and processes. The principle for which we should seek a new interpretation and application is this: that the power of a government to tax ought never to be used to confer privileges upon individuals or groups of individuals, but should be used always and only to secure general benefits, the benefit of the taxpayers as a whole or of the nation as an organism. This general benefit and development was the object sought by our policy of protective tariff as it was originally conceived by Alexander Hamilton, and all valid arguments for that system are simply reiterations of his argument in his masterful Report on Manufactures. But there came a time, and it came very early in the history of our actual tariff legislation, when the adjustment of import duties became a matter of contest and bargain, of give and take, amongst the various interests which sought its advantages. The Tariff of 1828 was called the Tariff of Abominations, because it was thought not to be made in the general interest but to be a miscellaneous piling together of the various duties which manufacturers of different kinds desired, and the tariffs of more recent date have been touched with the same disfigurement alike of symmetry and of principle. We need not stop to inquire when or where the line was crossed. Suffice it to say that it is the present general conviction that our more recent tariff legislation has been a doling out of privileges on the part of the government and that certain protected interests have been built up with no particular regard to the interests of the nation as a whole. When privileges have been created, governmental oversight and regulation are necessary. Those who act upon privilege or enjoy any artificial advantage must be controlled. Those who act upon right need not be. Half our present difficulties arise from the fact that privileged interests have threatened to become too strong for the general interest, and that, therefore, the government has had to step in to restrain those who enjoyed the very privileges which it itself granted. Reform, therefore, must come, not in the shape of a new adjustment of interests, but in the shape of a reconsideration of the general policy of the government in these matters which would square it with the general interest. This reform must proceed without injustice and with as little injury as possible. It must proceed, also, gradually and with a due regard to the maintenance of economic stability. And it must proceed upon the principle, not that all protection is to be withdrawn, but that all protection is to be adjusted to the general interest and withdrawn from the field of the granting of special privileges and advantages.

Take another principle which true conservatism demands should be revived and retranslated into the terms of our present life. The control of the government should be exercised by process of law and not by administrative discretion. This does not necessarily mean that the control of the government should be exercised only through the courts as we have known them, that is, only through the formal, elaborate, and somewhat tedious judicial processes which we have come to think of as characteristic of judicial action. The government may act less formally, more summarily, through commissions, without violation of any fundamental principle of liberty, provided only the action of the commissions be made real process of law and not a process of mere discretionary practical judgment on the part of those who compose them. This is the true meaning for us of the old Jeffersonian principle, "as little government as possible." For us that maxim means as little government by executive choice and preference, as little government of the kind that varies the footing upon which interests are dealt with, which chooses its measures differently, instance by instance, leaves some untouched and brings others up with a sharp turn. It means as little government by discretionary authority as possible. It is not hostile to regulated and equalized freedom or to any process of law which is a calculable process of rule and proceeds by defined standards.

Take again the question of the power of the general government as against the power of the governments of the States. We should not waste our time upon any pedantic discussion of what constitutes state rights. We know that we still have a singularly various country, that it would be folly to apply uniform rules of development to all parts of the country, that our strength has been in the elasticity of our institutions, in the almost infinite adaptability of our laws, that our vitality has consisted largely in the dispersion of political authority, in the necessity that communities should take care of themselves and work out their own order and progress. We know that in stating these things we are dealing with facts, not with abstract principles, and out of these facts we can draw a very definite rule of action, namely that in all that we do we should prefer a dispersion of governmental power to a concentration of it, that "home rule" should be the normal rule of life with us, that centralized authority should be the exception. We should not be afraid of it, as of a bugaboo, but we should not be in haste to set it up, and should be very sure that we were ready for a general rule before we set up a general authority.

And then, to take a final instance, I think that we can be sure that we are not done with the principle of individual initiative, of individual right. We can still be very sure that any set of measures based upon the purpose of allowing the government to coach or dictate to the individual unnecessarily, where individual action is still possible, will certainly turn out to be measures for the impoverishment of the nation in respect of everything that goes to make for its variety and energy and enrichment. It is hard to find the individual in many cases amidst the present confusion of conditions, but we know that he is the source of energy for the nation nevertheless, and that to smother him is to produce a general mediocrity and inertia. Any form of collectivism which submerges him will certainly be fatal to our progress no less than to our liberty. Whatever laws we may devise, we must make sure not to lose him by any collective process.

Such should be our handling of old principles. In this way should they be made our guides, not to recovering the past, for we are not going in that direction and do not wish to recover it, but to threading the present and making sure of wholesome and secure development in the future.

DOCUMENT 27

States' Rights

In his lectures on American government at Columbia University in 1907, Wilson provided a clear exposition of his distrust of federal authority and his preference for governmental action at the state or local level.

. . . The principle of the division of powers between State and Federal Governments is a very simple one when stated in its most general terms. It is that the Legislatures of the States shall have control of all the general subject-matter of law, of private rights of every kind, of local interests and of everything that directly concerns their people as communities, — free choice with regard to all matters of local regulation and development, and that Congress shall have control only of such matters as concern the peace and the commerce of the country as a whole. . . .

. . . Which parts of the many-sided processes of the nation's economic development shall be left to the regulation of the States, which parts shall be given over to the regulation of the Federal Government? I do not propound this as a mere question of choice, a mere question of statesmanship, but also as a question, a very fundamental question, of constitutional law. What, reading our Constitution in its true spirit, neither sticking in its letter nor yet forcing it arbitrarily to mean what we wish it to mean, shall be the answer of our generation to the old question of the distribution of powers between Congress and the States? For us, as for previous generations, it is a deeply critical question. The

---

Excerpts from Woodrow Wilson, "The States and the Federal Government," *North American Review*, CLXXXVII (May 1908), in *Public Papers*, II, 33–34, 36–38, 44–47, and 48. See also Woodrow Wilson, *Constitutional Government in the United States*, pp. 175, 178–180, 187–190, and 191–192.

very stuff of all our political principles, of all our political experience, is involved in it. In this all too indistinctly marked field of right choice our statesmanship shall achieve new triumphs or come to eventual shipwreck.

The old theory of the sovereignty of the States, which used so to engage our passions, has lost its vitality. The war between the States established at least this principle, that the Federal Government is, through its courts, the final judge of its own powers. Since that stern arbitrament it would be idle, in any practical argument, to ask by what law of abstract principle the Federal Government is bound and restrained. Its power is "to regulate commerce between the States," and the attempts now made during every session of Congress to carry the implications of that power beyond the utmost boundaries of reasonable and honest inference show that the only limits likely to be observed by politicians are those set by the good sense and conservative temper of the country.

The proposed Federal legislation with regard to the regulation of child labor affords a striking example. If the power to regulate commerce between the States can be stretched to include the regulation of labor in mills and factories, it can be made to embrace every particular of the industrial organization and action of the country. The only limitation Congress would observe, should the Supreme Court assent to such obviously absurd extravagances of interpretation, would be the limitations of opinion and of circumstance.

It is important, therefore, to look at the facts and to understand the real character of the political and economic materials of our own day with a clear and statesmanlike vision, as the makers of the Constitution understood the conditions they dealt with. If the jealousies of the colonies and of the little States which sprang out of them had not obliged the makers of the Constitution to leave the greater part of legal regulation in the hands of the States it would have been wise, it would even have been necessary, to invent such a division of powers as was actually agreed upon. It is not, at bottom, a question of sovereignty or of any other political abstraction; it is a question of vitality. Uniform regulation of the economic conditions of a vast territory and a various people like the United States would be mischievous, if not impossible. The statesmanship which really attempts it is premature and unwise. Undoubtedly the recent economic development of the country, particularly the development of the last two decades, has obliterated many boundaries, made many interests national and common which until our own day were separate and distinct; but the lines of these great changes we have not yet clearly traced or studiously enough considered. To distinguish them and provide for them is the task which is to test the statesmanship of our generation; and it is already plain that, great as they are, these new combinations of interest have not yet gone so far as to make the States mere units of local government. Not our legal conscience merely, but our practical interests as well, call upon us to discriminate and be careful, with the care of men who handle the vital stuff of a great constitutional system.

The United States are not a single, homogeneous community. In spite of a certain superficial sameness which seems to impart to Americans a common type and point of view, they still contain communities at almost every stage of development, illustrating in their social and economic structure almost every modern variety of interest and prejudice, following occupations of every kind, in climates of every sort that the temperate zone affords. This variety of fact and condition, these substantial economic and social contrasts, do not in all cases follow State lines. They are often contrasts between region and region rather than State and State. But they are none the less real, and are in many instances permanent and ineradicable. . . .

We are an industrial people. The development of the resources of the country, the command of the markets of the world, is for the time being more important in our eyes than any political theory or lawyer's discrimination of functions. We are intensely "practical," moreover, and insist that every obstacle, whether of law or fact, be swept out of the way. It is not the right temper for constitutional understandings. Too "practical" a purpose may give us a government such as we never should have chosen had we made the choice more thoughtfully and deliberately. We cannot afford to belie our reputation for political sagacity and self-possession by any such hasty processes as those into which such a temper of mere impatience seems likely to hurry us.

The remedy for ill-considered legislation by the States, the remedy alike for neglect and mistake on their part, lies, not outside the States, but within them. The mistakes which they themselves correct will sink deeper into the consciousness of their people than the mistakes which Congress may rush in to correct for them, thrusting upon them what they have not learned to desire. They will either themselves learn their mistakes, by such intimate and domestic processes as will penetrate very deep and abide with them in convincing force, or else they will prove that what might have been a mistake for other States or regions of the country was no mistake for them, and the country will have been saved its wholesome variety. In no case will their failure to correct their own measures prove that the Federal Government might have forced wisdom upon them.

There is, however, something else that comes to the surface, and that explains not a little of our present dissatisfaction with State legislation upon matters of vital national importance. Their failure to correct their own processes may prove that there is something radically wrong with the structure and operation of their governments, — that they have ceased to be sensitive and efficient instruments for the creation and realization of opinions, — the real function of constitutional governments.

It is better to learn the true political lesson than merely to improve business. There is something involved which is deeper than the mere question of the distribution of legislative powers within our Federal system. We have come to the test of the intimate and detailed processes of self-government to which it was supposed that our principles and our experience had committed us. There are many evidences that we are losing confidence in our State Legislatures, and yet it is evident that it is through them that we attempt all the more intimate measures of self-government. To lose faith in them is to lose faith in our very system of government, and that is a very serious matter. It is this loss of confidence in our local legislatures that has led our people to give so much heed to the radical suggestions of change made by those who advocate the use of the initiative and the referendum in our processes of legislation, the virtual abandonment of the representative principle and the attempt to put into the hands of the voters themselves the power to initiate and negative laws, — in order to enable them to do for themselves what they have not been able to get satisfactorily done through the representatives they have hitherto chosen to act for them.

Such doubts and such consequent proposals of reform should make us look deeper into this question than we have hitherto looked. It may turn out, upon examination, that what we are really dissatisfied with is not the present distribution of powers between the State and Federal authorities, but the character of our State governments. If they were really governments by the people we should not be dissatisfied with them. We are impatient of State Legislatures because they seem to us less representative of the thoughtful opinion of the country than Congress is. We know that our Legislatures do not think alike, but we are not sure that our people do not think alike. If there is a real variety of opinion among our people in the several regions of the country, we would be poor lovers of democratic self-government were we to wish to see those differences over-ridden by the majorities of a central Legislature. It is to be hoped that we still sufficiently understand the real proc-esses of political life to know that a growing country must grow, that opinion such as government can be based upon develops by experience, not by authority, that a region forced is a region dissatisfied, and that spontaneous is bet-ter, more genuine, more permanent than forced agreement.

The truth is that our State governments are many of them no longer truly representative governments. We are not, in fact, dissatisfied with local representative assem-blies and the government which they impose; we are dissatisfied, rather, with regulations imposed by commis-sions and assemblies which are no longer representative. It is a large subject, of many debatable parts, and I can only touch upon it here, but the fact is that we have im-posed an impossible task upon our voters, and that because it is impossible they do not perform it. It is impossible for the voters of any busy community actually to pick out or in any real sense choose the very large number of per-sons we call upon them under our present State Con-stitutions to elect. They have neither the time nor the quick and easy means of co-operation which would enable them to make up the long lists of candidates for offices local and national upon which they are expected to act. They must of necessity leave the selection to a few per-sons who, from one motive or another, volunteer to make a business of it. These are the political bosses and managers whom the people obey and affect to despise. It is unjust to despise them. Under a system of innumerable nominations they are indispensable. A system of so-called popular elec-tions like ours could not be operated successfully without them. But it is true that by their constant and professional attention to the business of nomination a real popular choice of candidates is done away with entirely, and that our State officers and legislators are in effect appointed, not elected.

The question at an election is only which set of appointees shall be put into office, those appointed by the managers and bosses of this party or of that. It is this, whether our people are distinctly conscious of it or not, which has so seriously impaired their confidence in the State Legislatures and which has made them look about for new means by which to obtain a real choice in affairs. . . .

It would be fatal to our political vitality really to strip the States of their powers and transfer them to the Federal Government. It cannot be too often repeated that it has been the privilege of separate development secured to the several regions of the country by the Constitution, and not the privilege of separate development only, but also that other more fundamental privilege that lies back of it, the privilege of independent local opinion and individual conviction, which has given speed, facility, vigor, and certainty to the processes of our economic and political growth. To buy temporary ease and convenience for the performance of a few great tasks of the hour at the expense of that would be to pay too great a price and to cheat all generations for the sake of one.

4. To Recapture the Democratic Party from the Bryan Radicals

DOCUMENT 28

"An Alien Faction"

In the period before 1910 Wilson thoroughly disapproved of William Jennings Bryan's leadership of the Democratic

---

Excerpt from "On the Political Future of the South," address to the Society of the Virginians, New York, November 29, 1904, *Princeton Alumni Weekly*, V (December 3, 1904), 161.

Party. He opposed Bryan's first bid for the Presidency, voting instead for the Gold Democratic ticket, and there-after he worked to eliminate what he considered to be Bryan's radical influence in public affairs. The conservative and solid South, he told an audience of Virginians in 1904, might be the means of restoring the Democratic Party to sound doctrine.

. . . No one can justly wonder at the present impatience of the Southern political leaders at finding themselves with-out real independence or influence in the politics of the country; the only section of the country which did not make a real choice of its political actions in the recent elections. But the only remedy suggested would put the Southern States in a still worse position.

To act independently of old party affiliations, as some of their leaders have recently proposed that they should act, would be to make them, if they still hung together and acted in concert, a third party in the politics of the country, and not a party of principle at that, but a geographical party, a sectional party, which would act in isolation and draw upon itself afresh old enmities and suspicions.

The real opportunity of the South is of another sort. It has now a unique opportunity to perform a great national ser-vice. As the only remaining part of the Democratic party that can command a majority of the votes in its constitu-encies, let the South demand a rehabilitation of the Demo-cratic party on the only lines that can restore it to dignity and power.

Since 1896 the Democratic party has permitted its name to be used by men who ought never to have been admitted to its counsels, men who held principles and professed purposes which it had always hitherto repudiated.

By themselves and under their proper designation as populists and radical theorists, contemptuous alike of principle and of experience, these men could never have played any role in national politics but that of a noisy minority. Since they forced themselves into the councils of the party and got the use of its name, every doubtful State has been turned into an enthusiastic supporter of the Republican party. Until it has read them out of the party as an alien faction there will be no doubtful States again.

It is now high time that the South, which has endured most by way of humiliation at the hands of this faction, should demand that it be utterly and once for all thrust out of Democratic counsels; that the men of New York, New Jersey, Connecticut, Massachusetts, Indiana and the prosperous States beyond the Mississippi who wish for reform without loss of stability should join with it to reassert the principles and return to the practices of the historic party which has always stood for thoughtful moderation in affairs and a careful use of the powers of the Federal Government in the interest of the whole people of whatever class or occupation.

There is no longer any Democratic party either in the South or in any Northern State which the discredited radicals can use. The great body of one-time Democrats that musters strong enough to win elections has revolted and will act with no organization which harbors the radicals — as the radicals themselves did not in fact act with the organization they themselves had discredited in the recent campaign, when the whole country felt that the Democratic party was still without definite character or make-up.

The country, as it moves forward in its great material progress, needs and will tolerate no party of discontent or radical experiment; but it does need a party of conservative reform, acting in the spirit of law and of ancient institutions. Hosts of voters are waiting and ready to flock back to the standard of such a party when once they see it come upon the field properly purged and authenticated.

The old Democratic party stood by the South through good report and ill; the South has now an opportunity to requite its thankless services by recalling it to its old counsel and spirit. To do this would be to render a real national service conceived in the interest of the whole country of whatever opinion; for the politics of the nation cannot go normally and healthfully forward without the stimulation and contest of two parties of principle.

DOCUMENT 29

"To Knock Mr. Bryan, Once for All, into a Cocked Hat"

Wilson's distrust of Bryan was revealed in a frank 1907 letter to a conservative member of the Princeton board of trustees who shared his view. Later, when Wilson was seeking the Democratic nomination for President in 1912 and needed at least Bryan's benevolent neutrality if not his outright support, the letter was released to the press in an effort to damage Wilson's candidacy. (See Document 34.)

Thank you very much for sending me your address at Parsons, Kansas, before the Board of Directors, of the Missouri, Kansas and Texas Railroad Company. I have read it with relish, and am in entire agreement. Would that we could do something, at once, dignified and effective, to knock Mr. Bryan, once for all, into a cocked hat.

Letter to Adrian H. Joline, April 29, 1907, in Baker, *Wilson, Life and Letters*, III, 23.

B. THE RISE OF A PROGRESSIVE GOVERNOR

DOCUMENT 30

The Catharsis of Campaigning

Wilson owed his nomination for the governorship of New Jersey chiefly to two things: his oft-stated orthodox views, which had persuaded Colonel George Harvey and other conservative Democrats that he might be the means of purging the party of Bryan's radical influence, and the New Jersey Democratic bosses' recognition that a candidate of Wilson's stature might enable the party to return to power after nearly a generation of Republican governors. Yet Wilson was clearly no ordinary machine candidate, and he quickly showed his independence. He had always championed individual rights and effective representative government, and as the campaign developed he found himself in agreement with many of the goals sought by New Jersey progressives of both parties. When challenged by a prominent Republican progressive, George L. Record, to state his position on a number of issues, Wilson responded with a disarmingly frank and unequivocal statement of his views. His letter to Record was circulated widely throughout the state as a campaign flyer and did much to assure his victory by a 50,000-vote margin. The letter is an important document marking the gradual conversion of Wilson to progressivism.

I am sincerely sorry that I have been obliged to wait so long before replying to your letter of the 17th. The delay has been due entirely to the fact of my necessary absorption in the actual engagements of the campaign.

Letter to George L. Record, October 24, 1910, in *Trenton True American*, October 26, 1910.

In order to reply as clearly as possible to your questions, I will quote them and append the answers:

1 – "That the public utilities commission should have full power to fix just and reasonable rates to be charged by all public service corporations. Do you favor this?"

Answer to Question One – Yes.

2 – "That the physical property of each public utility corporation which is devoted to a public use should be valued by the State. Do you favor this?"

Answer to Question Two – Yes.

3 – "That such physical valuation should be taken as the assessment upon which such corporation shall pay local taxes. Do you favor this?"

Answer to Question Three – Yes.

4 – "That such valuation should be used as a basis for fixing rates to be charged by these corporations and that such rates should be limited as to allow them to earn not exceeding six per cent. upon this valuation. Do you favor this?"

Answer to Question Four – No. I think that such valuation should form a very important part of the basis upon which rates should be fixed, but not the whole basis. All the financial, physical and economic circumstances of the business should be taken into consideration. The percentage of profit should be determined by the commission after full inquiry, and not by statute.

5 – "That the present primary law should be extended to the selection of candidates for party nominations for Governor, Congressman and delegates to national conventions. Do you favor this?"

Answer to Question Five – Yes, though I should wish a better primary law than the pesent.

6 – "That United States Senators should be elected by popular vote. Do you favor this?"

Answer to Question Six – Yes.

7 – "To apply this principle, I favor a law compelling all

candidates for nomination to the legislature to file a pledge to vote for that candidate of their party for United States Senator who shall receive the highest number of votes under the present primary law. Do you favor this?"

Answer to Question Seven — In principle, yes, but I fear that a law "compelling" this would be unconstitutional. Surely, the voters can exact this pledge, and have the matter in their own hands. A better primary law than the present would facilitate this exaction on the part of the voters by obliging the candidate for the State Legislature to state his intention in this matter when accepting his own nomination.

8 — "That the names of all candidates at election should be printed on a blanket ballot, and that all ballots shall be distributed to the voter by mail at public expense, or confined to the polling place. Do you favor this?"

Answer to Question Eight — I believe that the ballots should be given out only at the polling places and only by the election officers, and that, while the blanket ballot is the best form yet devised, experience has proved that it is best to put some indication of the source of the nomination after each name. A mere alphabetical list results usually in the election of the top of the alphabet, and there are actually cases on record of would-be candidates who have had their names changed to begin with the first letter of the alphabet in order to increase their chances of election. Amidst a multitude of names on our long ballots the ordinary voter needs some guidance.

9 — "That primary and election officers should be appointed by some impartial agency, like a court. Do you favor that?"

Answer to Question Nine — Yes.

10 — "There should be a drastic corrupt practices act, forbidding all political expenditures except for the objects named in the act, with drastic penalties for the violation of the act; prohibiting the employment of more than two

workers or watchers at the polls on primary day or election day representing any one party or group of candidates; prohibiting the hiring of vehicles for transporting voters; limiting the amount to be expended by candidates; prohibiting political contributions by corporations. Do you favor this?"

Answer to Question Ten—Yes.

11—"That every industry employing workmen shall be compelled to bear the expense of all injuries to employes which happen in the industry without wilful negligence of such employe. Do you favor this?"

Answer to Question Eleven—Yes.

12—"That the County Board of Elections law and the Hillery maximum tax law should be repealed. Do you favor this?"

Answer to Question Twelve—Yes.

13—"Does the Democratic platform declare for the choice of candidates for all elective officers by the direct vote system?

Answer to Question Thirteen—Yes; I so understand it. If it does not, I do.

14—"Do you admit that the boss system exists as I have described it? If so, how do you propose to abolish it?"

Answer to Question Fourteen—Of course, I admit it. Its existence is notorious. I have made it my business for many years to observe and understand that system, and I hate it as thoroughly as I understand it. You are quite right in saying that the system is bi-partisan; that it constitutes "the most dangerous condition in the public life of our State and nation today;" and that it has virtually, for the time being, "destroyed representative government and in its place set up a government of privilege." I would propose to abolish it by the above reforms, by the election to office of men who will refuse to submit to it and bend all their energies to break it up, and by pitiless publicity.

15—"In referring to the Board of Guardians, do you

mean such Republican leaders as Baird, Murphy, Kean and Stokes? Wherein do the relations to the special interests of such leaders differ from the relations to the same interests of such Democratic leaders as Smith, Nugent and Davis?"

Answer to Question Fifteen—I refer to the men you name. They differ from the others in this, that they are in control of the government of the State while the others are not and cannot be if the present Democratic ticket is elected.

16—"I join you in condemning the Republican Board of Guardians. I have been fighting them for years and shall continue to fight them. Will you join me in denouncing the Democratic Overlords, as parties to the same political system? If not, why not?

Answer to Question Sixteen—Certainly; I will join you or any one else in denouncing and fighting any and every one, of either party, who attempts such outrages against the government and public morality.

17—"You say the Democratic party has been reorganized, and the Republican party has not. Can a political party be reorganized without changing either its leaders, or its old leaders changing their point of view and their political character? Will you claim that either of these events has taken place in the Democratic party? If yes, upon what do you base that conclusion?"

Answer to Question Seventeen—I do not remember saying that the Democratic party has been reorganized. I remember saying that it was seeking reorganization, and was therefore at the threshold of a new era. I said this because it is seeking to change its leaders, and will obviously change them if successful at this election. If I am elected, I shall understand that I am chosen leader of my party and the direct representative of the whole people in the conduct of the government. All of this was distinctly understood at the very outset, when my nomination was first proposed, and there has never been the slightest intimation from any quarter to the contrary since. The Republican party is not seeking to change its leaders, and, therefore, is not even seeking reorganization.

18—"Is there any organized movement in the Democratic party in this State which corresponds to the Progressive Republican movement of which you have already spoken?"

Answer to Question Eighteen—I understand the present platform and the present principal nominations of the Democratic party in this State to be such an organized movement. It will be more fully organized if those nominees are elected. This is, as I interpret it, the spirit of the whole remarkable Democratic revival which we are witnessing not only in New Jersey, but in many other States.

Before I pass to the next question, will you not permit me to frame one which you have not asked, but which I am sure lies implied in those I have just answered? You wish to know what my relations would be with the Democrats whose power and influence you fear, should I be elected Governor, particularly in such important matters as appointments and the signing of bills, and I am very glad to tell you. If elected, I shall not, either in the matter of appointments to office or assent to legislation, or in shaping any part of the policy of my administration, submit to the dictation of any person, or persons, special interest or organization. I will always welcome advice and suggestions from any citizen, whether boss, leader, organization man or plain citizen, and I shall constantly seek the advice of influential and disinterested men, representative of their communities and disconnected from political "organizations" entirely; but all suggestions and all advice will be considered on their merits, and no additional weight will be given to any man's advice or suggestion because of his exercising or supposing that he exercises some sort of political influence or control. I should deem myself forever disgraced should I in even the slightest degree co-operate in any such system or any such transactions as you describe in your characterization of the "boss" system. I regard myself as pledged to the regeneration of the Democratic party which I have forecast above.

19 – "Will you agree to publicly call upon the Republican and Democratic candidates for the legislature to pledge themselves in writing prior to election in favor of such of the foregoing reforms as you personally favor? If not, why not?"

Answer to Question Nineteen – I will not. Because I think it would be most unbecoming to me to do so. That is the function of the voters in the several counties. Let them test and judge the men, and choose those who are sincere.

Allow me to thank you for this opportunity to express with the greatest possible definiteness my convictions upon the issues of the present campaign and also for your very kind expression of confidence and regard, which I highly appreciate.

DOCUMENT 31

A Mandate for Reform

Following his election as governor, Wilson swiftly consolidated his control of the party and proceeded to cajole and pressure the legislature into enacting a sweeping program of reform. His inaugural address on January 17, 1911, sounded the call to action in lofty Wilsonian prose and provided further evidence of his emergence as a progressive.

Public Papers, II, 270–282.

Gentlemen of the Legislature: I assume the great office of Governor of the State with unaffected diffidence. Many great men have made this office illustrious. A long tradition of honourable public service connects each incumbent of it with the generation of men who set up our governments here in free America, to give men perpetual assurance of liberty and justice and opportunity. No one dare be sure that he is qualified to play the part expected of him by the people of the commonwealth in the execution of this high trust. It is best for him, as he sets out, to look away from himself and to concentrate his thought upon the people whom he serves, the sacred interests which are entrusted to his care, and the day in which he is to work, its challenge, its promise, its energies of opinion and of purpose, its sustaining hopes and exciting expectations. The scene will inspire him, not thought of himself.

The opportunity of our day in the field of politics no man can mistake who can read any, even the most superficial, signs of the times. We have never seen a day when duty was more plain, the task to be performed more obvious, the way in which to accomplish it more easy to determine. The air has in recent months cleared amazingly about us, and thousands, hundreds of thousands, have lifted their eyes to look about them, to see things they never saw before, to comprehend things that once seemed vague and elusive. The whole world has changed within the lifetime of men not yet in their thirties; the world of business, and therefore the world of society and the world of politics. The organization and movement of business are new and upon a novel scale. Business has changed so rapidly that for a long time we were confused, alarmed, bewildered, in a sort of terror of the things we had ourselves raised up. We talked about them either in sensational articles in the magazines which distorted every line of the picture, or in conservative editorials in our newspapers, which stoutly

denied that anything at all had happened, or in grave dis-
courses which tried to treat them as perfectly normal phe-
nomena, or in legislative debates which sought to govern
them with statutes which matched them neither in size nor
in shape.

But, if only by sheer dint of talking about them, either to
frighten or to reassure one another, or to make ourselves
out wiser or more knowing than our fellows, we have at
last turned them about and looked at them from almost
every angle and begin to see them whole, as they are.
Corporations are no longer hobgoblins which have sprung
at us out of some mysterious ambush, nor yet unholy in-
ventions of rascally rich men, nor yet the puzzling devices
by which ingenious lawyers build up huge rights out of a
multitude of small wrongs; but merely organizations of a
perfectly intelligible sort which the law has licensed for
the convenience of extensive business; organizations
which have proved very useful but which have for the
time being slipped out of the control of the very law that
gave them leave to be and that can make or unmake them
at pleasure. We have now to set ourselves to control them,
soberly but effectively, and to bring them thoroughly
within the regulation of the law.

There is a great opportunity here; for wise regulation,
wise adjustment, will mean the removal of half the difficulties that now beset us in our search for justice and
equality and fair chances of fortune for the individuals
who make up our modern society. And there is a great
obligation as well as a great opportunity, an imperative
obligation, from which we cannot escape if we would.
Public opinion is at last wide awake. It begins to understand the problems to be dealt with; it begins to see very
clearly indeed the objects to be sought. It knows what has
been going on. It sees where resistance has come from
whenever efforts at reform have been made, and knows

also the means of resistance that have been resorted to. It is watchful, insistent, suspicious. No man who wishes to enjoy the public confidence dare hold back, and, if he is wise, he will not resort to subterfuge. A duty is exacted of him which he must perform simply, directly, immediately. The gate of opportunity stands wide open. If we are foolish enough to be unwilling to pass through it, the whip of opinion will drive us through.

No wise man will say, of course, that he sees the whole problem of reform lying plain before him, or knows how to frame the entire body of law that will be necessary to square business with the general interest, and put right and fairness and public spirit in the saddle again in all the transactions of our new society; but some things are plain enough, and upon these we can act.

In the first place, it is plain that our laws with regard to the relations of employer and employe are in many respects wholly antiquated and impossible. They were framed for another age, which nobody now living remembers, which is, indeed, so remote from our life that it would be difficult for many of us to understand it if it were described to us. The employer is now generally a corporation or huge company of some kind; the employe is one of hundreds or of thousands brought together, not by individual masters whom they know and with whom they have personal relations, but by agents of one sort or another. Workingmen are marshalled in great numbers for the performance of a multitude of particular tasks under a common discipline. They generally use dangerous and powerful machinery, over whose repair and renewal they have no control. New rules must be devised with regard to their obligations and their rights, their obligations to their employers and their responsibilities to one another. New rules must be devised for their protection, for their compensation when injured, for their support when disabled.

We call these questions of employers' liability, questions of workingmen's compensation, but those terms do not suggest quite the whole matter. There is something very new and very big and very complex about these new relations of capital and labour. A new economic society has sprung up, and we must effect a new set of adjustments. We must not pit power against weakness. The employer is generally in our day, as I have said, not an individual, but a powerful group of individuals, and yet the workingman is still, under our existing law, an individual when dealing with his employer, in case of accident, for example, or of loss or of illness, as well as in every contractual relationship. We must have a workingman's compensation act which will not put upon him the burden of fighting powerful composite employers to obtain his rights, but which will give him his rights without suit, directly, and without contest, by automatic operation of law, as if of a law of insurance.

This is the first adjustment needed, because it affects the rights, the happiness, the lives and fortunes of the largest number, and because it is the adjustment for which justice cries loudest and with the most direct appeal to our hearts as well as to our consciences.

But there is regulation needed which lies back of that and is much more fundamental. The composite employer himself needs to have his character and powers overhauled, his constitution and rights reconsidered, readjusted to the fundamental and abiding interests of society. If I may speak very plainly, we are much too free with grants of charters to corporations in New Jersey: A corporation exists, not of natural right, but only by license of law, and the law, if we look at the matter in good conscience, is responsible for what it creates. It can never rightly authorize any kind of fraud or imposition. It cannot righteously allow the setting up of a business which has no sound basis, or which follows methods which in any way outrage justice or fair dealing or the principles of honest industry. The law cannot give its license to things of that kind. It thereby authenticates what it ought of right to forbid.

I would urge, therefore, the imperative obligation of public policy and of public honesty we are under to effect such changes in the law of the State as will henceforth effectually prevent the abuse of the privilege of incorporation which has in recent years brought so much discredit upon our State. In order to do this it will be necessary to regulate and restrict the issue of securities, to enforce regulations with regard to bona fide capital, examining very rigorously the basis of capitalization, and to prescribe methods by which the public shall be safeguarded against fraud, deception, extortion, and every abuse of its confidence.

And such scrutiny and regulation ought not to be confined to corporations seeking charters. They ought also to be extended to corporations already operating under the license and authority of the State. For the right to undertake such regulation is susceptible of easy and obvious justification. A modern corporation—that is, a modern joint stock company—is in no proper sense an intimate or private concern. It is not set up on the risk and adventure of a few persons, the persons who originated it, manage it, carry it to failure or success. On the contrary, it is set up at what may be called the common risk. It is a risk and adventure in which the public are invited to share, and the hundreds, perhaps thousands, who subscribe to the stock do in fact share in it, oftentimes without sharing also, in any effectual manner, in the control and development of the business in which their risk is taken. Moreover, these modern enterprises, with their exchequers replenished out of the common store of the savings of the nation, conduct business transactions whose scope and influence are as wide as whole regions of the Union, often as wide as the nation itself. They affect sometimes the lives and fortunes of whole communities, dominate prices, determine land values, make and unmake markets, develop or check the growth of city and of countryside. If law is at liberty to adjust the general conditions of society itself, it is at liberty to control these great instrumentalities which nowadays, in so large part, determine the character of society. Wherever we can find what the common interest is in respect of them we shall find a solid enough basis for law, for reform.

The matter is most obvious when we turn to what we have come to designate public service, or public utility, corporations—those which supply us with the means of transportation and with those common necessaries, water, light, heat, and power. Here are corporations exercising peculiar and extraordinary franchises, and bearing such a relation to society in respect of the services they render that it may be said that they are the very medium of its life. They render a public and common service of which it is necessary that practically everybody should avail himself.

We have a Public Utilities Commission in New Jersey, but it has hardly more than powers of inquiry and advice. It could even as it stands be made a powerful instrument of publicity and of opinion, but it may also modestly wait until it is asked before expressing a judgment, and in any case it will have the uncomfortable consciousness that its opinion is gratuitous, and carries no weight of effective authority. This will not do. It is understood by everybody who knows anything of the common interest that it must have complete regulative powers: the power to regulate rates, the power to learn and make public everything that should furnish a basis for the public judgment with regard to the soundness, the efficiency, the economy of the business—the power, in brief, to adjust such service at every point and in every respect, whether of equipment or charges or methods of financing or means of service, to the general interest of the communities affected. This can be done, as experience elsewhere has demonstrated, not only without destroying the profits of such business, but also with the effect of putting it upon a more satisfactory footing for those who conduct it no less than for those who make use of it day by day.

Such regulation, based on thorough and authoritative inquiry, will go far towards disclosing and establishing those debatable values upon which so many questions of taxation turn. There is an uneasy feeling throughout the State, in which, I dare say, we all share, that there are glaring inequalities in our system—or, at any rate, in our practice—of taxation. The most general complaint is, that there is great inequality as between individuals and corporations. I do not see how anyone can determine whether there are or not, for we have absolutely no uniform system of assessment. It would seem that in every locality there is some local variety of practice, in the rate, the ratio of assessment value to market value, and that every assessor is a law unto himself. Our whole system of taxation, which is no system at all, needs overhauling from top to bottom. There can be no system, no safety, no regulation in a multitude of boards. An efficient Public Utilities Commission will be a beginning towards a system of taxation as well as towards a system of corporate control. We cannot fairly tax values until we have ascertained and established them.

And the great matter of conservation seems to me like a part of the same subject. The safeguarding of our water supply, the purification of our streams in order to maintain them as sources of life, and their protection against those who would divert them or diminish their volume for private profit, the maintenance of such woodlands as are left us and the reforestation of bare tracts more suited for forest than for field, the sanitation of great urban districts such as cover the northern portions of our State, by thorough systems of drainage and of refuse disposal, the protection of the public health and the facilitation of urban and suburban life—these are all public obligations which fall sooner or later upon you as the lawmakers of the commonwealth, and they are all parts of the one great task of adjustment which has fallen to our generation. Our business is to adjust right to right, interest to interest, and to systematize right and convenience, individual rights and corporate privileges, upon the single basis of the general good, the good of whole communities, the good which no one will look after or suffice to secure if the legislator does not, the common good for whose safeguarding and maintenance government is intended.

This readjustment has not been going on very fast or very favorably in New Jersey. It has been observed that it limped, or was prevented, or neglected, in other States as well. Everywhere there has been confusion of counsel and many a sad miscarriage of plan. There have, consequently, been some very radical criticisms of our methods of political action. There is widespread dissatisfaction with what our legislatures do, and still more serious dissatisfaction with what they do not do. Some persons have said that representative government has proved too indirect and clumsy an instrument, and has broken down as a means of popular control. Others, looking a little deeper, have said that it was not representative government that had broken down, but the effort to get it. They have pointed out that with our present methods of machine nomination and our present methods of elections, which were nothing more than a choice between one set of machine nominees and another, we did not get representative government at all—at least not government representative of the people, but government representative of political managers who served their own interests and the interests of those with whom they found it profitable to establish partnerships.

Obviously this is something that goes to the root of the whole matter. Back of all reform lies the method of getting it. Back of the question what you want lies the question, the fundamental question of all government, how are you going to get it? How are you going to get public servants who will obtain it for you? How are you going to get genuine representatives who will serve your real interests, and not their own or the interests of some special group or body of your fellow-citizens whose power is of the few and not of the many? These are the queries which have drawn the attention of the whole country to the subject of the direct primary, the direct choice of representatives by the people, without the intervention of the nominating machine, the nominating organization.

I earnestly commend to your careful consideration in this connection the laws in recent years adopted in the State of Oregon, whose effect has been to bring government back to the people and to protect it from the control of the representatives of selfish and special interests. They seem to me to point the direction which we must also take before we have completed our regeneration of a government which has suffered so seriously and so long as ours has here in New Jersey from private management and organized selfishness. Our primary laws, extended and perfected, will pave the way. They should be extended to every elective office, and to the selection of every party committee or official as well, in order that the people may once for all take charge of their own affairs, their own political organization and association; and the methods of primary selection should be so perfected that the primaries will be put upon the same free footing that the methods of election themselves are meant to rest upon.

We have here the undoubtedly sound chain and sequency of reforms: an actual direct choice by the people of the men who are to organize alike their parties and their government, and those measures which true representatives of the people will certainly favour and adopt—systematic compensation for injured workingmen; the careful regulation in the common interest of all corporations, both in respect of their organization and of their methods of business, and especially of public service corporations; the equalization of taxes; and the conservation of the natural resources of the State and of the health and safety of its people.

Another matter of the most vital consequence goes with all these: namely, systematic ballot reform and thorough and stringent provisions of law against corrupt practices in connection alike with primaries and with elections. We have lagged behind our sister States in these important matters, and should make haste to avail ourselves of their example and their experience. Here, again, Oregon may be our guide.

This is a big programme, but it is a perfectly consistent programme, and a perfectly feasible programme, and one upon whose details it ought to be possible to agree even within the limits of a single legislative session. You may count upon my coöperation at every step of the work.

I have not spoken of the broad question of economy in the administration of the State government, an economy which can probably be effected only through a thorough reorganization upon business principles, the familiar business principles so thoroughly understood and so intelligently practised by Americans, but so seldom applied to their governments. We make offices for party purposes too often, instead of conducting our public business by the organization best adapted to efficiency and economy. I have not dwelt upon the subject in this address because it is a very complicated one, hardly suited for brief exposition, and because so obvious a requirement of honest government needs hardly more than to be mentioned to be universally endorsed by the public. I shall try to point out to you from time to time the means by which reorganizaion and economy may be secured with benefit to the public service.

But there is a subject which lies a little off the beaten track to which I do wish to turn for a moment before I close. The whole country has remarked the extraordinary rise in the prices of foodstuffs in recent years, and the fact that prices are successfully maintained at an intolerably high level at all seasons, whether they be the seasons of plenty or of scarcity. We have a partial remedy at our own hand—a remedy which was proposed to the Legislature last year by Mr. James, of Hudson county, but which is said to have been defeated in some questionable fashion in the last hours of the session. It is estimated that most of the food supply of the people of northern New Jersey, and half the food supply for New York City, is kept in cold-storage warehouses in Hudson county, awaiting the desired state of the market. There is abundant reason to believe that it is the practice of dealers to seclude immense quantities of beef and other meats, poultry, eggs, fish, etc., in cold-storage in times of abundance in order that the price of these indispensable foods may be kept high and the foods dealt out only when the market is satisfactory for that purpose, even if the meats and eggs have to be kept for years together before being sold. Figures, said to be actually of record, foot up almost incredible totals of the amounts thus held in waiting, running into millions of heads of cattle, of sheep and lambs, of hogs, millions of pounds of poultry, and hundreds of millions of eggs.

The result is not only to control prices but also to endanger health, because of the effect of too long storage upon the foodstuffs themselves, and because of the deleterious effects of taking them out of cold-storage and exposing them to thaw in the markets. The least effect is loss of nutritious quality; the worst, the generation of actual poisons by decay and even putrefaction.

No limit at all is put upon this abuse by law, and strong

influences are brought to bear by interested parties to prevent the enactment of remedial legislation. Indictments were brought in Hudson county, but there was no sufficient law to sustain them. A bill was introduced, as I have said, at the last session of the Legislature, but was, I am told, after lingering a very long time in the Assembly committee, mysteriously lost when called up for passage in the Senate during the last hours of the session. I earnestly urge that the Legislature take up this important matter at the earliest possible time, and push some effective law of inspection and limitation to enactment. It would give me great pleasure to sign a bill that would really accomplish the purpose.

We are servants of the people, of the whole people. Their interest should be our constant study. We should pursue it without fear or favour. Our reward will be greater than that to be obtained in any other service: the satisfaction of furthering large ends, large purposes, of being an intimate part of that slow but constant and ever hopeful force of liberty and of enlightenment that is lifting mankind from age to age to new levels of progress and achievement, and of having been something greater than successful men. For we shall have been instruments of humanity, men whose thought was not for themselves, but for the true and lasting comfort and happiness of men everywhere. It is not the foolish ardour of too sanguine or too radical reform that I urge upon you, but merely the tasks that are evident and pressing, the things we have knowledge and guidance enough to do; and to do with confidence and energy. I merely point out the present business of progressive and serviceable government, the next stage on the journey of duty. The path is as inviting as it is plain. Shall we hesitate to tread it? I look forward with genuine pleasure to the prospect of being your comrade upon it.

DOCUMENT 32

"Like a Servant Who Has Kept Faith . . ."

Wilson's feeling of exultation over his triumph with the New Jersey legislature, as well as his larger ambitions for the future, were revealed in a letter to an old family friend.

The Legislature adjourned yesterday morning at three o'clock, with its work done. I got absolutely everything I strove for, — and more besides: all four of the great acts that I had set my heart on (the primaries and election law, the corrupt practices act, as stringent as the English, the workingmen's compensation act, and the act giving a public commission control over the railways, the trolley lines, the water companies, and the gas and electric light and power companies), and besides them I got certain fundamental school reforms and an act enabling any city in the State to adopt the commission form of government, which simplifies the electoral process and concentrates responsibility. Everyone, the papers included, are saying that none of it could have been done, if it had not been for my influence and tact and hold upon the people. Be that as it may, the thing was done, and the result was as complete a victory as has ever been won, I venture to say, in the history of the country. I wrote the platform, I had the measures formulated to my mind, I kept the pressure of opinion constantly on the legislature, and the programme was carried out to its last detail. This with the senatorial business seems, in the minds of the people looking on little less than a miracle, in the light of what has been the history of reform hitherto in this State. As a matter of fact, it is just a bit of

Letter to Mrs. Mary A. Hulbert, April 23, 1911, in Baker, *Wilson, Life and Letters*, III, 169–172.

natural history. I came to the office in the fulness of time, when opinion was ripe on all these matters, when both parties were committed to these reforms, and by merely standing fast, and by never losing sight of the business for an hour, but keeping up all sorts of (legitimate) pressure *all the time*, kept the mighty forces from being diverted or blocked at any point. The strain has been immense, but the reward is great. I feel a great reaction to-day, for I am, of course, exceedingly tired, but I am quietly and deeply happy that I should have been of just the kind of service I wished to be to those who elected and trusted me. I can look them in the face, like a servant who has kept faith and done all that was in him, given every power he possessed, to them and their affairs. There could be no deeper source of satisfaction and contentment! I have no doubt that a good deal of the result was due to the personal relations I established with the men in the Senate, the Republican Senate which, it was feared at the outset, might be the stumbling block. You remember the dinner in New York and the supper at the Trenton country club which I described to you. Those evenings undoubtedly played their part in the outcome. They brought us all close together on terms not unlike friendly intimacy; made them realize just what sort of *person* I was. Since then Republicans have resorted to my office for counsel and advice almost as freely as Democrats (an almost unprecedented circumstance at Trenton) and with several of them I have established relations almost of affection. Otherwise I do not believe that the extraordinary thing that happened could possibly have come about: for all four of the great "administration" measures passed the Senate *without a dissenting voice!* The newspaper men seemed dazed. They do not understand how such things *could* happen. They were impressed, too, with the orderly and dignified way in which the session ended, despite the long strain of the closing night, when the houses sat from eight until three. Generally there is wild horseplay, like that on the stock exchange, but this time everything was done decently and with an air of self-respect. I took several naps in my office during the long hours of the session, coming out into the outer office in the intervals to talk and swap stories with the men who were sitting there, my secretary, the reporters who were coming and going, and interested friends who had come down to see how things ended. Then a committee from each House called on me to ask if there was anything more I had to lay before them before adjournment,—and the session was over. Most of the members dropped in to say good bye, and by four o'clock your tired and happy friend was in bed in the noisy little Hotel Sterling, with the strong odours of late suppers in his nostrils, floating in at the open window. It's a great game, thoroughly worth playing!

I literally have not had five minutes time to drop in and see the Roeblings. I have thought of them almost every day, and have wanted to go very sincerely. I think Mrs. R. charming. But I have not felt that I could relax my attention for a moment while the session lasted,—and it had already begun when I was inaugurated, you know, and plunged into the first fight, the fight for the senatorship. Winning that, by the way, made all the rest easier; but it also made the session some two weeks longer than usual. What a vigil it has been! I am certainly in training for almost anything that may come to me by way of public tasks. There are serious times ahead. It daunts me to think of the possibility of my playing an influential part in them. There is no telling what deep waters may be ahead of me. The forces of greed and the forces of justice and humanity are about to grapple for a bout in which men will spend all the life that is in them. God grant I may have strength enough to count, to tip the balance in the unequal and tremendous struggle! This week I turn to speech-making again (much the easier task of the two) and to preparation for my western trip. All through everything, as the days come and go with their tale of tasks, runs a constant thought of you, a constant solicitude for you, and an abiding consciousness of being (and of being blessed by being),

Your devoted friend, . . .

DOCUMENT 33

A National Reform Program

Following the adoption of his legislative program in New Jersey, Wilson embarked on a national speaking-tour designed to win support for his bid for the Democratic Presidential nomination in 1912. At a rally of Democratic clubs at Harrisburg, Pennsylvania, on June 15, 1911, he outlined a broad program of national reform.

We are met here to renew our allegiance to the great party which we serve and to take counsel with regard to its welfare. A great work waits to be done for the country — a great work of counsel and of action. It calls its challenge to every man who desires to serve and has no fear. Are we wise and strong and sober and united enough to do it? Have we the knowledge, the self-possession, the poise, the courage? Are we the men? The country shall decide, but it is within our choice to deserve its confidence and concert a course of patriotic action which should commend us to all just and purposeful men.

Public Papers, II, 303–309.

There has, first and last, been a great deal of idle talk about divisions in the Democratic party, and men here and there have spoken as if it were possible for this individual or that to disrupt it and to break the splendid continuity of its history. Men who speak such empty predictions are forgetful of the history of the party. It is the one party in the United States which has continued unbroken from the beginning of our national history until now. Other parties have risen and fallen, have come into existence and passed utterly away, but the Democratic party has renewed itself from generation to generation with an indomitable youth. It is never the party of the past, but always the party of the present and the future, always taking new life with the changing circumstances of the nation.

Whenever things are to be done in a new way, in response to a new popular impulse, in obedience to the great democratic traditions of the nation itself, it is to the Democratic party that the country naturally turns. It has been spoken of as the party of opposition, the party of protest, and its long, unbroken party history has been attributed to the fact that it did not attempt a constructive programme, but was always critical and on the defensive, always harking back to ideals set up at the foundation of the government, to which it was never wholly possible for it to adjust its own actual policies. But, although there have been times when this characterization of it would seem to have been justified by the fact, the history of the country abounds in instances when our great party showed itself constructive and aggressive, not protesting, but performing, not criticising, but projecting great reforms. Other parties have tied themselves up to particular lines of action to which they presently became wholly subject, upon which they at length became dependent, but the Democratic party has remained free to act, free to take on the new elements of popular impulse, free to read new times in new terms.

Its freedom is now about to serve it in an extraordinary degree. Those who look about them see parties apparently breaking up; but if they will look closer what they will see is simply this, that men are turning away by the thousands from those courses of policy and of action to which the alliances and practices of the Republican party have at last bound the country as if with a grip of iron. The free elements of thought in the country are asserting themselves with an extraordinary energy and majesty that must presently work profound changes and mark this as one of the most noteworthy eras of our politics. But they are not exerting themselves to destroy, they are exerting themselves, rather, to find means of coöperation and action. Some men among the Republican leaders see what it is necessary to do, but they are not numerous enough to dominate their party counsels; they cannot turn or guide the great organization of their party in the direction of the desired reforms. The great mass of voters in the country perceive this. They are looking, therefore, with great expectation toward the Democratic party to see if it will now, at this critical juncture, prove true to its traditions and supply them with men and measures.

The Democratic party has always had the impulse of reform because it has always been based upon deep and fundamental sympathy with the interests of the people at large. It has now only to prove that its impulse can find expression in a wise and feasible programme in order to capture both the imagination and the allegiance of the country. It is this power of self-removal, this power of looking forward, this power of realizing the present and projecting itself into the future that has kept it young and which must now make it the party of young men, the party to which those must resort who are coming for the first time into the activities of politics; with which those must ally themselves whose hopes are forming into purposes, whose impulses are framing themselves by sober thought into concrete judgments, who know what they want and are fast finding out by what means they can get what they want.

If we recount the items of the liberal programme to which the country is now looking forward, it will be easy to see that it is already the programme of the Democratic party. The first item of that programme is that the *machinery of political control must be put in the hands of the people.* That means, translated into concrete terms, direct primaries, a short ballot, and, wherever necessary, the initiative, the referendum, and the recall. These things are being desired and obtained, not by way of revolution, not even with a desire to effect any fundamental change in our governmental system, but for the purpose of recovering what seems to have been lost—the people's control of their own instruments, their right to exercise a free and constant choice in the management of their own affairs.

Another great item of the programme is that the service rendered the people by the *national government must be of a more extended sort and of a kind* not only to protect it against monopoly, but also to facilitate its life. We are, therefore, in favour of postal savings banks and of a parcel post, and feel with some chagrin that we have lagged behind the other free nations of the world in establishing those manifestly useful and necessary instruments of our common life.

The revision of the tariff, of course, looms big and central in the programme, *because it is in the tariff schedules that half the monopolies* of the country have found covert and protection and opportunity. We *do not mean to strike at any essential economic arrangement,* but we do mean to drive all beneficiaries of governmental policy into the open and demand of them by what principle of national advantage, as contrasted with selfish privilege, they enjoy the extraordinary assistance extended to them.

The *regulation of corporations* is hardly less significant

and central. We have made many experiments in this difficult matter, and some of them have been crude and hurtful, but our thought is slowly clearing. We are beginning to see, for one thing, how public service corporations, at any rate, can be governed with great advantage to the public and without serious detriment to themselves, as undertakings of private capital. Experience is removing both prejudice and fear in this field, and it is likely that within the very near future we shall have settled down to some common, rational and effective policy. The regulation of corporations of other sorts lies intimately connected with the general question of monopoly, a question which ramifies in a thousand directions, but the intricate threads of which, we are slowly beginning to perceive, constitute a decipherable pattern. Measures will here also frame themselves soberly enough as we think our way forward.

Again there is the great question of *conservation.* We are not yet clear as to all the methods, but we are absolutely clear as to the principle and the intention and shall not be satisfied until we have found the way, not only to preserve our great national resources, but also to conserve the strength and health and energy of our people themselves by protection against wrongful forms of labour and by securing them against the myriad forms of harm which have come from the selfish uses of economic power.

Beyond all these, waiting to be solved, lying as yet in the hinterland of party policy, *lurks the great question of banking reform.* The plain fact is that control of credit—at any rate of credit upon any large scale—is dangerously concentrated in this country. The large money resources of the country are not at the command of those who do not submit to the direction and domination of small groups of capitalists, who wish to keep the economic development of the country under their own eye and guidance. The great monopoly in this country *is the money monopoly.* So long as that exists our old variety and freedom and individual energy of development are out of the question. A great industrial nation is controlled by its system of credit. Our system of credit is concentrated. The growth of the nation, therefore, and all our activities are in the hands of a few men who, even if their action be honest and intended for the public interest, are necessarily concentrated upon the great undertakings in which their own money is involved and who necessarily, by very reason of their own limitations, chill and check and destroy genuine economic freedom. This is the greatest question of all, and to this statesmen must address themselves with an earnest determination to serve the long future and the true liberties of men.

I have said that the Democratic party is now to attempt constructive statesmanship. There are well-known conditions which surround so great a task. In the first place it cannot be executed if attempted with inconsiderate haste. That is not constructive which is loosely or hastily put together. Its parts must be sound, and their combination must be true and vital. No man can in a moment put great policies together and reconstruct a whole order of life.

We must remember that the abuses we seek to remedy have come into existence as incidents of the great structure of industry we have built up. This structure is the work of our own hands; our own lives are involved in it. Reckless attacks upon it, destructive assaults against it would jeopardize our own lives and disturb, it might be fatally, the very progress we seek to attain. It would be particularly fatal to any successful programme to admit into our minds, as we pursue it, any spirit of revenge, any purpose to wreak our displeasure upon the persons and the institutions who now represent the abuses we deprecate and seek to destroy. I do not say these things because I feel that there is danger of vengeful action or of revolutionary haste, but merely because we ought always to recognize that it is of the very essence of constructive statesmanship that we should think and act temperately, wisely, justly, in

the spirit of those who reconstruct and amend, not in the
spirit of those who destroy and seek to build from the
foundations again.

The American people are an eminently just and an in
tensely practical people. They do not wish to lay violen
hands upon their own affairs, but they do claim the right to
look them over with close and frank and fearless scrutiny
from top to bottom; to look at them from within as well as
from without, in their most intimate and private details, as
well as in their obvious exterior proportions; and they do
hold themselves at liberty, attacking one point at a time, to
readjust, correct, purify, rearrange; not destroying or even
injuring the elements, but filling their altered combination
with a new spirit. This is the task of the Democratic party
It is the task of all statesmanship. It is a task which just a
this particular juncture in our affairs looms particularly big
It is not ominous, but inviting; not alarming, but inspirit
ing. We should congratulate ourselves that we have an
opportunity to take part in the true spirit of those who
would serve a great country, in a task which may recover
for America her old happiness and confidence, her old
spirit of triumphant democracy.

DOCUMENT 34

A Revised View of Bryan

As Wilson became more outspokenly progressive, he began
to revise his views of William Jennings Bryan and other
reform Democrats whom he had once considered danger-

Excerpt from address at Jackson Day dinner, Washington, D. C., January
8, 1912. *Public Papers*, II, 344–345.

ously radical. His original conservative supporters, led by Colonel Harvey, began to lose interest in his candidacy. On January 7, 1912, the conservative New York *Sun* created consternation among Democrats by publishing a five-year-old letter in which Wilson had denounced Bryan (See Document 29). The move was cleverly timed to do maximum damage to Wilson's political hopes, because he was scheduled to address a Jackson Day dinner in Washington the next day—a dinner at which the Commoner would also be present. But Wilson met the challenge head-on. He began his address with an eloquent tribute that greatly moved Bryan and effectively disarmed the trap Wilson's enemies had set for him.

Mr. Toastmaster and fellow Democrats, we are met to celebrate an achievement. It is an interesting circumstance that principles have no anniversaries. Only the men who embody principles are celebrated upon occasions like this and only the events to which their concerted action gave rise excite our enthusiasm. You know that the principles of the Democratic party are professed by practically the whole population of the United States. The test of a Democrat is whether he lives up to those principles or not. I have no doubt there are some people in the United States who covertly question the doctrines of Democracy, but nobody challenges them openly. It goes without saying, therefore, that we have not come together merely to state the abstract principles of our party. We have come together to take counsel as to how it is possible, by courageous and concerted action, to translate them into policy and law. The Democratic party has had a long period of disappointment and defeat and I think that we can point out the reason. We do not live in simple times. We live in very conflicting times indeed. No man can be certain that he can say how to weave the threads of Democratic principle throughout all the complicated garment of our civilization, and the reason that the Democratic party has had this period of successive disturbance is that it has been divided into groups just as it was as to the method of fulfilling the principles.

We have differed as to measures; it has taken us sixteen years and more to come to any comprehension of our community of thought in regard to what we ought to do. What I want to say is that one of the most striking things in recent years is that with all the rise and fall of particular ideas, with all the ebb and flow of particular proposals, there has been one interesting fixed point in the history of the Democratic party, and that fixed point has been the character and the devotion and the preachings of William Jennings Bryan.

I, for my part, never want to forget this: That while we have differed with Mr. Bryan upon this occasion and upon that in regard to the specific things to be done, he has gone serenely on pointing out to a more and more convinced people what it was that was the matter. He has had the steadfast vision all along of what it was that was the matter and he has, not any more than Andrew Jackson did, not based his career upon calculation, but has based it upon principle.

Now, what has been the matter? The matter has been that the Government of this country was privately controlled and that the business of this country was privately controlled; that we did not have genuine representative government and that the people of this country did not have the control of their own affairs.

What do we stand for here to-night and what shall we stand for as long as we live? We stand for setting the Government of this country free and the business of this country free. The facts have been disputed by a good many sections of the Democratic party for the last half generation, but they were not clearly recognized. . . .

PART IV

The New Freedom Enunciated

THE CAMPAIGN OF 1912

Although Wilson received the Democratic nomination for President in 1912 only after a lengthy and spirited contest, the battle for the nomination did not rupture the party. This was not the case with the Republicans, who were badly split between the Old Guard wing headed by President William Howard Taft and an insurgent faction led by former President Theodore Roosevelt. Taft took little part in the ensuing campaign, content that his candidacy should frustrate the ambitions of his former friend and patron, Roosevelt. Wilson and Roosevelt, on the other hand, engaged in a hard-hitting debate over the nature and future course of the progressive movement. Wilson stressed the need to free the individual from monopolistic power. He called his program the New Freedom — in contrast to Roosevelt's New Nationalism, which proposed a great extension of governmental regulation to curb the trusts and cure various social ills.

DOCUMENT 35

Restoration of Competition,
Not Regulation of Monopolies

In a Labor Day campaign speech Wilson stressed the differences between Roosevelt and himself on the question of controlling the trusts, a major campaign issue.

. . . We are not afraid of those who pursue legitimate pursuits provided they link those pursuits in at every turn with the interest of the community as a whole; and no man can conduct a legitimate business, if he conducts it in the interest of a single class. I want, therefore, to look at the nation as a whole today. I would like always to look at it as a whole, not divide it up into sections and classes, but I want particularly to discuss with you today the things which interest the wage earner. That is merely looking at the country as a whole from one angle, from one point of view, to which for the time being we will confine ourselves.

I want as a means of illustration, not as a means of contest, to use the platform of the third party as the means of expounding what I have to say today. I want you to read that platform very carefully, and I want to call your attention to the fact that it really consists of two parts. In one part of it, it declares the sympathy of the party with a certain great program of social reform, and promises that all the influence of that party, of the members of that party,

Excerpt from address at Buffalo, N. Y., September 2, 1912, *A Crossroads of Freedom: The 1912 Campaign Speeches of Woodrow Wilson*, ed. John Wells Davidson (New Haven, Conn.: Yale University Press, 1956), pp. 74–80. Reprinted with the permission of John Wells Davidson.

will be used for the promotion of that program of social reform. In the other part, it itself lays down a method of procedure, and what I want you to soberly consider is whether the method of procedure is a suitable way of laying the foundations for the realization of that social program — with regard to the social program, the betterment of the condition of men in this occupation and the other, the protection of women, the shielding of children, the bringing about of social justice here, there, and elsewhere. With that program who can differ in his heart, who can divorce himself in sympathy from the great project of advancing the interests of human beings, wherever it is possible to advance them?

But there is a central method, a central purpose, in that platform from which I very seriously dissent. I am a Democrat as distinguished from a Republican because I believe (and I think that it is generally believed) that the leaders of the Republican party — for I always distinguish them from the great body of the Republican voters who have been misled by them — I say not the Republican party, but the leaders of the Republican party have allowed themselves to become so tied up in alliances with special interests that they are not free to serve us all. And that the immediate business, if you are to have any kind of reform at all, is to set your government free, is to break it away from the partnerships and alliances and understandings and [purchases] which have made it impossible for it to look at the country as a whole and made it necessary to serve special interests one at a time. Until that has been done, no program of social reform is possible because a program of social reform depends upon universal sympathy, universal justice, universal cooperation. It depends upon our understanding one another and serving one another.

What is this program? What is the program of the third party with regard to the disentanglement of the government? Mr. Roosevelt has said, and up to a certain point I sympathize with him, that he does not object, for example, to the system of protection except in this circumstance — that it has [not] inured to the benefit of the workingman of this country. It is very interesting to have him admit that because the leaders of the Republican party have been time out of mind putting this bluff up on you men that the protective policy was for your sake, and I would like to know what you ever got out of it that you didn't get out of the better effort of organized labor. I have yet to learn of any instance where you got anything without going and taking it. And the process of our society instead of being a process of peace has sometimes too much resembled a process of war because men felt obliged to go and insist in organized masses upon getting the justice which they couldn't get any other way.

It is interesting, therefore, to have Mr. Roosevelt admit that not enough of the "prize money," as he frankly calls it, has gone into the pay envelope. He admits that not enough of the money has gone into the envelope. I wish it were not prize money, because dividing up prize money and dividing up earnings are two very different things. And it is very much simpler to divide up earnings than to divide up prize money, because the money is prize money for the [reason] that a limited number of men banded themselves together and got it from the Ways and Means Committee of the House and the Finance Committee of the Senate, and we paid the bills.

But Mr. Roosevelt says that his [object] will be to see that a larger proportion gets into the pay envelope. And how does he propose to do it? (For I am here not to make a speech; I am here to argue this thing with you gentlemen.) How does he propose to do it? I don't find any suggestion anywhere in that platform of the way in which he is going to do it, except in one plank. One plank says that the party will favor a minimum wage for women; and then it goes on to say by a minimum wage it means a living wage, enough to live on.

I am going to assume, for the sake of argument, that it proposed more than that, that it proposed to get a minimum wage for everybody, men as well as women; and I want to call your attention to the fact that just as soon as a minimum wage is established by law, the temptation of every employer in the United States will be to bring his wages down as close to that minimum as he dares, because you can't strike against the government of the United States. You can't strike against what is in the law. You can strike against what is in your agreement with your employer, but if underneath that agreement there is the steel and the adamant of federal law, you can't tamper with that foundation. And who is going to pay these wages? You know that the great difficulty about wages, one of the great difficulties about wages now, is that the control of industry is getting into fewer and fewer hands. And that, therefore, a smaller and smaller number of men are able to determine what wages shall be. In other words, one of the entanglements of our government is that we are dealing not with a community in which men may take their own choice of what they shall do, but in a community whose industry is very largely governed by great combinations of capital in the hands of a comparatively small number of men; that, in other words, we are in the hands, in many industries, of monopoly itself. And the only way in which the working-man can gain more wages is by getting them from the monopoly.

Very well then, what does this platform propose to do? Break up the monopolies? Not at all. It proposes to legal-ize them. It says in effect: You can't break them up, the only thing you can do is to put them in charge of the fed-eral government. It proposes that they shall be adopted and regulated. And that looks to me like a consummation of the partnership between monopoly and government. Because, when once the government regulates monopoly, then monopoly will have to see to it that it regulates the government. This is a [beautiful] circle of change.

We now complain that the men who control these monopolies control the government, and it is in turn proposed that the government should control them. I am perfectly willing to be controlled if it is I, myself, who control me. If this partnership can be continued, then this control can be manipulated and adjusted to its own pleasure. Therefore, I want to call your attention to this fact that these great combined industries have been more inimical to organized labor than any other class of employers in the United States. Is not that so?

These monopolies that the government, it is proposed, should adopt are the men who have made your independent action most difficult. They have made it most difficult that you should take care of yourselves; and let me tell you that the old adage that God takes care of those who take care of themselves is not gone out of date. No federal legislation can change that thing. The minute you are taken care of by the government you are wards, not independent men. And the minute they are legalized by the government, they are protégés and not monopolies. They are the guardians and you are the wards. Do you want to be taken care of by a combination of the government and the monopolies? [*A voice from the audience: "No."*] Because the workingmen of this country are perfectly aware that they sell their commodity, that is to say labor, in a perfectly open market. There is free trade in labor in the United States. The laboring men of all the world are free to come and offer their labor here and you are similarly free to go and offer your labor in most parts of the world. And the world demand is what establishes for the most part the rate of wages, at the same time that these gentlemen who are paying the wages in a free-trade market are protected by an unfree market against the competition that would make them [bid] higher because [bid] in competition and not [bid] under protection. If I am obliged to refrain from going into a particular industry by reason of the combination that already exists in it, I can't become an employer of labor, and I can't compete with these gentlemen for the employment of labor. And the whole business of the level of wages is artificially and arbitrarily determined.

Now, I say, gentlemen, that a party that proposes that program cannot, if it carries out that program, be forwarding these other industrial purposes of social regeneration, because they have crystallized, they have hardened, they have narrowed the government which is to be the source of this thing. After all this is done, who is to guarantee to us that the government is to be pitiful, that the government is to be righteous, that the government is to be just? Nothing will then control the power of the government except open revolt, and God forbid that we should bring about a state of politics in which open revolt should be substituted for the ballot box.

I believe that the greatest force for peace, the greatest force for righteousness, the greatest force for the elevation of mankind, is organized opinion, is the thinking of men, is the great force which is in the soul of men, and I want men to breathe a free and pure air. And I know that these monopolies are so many cars of juggernaut which are in our very sight being driven over men in such ways as to crush their life out of them. And I don't look forward with pleasure to the time when the juggernauts are licensed. I don't look forward with pleasure to the time when the juggernauts are driven by commissioners of the United States. I am willing to license automobiles, but not juggernauts, because if any man ever dares take a joy ride in one of them, I would like to know what is to become of the rest of us; because the road isn't wide enough for us to get out of the way. We would have to take to the woods and then set the woods afire. I am speaking partly in pleasantry but underneath, gentlemen, there is a very solemn sense in my mind that we are standing at a critical turning point in our [choice].

Now you say on the other hand, what do the Democrats propose to do? I want to call your attention to the fact that those who wish to support these monopolies by adopting them under the regulation of the government of the United States are the very men who cry out that competition is destructive. They ought to know because it is competition as they conducted it that destroyed our economic freedom. They are certainly experts in destructive competition. And the purpose of the Democratic leaders is this: not to legislate competition into existence again—because statutes can't make men do things—but to regulate competition.

What has created these monopolies? Unregulated competition. It has permitted these men to do anything that they chose to do to squeeze their rivals out and to crush their rivals to the earth. We know the processes by which they have done these things. We can prevent those processes by remedial legislation, and that remedial legislation will so restrict the wrong use of competition that the right use of competition will destroy monopoly. In other words, ours is a program of liberty and theirs is a program of regulation. Ours is a program by which we find we know the wrongs that have been committed and we can stop those wrongs. And we are not going to adopt into the governmental family the men who forward the wrongs and license them to do the whole business of the country.

I want you men to grasp the point because I want to say to you right now the program that I propose doesn't look quite as much like acting as a Providence for you as the other program looks. But I want to frankly say to you that I am not big enough to play Providence, and my objection to the other program is that I don't believe that there is any other man that is big enough to play Providence. I have never known any body of men, any small body of men, that understood the United States. And the only way the United States is ever going to be taken care of is by having the voice of all the men in it constantly clamorous for the recognition of what is justice as they see life. . . .

DOCUMENT 36

An Analysis of the Republican
and Progressive Parties

Wilson argued that of the three major parties only the Democrats could be counted on to restore freedom of opportunity and preserve the rights of the individual. Roosevelt made much of Wilson's statement—near the end of this excerpt—that "the history of liberty is a history of the limitation of governmental power, not the increase of it." While Wilson was stressing the need to end government favoritism to one class, business, his "history of liberty" comment suggested that he still had serious reservations about a substantial increase of federal authority.

. . . When we set up this government, we deliberately set ourselves at the front of the enterprises of civilization and of humanity. We said: "Governments hitherto have not been suited to the general interest. We are going to set

Excerpt from address to the New York Press Club, September 9, 1912. *Crossroads*, ed. Davidson, pp. 125–130.

up a government that is. Governments hitherto have not been interested in the general advancement of the welfare of men of all classes and conditions. This government shall be." We are not at liberty as Americans, if we maintain the standards which we professed at the outset, to treat our government as if it were merely the instrument for party control, and as if parties were merely the instruments for putting first the interests of this class and then the interests of the other at the front.

Now, if we are to free our government to serve civilization and humanity, what are we going to do in the present campaign? I am not going to pretend that we shall find a perfect means of doing either of these things. I simply want to put before us a comparative study of the means that are at our disposal to accomplish this thing. I am going to discuss the claims of three parties as the condition to undertake this task. I am leaving out the other parties, of which there are a number, not out of any disrespect to them, for some of them profess very noble purposes, but merely because of the more than likelihood, the certainty, that they will not be able to get control of the government of the country. Let's confine ourselves then to three parties.

If you want to set the government free, can you employ the party that entangled it? Can you employ the regular Republican party? My implication in asking that question is not that any set of our public men deliberately made partnerships which rendered it impossible for them to serve the people. Moreover, I want in every such discussion to discriminate between that great part of my fellow citizens who have usually voted the Republican ticket and that small body of my fellow citizens who have usually misled them into voting it. For the leaders of the Republican party are one thing; and the Republican party's rank and file is a very different thing, constituting some half of

the American nation. And I am quite ready to admit that
the leaders who have led these voters to do things which
would not inure to the interests of the country would not
intend to pursue any impolitic or deleterious course. I am
not uttering an indictment. I am simply pointing out what
I believe most of you will admit to be the facts.

The Republican party by reason of the tariff policy in
particular has tied the administration of this government
up to certain great interests, chiefly by the means of campaign contributions, so thoroughly and in such a complicated fashion that it is unreasonable to suppose that the
very next administration should seek to do what this administration has not even attempted to do. If there were
symptoms that the present administration had attempted to
do this, if there were symptoms that the present administration had pursued any consistent course whatever by
which we would be able to calculate the orbit of another
administration of the same sort, then perhaps the case
would need argument. But it does not seem to me to need
argument. It speaks for itself.

I am not going to detain you to analyze further the answer to the question, "Can we set the government free and
save civilization and humanity through the Republican
party?"

I am . . . one of those who entertain a very great respect for the history of the Republican party. I do not see
how any man though like myself bred a Democrat from the
beginning, can fail to realize with how great a purpose it
came into existence and how high a destiny for the time it
pursued. The entanglements of modern economic development set a very different scene for the Republican party
from that which was set forth when it came upon the field
of action. I am discussing only the year 1912 and trying to
forecast the years which will follow the year 1912.

Well, if not the regular Republican party, to whom shall

we turn? There is a new party which it is difficult to characterize because it is made up of several elements. As I see it, it is made up of three elements in particular. The first consists of those Republicans whose consciences and whose stomachs couldn't stand what the regular Republicans were doing. They were called at first in New Jersey "New Idea" Republicans, when it was a new idea that a Republican could do wrong. Later in other states they came to be called "insurgent Republicans" — Republicans, that is to say, [who] were setting up an insurrection against the control of their own party. And now the insurrectos are outside and have set up for themselves and constitute a very important element, perhaps the largest element in the new party.

But added to this element is one that interests me very deeply. A great many men and women of noble character, of the most elevated purpose, have joined themselves to that party because in the platform adopted by that party most of the reforms (which ought a long time ago to have been undertaken but most of which have been absolutely ignored by political parties) have been embodied. Irrespective of the present, I venture to conjecture, these high-spirited men and women believe that this combination of forces may in the future bring them out upon a plane [where] they can accomplish these things which their hearts have so long desired. I take off my hat to those people. I sympathize with their impulses. I have not a word of criticism of them for allying themselves with any force, any honorable force, which they think can accomplish these things.

Then there is a third element in the new party of which the less said the better. To discuss it would be interesting only if I could mention names and I have forbidden myself that indulgence.

It is not a homogeneous party, therefore. You see it is made up of elements old and new, made up of some elements that are only absolutely new in politics, because they have never before distinctly aligned themselves with a political party.

And the question that arises when we ask ourselves, "Shall we put the government in the hands of that party?" is this: Can it carry out this program of social betterment and reform? I don't know how to test that matter out, to answer that question, except by examining the portion of the program which seems to be distinctly political rather than social. Because let me remind you that the problem we start out with is: We want a free political instrument by which to do these things. If we can't get it, that can't be the party instrument.

You have in this new party two things: a political party and a body of social reformers. Will the political party contained in it be serviceable to the social reformers? I do not think that I am mistaken in picking out as the political part of that platform the part which determines how the government is going to stand related to the central problems upon which its freedom depends. The freedom of the government of the United States depends upon getting separated from, disentangled from, those interests which have enjoyed, chiefly enjoyed, the patronage of that government. Because the trouble with the tariff is not that it has been protective, for in recent years it has been much more than protective. It has been one of the most colossal systems of deliberate patronage that has ever been conceived. And the main trouble with it is that the protection stops where the patronage begins; and that if you could lop off the patronage, you would have taken away most of the objectionable features of the so-called protection.

This patronage, this special privilege, these favors doled

out to some persons and not to all, have been the basis of
the control which has been set up over the industries and
enterprises of this country by great combinations; because
we forgot, in permitting a regime of free competition to
last so long, that the competitors had ceased to be individuals or small groups of individuals, and it had come to be a
competition between individuals or small groups on the
one hand and enormous aggregations of individuals and
capital on the other; and that, after that contrast in strength
had been created in fact, competition, free competition,
was out of the question — that it was then possible for the
powerful to crush the weak.

That isn't competition; that is warfare. And because we
did not check the free competition soon enough, because
we did not check it at the point where pigmies entered the
field against giants, we have created a condition of affairs
in which the control of industry, and to a large extent the
control of credit in this country upon which industry feeds
and in which all new enterprises must be rooted, is in the
hands of a comparatively small and very compact body of
men. These are the gentlemen who have in some instances, perhaps in more than has been exhibited by legal
proof, engaged in what we are now expected to call
"unreasonable combinations in restraint of trade." They
have indulged themselves beyond reason in the exercise
of that power which makes competition practically
impossible.

Very well then, the test of our freedom for the next generation lies here. Are we going to take that power away
from them or are we going to leave it with them? You can
take it away from them if you regulate competition and
make it impossible for them to do some of the things
which they have been doing. You leave it with them if you
legitimatize and regulate monopoly. And what the plat-

form of the new party proposes to do is exactly that.

It proposes to start where we are, and without altering the established conditions of competition which are conditions which affect it. We shall say what these giants shall do and to what the pigmies shall submit. We shall do that not by law, for if you will read the plank in its candid statement (for it is perfectly candid) you will find that it rejects regulation by law and proposes a commission which shall have the discretion itself to undertake what the plank calls "constructive regulation." It shall make its rules as it goes along. As it handles these giants so shall it shape its course. That, gentlemen, is nothing more than a legitimated continuation of the present order of things, with the alliance between the great interests and the government open instead of covered.

There will then be nothing wrong in the alliance. The alliance will be accepted into the policy of the nation, and we shall simply say to one another, "Big as these men are, the federal government is bigger than they are; and we will depend upon the federal government to take care of them." But, gentlemen, that depends upon who takes care of the federal government. If you make it necessary, in order that they may have a comparatively free hand in the conduct of their colossal business, that they control the government, what is to prevent their controlling a government which for a generation they have already controlled? In other words, instead of setting your government free you have consented to a continuation and perpetuation of the existing alliance between the government and big business.

This alliance may be perfectly unimpeachable on the ground of honesty, and I am not intimating that there will be colossal corruption. I am merely pointing out that there will be a union of power between them, an inevitable union of power. And I say to these noble men and women who have allied themselves with that party because of the social program: Who will guarantee to us that this machine will be just and pitiful? Do we conceive social betterment to lie in the pitiful use of irresistible power? Or do we conceive it to arise out of the irresistible might of a body of free men? Has justice ever grown in the soil of absolute power? Has not justice always come from the press of the heart and spirit of men who resist power?

Liberty has never come from the government. Liberty has always come from the subjects of the government. The history of liberty is a history of resistance. The history of liberty is a history of the limitation of governmental power, not the increase of it. Do these gentlemen dream that in the year 1912 we have discovered a unique exception to the movement of human history? Do they dream that the whole character of those who exercise power has changed, that it is no longer a temptation? Above all things else, do they dream that men are bred great enough now to be a Providence to the people over whom they preside?

Great kings have been born into the world, gentlemen, men with big enough hearts to include their kingdoms, men with big enough brains to comprehend anything that can come within the scope of their understanding. But there are only twenty-four hours in the day of a king, as there are only twenty-four hours in the day of the humblest workman. And no brain in its twenty-four-hour day can comprehend the complex business of a nation.

Representative government, representative assemblies are necessary; not because their individual units are wise, but because their individual units are various; because, picked out of every class and condition, they speak what no ordinary man can speak—the voice of all classes and conditions. . . .

DOCUMENT 37

The Trustee Theory of the Republican Party

The Democrats, Wilson told the voters in 1912, were the
party of the people, whereas the Republicans were the
trustees of the great propertied interests of the country.
What was needed was a return to genuine representative
government, government that would represent people and
not merely property.

. . . I am not one of those who can draw up an indictment
against a great body of my fellow citizens because I don't
agree with them. But I am here to assert that the men who
have recently been leading the great Republican party
have gone upon a false theory in the leadership which
they have followed. That theory I am going to try to expose, if I can, with perfect candor, and yet at the same time
with perfect fairness.

In the first place, I want you to understand that when I
speak of the Republican party I am not speaking of that
great body of my fellow citizens who have been in the
habit of voting [for] the Republican party. I am speaking of
that comparatively small body of my fellow countrymen
who have been in the habit of misleading them, and whom
they have allowed to put it over them.

The theory that they have been themselves guided by is
a perfectly tenable theory. It isn't sound, but you can make
a very good argument for it—and you can make all the bad
argument for it—because men have presented the argument time out of mind. It is an argument as old as the
history of political systems. It is this: that only those men

---

Excerpts from address at Minneapolis, Minn., September 18, 1912.
Crossroads, ed. Davidson, pp. 187–189, 190–191.

who have the biggest material stake in the community understand what is good for that community. That is a rather plausible theory. If my business covers the United States not only, but covers the world, it is to be presumed that I have a pretty wide scope in my vision of business. But the flaw is that it is my business that I have a vision of, and not the business of the men who lie outside of the scope of those plans which I have made to make a profit out of the transactions I am connected with. And you can't by putting together a large number of men who understand their own business, no matter how large it is, make up a body of men who will understand the business of the nation; that is to say, who will see the interest of the nation as contrasted with their own interest.

In other words, the leaders of politics in this country in recent years have thought that we were safe only in the hands of trustees, and the trustees have become so conspicuous that we could write out a list of them. They have become so conspicuous that their names are mentioned upon almost every political platform. We know who the men are who have undertaken the interesting job of taking care of us.

I am one of those who absolutely reject that theory. I have never found a man who knew how to take care of me, and reasoning from that point out, I conjecture that there isn't any man who knows how to take care of all the people of the United States. I suspect that the people of theUnited States understand their own interest better than any group of men in the confines of the country. I don't have to prove that. You all know that that is so. Not only that, but I know this: that the men who are on the make, the men who are swimming against the stream, the men who are sweating blood to get their foothold in the world of endeavor, understand the conditions of business in the United States very much better than the men who have arrived and are at the top. They know what the thing is that they are struggling against. They know how many blind walls they come up against. They know how difficult it is to start a new enterprise. They know how far they have to search for any kind of big credit that will put them upon an even start and footing with the men who have already built up industry in this country. They know that somewhere, by somebody, the development of industry in this country is being controlled; and they want to know how they are going to get into the enterprise themselves.

The trustees have charge of it. And the gentlemen who are running politics are the trustees. And the gentlemen who are running politics are generally known as bosses. I have met bosses in my time. I know exactly what they are. I know that you only have to state in public in their presence what they are to put them out of business. They are the agents of special interests to see that nobody gets into office who won't serve those special interests, and that no law gets on the statute book that is inimical to the men who are at the head of those interests. That is what a boss is. A boss isn't a leader of a party. Parties don't meet in back rooms; parties don't have private understandings; parties don't make arrangements which never get into the newspapers. Parties, if you reckon them by voting strength, are great masses of men who because they can't vote any other ticket, or can't find any other ticket to vote, vote the ticket that was prepared for them by the aforesaid arrangement in the aforesaid back room in accordance with the aforesaid understanding.

Now, the thing that you have to do is to turn those back rooms wrong side out. I have said, and I want to repeat it, that the cure for bad politics is the same as the cure for tuberculosis. It is living in the open. So there can't be any germs of bad politics around here today. Our lungs have

God's air in them, and we are able to see things in the light of God's sun. . . .

The strength of America is proportionate to the health, the buoyancy, the elasticity, the hope, the energy of the American people. What would our forests be worth without these intelligent bodies of ambitious men to make use of them? Why should we conserve our natural resources if we could by a sort of magic of industry transmute them into the wealth of the world? Who transmutes them into that wealth, if not the skill and the touch of the great bodies of men who go daily to their toil and who constitute the great body of the American people? What I am interested in is having the government of the United States more concerned about human rights than about property rights. Property is an instrument of humanity. Humanity isn't an instrument of property. And yet when you see some men engaged in some kinds of industries riding their great industries as if they were driving a car of juggernaut, not looking to see what multitudes prostrate themselves before the car and lose their lives in the crushing effect of their industry, you wonder how long men are going to be permitted to think more of their machinery than they think of their men. Did you never think of it? Men are cheap and machinery is dear, and many a superintendent will be dismissed for overdriving a delicate machine, who wouldn't be dismissed for overdriving an overtaxed man. Because you can discard one man and replace him; there are others ready to come into his place; but you can't without great cost discard your machine and put a new one in its place. You are not looking upon your men as the essential and vital foundation part of your whole business. I say, therefore, that property as compared with humanity, as compared with the vital red blood in the American people, must take second place, not first place; and that we must see to it that there is no overcrowding, that there is no bad sanitation, that there is no unnecessary spread of avoidable diseases, that there is every safeguard against accidents, that women are not driven to impossible tasks and children not permitted to spend their energy before it is fit to be spent, that all the hope of the race must be preserved, and that men must be preserved according to their individual needs and not according to the programs of industry merely. Because, what is the use having industry if we die in producing it? If we die in trying to feed ourselves, why should we feed ourselves? If we die trying to get a foothold in the crowd, why not let the crowd trample us sooner and be done with it? I tell you, gentlemen, that there is beginning to beat in this nation a great pulse of irresistible sympathy which is going to transform the process of government amongst us. . . .

DOCUMENT 38

The Need for a Team Victory

To progressive Republicans and independents, Wilson shrewdly pointed out that he was the only Presidential candidate with any hope of having a unified party behind him in Congress. Hence he was the only candidate likely to be able to accomplish his program.

. . . You have only to examine the platforms of all the parties, for they are multiplying fast now, in order to see that they are all realizing more or less distinctly the new duty that is laid upon government. We used to think in the old-fashioned days when life was very simple that all that

Excerpt from address at Fall River, Mass., September 26, 1912. *Cross-roads*, ed. Davidson, pp. 275–277.

government had to do was to put on a policeman's uniform and say, "Now, don't anybody hurt anybody else." We used to say that the ideal of government was for every man to be left alone and not interfered with, only when he interfered with somebody else; and that the best government was the government that did as little governing as possible. But we are coming now to realize that life is so complicated that we are not dealing with the old conditions, and that the law has to step in and create the conditions under which we live, the conditions which will make it tolerable for us to live. And the reason that you have now to be very careful in the way you are going to vote on the fifth of November is that you are going to choose a method of justice.

All the parties are offering you justice. But it is one thing to offer it to you and it is another thing to know how to give it to you. In the first place, I want to present this consideration to you: There is only one party that is ready to give it to you. Have you heard anybody predict that the third party is going to have a majority in the House of Representatives? Have you heard anybody predict, in his wildest enthusiasm, that it is going to have a majority in the Senate of the United States? Don't you know just as well as you are sitting there that if the leader of the third party should be elected President, he would be one of the most [lonely] officials in the United States? In all probability, in a probability so strong as to amount to a practical certainty, he would have associated with him a Democratic House and a Democratic Senate. He would be just as lonely and just as unserviceable as the present President of the United States. I beg that you won't think that that is said with disrespect, for it is not. I am merely stating a fact. The House of Representatives is Democratic; there is a sufficient number of Republicans in the Senate to vote on all important matters with the Democrats in the Senate to make a majority, and the chief legislation of the past session has not been Republican and has therefore not been acceptable to the President; and almost all the chief measures intended for the relief of voters and buyers of this country have been vetoed by the President. So that you know what I mean. The present President is lonely. He occupies simply a post of resistance. He hasn't got a team behind him; he isn't associated with a team.

And the only President you can associate with a team in the coming years is a Democratic President. Now, I don't know what kind of a captain of the team the candidate would make. I have played quarterback and captain on a smaller team of the same kind, and I found it easy to teach the team the signals, and I found that they responded to the signals with a good deal of spirit. But this is another and a bigger job, and I am not going to pretend to you that I know whether the Democratic candidate would be successful or not. All that I know is that he would have a team back of him, and that no other President you can choose at this juncture would have. Therefore, if you are going to get justice that isn't mixed with all kinds of programs, if you aren't going to keep things at a standstill, if you don't want to wait at least two years, and perhaps four years, to get any program, the only thing you can do in common sense is to elect a Democratic President. Think that over. If I am wrong about it, I want to be corrected.

DOCUMENT 39

"A Day of Dedication"

Wilson won the Presidency by a narrow margin, receiving only a little more than 42 per cent of the popular vote (though his majority in the Electoral College was much more impressive, thanks to the Republican split). Despite the fact that he was a minority President, Wilson considered his election a mandate for reform. In his inaugural address on March 4, 1913, he eloquently summoned the nation to enlist in his crusade.

My fellow citizens:

There has been a change of government. It began two years ago, when the House of Representatives became Democratic by a decisive majority. It has now been completed. The Senate about to assemble will also be Democratic. The offices of President and Vice-President have been put into the hands of Democrats. What does the change mean? That is the question that is uppermost in our minds to-day. That is the question I am going to try to answer, in order, if I may, to interpret the occasion.

It means much more than the mere success of a party. The success of a party means little except when the Nation is using that party for a large and definite purpose. No one can mistake the purpose for which the Nation now seeks to use the Democratic Party. It seeks to use it to interpret a change in its own plans and point of view. Some old things with which we had grown familiar, and which had begun to creep into the very habit of our thought and of our lives, have altered their aspect as we have latterly looked critically upon them, with fresh, awakened eyes; have dropped their disguises and shown themselves alien and sinister. Some new things, as we look frankly upon them, willing to comprehend their real character, have come to assume the aspect of things long believed in and familiar, stuff of our own convictions. We have been refreshed by a new insight into our own life.

We see that in many things that life is very great. It is incomparably great in its material aspects, in its body of wealth, in the diversity and sweep of its energy, in the industries which have been conceived and built up by the genius of individual men and the limitless enterprise of groups of men. It is great, also, very great, in its moral force.

Nowhere else in the world have noble men and women exhibited in more striking forms the beauty and the energy of sympathy and helpfulness and counsel in their efforts to rectify wrong, alleviate suffering, and set the weak in the way of strength and hope. We have built up, moreover, a great system of government, which has stood through a long age as in many respects a model for those who seek to set liberty upon foundations that will endure against fortuitous change, against storm and accident. Our life contains every great thing, and contains it in rich abundance.

But the evil has come with the good, and much fine gold has been corroded.. With riches has come inexcusable waste. We have squandered a great part of what we might have used, and have not stopped to conserve the exceeding bounty of nature, without which our genius for enterprise would have been worthless and impotent, scorning to be careful, shamefully prodigal as well as admirably efficient. We have been proud of our industrial achievements, but we have not hitherto stopped thoughtfully enough to count the human cost, the cost of lives snuffed out, of energies overtaxed and broken, the fearful physical and spiritual cost to the men and women and children upon whom the dead weight and burden of it all has fallen pitilessly the years through. The groans and agony of it all had not yet reached our ears, the solemn, moving undertone of our life, coming up out of the mines and factories and out of every home where the struggle had its intimate and familiar seat. With the great Government went many deep secret things which we too long delayed to look into and scrutinize with candid, fearless eyes. The great Government we loved has too often been made use of for private and selfish purposes, and those who used it had forgotten the people.

At last a vision has been vouchsafed us of our life as a whole. We see the bad with the good, the debased and decadent with the sound and vital. With this vision we approach new affairs. Our duty is to cleanse, to reconsider to restore, to correct the evil without impairing the good to purify and humanize every process of our common life without weakening or sentimentalizing it. There has been something crude and heartless and unfeeling in our haste to succeed and be great. Our thought has been "Let every man look out for himself, let every generation look out for itself," while we reared giant machinery which made it impossible that any but those who stood at the levers of control should have a chance to look out for themselves We had not forgotten our morals. We remembered well enough that we had set up a policy which was meant to serve the humblest as well as the most powerful, with an eye single to the standards of justice and fair play, and remembered it with pride. But we were very heedless and in a hurry to be great.

We have come now to the sober second thought. The scales of heedlessness have fallen from our eyes. We have made up our minds to square every process of our national life again with the standards we so proudly set up at the beginning and have always carried at our hearts. Our work is a work of restoration.

We have itemized with some degree of particularity the things that ought to be altered and here are some of the chief items: A tariff which cuts us off from our proper part in the commerce of the world, violates the just principles of taxation, and makes the Government a facile instrument in the hands of private interests; a banking and currency system based upon the necessity of the Government to sell its bonds fifty years ago and perfectly adapted to concentrating cash and restricting credits; an industrial system which, take it on all its sides, financial as well as administrative, holds capital in leading strings, restricts the liberties and limits the opportunities of labor, and exploits without renewing or conserving the natural resources of the country; a body of agricultural activities never yet given the efficiency of great business undertakings or served as it should be through the instrumentality of science taken directly to the farm, or afforded the facilities of credit best suited to its practical needs; watercourses undeveloped, waste places unreclaimed, forests untended, fast disappearing without plan or prospect of renewal, unregarded waste heaps at every mine. We have studied as perhaps no other nation has the most effective means of production, but we have not studied cost or economy as we should either as organizers of industry, as statesmen, or as individuals.

Nor have we studied and perfected the means by which government may be put at the service of humanity, in safeguarding the health of the Nation, the health of its men and its women and its children, as well as their rights in the struggle for existence. This is no sentimental duty. The firm basis of government is justice, not pity. These are matters of justice. There can be no equality or opportunity, the first essential of justice in the body politic, if men and women and children be not shielded in their lives, their very vitality, from the consequences of great industrial and social processes which they can not alter, control, or singly cope with. Society must see to it that it does not itself crush or weaken or damage its own constituent parts. The first duty of law is to keep sound the society it serves. Sanitary laws, pure food laws, and laws determining conditions of labor which individuals are powerless to determine for themselves are intimate parts of the very business of justice and legal efficiency.

These are some of the things we ought to do, and not leave the others undone, the old-fashioned, never-to-be-neglected, fundamental safeguarding of property and of individual right. This is the high enterprise of the new day: To lift everything that concerns our life as a Nation to the light that shines from the hearthfire of every man's conscience and vision of the right. It is inconceivable that we should do this as partisans; it is inconceivable we should do it in ignorance of the facts as they are or in blind haste. We shall restore, not destroy. We shall deal with our economic system as it is and as it may be modified, not as it might be if we had a clean sheet of paper to write upon; and step by step we shall make it what it should be, in the spirit of those who question their own wisdom and seek counsel and knowledge, not shallow self-satisfaction or the excitement of excursions whither they can not tell. Justice, and only justice, shall always be our motto.

And yet it will be no cool process of mere science. The Nation has been deeply stirred, stirred by a solemn passion, stirred by the knowledge of wrong, of ideals lost, of government too often debauched and made an instrument of evil. The feelings with which we face this new age of right and opportunity sweep across our heartstrings like some air out of God's own presence, where justice and mercy are reconciled and the judge and the brother are one. We know our task to be no mere task of politics but a task which shall search us through and through, whether we be able to understand our time and the need of our people, whether we be indeed their spokesmen and interpreters, whether we have the pure heart to comprehend and the rectified will to choose our high course of action.

This is not a day of triumph; it is a day of dedication.

Here muster, not the forces of party, but the forces of humanity. Men's hearts wait upon us; men's lives hang in the balance; men's hopes call upon us to say what we will do. Who shall live up to the great trust? Who dares fail to try? I summon all honest men, all patriotic, all forward-looking men, to my side. God helping me, I will not fail them, if they will but counsel and sustain me!

PART V

The New Freedom Enacted

A. TARIFF REFORM

DOCUMENT 40

An Early View

Wilson's first goal as President was the reduction of the tariff, which he believed had fostered the trusts. He had long advocated a tariff that would be used for revenue purposes only, and as a young lawyer in Atlanta had criticized the protective principle before the Tariff Commission.

It is not my purpose to represent or advocate any particular interest, but only to say a few words upon the general issues before you on the subject of protection or free trade. This question of the tariff is one which has been under consideration in Congress for 90 odd years. Early in the century protection was introduced for the purpose of fostering new manufactures in this country. That system was continued

---

Excerpts from testimony before the U.S. Tariff Commission, Atlanta, Ga., September 22, 1882. *Public Papers*, I, 89–90, 90–91.

down to the time of the war; but since the war it has been upheld professedly for the purpose of raising revenue, and to enable the government to recover from the indebtedness caused by the war. Free trade, therefore, has been a slumbering question, but it will soon become one of the leading questions in all political discussions, because, now that peace has come, the people of the South will insist upon having the fruits of peace, and not being kept down under the burdens of war.

As you have already been told, there is a great deal of ignorance and indifference in regard to these questions in the South. The people here have been content to let things remain as they were. Probably this has resulted from the fact that the tariff is an indirect way of placing taxes upon the people, and they do not feel the immediate effects of it. But when the farmers and others begin to investigate these matters, they soon discover that they are, after all, paying these duties for the benefit of a few manufacturing classes. When a farmer discovers that he can buy a jack-knife of English manufacture for $1.30, while he has to pay $2 for a knife of American manufacture of the same quality, in order that the American manufacturer of cutlery may compete on equal terms with the British, then he feels that he has a personal interest in these subjects. . . .

No man with his senses about him would recommend perfect freedom of trade in the sense that there should be no duties whatever laid on imports. The only thing that free traders contend for is, that there shall be only so much duty laid as will be necessary to defray the expenses of the government, reduce the public debt, and leave a small surplus for accumulation. But that surplus should be so small that it will not lead to jobbery and corruption of the worst sort. . . .

DOCUMENT 41

A Direct Charge to Congress

One of the President's first acts was to call a special session of Congress, and when the lawmakers assembled he went dramatically before them to request a reduction of tariff duties. No President since John Adams had addressed Congress directly. Wilson chose to break precedent in order to emphasize his great interest in the matter as well as his desire to establish a close working relationship with the legislative branch.

GENTLEMEN OF THE CONGRESS:

I am very glad indeed to have this opportunity to address the two Houses directly and to verify for myself the impression that the President of the United States is a person, not a mere department of the Government hailing Congress from some isolated island of jealous power, sending messages, not speaking naturally and with his own voice—that he is a human being trying to co-operate with other human beings in a common service. After this pleasant experience I shall feel quite normal in all our dealings with one another.

I have called the Congress together in extraordinary session because a duty was laid upon the party now in power at the recent elections which it ought to perform promptly, in order that the burden carried by the people under existing law may be lightened as soon as possible, and in order, also, that the business interests of the country may not be kept too long in suspense as to what the fiscal changes are to be to which they will be required to adjust

---

First special address to Congress, April 8, 1913. *Public Papers*, III, 32–35.

themselves. It is clear to the whole country that the tariff duties must be altered. They must be changed to meet the radical alteration in the conditions of our economic life which the country has witnessed within the last generation. While the whole face and method of our industrial and commercial life were being changed beyond recognition the tariff schedules have remained what they were before the change began, or have moved in the direction they were given when no large circumstance of our industrial development was what it is to-day. Our task is to square them with the actual facts. The sooner that is done the sooner we shall escape from suffering from the facts and the sooner our men of business will be free to thrive by the law of nature—the nature of free business —instead of by the law of legislation and artificial arrangement.

We have seen tariff legislation wander very far afield in our day—very far indeed from the field in which our prosperity might have had a normal growth and stimulation. No one who looks the facts squarely in the face or knows anything that lies beneath the surface of action can fail to perceive the principles upon which recent tariff legislation has been based. We long ago passed beyond the modest notion of "protecting" the industries of the country and moved boldly forward to the idea that they were entitled to the direct patronage of the Government. For a long time—a time so long that the men now active in public policy hardly remember the conditions that preceded it—we have sought in our tariff schedules to give each group of manufacturers or producers what they themselves thought that they needed in order to maintain a practically exclusive market as against the rest of the world. Consciously or unconsciously, we have built up a set of privileges and exemptions from competition behind which it was easy by any, even the crudest, forms of combination to organize monopoly; until at last nothing is normal, nothing is obliged to stand the tests of efficiency and economy, in our world of big business, but everything thrives by concerted arrangement. Only new principles of action will save us from a final hard crystallization of monopoly and a complete loss of the influences that quicken enterprise and keep independent energy alive.

It is plain what those principles must be. We must abolish everything that bears even the semblance of privilege or of any kind of artificial advantage, and put our business men and producers under the stimulation of a constant necessity to be efficient, economical, and enterprising, masters of competitive supremacy, better workers and merchants than any in the world. Aside from the duties laid upon articles which we do not, and probably can not, produce, therefore, and the duties laid upon luxuries and merely for the sake of the revenues they yield, the object of the tariff duties henceforth laid must be effective competition, the whetting of American wits by contest with the wits of the rest of the world.

It would be unwise to move toward this end headlong, with reckless haste, or with strokes that cut at the very roots of what has grown up amongst us by long process and at our own invitation. It does not alter a thing to upset it and break it and deprive it of a chance to change. It destroys it. We must make changes in our fiscal laws, in our fiscal system, whose object is development, a more free and wholesome development, not revolution or upset or confusion. We must build up trade, especially foreign trade. We need the outlet and the enlarged field of energy more than we ever did before. We must build up industry as well, and must adopt freedom in the place of artificial stimulation only so far as it will build, not pull down. In dealing with the tariff the method by which this may be done will be a matter of judgment exercised item by item.

To some not accustomed to the excitements and responsibilities of greater freedom our methods may in some respects and at some points seem heroic but remedies may be heroic and yet be remedies. It is our business to make sure that they are genuine remedies. Our object is clear. If our motive is above just challenge and only an occasional error of judgment is chargeable against us, we shall be fortunate.

We are called upon to render the country a great service in more matters than one. Our responsibility should be met and our methods should be thorough, as thorough as moderate and well considered, based upon the facts as they are, and not worked out as if we were beginners. We are to deal with the facts of our own day, with the facts of no other and to make laws which square with those facts. It is best, indeed it is necessary, to begin with the tariff. I will urge nothing upon you now at the opening of your session which can obscure the first object or divert our energies from that clearly defined duty. At a later time I may take the liberty of calling your attention to reforms which should press close upon the heels of the tariff changes, if not accompany them, of which the chief is the reform of our banking and currency laws; but just now I refrain. For the present, I put these matters on one side and think only of this one thing — of the changes in our fiscal system which may best serve to open once more the free channels of prosperity to a great people whom we would serve to the utmost and throughout both rank and file.

I sincerely thank you for your courtesy.

DOCUMENT 42

Close Attention to Detail

As he had while governor of New Jersey, Wilson kept in close touch with legislative leaders, conferring with them frequently by telephone and at the White House and the Capitol. He mastered the intricacies of tariff schedules and intervened whenever he thought his objectives might be endangered, as this letter to Oscar W. Underwood, the Democratic floor leader and chairman of the House Ways and Means Committee, indicates.

Ready made clothing under the proposed bill carries a duty of thirty-five per cent. ad valorem; and Paragraph 304 includes everything, apparently, from a ten dollar suit up to a Parisian gown if wool is the chief material. I suppose that this would include shawls and workmen's cheap suits.

I beg your pardon for calling your attention to this so late in the game, but I write chiefly to inquire if this were a deliberate arrangement the consequences of which with regard to the price of the cheaper sort of clothing were analyzed.

I know that you will pardon my calling these matters to your attention as they come up.

DOCUMENT 43

Routing the Lobbyists

When the low-tariff bill passed by the House of Representatives seemed likely to run afoul of a strong protectionist

Letter to Oscar W. Underwood, April 19, 1913, in Wilson MSS, Library of Congress.

lobby working on the Senate, Wilson appealed to the country for support. His attack angered some Senators but in the long run insured the passage of the administration's bill. Wilson's attempts to mobilize public opinion were not always so successful as in this case, but they were a characteristic element of his Presidential leadership. The incident also revealed two other Wilson characteristics: his tendency to moralize an issue, and his belief that he spoke for the "people" as opposed to the "interests."

I think that the public ought to know the extraordinary exertions being made by the lobby in Washington to gain recognition for certain alterations of the Tariff bill. Washington has seldom seen so numerous, so industrious or so insidious a lobby. The newspapers are being filled with paid advertisements calculated to mislead the judgment of public men not only, but also the public opinion of the country itself. There is every evidence that money without limit is being spent to sustain this lobby and to create an appearance of a pressure of opinion antagonistic to some of the chief items of the Tariff bill.

It is of serious interest to the country that the people at large should have no lobby and be voiceless in these matters, while great bodies of astute men seek to create an artificial opinion and to overcome the interests of the public for their private profit. It is thoroughly worth the while of the people of this country to take knowledge of this matter. Only public opinion can check and destroy it.

The Government in all its branches ought to be relieved from this intolerable burden and this constant interruption to the calm progress of debate. I know that in this I am speaking for the members of the two houses, who would rejoice as much as I would to be released from this unbearable situation.

Press statement, May 26, 1913. *Public Papers*, III, 36.

B. BANKING AND CURRENCY REFORM

DOCUMENT 44

"So That the Banks May Be
the Instruments, Not the Masters . . ."

Even before the Senate had completed work on the Underwood-Simmons Tariff, the President was hard at work on a more ambitious and complex task—reform of the nation's banking system. His address to Congress on the subject was deliberately vague as to details, but Wilson was very much involved in the legislative work that resulted in the passage of the Federal Reserve Act late in 1913. This Act was the most important domestic achievement of the Wilson administration.

GENTLEMEN OF THE CONGRESS:

It is under the compulsion of what seems to me a clear and imperative duty that I have a second time this session sought the privilege of addressing you in person. I know, of course, that the heated season of the year is upon us, that work in these Chambers and in the committee rooms is likely to become a burden as the season lengthens, and that every consideration of personal convenience and personal comfort, perhaps, in the cases of some of us, considerations of personal health even, dictate an early conclusion of the deliberations of the session; but there are occasions of public duty when these things which touch us privately seem very small; when the work to be done is so pressing

---

Excerpts from address to Congress, June 23, 1913, *Public Papers*, III, 37–38, 39–40.

and so fraught with big consequence that we know that we are not at liberty to weigh against it any point of personal sacrifice. We are now in the presence of such an occasion. It is absolutely imperative that we should give the business men of this country a banking and currency system by means of which they can make use of the freedom of enterprise and of individual initiative which we are about to bestow upon them.

We are about to set them free; we must not leave them without the tools of action when they are free. We are about to set them free by removing the trammels of the protective tariff. Ever since the Civil War they have waited for this emancipation and for the free opportunities it will bring with it. It has been reserved for us to give it to them. Some fell in love, indeed, with the slothful security of their dependence upon the Government, some took advantage of the shelter of the nursery to set up a mimic mastery of their own within its walls. Now both the tonic and the discipline of liberty and maturity are to ensue. There will be some readjustments of purpose and point of view. There will follow a period of expansion and new enterprise, freshly conceived. It is for us to determine now whether it shall be rapid and facile and of easy accomplishment. This it can not be unless the resourceful business men who are to deal with the new circumstances are to have at hand and ready for use the instrumentalities and conveniences of free enterprise which independent men need when acting on their own initiative. . . .

The principles upon which we should act are also clear. The country has sought and seen its path in this matter within the last few years — sees it more clearly now than it ever saw it before — much more clearly than when the last legislative proposals on the subject were made. We must have a currency, not rigid as now, but readily, elastically responsive to sound credit, the expanding and contracting credits of everyday transactions, the normal ebb and flow

of personal and corporate dealings. Our banking laws must
mobilize reserves; must not permit the concentration anywhere in a few hands of the monetary resources of the
country or their use for speculative purposes in such volume as to hinder or impede or stand in the way of other
more legitimate, more fruitful uses. And the control of the
system of banking and of issue which our new laws are to
set up must be public, not private, must be vested in the
Government itself, so that the banks may be the instruments, not the masters, of business and of individual enterprise and initiative. . . .

C. REGULATION OF BUSINESS

DOCUMENT 45

The Trade-Commission Concept

During the 1912 campaign Theodore Roosevelt had em-
phasized the need for a federal trade commission to supervise business practices and prevent unfair competition. Still
essentially a states'-rights Democrat, Wilson had not rejected the idea outright, but he had expressed serious reservations about the trade-commission approach to the trust
problem.

. . . The starting point is plain. The road is pointed out
with some degree of particularity. But where we shall get
at the end of the road is left in convenient doubt. And it is
all the more important that we should resolve that doubt;
because we as a nation are now about to undertake what

Excerpts from address at Boston, September 27, 1912, *Crossroads*, ed.
Davidson, pp. 286–287, 291–292.

will be regarded as the most difficult part of our governmental undertakings. We have gone along so far without very much assistance from our government. We have felt it, felt more and more in recent months, that the American people were at a certain disadvantage as compared with the people of other countries because of what the governments of other countries were doing for them and our government omitting to do for us.

It is perfectly clear to every man who has any vision of the immediate future, who can forecast any part of it from the indications of the present, that we are just upon the threshold of a time when the systematic life of this country will be sustained at every point by governmental activity. We have now to determine what kind of governmental activity it shall be: whether in the first place it shall be direct from the government itself, or whether it shall be indirect through instrumentalities which have already constituted themselves and have already offered to supersede the government. For as I see the difference between the Democratic plan and the Republican plan it is not a difference of machinery, as some of the debaters in this great campaign would have you believe. It is not that the Democratic party, for example, does not care to have an administrative industrial commission; but that it does not intend that an administrative industrial commission shall exercise the power of the government through the trusts; but does intend that that commission, if it is set up, shall be the instrument of a free government, a government free to serve the interests of the people and quickly responsive to the opinions of the people, with no intermediaries to interpret the interests of business and to check the rise of new industries and the entrance into the field of initiative of the individual himself. . . .

Now, did you ever look into the way a trust was made? It is very natural, in one sense, in the same sense in which human greed is fundamentally natural. If I haven't efficiency enough to beat my rivals, if I can't get money enough to beat my rivals, if I can't economize enough to undersell my rivals, then the thing I am inclined to do is to get together with my rivals and say: "Here, don't let's cut each other's throats; let's combine and determine prices for ourselves and determine the output, and thereby determine the prices, and so dominate and control the market." That is very natural. That has been done ever since freebooting was established. That has been done ever since power was used to get control. The reason that they have shut out competition is that the only basis of control under competition is brains and efficiency. I admit that anything that is built up by the legitimate processes of business, by working capital, by economy, by efficiency, by growth, is natural; and I am not afraid of it, no matter how big it gets, because it can stay big only by doing its work more thoroughly than anybody else. Because there is a point of bigness—as every businessman in this country knows, though some of them will not admit it— . . .where you pass the point of efficiency and get to the point of clumsiness and unwieldiness. You get a thing that you can't digest into a single system. You get so many pieces to it that they won't tie together. You can't assemble them as you would an effective piece of machinery. Therefore, the point of efficiency is overstepped in the process of development oftentimes, and it has been overstepped many, many times in the formation of trusts.

DOCUMENT 46

Curbing Trusts and Monopolies

Wilson spelled out his program for business reform in an address to Congress early in 1914. He called for a tight-

Special address to Congress, January 20, 1914, *Public Papers*, III, 81–88.

ening of the antitrust law to prohibit a variety of monopolistic practices, and he also urged the creation of a fact-
gathering trade commission to provide information and
publicity about business matters. In time the President was
persuaded that such a commission ought to be empowered
(as Roosevelt had suggested) to investigate abuses and to
issue cease-and-desist orders against unfair or monopolistic
practices. The result was the Clayton Antitrust Act, and also
a much more powerful Federal Trade Commission Act than
Wilson had originally contemplated. The gap between the
New Freedom and the New Nationalism was rapidly nar-
rowing.

GENTLEMEN OF THE CONGRESS:

In my report "on the state of the Union," which I had
the privilege of reading to you on the 2d of December last,
I ventured to reserve for discussion at a later date the
subject of additional legislation regarding the very difficult
and intricate matter of trusts and monopolies. The time
now seems opportune to turn to that great question, not
only because the currency legislation, which absorbed
your attention and the attention of the country in December, is now disposed of, but also because opinion seems to
be clearing about us with singular rapidity in this other
great field of action. In the matter of the currency it
cleared suddenly and very happily after the much-debated
act was passed; in respect of the monopolies which have
multiplied about us and in regard to the various means by
which they have been organized and maintained, it seems
to be coming to a clear and all but universal agreement in
anticipation of our action, as if by way of preparation,
making the way easier to see and easier to set out upon
with confidence and without confusion of counsel.

Legislation has its atmosphere like everything else, and
the atmosphere of accommodation and mutual understanding which we now breathe with so much refreshment is

matter of sincere congratulation. It ought to make our task very much less difficult and embarrassing than it would have been had we been obliged to continue to act amidst the atmosphere of suspicion and antagonism which has so long made it impossible to approach such questions with dispassionate fairness. Constructive legislation, when successful, is always the embodiment of convincing experience and of the mature public opinion which finally springs out of that experience. Legislation is a business of interpretation, not of origination; and it is now plain what the opinion is to which we must give effect in this matter. It is not recent or hasty opinion. It springs out of the experience of a whole generation. It has clarified itself by long contest, and those who for a long time battled with it and sought to change it are now frankly and honorably yielding to it and seeking to conform their actions to it. The great business men who organized and financed monopoly and those who administered it in actual everyday transactions have, year after year until now, either denied its existence or justified it as necessary for the effective maintenance and development of the vast business processes of the country in the modern circumstances of trade and manufacture and finance; but all the while opinion has made head against them. The average business man is convinced that the ways of liberty are also the ways of peace and the ways of success as well; and at last the masters of business on the great scale have begun to yield their preference and purpose, perhaps their judgment also, in honorable surrender.

What we are purposing to do, therefore, is, happily, not to hamper or interfere with business as enlightened business men prefer to do it, or in any sense to put it under the ban. The antagonism between business and Government is over. We are now about to give expression to the best business judgment of America, to what we know to be the business conscience and honor of the land. The Government and business men are ready to meet each other halfway in a common effort to square business methods with both public opinion and the law. The best-informed men of the business world condemn the methods and processes and consequences of monopoly as we condemn them, and the instinctive judgment of the vast majority of business men everywhere goes with them. We shall now be their spokesmen. That is the strength of our position and the sure prophecy of what will ensue when our reasonable work is done.

When serious contest ends, when men unite in opinion and purpose, those who are to change their ways of business joining with those who ask for the change, it is possible to effect it in the way in which prudent and thoughtful and patriotic men would most wish to see it brought about, with as few, as slight, as easy and simple business readjustments as possible in the circumstances, nothing essential disturbed, nothing torn up by the roots, no parts rent asunder which can be left in wholesome combination. Fortunately, no measures of sweeping or novel change are necessary. It will be understood that our object is *not* to unsettle business or anywhere seriously to break its established courses athwart. On the contrary, we desire the laws we are now about to pass to be the bulwarks and safeguards of industry against the forces that now disturb them. What we have to do can be done in a new spirit, in quiet moderation, without revolution of any untoward kind.

We are all agreed that "private monopoly is indefensible and intolerable," and our program is founded upon that conviction. It will be a comprehensive but not a radical or unacceptable program and these are its items, the changes which opinion deliberately sanctions and for which business waits:

It waits with acquiescence, in the first place, for laws which will effectually prohibit and prevent such interlockings of the *personnel* of the directorates of great corporations—banks and railroads, industrial, commercial, and public service bodies—as in effect result in making those who borrow and those who lend practically one and the same, those who sell and those who buy but the same persons trading with one another under different names and in different combinations, and those who affect to compete in fact partners and masters of the whole field of particular kinds of business. Sufficient time should be allowed, of course, in which to effect these changes of organization without inconvenience or confusion.

Such a prohibition will work much more than a mere negative good by correcting the serious evils which have arisen because, for example, the men who have been the directing spirits of the great investment banks have usurped the place which belongs to independent industrial management working in its own behoof. It will bring new men, new energies, a new spirit of initiative, new blood, into the management of our great business enterprises. It will open the field of industrial development and origination to scores of men who have been obliged to serve when their abilities entitled them to direct. It will immensely hearten the young men coming on and will greatly enrich the business activities of the whole country.

In the second place, business men as well as those who direct public affairs now recognize, and recognize with painful clearness, the great harm and injustice which has been done to many, if not all, of the great railroad systems of the country by the way in which they have been financed and their own distinctive interests subordinated to the interests of the men who financed them and of other business enterprises which those men wished to promote. The country is ready, therefore, to accept, and accept with relief as well as approval, a law which will confer upon the Interstate Commerce Commission the power to superintend and regulate the financial operations by which the railroads are henceforth to be supplied with the money they need for their proper development to meet the rapidly growing requirements of the country for increased and improved facilities of transportation. We cannot postpone action in this matter without leaving the railroads exposed to many serious handicaps and hazards; and the prosperity of the railroads and the prosperity of the country are inseparably connected. Upon this question those who are chiefly responsible for the actual management and operation of the railroads have spoken very plainly and very earnestly, with a purpose we ought to be quick to accept. It will be one step, and a very important one, towards the necessary separation of the business of production from the business of transportation.

The business of the country awaits also, has long awaited and has suffered because it could not obtain, further and more explicit legislative definition of the policy and meaning of the existing antitrust law. Nothing hampers business like uncertainty. Nothing daunts or discourages it like the necessity to take chances, to run the risk of falling under the condemnation of the law before it can make sure just what the law is. Surely we are sufficiently familiar with the actual processes and methods of monopoly and of the many hurtful restraints of trade to make definition possible, at any rate up to the limits of what experience has disclosed. These practices, being now abundantly disclosed, can be explicitly and item by item forbidden by statute in such terms as will practically eliminate uncertainty, the law itself and the penalty being made equally plain.

And the business men of the country desire something more than that the menace of legal process in these matters be made explicit and intelligible. They desire the advice, the definite guidance, and information which can be supplied by an administrative body, an interstate trade commission.

The opinion of the country would instantly approve of such a commission. It would not wish to see it empowered to make terms with monopoly or in any sort to assume control of business, as if the Government made itself responsible. It demands such a commission only as an indispensable instrument of information and publicity, as a clearing house for the facts by which both the public mind and the managers of the great business undertakings should be guided, and as an instrumentality for doing justice to business where the processes of the courts or the natural forces of correction outside the courts are inadequate to adjust the remedy to the wrong in a way that will meet all the equities and circumstances of the case.

Producing industries, for example, which have passed the point up to which combination may be consistent with the public interest and the freedom of trade, can not always be dissected into their component units as readily as railroad companies or similar organizations can be. Their dissolution by ordinary legal process may oftentimes involve financial consequences likely to overwhelm the security market and bring upon it breakdown and confusion. There ought to be an administrative commission capable of directing and shaping such corrective processes, not only in aid of the courts but also by independent suggestion, if necessary.

Inasmuch as our object and the spirit of our action in these matters is to meet business half way in its processes of self-correction and disturb its legitimate course as little as possible, we ought to see to it, and the judgment of practical and sagacious men of affairs everywhere would applaud us if we did see to it, that penalties and punishments should fall not upon business itself, to its confusion and interruption, but upon the individuals who use the instrumentalities of business to do things which public policy and sound business practice condemn. Every act of business is done at the command or upon the initiative of some ascertainable person or group of persons. These should be held individually responsible and the punishment should fall upon them, not upon the business organization of which they make illegal use. It should be one of the main objects of our legislation to divest such persons of their corporate cloak and deal with them as with those who do not represent their corporations, but merely by deliberate intention break the law. Business men the country through would, I am sure, applaud us if we were to take effectual steps to see that the officers and directors of great business bodies were prevented from bringing them and the business of the country in general into disrepute and danger.

Other questions remain which will need very thoughtful and practical treatment. Enterprises in these modern days of great individual fortunes are oftentimes interlocked, not by being under the control of the same directors but by the fact that the greater part of their corporate stock is owned by a single person or group of persons who are in some way intimately related in interest. We are agreed, I take it, that holding *companies* should be prohibited, but what of the controlling private ownership of individuals or actually co-operative groups of individuals? Shall the private owners of capital stock be suffered to be themselves in effect holding companies? We do not wish, I suppose, to forbid the purchase of stocks by any person who pleases to buy them in such quantities as he can afford, or in any way arbitrarily to limit the sale of stocks to bona fide purchasers. Shall we require the owners of stock, when their voting power in several companies which ought to be independent of one another would constitute actual control, to make election in which of them they will exercise their right to vote? This question I venture for your consideration.

There is another matter in which imperative considerations of justice and fair play suggest thoughtful remedial action. Not only do many of the combinations effected or sought to be effected in the industrial world work an injustice upon the public in general; they also directly and seriously injure the individuals who are put out of business in one unfair way or another by the many dislodging and exterminating forces of combination. I hope that we shall agree in giving private individuals who claim to have been injured by these processes the right to found their suits for redress upon the facts and judgments proved and entered in suits by the Government where the Government has upon its own initiative sued the combinations complained of and won its suit, and that the statute of limitations shall be suffered to run against such litigants only from the date of the conclusion of the Government's action. It is not fair that the private litigant should be obliged to set up and establish again the facts which the Government has proved. He cannot afford, he has not the power, to make use of such processes of inquiry as the Government has command of. Thus shall individual justice be done while the processes of business are rectified and squared with the general conscience.

I have laid the case before you, no doubt, as it lies in your own mind, as it lies in the thought of the country. What must every candid man say of the suggestions I have laid before you, of the plain obligations of which I have reminded you? That these are new things for which the country is not prepared? No; but that they are old things, now familiar, and must of course be undertaken if we are to square our laws with the thought and desire of the country. Until these things are done, conscientious business men the country over will be unsatisfied. They are in these things our mentors and colleagues. We are now about to write the additional articles of our constitution of peace, the peace that is honor and freedom and prosperity.

D. THE RIGHTS OF LABOR

DOCUMENT 47

The Legal Right to Organize

Wilson's New Freedom program stressed "special privilege to none," meaning no class legislation. There were exceptions, of course, and Wilson noted one in a 1912 campaign speech to a group of enthusiastic workingmen at Fall River, Massachusetts.

. . . But the point I want to return to is that with this ability to shut up shops, with this ability to shut off labor in certain parts of the country, with unlimited means to live (while the men shut out can't live because they haven't unlimited means), they have used that awful power to break up the right to organize. That is my point. Because, if it isn't a right on the part of a workingman to organize, then there oughtn't to be a right on the part of capital to organize. It is organization that makes capital strong, and it isn't fair from the legal point of view, or any other point of view, to prevent the rest of the men dealing with capital

---

Excerpt from address at Fall River, Mass., September 26, 1912, *Crossroads*, ed. Davidson, pp. 279–280.

rom getting the strength which organization, and only
organization, can bring.

So that you don't have to defend all the things that organized labor has done. Organized labor has been unwise
n some things, but the point is this, that the right of organization on the part of labor is not recognized even by
he laws of the United States. And nowhere in the third-
party platform is it promised that that right will be granted.
There is a plank in which it is said: "We are in favor of the
organization of labor"—I have forgotten the exact words,
but that is what it means—"We are in favor of the organization of labor"; that is to say, "We approve of the practice," but it doesn't anywhere promise to buttress that
practice with the structural steel of law. And this is the law
at present: In most of the states of the Union, so far as I
know in all of them, for I haven't been able to examine all
the decisions of the courts, any corporation, any employer
of any kind, has the right under our law to dismiss not only
one of his workingmen or a group of them, but all of them,
for no other reason whatever than that they belong to a
union. He doesn't have to show that they are not good
workmen; he doesn't have to show that they have been
negligent, broken the machinery, or done anything that
they oughtn't to do. He can dismiss them wholesale,
merely because they belong to a union.

Now, a union can't oppose an employer merely on the
ground that he is employing men who don't belong to a
union. And so the thing is absolutely one-sided. The courts
have held that union labor has not the right to boycott a
concern because it is employing nonunion labor, and yet it
says that the concern may boycott them because they are
unionized. I believe that we ought to hold a brief for the
right, the legal right, to organize. Of course, we can go to
the opposite extreme. We can say that capital shall not
organize, but imagine the howl that would create. Do you

think you could get through a law that capital couldn't organize? Well, what is sauce for the goose is sauce for the gander; and if capital can organize, then it stands to every standard of justice that I have ever heard of that anybody else who has a legitimate object may organize. There ought to be an absolute equality in regard to that right. Of course, the law must regulate what capital must do with its organization, and we will all of us agree that the law ought also to regulate what organized labor can do with its organization. But that is another story. At present there is no legal right to organize. That is an extraordinary circumstance. . . .

DOCUMENT 48

To End Antagonism Between Capital and Labor

Wilson's endorsement of labor's right to organize did not mean that he was an all-out supporter of trade unions. He declined to write into the Clayton Act a clear immunity for labor and farm organizations from antitrust prosecution, for example, and he withheld support from certain other labor objectives. Still, organized labor made large gains under the Wilson administration, especially during the war years when the government gave tacit support to union-organizing drives. Wilson was more concerned with foreign than with domestic problems after the war, and his subordinates were notably unsuccessful in coping with the postwar wave of labor strife. In his annual message to Congress in 1919, however, the President addressed himself to the question of labor-management relations.

Excerpts from annual message to Congress, December 2, 1919, *Public Papers*, VI, 437–440.

. . No one who has observed the march of events in the last year can fail to note the absolute need of a definite program to bring about an improvement in the conditions of labor. There can be no settled conditions leading to increased production and a reduction in the cost of living if labor and capital are to be antagonists instead of partners. Sound thinking and an honest desire to serve the interests of the whole Nation, as distinguished from the interests of a class, must be applied to the solution of this great and pressing problem. The failure of other nations to consider this matter in a vigorous way has produced bitterness and jealousies and antagonisms, the food of radicalism. The only way to keep men from agitating against grievances is to remove the grievances. An unwillingness even to discuss these matters produces only dissatisfaction and gives comfort to the extreme elements in our country which endeavor to stir up disturbances in order to provoke Governments to embark upon a course of retaliation and repression. The seed of revolution is repression. The remedy for these things must not be negative in character. It must be constructive. It must comprehend the general interest. The real antidote for the unrest which manifests itself is not suppression, but a deep consideration of the wrongs that beset our national life and the application of a remedy.

Congress has already shown its willingness to deal with these industrial wrongs by establishing the eight-hour day as the standard in every field of labor. It has sought to find a way to prevent child labor. It has served the whole country by leading the way in developing the means of preserving and safeguarding lives and health in dangerous industries. It must now help in the difficult task of finding a method that will bring about a genuine democratization of industry based upon the full recognition of the right of those who work, in whatever rank, to participate in some organic way in every decision which directly affects their welfare. It is with this purpose in mind that I called a conference to meet in Washington on December 1, to consider these problems in all their broad aspects, with the idea of bringing about a better understanding between these two interests.

The great unrest throughout the world, out of which has emerged a demand for an immediate consideration of the difficulties between capital and labor, bids us put our own house in order. Frankly, there can be no permanent and lasting settlements between capital and labor which do not recognize the fundamental concepts for which labor has been struggling through the years. The whole world gave its recognition and endorsement to these fundamental purposes in the League of Nations. The statesmen gathered at Versailles recognized the fact that world stability could not be had by reverting to industrial standards and conditions against which the average workman of the world had revolted. It is, therefore, the task of the statesmen of this new day of change and readjustment to recognize world conditions and to seek to bring about, through legislation, conditions that will mean the ending of age-long antagonisms between capital and labor and that will hopefully lead to the building up of a comradeship which will result not only in greater contentment among the mass of workmen but also bring about a greater production and a greater prosperity to business itself.

To analyze the particulars in the demands of labor is to admit the justice of their complaint in many matters that lie at their basis. The workman demands an adequate wage, sufficient to permit him to live in comfort, unhampered by the fear of poverty and want in his old age. He demands the right to live and the right to work amidst sanitary surroundings, both in home and in workshop, surroundings that develop and do not retard his own health and well-being; and the right to provide for his children's wants in the matter of health and education. In other words, it is his desire to make the conditions of his life and the lives of those dear to him tolerable and easy to bear.

The establishment of the principles regarding labor laid down in the Covenant of the League of Nations offers us the way to industrial peace and conciliation. No other road lies open to us. Not to pursue this one is longer to invite enmities, bitterness, and antagonisms which in the end only lead to industrial and social disaster. The unwilling workman is not a profitable servant. An employee whose industrial life is hedged about by hard and unjust conditions, which he did not create and over which he has no control, lacks that fine spirit of enthusiasm and volunteer effort which are the necessary ingredients of a great producing entity. Let us be frank about this solemn matter. The evidences of world-wide unrest which manifest themselves in violence throughout the world bid us pause and consider the means to be found to stop the spread of this contagious thing before it saps the very vitality of the nation itself. Do we gain strength by withholding the remedy? Or is it not the business of statesmen to treat these manifestations of unrest which meet us on every hand as evidences of an economic disorder and to apply constructive remedies wherever necessary, being sure that in the application of the remedy we touch not the vital tissues of our industrial and economic life? There can be no recession of the tide of unrest until constructive instrumentalities are set up to stem that tide.

Governments must recognize the right of men collectively to bargain for humane objects that have at their base the mutual protection and welfare of those engaged in all industries. Labor must not be longer treated as a commodity. It must be regarded as the activity of human beings, possessed of deep yearnings and desires. The business man gives his best thought to the repair and replenishment of his machinery, so that its usefulness will not be impaired and its power to produce may always be at its height and kept in full vigor and motion. No less regard ought to be paid to the human machine, which after all propels the machinery of the world and is the great dynamic force that lies back of all industry and progress. Return to the old standards of wage and industry in employment is unthinkable. The terrible tragedy of war which has just ended and which has brought the world to the verge of chaos and disaster would be in vain if there should ensue a return to the conditions of the past. Europe itself, whence has come the unrest which now holds the world at bay, is an example of standpatism in these vital human matters which America might well accept as an example, not to be followed but studiously to be avoided. Europe made labor the differential, and the price of it all is enmity and antagonism and prostrated industry. The right of labor to live in peace and comfort must be recognized by governments and America should be the first to lay the foundation stones upon which industrial peace shall be built. . . .

E. RACE RELATIONS

DOCUMENT 49

"I Sincerely Believe It to Be

in Their Interest"

Wilson's New Freedom put great stress on individual rights, but the program had at least one glaring blind spot.

Letter to Oswald Garrison Villard, July 23, 1913, in Baker, *Wilson, Life and Letters*, IV, 221.

Several members of Wilson's cabinet were, like the President himself, Southerners who took a narrow, sectional view of race relations. Led by Secretary of the Treasury William G. McAdoo, a Georgian, and Postmaster General Albert S. Burleson, a Texan, both of whose departments had hitherto employed a significant number of Negro workers, the administration not only cut back the number and level of jobs open to Negroes but also adopted a policy of racial segregation in federal employment. Strong protests from some white progressives—notably Oswald Garrison Villard, publisher of the New York *Evening Post* and board chairman of the National Association for the Advancement of Colored People—forced the administration to backtrack a bit, but Wilson's attitude on this matter remained distinctively Southern. The New Freedom was for whites only, it appeared, and in fact Wilson saw a positive virtue in Jim Crowism, as the following letter to Villard indicates.

It is true that the segregation of the colored employees in the several departments was begun upon the initiative and at the suggestion of several of the heads of departments, but as much as in the interest of the negroes as for any other reason, with the approval of some of the most influential negroes I know, and with the idea that the friction, or rather the discontent and uneasiness, which had prevailed in many of the departments would thereby be removed. It is as far as possible from being a movement *against* the negroes. I sincerely believe it to be in their interest. And what distresses me about your letter is to find that you look at it in so different a light.

I am sorry that those who interest themselves most in the welfare of the negroes should misjudge this action on the part of the departments, for they are seriously misjudging it. My own feeling is, by putting certain bureaus and sections of the service in the charge of negroes we are rendering them more safe in their possession of office and less likely to be discriminated against.

F. IMMIGRATION

DOCUMENT 50

Exclusion of Orientals

Wilson was also race-conscious on the question of Oriental immigration, as this letter written during the campaign of 1912 suggests. Phelan, a former mayor of San Francisco, was a prominent California Democrat.

In the matter of Chinese and Japanese coolie immigration I stand for the national policy of exclusion. The whole question is one of assimilation of diverse races. We cannot make a homogeneous population out of people who do not blend with the Caucasian race. Their lower standards of living as laborers will crowd out the white agriculturists and will in other fields prove a most serious industrial menace. The success of free democratic institutions demands of our people education, intelligence, patriotism, and the State should protect them against unjust and impossible competition. United labor is the basis of contentment. Democracy rests on equality of the citizens. Oriental coolieism will give us another race problem to solve, and surely we have had our lessons.

Letter to James D. Phelan, in *Independent*, LXXIII (October 10, 1912), 863.

DOCUMENT 51

Veto of the Literacy Test

Although Wilson applied racial value-judgments to some immigrant groups, he was no narrow exclusionist. In 1915 he vetoed a bill seeking to restrict immigration by means of a literacy test; the President believed that the bill unwisely and unfairly discriminated against those whose disability resulted from a previous lack of opportunity and not from any defect of character. His veto message also pointed out that this was an issue on which the American people neither had been adequately consulted nor had expressed a clear opinion. When Congress passed a similar literacy test in 1917, the restrictionists were able to muster enough votes to override Wilson's second veto. The President's views were cogently expressed in his 1915 veto.

To THE HOUSE OF REPRESENTATIVES:

It is with unaffected regret that I find myself constrained by clear conviction to return this bill (H. R. 6060, "An act to regulate the immigration of aliens to and the residence of aliens in the United States") without my signature. Not only do I feel it to be a very serious matter to exercise the power of veto in any case, because it involves opposing the single judgment of the President to the judgment of a majority of both the Houses of the Congress, a step which no man who realizes his own liability to error can take without great hesitation, but also because this particular bill is in so many important respects admirable, well conceived, and desirable. Its enactment into law would undoubtedly enhance the efficiency and improve the meth-

---

Message to the House of Representatives, January 28, 1915, *Public Papers*, III, 252–254.

ods of handling the important branch of the public service to which it relates. But candor and a sense of duty with regard to the responsibility so clearly imposed upon me by the Constitution in matters of legislation leave me no choice but to dissent.

In two particulars of vital consequence this bill embodies a radical departure from the traditional and long-established policy of this country, a policy in which our people have conceived the very character of their Government to be expressed, the very mission and spirit of the Nation in respect of its relations to the peoples of the world outside their borders. It seeks to all but close entirely the gates of asylum which have always been open to those who could find nowhere else the right and opportunity of constitutional agitation for what they conceived to be the natural and inalienable rights of men; and it excludes those to whom the opportunities of elementary education have been denied, without regard to their character, their purposes, or their natural capacity.

Restrictions like these, adopted earlier in our history as a Nation, would very materially have altered the course and cooled the humane ardors of our politics. The right of political asylum has brought to this country many a man of noble character and elevated purpose who was marked as an outlaw in his own less fortunate land, and who has yet become an ornament to our citizenship and to our public councils. The children and the compatriots of these illustrious Americans must stand amazed to see the representatives of their Nation now resolved, in the fullness of our national strength and at the maturity of our great institutions, to risk turning such men back from our shores without test of quality or purpose. It is difficult for me to believe that the full effect of this feature of the bill was realized when it was framed and adopted, and it is impossible for me to assent to it in the form in which it is here cast.

The literacy test and the tests and restrictions which accompany it constitute an even more radical change in the policy of the Nation. Hitherto we have generously kept our doors open to all who were not unfitted by reason of disease or incapacity for self-support or such personal records and antecedents as were likely to make them a menace to our peace and order or to the wholesome and essential relationships of life. In this bill it is proposed to turn away from tests of character and of quality and impose tests which exclude and restrict; for the new tests here embodied are not tests of quality or of character or of personal fitness, but tests of opportunity. Those who come seeking opportunity are not to be admitted unless they have already had one of the chief of the opportunities they seek, the opportunity of education. The object of such provisions is restriction, not selection.

If the people of this country have made up their minds to limit the number of immigrants by arbitrary tests and so reverse the policy of all the generations of Americans that have gone before them, it is their right to do so. I am their servant and have no license to stand in their way. But I do not believe that they have. I respectfully submit that no one can quote their mandate to that effect. Has any political party ever avowed a policy of restriction in this fundamental matter, gone to the country on it, and been commissioned to control its legislation? Does this bill rest upon the conscious and universal assent and desire of the American people? I doubt it. It is because I doubt it that I make bold to dissent from it. I am willing to abide by the verdict, but not until it has been rendered. Let the platforms of parties speak out upon this policy and the people pronounce their wish. The matter is too fundamental to be settled otherwise.

I have no pride of opinion in this question. I am not foolish enough to profess to know the wishes and ideals of

America better than the body of her chosen representatives know them. I only want instruction direct from those whose fortunes, with ours and all men's, are involved.

G. WOMAN SUFFRAGE

DOCUMENT 52

"Democracy Means that Women Shall Play Their Part. . . ."

Just as the New Freedom did not include Negroes, so it did not initially include women, or at least the enfranchisement of women. Wilson was too much a tradition-minded Southern gentleman to accept easily the notion that women ought to play a significant role in public affairs. To evade the question, he argued that suffrage qualifications were matters to be determined by the states. When a suffrage amendment came before the voters of his own state of New Jersey in 1915, the President was obliged to take a public stand. He declared his intention to vote in favor of the measure. Beyond this he refused to go, however, until increasing pressure from militant suffragettes during his second term forced him to make a stronger endorsement. Using somewhat heavy-handed wartime arguments. he appealed to the Senate to approve a woman-suffrage amendment.

The unusual circumstances of a world war in which we stand and are judged in the view not only of our own people and our own consciences but also in the view of all

---

Address to the Senate, September 30, 1918, *Public Papers*, V, 263–267.

nations and peoples will, I hope, justify in your thought, as it does in mine, the message I have come to bring you. I regard the concurrence of the Senate in the constitutional amendment proposing the extension of the suffrage to women as vitally essential to the successful prosecution of the great war of humanity in which we are engaged. I have come to urge upon you the considerations which have led me to that conclusion. It is not only my privilege, it is also my duty to apprise you of every circumstance and element involved in this momentous struggle which seems to me to affect its very processes and its outcome. It is my duty to win the war and to ask you to remove every obstacle that stands in the way of winning it.

I had assumed that the Senate would concur in the amendment because no disputable principle is involved, but only a question of the method by which the suffrage is to be extended to women. There is and can be no party issue involved in it. Both of our great national parties are pledged, explicitly pledged, to equality of suffrage for the women of the country. Neither party, therefore, it seems to me, can justify hesitation as to the method of obtaining it, can rightfully hesitate to substitute federal initiative for state initiative, if the early adoption of this measure is necessary to the successful prosecution of the war and if the method of state action proposed in the party platforms of 1916 is impracticable within any reasonable length of time, if practicable at all. And its adoption is, in my judgment, clearly necessary to the successful prosecution of the war and the successful realization of the objects for which the war is being fought.

That judgment I take the liberty of urging upon you with solemn earnestness for reasons which I shall state very frankly and which I shall hope will seem as conclusive to you as they seem to me.

This is a peoples' war and the peoples' thinking constitutes its atmosphere and morale, not the predilections of
the drawing room or the political considerations of the
caucus. If we be indeed democrats and wish to lead the
world to democracy, we can ask other peoples to accept in
proof of our sincerity and our ability to lead them whither
they wish to be led nothing less persuasive and convincing
than our actions. Our professions will not suffice. Verification must be forthcoming when verification is asked for.
And in this case verification is asked for, — asked for in this
particular matter. You ask by whom? Not through diplomatic channels; not by Foreign Ministers. Not by the intimations of parliaments. It is asked for by the anxious,
expectant, suffering peoples with whom we are dealing
and who are willing to put their destinies in some measure
in our hands, if they are sure that we wish the same things
that they do. I do not speak by conjecture. It is not alone
the voices of statesmen and of newspapers that reach me,
and the voices of foolish and intemperate agitators do not
reach me at all. Through many, many channels I have
been made aware what the plain, struggling, workaday folk
are thinking upon whom the chief terror and suffering of
this tragic war falls. They are looking to the great, powerful, famous Democracy of the West to lead them to the
new day for which they have so long waited; and they
think, in their logical simplicity, that democracy means
that women shall play their part in affairs alongside men
and upon an equal footing with them. If we reject measures like this, in ignorance or defiance of what a new age
has brought forth, of what they have seen but we have not,
they will cease to believe in us; they will cease to follow
or to trust us. They have seen their own Governments
accept this interpretation of democracy, — seen old Governments like that of Great Britain, which did not profess
to be democratic, promise readily and as of course this

justice to women, though they had before refused it, the strange revelations of this war having made many things new and plain, to governments as well as to peoples.

Are we alone to refuse to learn the lesson? Are we alone to ask and take the utmost that our women can give,— service and sacrifice of every kind,— and still say we do not see what title that gives them to stand by our sides in the guidance of the affairs of their Nation and ours? We have made partners of the women in this war; shall we admit them only to a partnership of suffering and sacrifice and toil and not to a partnership of privilege and right? This war could not have been fought, either by the other nations engaged or by America, if it had not been for the services of the women,— services rendered in every sphere,— not merely in the fields of effort in which we have been accustomed to see them work, but wherever men have worked and upon the very skirts and edges of the battle itself. We shall not only be distrusted but shall deserve to be distrusted if we do not enfranchise them with the fullest possible enfranchisement, as it is now certain that the other great free nations will enfranchise them. We cannot isolate our thought and action in such a matter from the thought of the rest of the world. We must either conform or deliberately reject what they propose and resign the leadership of liberal minds to others.

The women of America are too noble and too intelligent and too devoted to be slackers whether you give or withhold this thing that is mere justice; but I know the magic it will work in their thoughts and spirits if you give it them. I propose it as I would propose to admit soldiers to the suffrage, the men fighting in the field for our liberties and the liberties of the world, were they excluded. The tasks of the women lie at the very heart of the war, and I know how much stronger that heart will beat if you do this just thing and show our women that you trust them as much as you in fact and of necessity depend upon them.

Have I said that the passage of this amendment is a vitally necessary war measure, and do you need further proof? Do you stand in need of the trust of other peoples and of the trust of our own women? Is that trust an asset or is it not? I tell you plainly, as the commander-in-chief of our armies and of the gallant men in our fleets, as the present spokesman of this people in our dealings with the men and women throughout the world who are now our partners, as the responsible head of a great Government which stands and is questioned day by day as to its purposes, its principles, its hopes, whether they be serviceable to men everywhere or only to itself, and who must himself answer these questionings or be ashamed, as the guide and director of forces caught in the grip of war and by the same token in need of every material and spiritual resource this great Nation possesses,—I tell you plainly that this measure which I urge upon you is vital to the winning of the war and to the energies alike of preparation and of battle.

And not to the winning of the war only. It is vital to the right solution of the great problems which we must settle, and settle immediately, when the war is over. We shall need then in our vision of affairs, as we have never needed them before, the sympathy and insight and clear moral instinct of the women of the world. The problems of that time will strike to the roots of many things that we have not hitherto questioned, and I for one believe that our safety in those questioning days, as well as our comprehension of matters that touch society to the quick, will depend upon the direct and authoritative participation of women in our counsels. We shall need their moral sense to preserve what is right and fine and worthy in our system of life as well as to discover just what it is that ought to be purified and reformed. Without their counselings we shall be only half wise.

That is my case. This is my appeal. Many may deny its validity, if they choose, but no one can brush aside or answer the arguments upon which it is based. The executive tasks of this war rest upon me. I ask that you lighten them and place in my hands instruments, spiritual instruments, which I do not now possess, which I sorely need, and which I have daily to apologize for not being able to employ.

H. ECONOMY IN GOVERNMENT

DOCUMENT 53

"It Is Not Expenditure But Extravagance That We Should Fear. . . ."

Wilson believed that he was in a real sense the steward of the American people. As a long-time student of government, he was conscious of the danger of waste and costly inefficiency in laxly administered governmental activities. He therefore tried to maintain a close scrutiny over the expenses and operations of the various executive departments (See, for example, Documents 98 and 99). The President summarized his views on the need for prudent and economical government in his annual message to Congress in 1914, at a time when he was otherwise seeking to persuade businessmen of his financial prudence (See Documents 13 and 14).

Excerpt from annual message to Congress December 8, 1914, *Public Papers*, III, 222–223.

. . . The duty of economy is not debatable. It is manifest and imperative. In the appropriations we pass we are spending the money of the great people whose servants we are, — not our own. We are trustees and responsible stewards in the spending. The only thing debatable and upon which we should be careful to make our thought and purpose clear is the kind of economy demanded of us. I assert with the greatest confidence that the people of the United States are not jealous of the amount their Government costs if they are sure that they get what they need and desire for the outlay, that the money is being spent for objects of which they approve, and that it is being applied with good business sense and management.

Governments grow, piecemeal, both in their tasks and in the means by which those tasks are to be performed, and very few Governments are organized, I venture to say, as wise and experienced business men would organize them if they had a clean sheet of paper to write upon. Certainly the Government of the United States is not. I think that it is generally agreed that there should be a systematic reorganization and reassembling of its parts so as to secure greater efficiency and effect considerable savings in expense. But the amount of money saved in that way would, I believe, though no doubt considerable in itself, running, it may be, into the millions, be relatively small, — small, I mean, in proportion to the total necessary outlays of the Government. It would be thoroughly worth effecting, as every saving would, great or small. Our duty is not altered by the scale of the saving. But my point is that the people of the United States do not wish to curtail the activities of this Government; they wish, rather, to enlarge them; and with every enlargement, with the mere growth, indeed, of the country itself, there must come, of course, the inevitable increase of expense. The sort of economy we ought to practice may be effected, and ought to be effected, by a careful study and assessment of the tasks to be performed; and the money spent ought to be made to yield the best possible returns in efficiency and achievement. And, like good stewards, we should so account for every dollar of our appropriations as to make it perfectly evident what it was spent for and in what way it was spent.

It is not expenditure but extravagance that we should fear being criticized for; not paying for the legitimate enterprises and undertakings of a great Government whose people command what it should do, but adding what will benefit only a few or pouring money out for what need not have been undertaken at all or might have been postponed or better and more economically conceived and carried out. The Nation is not niggardly; it is very generous. It will chide us only if we forget for whom we pay money out and whose money it is we pay. These are large and general standards, but they are not very difficult of application to particular cases. . . .

I. THE NEW FREEDOM APPRAISED

DOCUMENT 54

"A Time of Healing . . ."

After the passage of the three main elements of his legislative program — reduction of the tariff, banking and currency reform, and increased regulation of business — Wilson considered the New Freedom essentially complete. He had achieved the major objectives of his 1912 platform and more besides, having adopted Roosevelt's proposal for a

Letter to William G. McAdoo, November 17, 1914, *Public Papers*, III, 210–214.

strong trade commission. What was needed now, he believed, was a period of comparative calm during which the country could adjust to the new reforms and the new regulatory agencies could be put into operation. The unsettled business conditions arising from the outbreak of war in Europe, moreover, reinforced the President's inclination to call a halt to further reform, and influenced him to appoint conservatives to the new agencies. In his private correspondence, and in a public letter to Secretary of the Treasury McAdoo upon the opening of the Federal Reserve banking system in November 1914, Wilson indicated his pride in the reforms accomplished and his faith that they had provided the means to correct the basic evils afflicting the country.

I warmly appreciate your letter of yesterday, for I share your feelings entirely about the significance of the opening of the Federal Reserve banks for business.

I do not know that any special credit belongs to me for the part I was privileged to play in the establishment of this new system of which we confidently hope so much; in it the labor and knowledge and forethought and practical experience and sagacity of many men are embodied, who have cooperated with unusual wisdom and admirable public spirit. None of them, I am sure, will be jealous of the distribution of the praise for the great piece of legislation upon which the new system rests; they will only rejoice unselfishly to see the thing accomplished upon which they had set their hearts.

It has been accomplished, and its accomplishment is of the deepest significance, both because of the things it has done away with and because of the things it has supplied that the country lacked, and had long needed. It has done away with agitation and suspicion, because it has done away with certain fundamental wrongs. It has supplied means of accommodation in the business world and an instrumentality by which the interests of all, without regard to class, may readily be served.

We have only to look back ten years or so to realize the deep perplexities and dangerous ill humors out of which we have now at last issued as if from a bewildering fog, a noxious miasma. Ten or twelve years ago the country was torn and excited by an agitation which shook the very foundations of her political life, brought her business ideals into question, condemned her social standards, denied the honesty of her men of affairs, the integrity of her economic processes, the morality and good faith of many of the things which her law sustained.

Those who had power, whether in business or in politics, were almost universally looked upon with suspicion, and little attempt was made to distinguish the just from the unjust. They in their turn seemed to distrust the people and to wish to limit their control. There was ominous antagonism between classes. Capital and labor were in sharp conflict without prospect of accommodation between them. Interests harshly clashed which should have cooperated.

This was not merely the work of irresponsible agitators. There were real wrongs which cried out to be righted and fearless men had called attention to them, demanding that they be dealt with by law. We were living under a tariff which had been purposely contrived to confer private favors upon those who were cooperating to keep the party that originated it in power and in all that too fertile soil all the bad, interlaced growth and jungle of monopoly had sprung up. Credit, the very life of trade, the very air men must breathe if they would meet their opportunities, was too largely in control of the same small groups who had planted and cultivated monopoly. The control of all big business and, by consequence, of all little business, too, was for the most part potentially, if not actually, in their hands. And the thing stood so until the Democrats came into power last year. The legislation of the past year and a half has in very large measure done away with these things. With a correction, suspicion and ill-will will pass away. For not only have these things been righted, but new things have been put into action which are sure to prove the instruments of a new life, in which the mists and distempers which have so embarrassed us will be cleared away; the wrongs and misunderstandings corrected which have brought distrust upon so many honest men unjustly. That is the main ground of my own satisfaction.

The tariff has been recast with a view to supporting the Government rather than supporting the favored beneficiaries of the Government. A system of banking and currency issues has been created which puts credit within the reach of every man who can show a going business, and the supervision and control of the system is in the hands of a responsible agency of the Government itself. A trade tribunal has been created by which those who attempt unjust and oppressive practices in business can be brought to book. Labor has been made something else in the view of the law than a mercantile commodity—something human and linked with the privileges of life itself. The soil has everywhere been laid bare out of which monopoly is slowly to be eradicated. And undoubtedly the means by which credit has been set free is at the heart of all these things—is the key piece of the whole structure.

This is the more significant because of its opportuneness. It is brought to its final accomplishment just as it is most imperatively needed. The war, which has involved the whole of the heart of Europe, has made it necessary that the United States should mobilize its resources in the most effective way possible and make her credit and her usefulness good for the service of the whole world. It has created, too, special difficulties, peculiar situations to be dealt with, like the great embarrassment in selling our immense cotton crop, which all the world needs, but against which, for the time being, the markets of the world are in danger of being artificially shut. The situation the bankers of the country are meeting as far as possible in a businesslike fashion and in the spirit of the new time which is opening before us.

The railroads of the country are almost as much affected, not so much because their business is curtailed as because their credit is called in question by doubt as to their earning capacity. There is no other interest so central to the business welfare of the country as this. No doubt, in the light of the new day, with its new understandings, the problems of the railroads will also be met and dealt with in a spirit of candor and justice.

For the future is clear and bright with promise of the best things. While there was agitation and suspicion and distrust and bitter complaint of wrong, groups and classes were at war with one another, did not see that their interests were common, and suffered only when separated and brought into conflict. Fundamental wrongs once righted, as they may now easily and quickly be, all differences will clear away.

We are all in the same boat, though apparently we have forgotten it. We now know the port for which we are bound. We have and shall have, more and more as our new understandings ripen, a common discipline of patriotic purpose. We shall advance, and advance together, with a new spirit, a new enthusiasm, a new cordiality of spirit and co-operation. It is an inspiring prospect. Our task is henceforth to work, not for any single interest, but for all the interests of the country as a united whole.

The future will be very different from the past, which we shall presently look back upon, I venture to say, as if upon a bad dream. The future will be different in action and different in spirit, a time of healing because a time of just dealing and co-operation between men made equal before the law in fact as well as in name. I am speaking of this because the new banking system seems to me to symbolize all of it. The opening of the Federal Reserve banks seems to me to be the principal agency we have created for the emancipation we seek. The 16th of November, 1914, will be notable as marking the time when we were best able to realize just what had happened.

In the anxious times through which we have been passing, you have, my dear Mr. Secretary, been able to do many noteworthy things to strengthen and facilitate the business operations of the country. Henceforth, you have a new instrument at hand which will render many parts of your task easy. I heartily congratulate you upon the part you yourself have played in its conception and creation and upon the successful completion of the difficult work of organization.

A new day has dawned for the beloved country whose lasting prosperity and happiness we so earnestly desire.

DOCUMENT 55

"The Test Is Contained in the Record"

During 1915 and the early months of 1916 Wilson was under heavy pressure from more advanced progressives to adopt further reforms aimed at various economic and social ills. He was also well aware that in order to be re-elected he would need to attract the votes of those independents and progressive Republicans who had followed Roosevelt in 1912. Partly out of political expediency, partly because

Address accepting renomination, September 2, 1916, *Public Papers*, IV, 275–291.

he became convinced of the justice of some of the proposals, Wilson accepted and pushed through Congress a number of reforms that he had previously considered not within the proper purview of the federal government. Some of the measures, moreover, were clearly "class legislation" of the sort Wilson had criticized in the 1912 campaign. The President's address accepting renomination in 1916 placed particular stress on his reform record and revealed how much his thinking on governmental responsibilities had changed within a decade.

I cannot accept the leadership and responsibility which the National Democratic Convention has again, in such generous fashion, asked me to accept without first expressing my profound gratitude to the party for the trust it reposes in me after four years of fiery trial in the midst of affairs of unprecedented difficulty, and the keen sense of added responsibility with which this honour fills (I had almost said burdens) me as I think of the great issues of national life and policy involved in the present and immediate future conduct of our Government. I shall seek, as I have always sought, to justify the extraordinary confidence thus reposed in me by striving to purge my heart and purpose of every personal and of every misleading party motive and devoting every energy I have to the service of the nation as a whole, praying that I may continue to have the counsel and support of all forward-looking men at every turn of the difficult business.

For I do not doubt that the people of the United States will wish the Democratic Party to continue in control of the Government. They are not in the habit of rejecting those who have actually served them for those who are making doubtful and conjectural promises of service. Least of all are they likely to substitute those who promised to render them particular services and proved false to that promise for those who have actually rendered those very services.

Boasting is always an empty business, which pleases nobody but the boaster, and I have no disposition to boast of what the Democratic Party has accomplished. It has merely done its duty. It has merely fulfilled its explicit promises. But there can be no violation of good taste in calling attention to the manner in which those promises have been carried out or in adverting to the interesting fact that many of the things accomplished were what the opposition party had again and again promised to do but had left undone. Indeed that is manifestly part of the business of this year of reckoning and assessment. There is no means of judging the future except by assessing the past. Constructive action must be weighed against destructive comment and reaction. The Democrats either have or have not understood the varied interests of the country. The test is contained in the record.

What is that record? What were the Democrats called into power to do? What things had long waited to be done, and how did the Democrats do them? It is a record of extraordinary length and variety, rich in elements of many kinds, but consistent in principle throughout and susceptible of brief recital.

The Republican party was put out of power because of failure, practical failure and moral failure; because it had served special interests and not the country at large; because, under the leadership of its preferred and established guides, of those who still make its choices, it had lost touch with the thoughts and the needs of the Nation and was living in a past age and under a fixed illusion of greatness. It had framed tariff laws based upon a fear of foreign trade, a fundamental doubt as to American skill, enterprise, and capacity, and a very tender regard for the profitable privileges of those who had gained control of domestic markets and domestic credits; and yet had enacted antitrust laws which hampered the very things they meant to foster, which were stiff and inelastic, and in part unintelligible. It had permitted the country throughout the long period of its control to stagger from one financial crisis to another under the operation of a national banking law of its own framing which made stringency and panic certain and the control of the larger business operations of the country by the bankers of a few reserve centers inevitable; had made as if it meant to reform the law but had faint-heartedly failed in the attempt, because it could not bring itself to do the one thing necessary to make the reform genuine and effectual, namely, break up the control of small groups of bankers. It had been oblivious, or indifferent, to the fact that the farmers, upon whom the country depends for its food and in the last analysis for its prosperity, were without standing in the matter of commercial credit, without the protection of standards in their market transactions, and without systematic knowledge of the markets themselves; that the labourers of the country, the great army of men who man the industries it was professing to father and promote, carried their labour as a mere commodity to market, were subject to restraint by novel and drastic process in the courts, were without assurance of compensation for industrial accidents, without federal assistance in accommodating labour disputes, and without national aid or advice in finding the places and the industries in which their labour was most needed. The country had no national system of road construction and development. Little intelligent attention was paid to the army, and not enough to the navy. The other republics of America distrusted us, because they found that we thought first of the profits of American investors and only as an afterthought of impartial justice and helpful friendship. Its policy was provincial in all things; its purposes were out of harmony with the temper and purpose of the people and the timely development of the nation's interests.

So things stood when the Democratic Party came into power. How do they stand now? Alike in the domestic field and in the wide field of the commerce of the world, American business and life and industry have been set free to move as they never moved before.

The tariff has been revised, not on the principle of repelling foreign trade, but upon the principle of encouraging it, upon something like a footing of equality with our own in respect of the terms of competition, and a Tariff Board has been created whose function it will be to keep the relations of American with foreign business and industry under constant observation, for the guidance alike of our businessmen and of our Congress. American energies are now directed towards the markets of the world.

The laws against trusts have been clarified by definition, with a view to making it plain that they were not directed against big business but only against unfair business and the pretense of competition where there was none; and a Trade Commission has been created with powers of guidance and accommodation which have relieved business men of unfounded fears and set them upon the road of hopeful and confident enterprise.

By the Federal Reserve Act the supply of currency at the disposal of active business has been rendered elastic, taking its volume, not from a fixed body of investment securities, but from the liquid assets of daily trade; and these assets are assessed and accepted, not by distant groups of bankers in control of unavailable reserves, but by bankers at the many centers of local exchange who are in touch with local conditions everywhere.

Effective measures have been taken for the re-creation of an American merchant marine and the revival of the American carrying trade indispensable to our emancipation from the control which foreigners have so long exercised over the opportunities, the routes, and the methods of our commerce with other countries.

The Interstate Commerce Commission has been reorganized to enable it to perform its great and important functions more promptly and more efficiently. We have created, extended and improved the service of the parcels post.

So much we have done for business. What other party has understood the task so well or executed it so intelligently and energetically? What other party has attempted it at all? The Republican leaders, apparently, know of no means of assisting business but "protection." How to stimulate it and put it upon a new footing of energy and enterprise they have not suggested.

For the farmers of the country we have virtually created commercial credit, by means of the Federal Reserve Act and the Rural Credits Act. They now have the standing of other business men in the money market. We have successfully regulated speculation in "futures" and established standards in the marketing of grains. By an intelligent Warehouse Act we have assisted to make the standard crops available as never before both for systematic marketing and as a security for loans from the banks. We have greatly added to the work of neighborhood demonstration on the farm itself of improved methods of cultivation, and, through the intelligent extension of the functions of the Department of Agriculture, have made it possible for the farmer to learn systematically where his best markets are and how to get at them.

The workingmen of America have been given a veritable emancipation, by the legal recognition of a man's labour as part of his life, and not a mere marketable commodity; by exempting labour organizations from processes of the courts which treated their members like fractional parts of mobs and not like accessible and responsible individuals; by releasing our seamen from involuntary servitude; by making adequate provision for compensation for industrial accidents; by providing suitable machinery for mediation and conciliation in industrial disputes; and by putting the Federal Department of Labor at the disposal of the workingman when in search of work.

We have effected the emancipation of the children of the country by releasing them from hurtful labour. We have instituted a system of national aid in the building of highroads such as the country has been feeling after for a century. We have sought to equalize taxation by means of an equitable income tax. We have taken the steps that ought to have been taken at the outset to open up the resources of Alaska. We have provided for national defense upon a scale never before seriously proposed upon the responsibility of an entire political party. We have driven the tariff lobby from cover and obliged it to substitute solid argument for private influence.

This extraordinary recital must sound like a platform, a list of sanguine promises; but it is not. It is a record of promises made four years ago and now actually redeemed in constructive legislation.

These things must profoundly disturb the thoughts and confound the plans of those who have made themselves believe that the Democratic Party neither understood nor was ready to assist the business of the country in the great enterprises which it is its evident and inevitable destiny to undertake and carry through. The breaking up of the lobby must especially disconcert them; for it was through the lobby that they sought and were sure they had found the heart of things. The game of privilege can be played successfully by no other means.

This record must equally astonish those who feared that the Democratic Party had not opened its heart to comprehend the demands of social justice. We have in four years come very near to carrying out the platform of the Progressive Party as well as our own; for we also are progressives.

There is one circumstance connected with this program

which ought to be very plainly stated. It was resisted at
every step by the interests which the Republican Party
had catered to and fostered at the expense of the country,
and these same interests are now earnestly praying for a
reaction which will save their privileges, — for the restoration of their sworn friends to power before it is too late to
recover what they have lost. They fought with particular
desperation and infinite resourcefulness the reform of the
banking and currency system, knowing that to be the cita-
del of their control; and most anxiously are they hoping
and planning for the amendment of the Federal Reserve
Act by the concentration of control in a single bank which
the old familiar group of bankers can keep under their eye
and direction. But while the "big men" who used to write
the tariffs and command the assistance of the Treasury
have been hostile — all but a few with vision — the average
business man knows that he has been delivered, and that
the fear that was once every day in his heart that the men
who controlled credit and directed enterprise from the
committee rooms of Congress would crush him, is there no
more, and will not return — unless the party that consulted
only the "big men" should return to power — the party of
masterly inactivity and cunning resourcefulness in standing pat to resist change.

The Republican Party is just the party that *cannot* meet
the new conditions of a new age. It does not know the way
and it does not wish new conditions. It tried to break away
from the old leaders and could not. They still select its
candidates and dictate its policy, still resist change, still
hanker after the old conditions, still know no methods of encouraging business but the old methods. When it changes
its leaders and its purposes and brings its ideas up to date
it will have the right to ask the American people to give it
power again; but not until then. A new age, an age of revolutionary change, needs new purposes and new ideas.

In foreign affairs we have been guided by principles clearly conceived and consistently lived up to. Perhaps they have not been fully comprehended because they have hitherto governed international affairs only in theory, not in practice. They are simple, obvious, easily stated, and fundamental to American ideals.

We have been neutral not only because it was the fixed and traditional policy of the United States to stand aloof from the politics of Europe and because we had had no part either of action or of policy in the influences which brought on the present war, but also because it was manifestly our duty to prevent . . . , if it were possible, the indefinite extension of the fires of hate and desolation kindled by that terrible conflict and seek to serve mankind by reserving our strength and our resources for the anxious and difficult days of restoration and healing which must follow, when peace will have to build its house anew.

The rights of our own citizens of course became involved: that was inevitable. Where they did, this was our guiding principle: that property rights can be vindicated by claims for damages when the war is over, and no modern nation can decline to arbitrate such claims; but the fundamental rights of humanity cannot be. The loss of life is irreparable. Neither can direct violations of a nation's sovereignty await vindication in suits for damages. The nation that violates these essential rights must expect to be checked and called to account by direct challenge and resistance. It at once makes the quarrel in part our own. These are plain principles and we have never lost sight of them or departed from them, whatever the stress or the perplexity of circumstance or the provocation to hasty resentment. The record is clear and consistent throughout and stands distinct and definite for anyone to judge who wishes to know the truth about it.

The seas were not broad enough to keep the infection of the conflict out of our own politics. The passions and intrigues of certain active groups and combinations of men amongst us who were born under foreign flags injected the poison of disloyalty into our own most critical affairs, laid violent hands upon many of our industries, and subjected us to the shame of divisions of sentiment and purpose in which America was contemned and forgotten. It is part of the business of this year of reckoning and settlement to speak plainly and act with unmistakable purpose in rebuke of these things, in order that they may be forever hereafter impossible. I am the candidate of a party, but I am above all things else an American citizen. I neither seek the favour nor fear the displeasure of that small alien element amongst us which puts loyalty to any foreign power before loyalty to the United States.

While Europe was at war our own continent, one of our own neighbours, was shaken by revolution. In that matter, too, principle was plain and it was imperative that we should live up to it if we were to deserve the trust of any real partisan of the right as free men see it. We have professed to believe, and we do believe, that the people of small and weak states have the right to expect to be dealt with exactly as the people of big and powerful states would be. We have acted upon that principle in dealing with the people of Mexico.

Our recent pursuit of bandits into Mexican territory was no violation of that principle. We ventured to enter Mexican territory only because there were no military forces in Mexico that could protect our border from hostile attack and our own people from violence, and we have committed there no single act of hostility or interference even with the sovereign authority of the Republic of Mexico herself. It was a plain case of the violation of our own sovereignty which could not wait to be vindicated by damages and for which there was no other remedy. The authorities of Mexico were powerless to prevent it.

Many serious wrongs against the property, many irreparable wrongs against the persons, of Americans have been committed within the territory of Mexico herself during this confused revolution, wrongs which could not be effectually checked so long as there was no constituted power in Mexico which was in a position to check them. We could not act directly in that matter ourselves without denying Mexicans the right to any revolution at all which disturbed us and making the emancipation of her own people await our own interest and convenience.

For it is their emancipation that they are seeking— blindly, it may be, and as yet ineffectually, but with profound and passionate purpose and within their unquestionable right, apply what true American principle you will —any principle that an American would publicly avow. The people of Mexico have not been suffered to own their own country or direct their own institutions. Outsiders, men out of other nations and with interests too often alien to their own, have dictated what their privileges and opportunities should be and who should control their land, their lives, and their resources—some of them Americans, pressing for things they could never have got in their own country. The Mexican people are entitled to attempt their liberty from such influences; and so long as I have anything to do with the action of our great Government I shall do everything in my power to prevent anyone standing in their way. I know that this is hard for some persons to understand; but it is not hard for the plain people of the United States to understand. It is hard doctrine only for those who wish to get something for themselves out of Mexico. There are men, and noble women, too, not a few, of our own people, thank God! whose fortunes are invested in great properties in Mexico who yet see the case with true vision and assess its issues with true American feeling. The rest can be left for the present out of the reckoning until this enslaved people has had its day of struggle towards the light. I have heard no one who was free from such influences propose interference by the United States with the internal affairs of Mexico. Certainly no friend of the Mexican people has proposed it.

The people of the United States are capable of great sympathies and a noble pity in dealing with problems of this kind. As their spokesman and representative, I have tried to act in the spirit they would wish me to show. The people of Mexico are striving for the rights that are fundamental to life and happiness—fifteen million oppressed men, overburdened women, and pitiful children in virtual bondage in their own home of fertile lands and inexhaustible treasure! Some of the leaders of the revolution may often have been mistaken and violent and selfish, but the revolution itself was inevitable and is right. The unspeakable Huerta betrayed the very comrades he served, traitorously overthrew the government of which he was a trusted part, impudently spoke for the very forces that had driven his people to the rebellion with which he had pretended to sympathize. The men who overcame him and drove him out represent at least the fierce passion of reconstruction which lies at the very heart of liberty; and so long as they represent, however imperfectly, such a struggle for deliverance, I am ready to serve their ends when I can. So long as the power of recognition rests with me the Government of the United States will refuse to extend the hand of welcome to any one who obtains power in a sister republic by treachery and violence. No permanency can be given the affairs of any republic by a title based upon intrigue and assassination. I declared that to be the policy of this Administration within three weeks after I assumed the presidency. I here again vow it. I am more interested in the fortunes of oppressed men and pitiful women and children than in any property rights whatever. Mistakes I have no doubt made in this perplexing business, but not in purpose or object.

More is involved than the immediate destinies of Mexico and the relations of the United States with a distressed and distracted people. All America looks on. Test is now being made of us whether we be sincere lovers of popular liberty or not and are indeed to be trusted to respect national sovereignty among our weaker neighbours. We have undertaken these many years to play big brother to the republics of this hemisphere. This is the day of our test whether we mean, or have ever meant, to play that part for our own benefit wholly or also for theirs. Upon the outcome of that test (its outcome in their minds, not in ours) depends every relationship of the United States with Latin America, whether in politics or in commerce and enterprise. These are great issues and lie at the heart of the gravest tasks of the future, tasks both economic and political and very intimately inwrought with many of the most vital of the new issues of the politics of the world. The republics of America have in the last three years been drawing together in a new spirit of accommodation, mutual understanding, and cordial co-operation. Much of the politics of the world in the years to come will depend upon their relationships with one another. It is a barren and provincial statesmanship that loses sight of such things!

The future, the immediate future, will bring us squarely face to face with many great and exacting problems which will search us through and through whether we be able and ready to play the part in the world that we mean to play. It will not bring us into their presence slowly, gently, with ceremonious introduction, but suddenly and at once, the moment the war in Europe is over. They will be new problems, most of them; many will be old problems in a new setting and with new elements which we have never dealt with or reckoned the force and meaning of before. They will require for their solution new thinking, fresh courage and resourcefulness, and in some matters radical reconsiderations of policy. We must be ready to mobilize our resources alike of brains and of materials.

It is not a future to be afraid of. It is, rather, a future to stimulate and excite us to the display of the best powers that are in us. We may enter it with confidence when we are sure that we understand it — and we have provided ourselves already with the means of understanding it.

Look first at what it will be necessary that the nations of the world should do to make the days to come tolerable and fit to live and work in; and then look at our part in what is to follow and our own duty of preparation. For we must be prepared both in resources and in policy.

There must be a just and settled peace, and we here in America must contribute the full force of our enthusiasm and of our authority as a nation to the organization of that peace upon world-wide foundations that cannot easily be shaken. No nation should be forced to take sides in any quarrel in which its own honour and integrity and the fortunes of its own people are not involved; but no nation can any longer remain neutral as against any wilful disturbance of the peace of the world. The effects of war can no longer be confined to the areas of battle. No nation stands wholly apart in interest when the life and interests of all nations are thrown into confusion and peril. If hopeful and generous enterprise is to be renewed, if the healing and helpful arts of life are indeed to be revived when peace comes again, a new atmosphere of justice and friendship must be generated by means the world has never tried before. The nations of the world must unite in joint guarantees that whatever is done to disturb the whole world's life must first be tested in the court of the whole world's opinion before it is attempted.

These are the new foundations the world must build for itself, and we must play our part in the reconstruction, generously and without too much thought of our separate interests. We must make ourselves ready to play it intelligently, vigorously and well.

One of the contributions we must make to the world's peace is this: We must see to it that the people in our insular possessions are treated in their own lands as we would treat them here, and make the rule of the United States mean the same thing everywhere — the same justice, the same consideration for the essential rights of men.

Besides contributing our ungrudging moral and practical support to the establishment of peace throughout the world we must actively and intelligently prepare ourselves to do our full service in the trade and industry which are to sustain and develop the life of the nations in the days to come.

We have already been provident in this great matter and supplied ourselves with the instrumentalities of prompt adjustment. We have created, in the Federal Trade Commission, a means of inquiry and of accommodation in the field of commerce which ought both to co-ordinate the enterprises of our traders and manufacturers and to remove the barriers of misunderstanding and of a too technical interpretation of the law. In the new Tariff Commission we have added another instrumentality of observation and adjustment which promises to be immediately serviceable. The Trade Commission substitutes counsel and accommodation for the harsher processes of legal restraint, and the Tariff Commission ought to substitute facts for prejudices and theories. Our exporters have for some time had the advantage of working in the new light thrown upon foreign markets and opportunities of trade by the intelligent inquiries and activities of the Bureau of Foreign and Domestic Commerce which the Democratic Congress so wisely created in 1912. The Tariff Commission completes the machinery by which we shall be enabled to open up our legislative policy to the facts as they develop.

We can no longer indulge our traditional provincialism. We are to play a leading part in the world drama whether we wish it or not. We shall lend, not borrow; act for ourselves, not imitate or follow; organize and initiate, not peep about merely to see where we may get in.

We have already formulated and agreed upon a policy of law which will explicitly remove the ban now supposed to rest upon co-operation amongst our exporters in seeking and securing their proper place in the markets of the world. The field will be free, the instrumentalities at hand. It will only remain for the masters of enterprise amongst us to act in energetic concert, and for the Government of the United States to insist upon the maintenance throughout the world of those conditions of fairness and of evenhanded justice in the commercial dealings of the nations with one another upon which, after all, in the last analysis, the peace and ordered life of the world must ultimately depend.

At home also we must see to it that the men who plan and develop and direct our business enterprises shall enjoy definite and settled conditions of law, a policy accommodated to the freest progress. We have set the just and necessary limits. We have put all kinds of unfair competition under the ban and penalty of the law. We have barred monopoly. These fatal and ugly things being excluded, we must now quicken action and facilitate enterprise by every just means within our choice. There will be peace in the business world, and, with peace, revived confidence and life.

We ought both to husband and to develop our natural resources, our mines, our forests, our water power. I wish we could have made more progress than we have made in this vital matter; and I call once more, with the deepest earnestness and solicitude, upon the advocates of a careful and provident conservation, on the one hand, and the advocates of a free and inviting field for private capital, on the other, to get together in a spirit of genuine accommodation and agreement and set this great policy forward at once.

We must hasten and quicken the spirit and efficiency of labour throughout our whole industrial system by everywhere and in all occupations doing justice to the labourer, not only by paying a living wage but also by making all the conditions that surround labour what they ought to be. And we must do more than justice. We must safeguard life and promote health and safety in every occupation in which they are threatened or imperilled. That is more than justice, and better, because it is humanity and economy.

We must co-ordinate the railway systems of the country for national use, and must facilitate and promote their development with a view to that co-ordination and to their better adaptation as a whole to the life and trade and defense of the Nation. The life and industry of the country can be free and unhampered only if these articles are open, efficient, and complete.

Thus shall we stand ready to meet the future as circumstances and international policy effect their unfolding, whether the changes come slowly or come fast and without preface.

I have not spoken explicitly, gentlemen, of the platform adopted at St. Louis; but it has been implicit in all that I have said. I have sought to interpret its spirit and meaning. The people of the United States do not need to be assured now that the platform is a definite pledge, a practical program. We have proved to them that our promises are made to be kept.

We hold very definite ideals. We believe that the energy and initiative of our people have been too narrowly coached and superintended; that they should be set free, as we have set them free, to disperse themselves throughout the Nation; that they should not be concentrated in the hands of a few powerful guides and guardians, as our opponents have again and again, in effect if not in purpose, sought to concentrate them. We believe, moreover, — who that looks about him now with comprehending eye can fail to believe? — that the day of Little Americanism, with its narrow horizons, when methods of "protection" and industrial nursing were the chief study of our provincial statesmen, are past and gone and that a day of enterprise has at last dawned for the United States whose field is the wide world.

We hope to see the stimulus of that new day draw all America, the republics of both continents, on to a new life and energy and initiative in the great affairs of peace. We are Americans for Big America, and rejoice to look forward to the days in which America shall strive to stir the world without irritating it or drawing it on to new antagonisms, when the nations with which we deal shall at last come to see upon what deep foundations of humanity and justice our passion for peace rests, and when all mankind shall look upon our great people with a new sentiment of admiration, friendly rivalry and real affection, as upon a people who, though keen to succeed, seeks always to be at once generous and just and to whom humanity is dearer than profit or selfish power.

Upon this record and in the faith of this purpose we go to the country.

PART VI

Moral Diplomacy: Theory and Practice

A. THE MORAL BASIS
OF AMERICAN DIPLOMACY

Given his belief in a personal God whose inflexible
moral law provided the guide for human conduct, it
was natural that Wilson should seek to justify his own
actions in terms of moral precepts. Nowhere was this
more evident than in the field of foreign affairs, where
his knowledge and experience were limited and he
consequently felt the need of guidance. American
diplomacy, Wilson contended, should be based on
simple Christian morality. The United States coveted
no territory, he said; neither did it desire selfish advantage in its dealings with its neighbors. Wilson
recognized that as a great power the United States
had certain strategic, economic, and political interests
to consider, but in pursuing these interests he had an
overriding concern to adopt only policies that were
morally defensible.

Under Wilson the United States changed its historic
basis for the diplomatic recognition of other governments. Instead of basing recognition upon the easily
ascertained *de facto* holding of power, Wilson established a new standard, the legitimacy and moral fitness
of a regime to govern. The old nonmoral and comparatively simple test now became a more complex
.value judgment subject to Presidential whims and

popular pressures. While Wilson was not averse to promoting trade and investment opportunities for American businessmen, and while he was fully aware of the strategic importance of the Panama Canal and other American overseas bases, he was chiefly concerned with developing foreign policies that would set a new standard for enlightened civilized behavior and would thereby establish America's claim to the moral leadership of the world. The difficulty of this approach to foreign affairs, of course, was that not all problems could be resolved in terms of black-and-white moral judgments, nor was it always easy to distinguish between conflicting interests. As a result, Wilson's performance in foreign affairs did not always square with his rhetoric.

DOCUMENT 56

"No Spirit of Aggrandizement. . . ."

This stress on moralism characterized most of Wilson's public statements on foreign affairs, as this excerpt from a 1916 address on preparedness suggests.

. . . Let no man dare to say, if he would speak the truth, that the question of preparation for national defense is a question of war or of peace. If there is one passion more deep-seated in the hearts of our fellow countrymen than another, it is the passion for peace. No nation in the world ever more instinctively turned away from the thought of war than this Nation to which we belong. Partly because in the plenitude of its power, in the unrestricted area of its

---

Excerpt from address to the Railway Business Association, New York, January 27, 1916, *Public Papers*, IV, 7–9.

opportunities, it has found nothing to covet in the possession and power of other nations. There is no spirit of aggrandizement in America. There is no desire on the part of
any thoughtful and conscientious American man to take
one foot of territory from any other nation in the world. I
myself share to the bottom of my heart that profound love
for peace. I have sought to maintain peace against very
great and sometimes very unfair odds. I have had many a
time to use every power that was in me to prevent such a
catastrophe as war coming upon this country. It is not
permissible for any man to say that anxiety for the defense
of the Nation has in it the least tinge of desire for a power
that can be used to bring on war.

But, gentlemen, there is something that the American
people love better than they love peace. They love the
principles upon which their political life is founded. They
are ready at any time to fight for the vindication of their
character and of their honor. They will not at any time
seek the contest, but they will at no time cravenly avoid it;
because if there is one thing that the individual ought to
fight for, and that the Nation ought to fight for, it is the
integrity of its own convictions. We can not surrender our
convictions. I would rather surrender territory than surrender those ideals which are the staff of life of the soul
itself.

And because we hold certain ideals we have thought
that it was right that we should hold them for others as
well as for ourselves. America has more than once given
evidence of the generosity and disinterestedness of its
love of liberty. It has been willing to fight for the liberty of
others as well as for its own liberty. The world sneered
when we set out upon the liberation of Cuba, but the
world sneers no longer. The world now knows, what it was
then loath to believe, that a nation can sacrifice its own
interests and its own blood for the sake of the liberty and
happiness of another people. Whether by one process or

another, we have made ourselves in some sort the champions of free government and national sovereignty in both continents of this hemisphere; so that there are certain obligations which every American knows that we have undertaken.

The first and primary obligation is the maintenance of the integrity of our own sovereignty. That goes as of course. There is also the maintenance of our liberty to develop our political institutions without hindrance; and, last of all, there is the determination and the obligation to stand as the strong brother of all those in this hemisphere who mean to maintain the same principles and follow the same ideals of liberty. . . .

B. THE OPEN DOOR IN CHINA

DOCUMENT 57

"A Door of Friendship and Mutual Advantage"

Wilson fully approved of the Open Door Policy established at the turn of the century by Secretary of State John Hay. Indeed, Wilson wished to apply the open door principle to other areas of the world besides the Far East. He interpreted the policy somewhat more idealistically than his predecessors, however, contending that the open door implied genuine respect for the rights and well-being of the host country, not simply the advantage of the visitor. One of Wilson's first acts as President was to inform a group of

---

Public statement, March 18, 1913. Department of State, *Papers Relating to the Foreign Relations of the United States, 1913* (Washington, D.C.: Government Printing Office, 1920), pp. 170–171. Hereafter cited as *Foreign Relations*.

American bankers that the government could not endorse their participation in an international loan to China, because he felt that the terms were unfair to the Chinese. The President's explanation of his stand reflected both his moral approach to foreign policy and his idealistic view of the open door principle.

We are informed that at the request of the last administration a certain group of American bankers undertook to participate in the loan now desired by the Government of China (approximately $125,000,000). Our Government wished American bankers to participate along with the bankers of other nations, because it desired that the good will of the United States toward China should be exhibited in this practical way, that American capital should have access to that great country, and that the United States should be in a position to share with the other powers any political responsibilities that might be associated with the development of the foreign relations of China in connection with her industrial and commercial enterprises. The present administration has been asked by this group of bankers whether it would also request them to participate in the loan. The representatives of the bankers through whom the administration was approached declared that they would continue to seek their share of the loan under the proposed agreements only if expressly requested to do so by the Government. The administration has declined to make such request, because it did not approve the conditions of the loan or the implications of responsibility on its own part which it was plainly told would be involved in the request.

The conditions of the loan seem to us to touch very nearly the administrative independence of China itself, and this administration does not feel that it ought, even by implication, to be a party to those conditions. The responsibility on its part which would be implied in requesting the bankers to undertake the loan might conceivably go

the length in some unhappy contingency of forcible interference in the financial, and even the political, affairs of that
great oriental State, just now awakening to a consciousness
of its power and of its obligations to its people. The conditions include not only the pledging of particular taxes,
some of them antiquated and burdensome, to secure the
loan, but also the administration of those taxes by foreign
agents. The responsibility on the part of our Government
implied in the encouragement of a loan thus secured and
administered is plain enough and is obnoxious to the principles upon which the government of our people rests.

The Government of the United States is not only willing, but earnestly desirous, of aiding the great Chinese
people in every way that is consistent with their untrammeled development and its own immemorial principles.
The awakening of the people of China to a consciousness
of their responsibilities under free government is the most
significant, if not the most momentous, event of our generation. With this movement and aspiration the American
people are in profound sympathy. They certainly wish to
participate, and participate very generously, in the opening to the Chinese and to the use of the world the almost
untouched and perhaps unrivaled resources of China.

The Government of the United States is earnestly desirous of promoting the most extended and intimate trade
relationship between this country and the Chinese Republic. The present administration will urge and support the
legislative measures necessary to give American merchants, manufacturers, contractors, and engineers the
banking and other financial facilities which they now lack
and without which they are at a serious disadvantage as
compared with their industrial and commercial rivals. This
is its duty. This is the main material interest of its citizens
in the development of China. Our interests are those of the
open door—a door of friendship and mutual advantage.
This is the only door we care to enter.

DOCUMENT 58

"Champions of the Sovereign Rights of China. . . ."

Wilson took a similar stand in support of the open door principle in 1915 when Japan, taking advantage of the preoccupation of the European powers with the World War, made a series of Twenty-one Demands upon China for various special concessions. Like Roosevelt and Taft before him, Wilson was not prepared to defend the open door with force; but when he realized the nature of the Japanese demands he protested strongly and ultimately forced them to give way on the most objectionable proposals. In the course of the affair, Wilson and Secretary of State Bryan formally restated the United States' commitment to the open door principle and the preservation of the political and territorial integrity of the Republic of China. They thus strengthened a tradition that would contribute to an outbreak of war with Japan in 1941. Wilson's views were summarized in a letter to Bryan on April 14, 1915, at the height of the crisis. Paul S. Reinsch, a former professor of political science at the University of Wisconsin, was the American Minister at Peking.

. . . I am very uneasy about what is going on, as reported by Mr. Reinsch. . . . I wish that you might find an opportunity to express to the Japanese ambassador the grave concern we feel at hearing that his government is insisting upon the acquiescence of the Chinese government in the "Requests," because they are so clearly incompatible with the administrative independence and autonomy of the

---

Letter to William Jennings Bryan, April 14, 1915, in Department of State, *Papers Relating to the Foreign Relations of the United States: The Lansing Papers, 1914–1920* (Washington: Government Printing Office, 1939–1940), II, 416–417. Hereafter cited as *Lansing Papers*.

Chinese Empire and with the maintenance of the policy of an open door to the world.

In short, I feel that we should be as active as the circumstances permit in showing ourselves to be champions of the sovereign rights of China, now as always, though with no thought of seeking any special advantage or privilege for ourselves. In this way only can we make good this message to Reinsch.

Has Reinsch been told definitely that it is not true that we have acquiesced in any of Japan's demands? Count Okuma has been quoted in the newspaper despatches as saying that we had acquiesced.

C. MORALISTIC MEDDLING IN LATIN AMERICA

1. General Aims

DOCUMENT 59

"Just Government Rests Always upon the Consent of the Governed. . . ."

From the very start of his administration Wilson took a special interest in Latin American affairs, especially in the region of the Caribbean. Here, more than in any other part of the world, American military power was decisive. Here, too, the United States possessed important interests, notably the nearly completed Panama Canal, a protectorate and bases in Cuba, and valuable mineral and agricultural properties held by Americans in a number of countries. Accordingly, there were both the justification and the means for an active policy with respect to the area. Wilson had little patience with the political instability characteristic of many

---

Public statement, March 11, 1913. *Foreign Relations, 1913*, p. 7.

Latin American states, nor did he approve of the unrepresentative and sometimes despotic nature of some of the Latin American governments. Only a week after his inauguration the President issued a public statement setting forth his policy toward Latin America. He stressed his interest in orderly and constitutional government, and he warned that the United States would view with disfavor any illegal seizures of power. Clearly foreshadowed in this statement was Wilson's intent to apply a test of moral fitness as the basis for diplomatic recognition.

One of the chief objects of my administration will be to cultivate the friendship and deserve the confidence of our sister republics of Central and South America, and to promote in every proper and honorable way the interests which are common to the peoples of the two continents. I earnestly desire the most cordial understanding and co-operation between the peoples and leaders of America and, therefore, deem it my duty to make this brief statement.

Cooperation is possible only when supported at every turn by the orderly processes of just government based upon law, not upon arbitrary or irregular force. We hold, as I am sure all thoughtful leaders of republican government everywhere hold, that just government rests always upon the consent of the governed, and that there can be no freedom without order based upon law and upon the public conscience and approval. We shall look to make these principles the basis of mutual intercourse, respect, and helpfulness between our sister republics and ourselves. We shall lend our influence of every kind to the realization of these principles in fact and practice, knowing that disorder, personal intrigues, and defiance of constitutional rights weaken and discredit government and injure none so much as the people who are unfortunate enough to have their common life and their common affairs so tainted and disturbed. We can have no sympathy with those who seek to seize the power of government to advance their own personal interests or ambition. We are the friends of peace, but we know that there can be no lasting or stable peace in such circumstances. As friends, therefore, we shall prefer those who act in the interest of peace and honor, who protect private rights, and respect the restraints of constitutional provision. Mutual respect seems to us the indispensable foundation of friendship between states, as between individuals.

The United States has nothing to seek in Central and South America except the lasting interests of the peoples of the two continents, the security of governments intended for the people and for no special group or interest, and the development of personal and trade relationships between the two continents which shall redound to the profit and advantage of both and interfere with the rights and liberties of neither.

From these principles may be read so much of the future policy of this Government as it is necessary now to forecast, and in the spirit of these principles I may, I hope, be permitted with as much confidence as earnestness to extend to the Governments of all the Republics of America the hand of genuine disinterested friendship, and to pledge my own honor and the honor of my colleagues to every enterprise of peace and amity that a fortunate future may disclose.

DOCUMENT 60

"Morality and Not Expediency

Is the Thing That Must Guide Us. . . ."

Wilson saw a great trade potential in Latin America once the Panama Canal had brought about a reorganization of the

Address to the Southern Commercial Congress, October 27, 1913. *Public Papers,* III, 64–69.

world's arteries of commerce. But such trade must be carried on, he warned, upon mutually advantageous terms. The old-fashioned foreign concession, with its special rights backed by foreign power, was now out of date so far as Latin America was concerned. Wilson made his most eloquent expression of these views in a speech to the Southern Commercial Congress at Mobile, Alabama, in the fall of 1913. His remarks were aimed as much at British and other foreign investors as at American overseas interests.

It is with unaffected pleasure that I find myself here today. I once before had the pleasure, in another southern city, of addressing the Southern Commercial Congress. I then spoke of what the future seemed to hold in store for this region, which so many of us love and toward the future of which we all look forward with so much confidence and hope. But another theme directed me here this time. I do not need to speak of the South. She has, perhaps, acquired the gift of speaking for herself. I come because I want to speak of our present and prospective relations with our neighbors to the south. I deemed it a public duty, as well as a personal pleasure, to be here to express for myself and for the Government I represent the welcome we all feel to those who represent the Latin American States.

The future, ladies and gentlemen, is going to be very different for this hemisphere from the past. These States lying to the south of us, which have always been our neighbors, will now be drawn closer to us by innumerable ties, and, I hope, chief of all, by the tie of a common understanding of each other. Interest does not tie nations together; it sometimes separates them. But sympathy and understanding does unite them, and I believe that by the new route that is just about to be opened, while we physically cut two continents asunder, we spiritually unite them. It is a spiritual union which we seek.

I wonder if you realize, I wonder if your imaginations have been filled with the significance of the tides of com-

merce. Your governor alluded in very fit and striking terms
to the voyage of Columbus, but Columbus took his voyage
under compulsion of circumstances. Constantinople had
been captured by the Turks and all the routes of trade with
the East had been suddenly closed. If there was not a way
across the Atlantic to open those routes again, they were
closed forever, and Columbus set out not to discover
America, for he did not know that it existed, but to discover the eastern shores of Asia. He set sail for Cathay and
stumbled upon America. With that change in the outlook
of the world, what happened? England, that had been at
the back of Europe with an unknown sea behind her,
found that all things had turned as if upon a pivot and she
was at the front of Europe; and since then all the tides of
energy and enterprise that have issued out of Europe have
seemed to be turned westward across the Atlantic. But you
will notice that they have turned westward chiefly north of
the Equator and that it is the northern half of the globe
that has seemed to be filled with the media of intercourse
and of sympathy and of common understanding.

Do you not see now what is about to happen? These
great tides which have been running along parallels of
latitude will now swing southward athwart parallels of
latitude, and that opening gate at the Isthmus of Panama
will open the world to a commerce that she has not known
before, a commerce of intelligence, of thought and sympathy between North and South. The Latin American States,
which, to their disadvantage, have been off the main lines,
will now be on the main lines. I feel that these gentlemen
honoring us with their presence to-day will presently find
that some part, at any rate, of the center of gravity of the
world has shifted. Do you realize that New York, for example, will be nearer the western coast of South America
than she is now to the eastern coast of South America? Do
you realize that a line drawn northward parallel with the

greater part of the western coast of South America will run only about 150 miles west of New York? The great bulk of South America, if you will look at your globes (not at your Mercator's projection), lies eastward of the continent of North America. You will realize that when you realize that the canal will run southeast, not southwest, and that when you get into the Pacific you will be farther east than you were when you left the Gulf of Mexico. These things are significant, therefore, of this, that we are closing one chapter in the history of the world and are opening another, of great, unimaginable significance.

There is one peculiarity about the history of the Latin American States which I am sure they are keenly aware of. You hear of "concessions" to foreign capitalists in Latin America. You do not hear of concessions to foreign capitalists in the United States. They are not granted concessions. They are invited to make investments. The work is ours, though they are welcome to invest in it. We do not ask them to supply the capital and do the work. It is an invitation, not a privilege; and States that are obliged, because their territory does not lie within the main field of modern enterprise and action, to grant concessions are in this condition, that foreign interests are apt to dominate their domestic affairs, a condition of affairs always dangerous and apt to become intolerable. What these States are going to see, therefore, is an emancipation from the subordination, which has been inevitable, to foreign enterprise and an assertion of the splendid character which, in spite of these difficulties, they have again and again been able to demonstrate. The dignity, the courage, the self-possession, the self-respect of the Latin American States, their achievements in the face of all these adverse circumstances, deserve nothing but the admiration and applause of the world. They have had harder bargains driven with them in the matter of loans than any other peoples in the world.

Interest has been exacted of them that was not exacted of anybody else, because the risk was said to be greater; and then securities were taken that destroyed the risk — an admirable arrangement for those who were forcing the terms! I rejoice in nothing so much as in the prospect that they will now be emancipated from these conditions, and we ought to be the first to take part in assisting in that emancipation. I think some of these gentlemen have already had occasion to bear witness that the Department of State in recent months has tried to serve them in that wise. In the future they will draw closer and closer to us because of circumstances of which I wish to speak with moderation and, I hope, without indiscretion.

We must prove ourselves their friends, and champions upon terms of equality and honor. You cannot be friends upon any other terms than upon the terms of equality. You cannot be friends at all except upon the terms of honor. We must show ourselves friends by comprehending their interest whether it squares with our own interest or not. It is a very perilous thing to determine the foreign policy of a nation in the terms of material interest. It not only is unfair to those with whom you are dealing, but it is degrading as regards your own actions.

Comprehension must be the soil in which shall grow all the fruits of friendship, and there is a reason and a compulsion lying behind all this which is dearer than anything else to the thoughtful men of America. I mean the development of constitutional liberty in the world. Human rights, national integrity, and opportunity as against material interests — that, ladies and gentlemen, is the issue which we now have to face. I want to take this occasion to say that the United States will never again seek one additional foot of territory by conquest. She will devote herself to showing that she knows how to make honorable and fruitful use of the territory she has, and she must regard it as one of the duties of friendship to see that from no quar-

ter are material interests made superior to human liberty
and national opportunity. I say this, not with a single
thought that anyone will gainsay it, but merely to fix in our
consciousness what our real relationship with the rest of
America is. It is the relationship of a family of mankind
devoted to the development of true constitutional liberty.
We know that that is the soil out of which the best enterprise springs. We know that this is a cause which we are
making in common with our neighbors, because we have
had to make it for ourselves.

Reference has been made here to-day to some of the
national problems which confront us as a Nation. What is
at the heart of all our national problems? It is that we have
seen the hand of material interest sometimes about to
close upon our dearest rights and possessions. We have
seen material interests threaten constitutional freedom in
the United States. Therefore we will now know how to
sympathize with those in the rest of America who have to
contend with such powers, not only within their borders
but from outside their borders also.

I know what the response of the thought and heart of
America will be to the program I have outlined, because
America was created to realize a program like that. This is
not America because it is rich. This is not America because
it has set up for a great population great opportunities of
material prosperity. America is a name which sounds in
the ears of men everywhere as a synonym with individual
opportunity because a synonym of individual liberty. I
would rather belong to a poor nation that was free than to a
rich nation that had ceased to be in love with liberty. But
we shall not be poor if we love liberty, because the nation
that loves liberty truly sets every man free to do his best
and be his best, and that means the release of all the
splendid energies of a great people who think for themselves. A nation of employees cannot be free any more
than a nation of employers can be.

In emphasizing the points which must unite us in sympathy and in spiritual interest with the Latin American peoples we are only emphasizing the points of our own life, and we should prove ourselves untrue to our own traditions if we proved ourselves untrue friends to them.

Do not think, therefore, gentlemen, that the questions of the day are mere questions of policy and diplomacy. They are shot through with the principles of life. We dare not turn from the principle that morality and not expediency is the thing that must guide us and that we will never condone iniquity because it is most convenient to do so. It seems to me that this is a day of infinite hope, of confidence in a future greater than the past has been, for I am fain to believe that in spite of all the things that we wish to correct the nineteenth century that now lies behind us has brought us a long stage toward the time when, slowly ascending the tedious climb that leads to the final uplands, we shall get our ultimate view of the duties of mankind. We have breasted a considerable part of that climb and shall presently—it may be in a generation or two—come out upon those great heights where there shines unobstructed the light of the justice of God.

2. Venezuela

DOCUMENT 61

"This Scoundrel Ought to Be Put Out"

Wilson's concern over the moral fitness of nearby Latin American regimes often led him to contemplate, and some-

---

Letter to Robert Lansing, February 16, 1918, in Baker, *Wilson, Life and Letters*, VII, 550.

times to consummate, unwise interference in the internal affairs of the country concerned, as when he advised Secretary of State Robert Lansing of his contempt for President Gomez of Venezuela.

I have read this Memorandum with the greatest concern, as I have also the many recent communications from our Minister in Venezuela. This scoundrel ought to be put out. Can you think of any way in which we can do it that would not upset the peace of Latin America more than letting him alone will?

3. Costa Rica

DOCUMENT 62

Morality as a Basis for Diplomatic Recognition

In January, 1917, Federico A. Tinoco, the Costa Rican Minister of War, overthrew the government and established himself as president. Wilson declined to recognize the Tinoco regime, and he persisted in this course despite pressure from the United Fruit Company and others — including, surprisingly, former Secretary of State William Jennings Bryan.

I value your long letter about the Costa Rican situation but beg to assure you in reply that no item of foreign policy has received more frequent or careful consideration by me or has been looked at from more angles, and I feel obliged to retain immovably my position that I will not and cannot

---

Letter to William Jennings Bryan, July 23, 1918, in Baker, *Wilson, Life and Letters*, VIII, 291–292.

recognize a government which originated in individual unconstitutional action. This is a test case and I am sure that my yielding in it would break down the whole morale of our relations, particularly with Central America.

I cannot tell you how many persons have been to me and laid the various aspects of this matter before me. The latest was Mr. Samuel Untermyer, who very earnestly urged the same course upon me that you are urging. But behind it all, my dear Mr. Bryan, there are contending business interests in the United States which we ought to be very careful to disappoint in what is nothing less than an attempt on their part to use the Government of Costa Rica for their own benefit.

I am always sorry to differ from you in any matter of importance, but this is a matter in which I feel bound both by principle and expediency.

4. *Intervention in the Dominican Republic and Haiti*

DOCUMENT 63

The Wilson Plan

Abhorring revolutionary strife and illegal seizure of power, Wilson naturally took a dim view of the chronic political chaos that existed in the two neighboring republics on the island of Hispaniola, the Dominican Republic and Haiti. In the Dominican Republic, Wilson's first impulse was to support the regime of President José Bordas Valdés, but he soon wavered in the face of Bordas' arbitrary treatment of his political foes and his evident intention to perpetuate

---

Arthur S. Link, *Wilson: The Struggle for Neutrality, 1914–1915* (Princeton, N.J.: Princeton University Press, 1960), pp. 512–514.

himself in power by means of rigged elections. By the spring of 1914 a revolt had broken out against Bordas, and it was clear that he neither deserved American support nor could survive without it. To prevent further disorder and bloodshed, early in August Wilson dispatched a commission to Santo Domingo with instructions to restore peace on the basis of a plan drafted by Wilson himself. Though it represented a remarkable interference in the internal affairs of a sovereign state, the Wilson Plan, backed by the threat of United States intervention, secured an uneasy peace for the next year and a half. In May of 1916, however, a new revolution broke out, and this time Wilson felt obliged to send American Marines to restore order, thus launching what became a full-fledged military occupation of the country. The Wilson Plan of August 1914 provides a revealing illustration of the distance Wilson was prepared to go in teaching Latin Americans to govern themselves.

The Government of the United States desires nothing for itself from the Dominican Republic and no concessions or advantages for its citizens which are not accorded citizens of other countries. It desires only to prove its sincere and disinterested friendship for the republic and its people and to fulfill its responsibilities as the friend to whom in such crises as the present all the world looks to guide Santo Domingo out of its difficulties.

It, therefore, makes the following earnest representations not only to the existing de facto Government of the Dominican Republic, but also to all who are in any way responsible for the present posture of affairs there:

I. It warns everyone concerned that it is absolutely imperative that the present hostilities should cease and that all who are concerned in them should disperse to their several homes, disbanding the existing armed forces and returning to the peaceful occupations upon which the welfare of the people of the republic depends. This is necessary, and necessary at once. Nothing can be successfully accomplished until this is done.

II. It is also necessary that there should be an immediate reconstitution of political authority in the republic. To this end the Government of the United States very solemnly advises all concerned with the public affairs of the republic to adopt the following plan.

(1) Let all those who have any pretensions to be chosen President of the Republic and who can make any sufficient show of exercising a recognized leadership and having an acknowledged following agree upon some responsible and representative man to act as Provisional President of the Republic, it being understood that Mr. Bordas will relinquish his present position and authority. If these candidates can agree in this matter, the Government of the United States will recognize and support the man of their choice as Provisional President. If they cannot agree, the Government of the United States will itself name a Provisional President, sustain him in the assumption of office, and support him in the exercise of his temporary authority. The Provisional President will not be a candidate for President.

(2) At the earliest feasible date after the establishment and recognition of the Provisional Government thus established let elections for a regular President and Congress be held under the authority and direction of the Provisional President, who will, it must of course be understood, exercise during his tenure of office the full powers of President of the Republic; but let it be understood that the Government of the United States will send representatives of its own choosing to observe the election throughout the republic and that it will expect those observers not only to be accorded a courteous welcome but also to be accorded the freest opportunities to observe the circumstances and processes of the election.

(3) Let it be understood that if the United States Government is satisfied that these elections have been free and fair and carried out under conditions which enable the people of the republic to express their real choice, it will recognize the President and Congress thus chosen as the legitimate and constitutional Government of the Republic and will support them in the exercise of their functions and authority in every way it can. If it should not be satisfied that elections of the right kind have been held, let it be understood that another election will be held at which the mistakes observed will be corrected.

III. A regular and constitutional government having thus been set up, the Government of the United States would feel at liberty thereafter to insist that revolutionary movements cease and that all subsequent changes in the Government of the Republic be effected by the peaceful processes provided in the Dominican Constitution. By no other course can the Government of the United States fulfill its treaty obligations with Santo Domingo or its tacitly conceded obligations as the nearest friend of Santo Domingo in her relations with the rest of the world.

DOCUMENT 64

"Nothing for It But to Take the Bull by the Horns and Restore Order"

In neighboring Haiti the situation deteriorated even more quickly into revolutionary chaos, resulting finally in such bloody anarchy in the summer of 1915 that Wilson felt

---

Excerpts from letter to Robert Lansing, August 4, 1915, in Link, *Wilson: The Struggle for Neutrality*, p. 536.

constrained to order American sailors to occupy the capital city of Port-au-Prince on July 28. Wilson's decision to proceed with a more ambitious program of pacification in Haiti was outlined in a letter to Secretary of State Lansing on August 4, 1915. Within a few weeks United States forces had occupied the port towns and taken control of most of the interior of the country.

. . . These are serious matters, and my own judgment is as much perplexed as yours.

I fear we have not the legal authority to do what we apparently ought to do; and that if we did do what is necessary it would constitute a case very much like that of Mr. Roosevelt's action in Santo Domingo, and have very much the same issue.

I suppose there is nothing for it but to take the bull by the horns and restore order. A long programme . . . involves legislation and the cooperation of the Senate in treaty-making, and must therefore await the session of our Congress.

In the meantime this is plain to me:

**1. We must send to Port au Prince a force sufficient to absolutely control the city not only but also the country immediately about it from which it draws its food. I would be obliged if you would ascertain from the Secretary of the Navy whether he has such a force available that can reach there soon.

2. We must let the present [Haitian] Congress know that we will protect it but that we will not recognize any action on its part which does not put men in charge of affairs whom we can trust to handle and put an end to revolution.

3. We must give all who now have authority there or desire to have it or who think they have it or [are] about to have it to understand that we shall take steps to prevent

the payment of debts contracted to finance revolution: in other words, that we consider it our duty to insist on constitutional government there and will, if necessary (that is, if they force us to it as the only way) take charge of elections and see that a real government is erected which we can support. . . .

**This will probably involve making the city authorities virtually subordinate to our commanders. They may hand the city government over to us voluntarily.

5. *The Mexican Quagmire*

DOCUMENT 65

United States Purposes in Mexico

Wilson's moral diplomacy met its most serious test in Mexico, where an uprising led by a moderate reformer, Francisco I. Madero, had toppled the dictatorial regime of aged Porfirio Díaz in 1911, ushering in what would turn out to be a decade of revolutionary strife. Only a month before Wilson was inaugurated, General Victoriano Huerta, heading a conservative counterrevolution, seized power by overthrowing and murdering President Madero. Wilson declined to recognize Huerta and sought to force him from office by moral and economic pressure. He made plain the objectives of this "watchful waiting" policy in a circular note sent to other interested governments on November 24, 1913.

Arthur S. Link, *Wilson: The New Freedom* (Princeton, N. J.: Princeton University Press, 1956), pp. 386–387.

OUR PURPOSES IN MEXICO

The purpose of the United States is solely and singly to secure peace and order in Central America by seeing to it that the processes of self-government there are not interrupted or set aside.

Usurpations like that of General Huerta menace the peace and development of America as nothing else could. They not only render the development of ordered self-government impossible; they also tend to set law entirely aside, to put the lives and fortunes of citizens and foreigners alike in constant jeopardy, to invalidate contracts and concessions in any way the usurper may devise for his own profit, and to impair both the national credit and all the foundations of business, domestic or foreign.

It is the purpose of the United States, therefore, to discredit and defeat such usurpations whenever they occur. The present policy of the Government of the United States is to isolate General Huerta entirely; to cut him off from foreign sympathy and aid and from domestic credit, whether moral or material, and so to force him out.

It hopes and believes that isolation will accomplish this end, and shall await the results without irritation or impatience. If General Huerta does not retire by force of circumstances, it will become the duty of the United States to use less peaceful means to put him out. It will give other governments notice in advance of each affirmative or aggressive step it has in contemplation, should it unhappily become necessary to move actively against the usurper; but no such step seems immediately necessary.

Its fixed resolve is, that no such interruptions of civil order shall be tolerated so far as it is concerned. Each conspicuous instance in which usurpations of this kind are prevented will render their recurrence less likely, and in the end a state of affairs will be secured in Mexico and elsewhere upon this continent which will assure the peace of America and the untrammeled development of its economic and social relations with the rest of the world.

Beyond this fixed purpose the Government of the United States will not go. It will not permit itself to seek any special or exclusive advantages in Mexico or elsewhere for its own citizens, but will seek, here as elsewhere, to show itself the consistent champion of the open door.

In the meantime it is making every effort that the circumstances permit to safeguard foreign lives and property in Mexico and is making the lives and fortunes of the subjects of other governments as much its concern as the lives and fortunes of its own citizens.

DOCUMENT 66

The Tampico Affair

Wilson's "watchful waiting" policy of moral and economic pressure did not greatly impress General Huerta, nor did it appreciably strengthen his opponents, the Constitutionalists of northern Mexico led by General Venustiano Carranza. By the spring of 1914, therefore, Wilson was ready to take more decisive action to effect the removal of the usurper Huerta. He found an excuse in the arrest and brief detention of a U.S. Navy boat crew by Huertista forces at Tampico, and he decided to back the demand of Admiral Henry T. Mayo for an apology and salute to the American flag. When Huerta declined to give such a salute unless it were returned, which would be tantamount to recognition, Wilson went before Congress on April 20, 1914, to ask for authority to use armed force against the Huerta regime. The next day, while Congress was still debating his request, the President learned that a large shipment of munitions for the

---

Excerpts from special address to Congress, April 20, 1914, *Public Papers*, III, 99, 100, and 101–102.

Huerta forces was due to be landed momentarily at Veracruz. Because these weapons might well be used against
American troops, Wilson ordered the immediate occupation of Veracruz by U.S. Navy forces in the vicinity, without
waiting for Congressional sanction. By April 22 the city was
in American hands, though at a cost of more than 400 Mexican and American casualties.

GENTLEMEN OF THE CONGRESS:

It is my duty to call your attention to a situation which
has arisen in our dealings with Gen. Victoriano Huerta at
Mexico City which calls for action, and to ask your advice
and co-operation in acting upon it.

On April 9 a Paymaster of the U.S.S. *Dolphin* landed at
the Iturbide bridge landing at Tampico with a whaleboat
and boat's crew to take off certain supplies needed by his
ship, and while engaged in loading the boat was arrested
by an officer and squad of men of the army of General
Huerta. . . .. Admiral Mayo regarded the arrest as so serious an affront that he was not satisfied with the apologies
offered, but demanded that the flag of the United States be
saluted with special ceremony by the military commander
of the port. . . .

The manifest danger of such a situation was that such
offenses might grow from bad to worse until something
happened of so gross and intolerable a sort as to lead directly and inevitably to armed conflict. It was necessary
that the apologies of General Huerta and his representatives should go much further, that they should be such as
to attract the attention of the whole population to their
significance, and such as to impress upon General Huerta
himself the necessity of seeing to it that no further occasion for explanations and professed regrets should arise. I,
therefore, felt it my duty to sustain Admiral Mayo in the
whole of his demand and to insist that the flag of the

United States should be saluted in such a way as to indicate a new spirit and attitude on the part of the Heurtistas.

Such a salute General Huerta has refused, and I have come to ask your approval and support in the course I now purpose to pursue.

This Government can, I earnestly hope, in no circumstances be forced into war with the people of Mexico. Mexico is torn by civil strife. If we are to accept the tests of its own Constitution, it has no government. General Huerta has set his power up in the City of Mexico, such as it is, without right and by methods for which there can be no justification. Only part of the country is under his control.

If armed conflict should unhappily come as a result of his attitude of personal resentment toward this Government, we should be fighting only General Huerta and those who adhere to him and give him their support, and our object would be only to restore to the people of the distracted republic the opportunity to set up again their own laws and their own government.

But I earnestly hope that war is not now in question. I believe that I speak for the American people when I say that we do not desire to control in any degree the affairs of our sister republic. Our feeling for the people of Mexico is one of deep and genuine friendship, and everything that we have so far done or refrained from doing has proceeded from our desire to help them, not to hinder or embarrass them. We would not wish even to exercise the good offices of friendship without their welcome and consent.

The people of Mexico are entitled to settle their own domestic affairs in their own way, and we sincerely desire to respect their right. The present situation need have none of the grave complications of interference if we deal with it promptly, firmly, and wisely.

No doubt I could do what is necessary in the circumstances to force respect for our Government without recourse to the Congress, and yet not exceed my constitutional power as President; but I do not wish to act in a matter possibly of so grave consequence except in close conference and co-operation with both the Senate and House. I therefore come to ask your approval that I should use the armed forces of the United States in such ways and to such an extent as may be necessary to obtain from General Huerta and his adherents the fullest recognition of the rights and dignity of the United States, even amid the distressing conditions now unhappily obtaining in Mexico.

There can in what we do be no thought of aggression or of selfish aggrandizement. We seek to maintain the dignity and authority of the United States only because we wish always to keep our great influence unimpaired for the uses of liberty, both in the United States and wherever else it may be employed for the benefit of mankind.

DOCUMENT 67

"I Am for the Eighty Per Cent!"

The Veracruz landing probably contributed to the abdication of Huerta in the summer of 1914 and his replacement by a Constitutionalist government headed by Carranza. But Wilson's intervention was unpopular in the United States and was thoroughly resented by all factions in Mexico. Accordingly, the President felt obliged to stress repeatedly that his concern was for the liberty and well-being of the submerged mass of the Mexican people.

. . . There is one thing I have got a great enthusiasm about, I might almost say a reckless enthusiasm, and that is human liberty. The Governor has just now spoken about watchful waiting in Mexico. I want to say a word about

Excerpt from Jackson Day address, Indianapolis, Ind., January 8, 1915, *Public Papers*, III, 247–249.

Mexico, or not so much about Mexico as about our attitude towards Mexico. I hold it as a fundamental principle, and so do you, that every people has the right to determine its own form of government; and until this recent revolution in Mexico, until the end of the Diaz reign, eighty per cent. of the people of Mexico never had a "look in" in determining who should be their governors or what their government should be. Now, I am for the eighty per cent! It is none of my business, and it is none of your business, how long they take in determining it. It is none of my business, and it is none of yours, how they go about the business. The country is theirs. The Government is theirs. The liberty, if they can get it, and Godspeed them in getting it, is theirs. And so far as my influence goes while I am President nobody shall interfere with them.

That is what I mean by a great emotion, the great emotion of sympathy. Do you suppose that the American people are ever going to count a small amount of material benefit and advantage to people doing business in Mexico against the liberties and the permanent happiness of the Mexican people? Have not European nations taken as-long as they wanted and spilt as much blood as they pleased in settling their affairs, and shall we deny that to Mexico because she is weak? No, I say! I am proud to belong to a strong nation that says, "This country which we could crush shall have just as much freedom in her own affairs as we have." If I am strong, I am ashamed to bully the weak. In proportion to my strength is my pride in withholding that strength from the oppression of another people. And I know when I speak these things, not merely from the generous response with which they have just [been] met from you, but from my long-time knowledge of the American people, that that is the sentiment of this great people. With all due respect to editors of great newspapers, I have to say to them that I seldom take my opinion of the American people from their editorials. So that when some great dailies not very far from where I am temporarily residing thundered with rising scorn at watchful waiting, Woodrow sat back in his chair and chuckled, knowing that he laughs best who laughs last—knowing, in short, what were the temper and principles of the American people. If I did not at least think I knew, I would emigrate, because I would not be satisfied to stay where I am. There may come a time when the American people have to judge whether I know what I am talking about or not, but at least for two years more I am free to think that I do, with a great comfort in immunity in the time being. . . .

DOCUMENT 68

"To Check What Is Futile
and Promote What Promises
Genuine Reform and Settled Peace"

The Constitutionalists soon divided into two factions, one headed by Carranza and the other led by his ablest general, Francisco "Pancho" Villa. Wilson had never liked Carranza's stubborn independence and had not forgiven his criticism of the Veracruz landing. The President was thus inclined to throw American support behind Villa, who appeared both more cooperative and more committed to social reform. In February 1915, the President dispatched a special agent, Duval West of San Antonio, Texas, to investigate the confused situation in Mexico. His instructions to West revealed that he was still determined to try to influence Mexican developments.

Letter to Duval West, February 5, 1915, in Wilson MSS, Library of Congress.

I do not believe that it is necessary for me to give you detailed suggestions as to your mission in my behalf in Mexico, for I know you have talked the matter over, I hope quite fully, with the Secretary of State.

My wish in general is this: To have you meet and, as far as possible, assess the character and purposes of the principle [*sic*] men down there of the several groups and factions, in the hope that you may be able to form a definite idea not only as to their relative strength and their relative prospects of success, but also as to their real purposes.

Above all, I want to find out just what prospects of a settlement there are and what sort of settlement it would be likely to be. If the settlement contemplated is not seriously intended for the benefit of the common people of the country, if the plans and ambitions of the leaders center upon themselves and not upon the people they are trying to represent, of course it will not be a permanent settlement but will simply lead to further distress and disorder. I am very anxious to know just what the moral situation is, therefore, and just what it behooves us to do to check what is futile and promote what promises genuine reform and settled peace. . . .

DOCUMENT 69

"To Help Mexico Save Herself
and Serve her People"

West's report of a Mexico devastated by hopeless civil war persuaded Wilson to issue a blunt warning on June 2, 1915, to the various Mexican factions. He admonished them to

Statement to the press, June 2, 1915, *Public Papers*, III, 339–340.

get together behind some responsible government or face United States intervention to restore order. The stage was now set for General John J. Pershing's futile and frustrating Punitive Expedition of 1916–1917.

FOR more than two years revolutionary conditions have existed in Mexico. The purpose of the revolution was to rid Mexico of men who ignored the constitution of the Republic and used their power in contempt of the rights of its people; and with these purposes the people of the United States instinctively and generously sympathized. But the leaders of the revolution, in the very hour of their success, have disagreed and turned their arms against one another. All professing the same objects, they are nevertheless unable or unwilling to co-operate. A central authority at Mexico City is no sooner set up than it is undermined and its authority denied by those who were expected to support it. Mexico is apparently no nearer a solution of her tragical troubles than she was when the revolution was first kindled. And she has been swept by civil war as if by fire. Her crops are destroyed, her fields lie unseeded, her work cattle are confiscated for the use of the armed factions, her people flee to the mountains to escape being drawn into unavailing bloodshed, and no man seems to see or lead the way to peace and settled order. There is no proper protection either for her own citizens or for the citizens of other nations resident and at work within her territory. Mexico is starving and without a government.

In these circumstances the people and Government of the United States cannot stand indifferently by and do nothing to serve their neighbor. They want nothing for themselves in Mexico. Least of all do they desire to settle her affairs for her, or claim any right to do so. But neither do they wish to see utter ruin come upon her, and they deem it their duty as friends and neighbors to lend any aid they properly can to any instrumentality which promises to be effective in bringing about a settlement which will embody the real objects of the revolution—constitutional government and the rights of the people. Patriotic Mexicans are sick at heart and cry out for peace and for every self-sacrifice that may be necessary to procure it. Their people cry out for food and will presently hate as much as they fear every man, in their country or out of it, who stands between them and their daily bread.

It is time, therefore, that the Government of the United States should frankly state the policy which in these extraordinary circumstances it becomes its duty to adopt. It must presently do what it has not hitherto done or felt at liberty to do, lend its active moral support to some man or group of men, if such may be found, who can rally the suffering people of Mexico to their support in an effort to ignore, if they cannot unite, the warring factions of the country, return to the constitution of the Republic so long in abeyance, and set up a government at Mexico City which the great powers of the world can recognize and deal with, a government with which the program of the revolution will be a business and not merely a platform. I, therefore, publicly and very solemnly, call upon the leaders of faction in Mexico to act, to act together, and to act promptly for the relief and redemption of their prostrate country. I feel it to be my duty to tell them that, if they cannot accommodate their differences and unite for this great purpose within a very short time, this Government will be constrained to decide what means should be employed by the United States in order to help Mexico save herself and serve her people.

PART VII

Neutrality and Preparedness

A. AMERICAN NEUTRALITY: GENERAL GOALS

The most serious test of Wilson's diplomacy came with the outbreak of a general European war in August of 1914. The President's immediate reaction was the same as that of most Americans—disbelief and profound shock over the senseless destruction and slaughter, and confident determination that the United States should remain outside the struggle. But the American melting pot had only partially digested the recent waves of immigrants, and many Americans still had strong ties to the various nations now engaged in a life-and-death struggle on the battlefields of Europe. Wilson accordingly set for his countrymen a difficult task—to be neutral in thought as well as in deed.

DOCUMENT 70

"Be Neutral in Fact as Well as in Name. . . ."

MY FELLOW COUNTRYMEN: I suppose that every thoughtful man in America has asked himself, during these last troubled weeks, what influence the European war may exert upon the United States, and I take the liberty of addressing

---

Appeal to the country, presented in the Senate, August 19, 1914, *Public Papers*, III, 157–159.

a few words to you in order to point out that it is entirely within our own choice what its effects upon us will be and to urge very earnestly upon you the sort of speech and conduct which will best safeguard the Nation against distress and disaster.

The effect of the war upon the United States will depend upon what American citizens say and do. Every man who really loves America will act and speak in the true spirit of neutrality, which is the spirit of impartiality and fairness and friendliness to all concerned. The spirit of the Nation in this critical matter will be determined largely by what individuals and society and those gathered in public meetings do and say, upon what newspapers and magazines contain, upon what ministers utter in their pulpits, and men proclaim as their opinions on the street.

The people of the United States are drawn from many nations, and chiefly from the nations now at war. It is natural and inevitable that there should be the utmost variety of sympathy and desire among them with regard to the issues and circumstances of the conflict. Some will wish one nation, others another, to succeed in the momentous struggle. It will be easy to excite passion and difficult to allay it. Those responsible for exciting it will assume a heavy responsibility, responsibility for no less a thing than that the people of the United States, whose love of their country and whose loyalty to its Government should unite them as Americans all, bound in honor and affection to think first of her and her interests, may be divided in camps of hostile opinion, hot against each other, involved in the war itself in impulse and opinion if not in action.

Such divisions amongst us would be fatal to our peace of mind and might seriously stand in the way of the proper performance of our duty as the one great nation at peace, the one people holding itself ready to play a part of impartial mediation and speak the counsels of peace and accommodation, not as a partisan, but as a friend.

I venture, therefore, my fellow countrymen, to speak a solemn word of warning to you against that deepest, most subtle, most essential breach of neutrality which may spring out of partisanship, out of passionately taking sides. The United States must be neutral in fact as well as in name during these days that are to try men's souls. We must be impartial in thought as well as in action, must put a curb upon our sentiments as well as upon every transaction that might be construed as a preference of one party to the struggle before another.

My thought is of America. I am speaking, I feel sure, the earnest wish and purpose of every thoughtful American that this great country of ours, which is, of course, the first in our thoughts and in our hearts, should show herself in this time of peculiar trial a Nation fit beyond others to exhibit the fine poise of undisturbed judgment, the dignity of self-control, the efficiency of dispassionate action; a Nation that neither sits in judgment upon others nor is disturbed in her own counsels and which keeps herself fit and free to do what is honest and disinterested and truly serviceable for the peace of the world.

Shall we not resolve to put upon ourselves the restraints which will bring to our people the happiness and the great and lasting influence for peace we covet for them?

DOCUMENT 71

No Abridgment of American Rights

Wilson believed that the United States, as the most powerful neutral nation, must lead the fight to compel the belligerents to respect the neutral rights of the non-warring world.

Letter to William J. Stone, February 24, 1916, *Public Papers*, IV, 122–124.

There could be no yielding or compromise on any of these rights, he argued, or the United States would lose respect and international law would be reduced to a meaningless shambles. But Wilson in fact reacted more strongly against German submarine activity than against the less spectacular British violations. His general views were summed up early in 1916 in an open letter to Senator William J. Stone, the chairman of the Senate Foreign Relations Committee. The letter was part of a successful effort to head off Congressional passage of the Gore-McLemore Resolution, which warned American citizens not to travel on armed belligerent ships. Wilson was opposed to such an abridgment of the right of Americans to travel in safety on the high seas on any passenger or merchant ship.

I very warmly appreciate your kind and frank letter of to-day, and feel that it calls for an equally frank reply.

You are right in assuming that I shall do everything in my power to keep the United States out of war. I think the country will feel no uneasiness about my course in that respect. Through many anxious months I have striven for that object, amidst difficulties more manifold than can have been apparent upon the surface; and so far I have succeeded. I do not doubt that I shall continue to succeed. The course which the central European powers have announced their intention of following in the future with regard to undersea warfare seems for the moment to threaten insuperable obstacles, but its apparent meaning is so manifestly inconsistent with explicit assurances recently given us by those powers with regard to their treatment of merchant vessels on the high seas that I must believe that explanations will presently ensue which will put a different aspect upon it. We have had no reason to question their good faith or their fidelity to their promises in the past, and I, for one, feel confident that we shall have none in the future.

But in any event our duty is clear. No nation, no group of nations, has the right while war is in progress to alter or disregard the principles which all nations have agreed upon in mitigation of the horrors and sufferings of war; and if the clear rights of American citizens should ever unhappily be abridged or denied by any such action, we should, it seems to me, have in honor no choice as to what our own course should be.

For my own part, I can not consent to any abridgment of the rights of American citizens in any respect. The honor and self-respect of the nation is involved. We covet peace, and shall preserve it at any cost but the loss of honor. To forbid our people to exercise their rights for fear we might be called upon to vindicate them would be a deep humiliation indeed. It would be an implicit, all but an explicit, acquiescence in the violation of the rights of mankind everywhere and of whatever nation or allegiance. It would be a deliberate abdication of our hitherto proud position as spokesmen even amidst the turmoil of war for the law and the right. It would make everything this Government has attempted and everything that it has achieved during this terrible struggle of nations meaningless and futile.

It is important to reflect that if in this instance we allowed expediency to take the place of principle, the door would inevitably be opened to still further concessions. Once accept a single abatement of right and many other humiliations would certainly follow, and the whole fine fabric of international law might crumble under our hands piece by piece. What we are contending for in this matter is of the very essence of the things that have made America a sovereign nation. She cannot yield them without conceding her own impotency as a nation and making virtual surrender of her independent position among the nations of the world.

I am speaking, my dear Senator, in deep solemnity, without heat, with a clear consciousness of the high responsibilities of my office, and as your sincere and devoted friend. If we should unhappily differ, we shall differ as friends; but where issues so momentous as these are involved we must, just because we are friends, speak our minds without reservation.

DOCUMENT 72

United States Goals and the War

While seeking to defend neutral rights, Wilson also set for the United States a role as the moral leader of the world in establishing a just and enduring peace (See, for example, Documents 76, 107–110). In his second inaugural address, delivered when Wilson was moving toward a decision to enter the war in response to Germany's resumption of unrestricted submarine warfare, the President summarized American objectives with lofty eloquence.

The four years which have elapsed since last I stood in this place have been crowded with counsel and action of the most vital interest and consequence. Perhaps no equal period in our history has been so fruitful of important reforms in our economic and industrial life or so full of significant changes in the spirit and purpose of our political action. We have sought very thoughtfully to set our house in order, correct the grosser errors and abuses of our industrial life, liberate and quicken the processes of our national genius and energy, and lift our politics to a broader view of the people's essential interests. It is a

Second inaugural address, March 5, 1917, *Public Papers*, V, 1–5.

record of singular variety and singular distinction. But I shall not attempt to review it. It speaks for itself and will be of increasing influence as the years go by. This is not the time for retrospect. It is time, rather, to speak our thoughts and purposes concerning the present and the immediate future.

Although we have centered counsel and action with such unusual concentration and success upon the great problems of domestic legislation to which we addressed ourselves four years ago, other matters have more and more forced themselves upon our attention, matters lying outside our own life as a nation and over which we had no control, but which, despite our wish to keep free of them, have drawn us more and more irresistibly into their own current and influence.

It has been impossible to avoid them. They have affected the life of the whole world. They have shaken men everywhere with a passion and an apprehension they never knew before. It has been hard to preserve calm counsel while the thought of our own people swayed this way and that under their influence. We are a composite and cosmopolitan people. We are of the blood of all the nations that are at war. The currents of our thoughts as well as the currents of our trade run quick at all seasons back and forth between us and them. The war inevitably set its mark from the first alike upon our minds, our industries, our commerce, our politics, and our social action. To be indifferent to it or independent of it was out of the question.

And yet all the while we have been conscious that we were not part of it. In that consciousness, despite many divisions, we have drawn closer together. We have been deeply wronged upon the seas, but we have not wished to wrong or injure in return; have retained throughout the consciousness of standing in some sort apart, intent upon an interest that transcended the immediate issues of the war itself. As some of the injuries done us have become intolerable we have still been clear that we wished nothing for ourselves that we were not ready to demand for all mankind, — fair dealing, justice, the freedom to live and be at ease against organized wrong.

It is in this spirit and with this thought that we have grown more and more aware, more and more certain that the part we wished to play was the part of those who mean to vindicate and fortify peace. We have been obliged to arm ourselves to make good our claim to a certain minimum of right and of freedom of action. We stand firm in armed neutrality since it seems that in no other way we can demonstrate what it is we insist upon and cannot forego. We may even be drawn on, by circumstances, not by our own purpose or desire, to a more active assertion of our rights as we see them and a more immediate association with the great struggle itself. But nothing will alter our thought or our purpose. They are too clear to be obscured. They are too deeply rooted in the principles of our national life to be altered. We desire neither conquest nor advantage. We wish nothing that can be had only at the cost of another people. We have always professed unselfish purpose and we covet the opportunity to prove that our professions are sincere.

There are many things still to do at home, to clarify our own politics and give new vitality to the industrial processes of our own life, and we shall do them as time and opportunity serve; but we realize that the greatest things that remain to be done must be done with the whole world for stage and in coöperation with the wide and universal forces of mankind, and we are making our spirits ready for those things. They will follow in the immediate wake of the war itself and will set civilization up again. We are provincials no longer. The tragical events of the thirty months of vital turmoil through which we have just passed have made us citizens of the world. There can be no turning back. Our own fortunes as a nation are involved, whether we would have it so or not.

And yet we are not the less Americans on that account. We shall be the more American if we but remain true to the principles in which we have been bred. They are not the principles of a province or of a single continent. We have known and boasted all along that they were the principles of a liberated mankind. These, therefore, are the things we shall stand for, whether in war or in peace:

That all nations are equally interested in the peace of the world and in the political stability of free peoples, and equally responsible for their maintenance;

That the essential principle of peace is the actual equality of nations in all matters of right or privilege;

That peace cannot securely or justly rest upon an armed balance of power;

That governments derive all their just powers from the consent of the governed and that no other powers should be supported by the common thought, purpose, or power of the family of nations.

That the seas should be equally free and safe for the use of all peoples, under rules set up by common agreement and consent, and that, so far as practicable, they should be accessible to all upon equal terms;

That national armaments should be limited to the necessities of national order and domestic safety;

That the community of interest and of power upon which peace must henceforth depend imposes upon each nation the duty of seeing to it that all influences proceeding from its own citizens meant to encourage or assist revolution in other states should be sternly and effectually suppressed and prevented.

I need not argue these principles to you, my fellow countrymen: they are your own, part and parcel of your own thinking and your own motive in affairs. They spring up native amongst us. Upon this as a platform of purpose and of action we can stand together.

And it is imperative that we should stand together. We are being forged into a new unity amidst the fires that now blaze throughout the world. In their ardent heat we shall, in God's providence, let us hope, be purged of faction and division, purified of the errant humors of party and of private interest, and shall stand forth in the days to come with a new dignity of national pride and spirit. Let each man see to it that the dedication is in his own heart, the high purpose of the Nation in his own mind, ruler of his own will and desire.

I stand here and have taken the high and solemn oath to which you have been audience because the people of the United States have chosen me for this august delegation of power and have by their gracious judgment named me their leader in affairs. I know now what the task means. I realize to the full the responsibility which it involves. I pray God I may be given the wisdom and the prudence to do my duty in the true spirit of this great people. I am their servant and can succeed only as they sustain and guide me by their confidence and their counsel. The thing I shall count upon, the thing without which neither counsel nor action will avail, is the unity of America,—an America united in feeling, in purpose, and in its vision of duty, of opportunity, and of service. We are to beware of all men who would turn the tasks and the necessities of the Nation to their own private profit or use them for the building up of private power; beware that no faction or disloyal intrigue break the harmony or embarrass the spirit of our people; beware that our Government be kept pure and incorrupt in all its parts. United alike in the conception of our duty and in the high resolve to perform it in the face of all men, let us dedicate ourselves to the great task to which we must now set our hands. For myself I beg your tolerance, your countenance, and your united aid. The shadows that now lie dark upon our path will soon be dispelled and we shall walk with the light all about us if we be but true to ourselves,—to ourselves as we have wished to be known in the counsels of the world and in the thought of all those who love liberty and justice and the right exalted.

B. TRADE WITH BELLIGERENTS

DOCUMENT 73

"One of the Most Perplexing Things I Have Had to Decide."

With the outbreak of the World War in 1914 one of Wilson's first tasks was to determine how to implement American neutrality and define the obligations of the United States. On the urging of Secretary of State Bryan he initially sought to discourage private American loans to the belligerents. This extremely narrow and unprecedented view of neutral obligations had the effect of favoring the Central Powers, because it tended to nullify the advantage of the Allies' control of the seas and hence their access to the American

---

Letter to Jacob H. Schiff, December 8, 1914, in Baker, *Wilson, Life and Letters,* V, 188–189.

market. By 1915 Wilson was persuaded that this prohibition was wrong, and he reversed himself to permit short-term commercial credits and, ultimately, long-term loans to facilitate belligerent (in practice, Allied) trade with American suppliers. Wilson fully supported the right of neutrals to trade with any nation, neutral or belligerent, in wartime. He had some difficulty deciding whether there ought to be any limits put on such trade, however, as this letter to a prominent financier indicates.

I fear you must have thought me guilty of a discourtesy in not replying sooner to your letter of November nineteenth, but the fact is I wanted to think out very carefully the matter about which you wrote.

Not that it was the first time that I had tried to think it out, for it is one of the most perplexing things I have had to decide. The law standing as it does, the most I can do is to exercise influence, and in the case of the lending of money I was directly applied to for advice and approval. There my duty was clear. It was my duty to discourage the loans to belligerents. In the matter of sales of goods of all kinds, however, the precedents of international law are so clear, the sales proceed from so many sources, and my lack of power is so evident, that I have felt that I could do nothing else than leave the matter to settle itself. In a single recent case I saw my way clear to act. When it came to the manufacture of constituent parts of submarines and their shipment abroad, complete, to be put together elsewhere, it seemed to me clearly my privilege, acting in the spirit of the *Alabama* case, to say that the government could not allow that, and the Fore River Ship Building Company which is said to have undertaken the contracts has canceled them.

I am sure that you realize the very great delicacy and difficulty of my task in matters of this sort, and I wanted to make a very frank statement of them to you.

C. GREAT BRITAIN
AND AMERICAN NEUTRAL RIGHTS

DOCUMENT 74

"This Government Is Greatly Disturbed. . . ."

One of Wilson's chief objectives following the outbreak of war was to preserve the greatest freedom of trade for American citizens. He accordingly sought to commit the belligerent nations to the so-called Declaration of London, which had been drafted by an international conference at London in 1908–1909 and which laid down an elaborate set of rules governing neutral rights and trade in wartime. Because the rules benefited neutrals and land-locked belligerents and operated to the disadvantage of maritime powers, neither Great Britain nor the United States had ratified the Declaration. It had little standing in international law. Now, upon Wilson's urging, the Central Powers promptly agreed to accept the Declaration; but the British understandably declined to be bound by all of its restrictions. Concerned by the evident intent of the British government to include in its blockade of the Central Powers such American export goods as cotton and copper, Wilson instructed Ambassador Page to make a strong protest. The cable to Page was drafted initially by Robert Lansing, the Department of State Counselor, and amended by the President. Wilson's deletions in Lansing's text are within brackets; Wilson's additions are in italics.

Strictly Confidential. You will immediately see Sir Edward Grey and state to him informally *and confidentially* that

---

Cabled instructions to Walter Hines Page, September 28, 1914, in Link, *Wilson: The Struggle for Neutrality*, pp. 112–113.

this Government [has given careful consideration to] *is greatly disturbed by* the intention of the British Government to change the provisions of the Declaration of London by the Order in Council of the twentieth August and to adopt the Declaration thus changed as the code of naval warfare for the present war. This Government [as the result of its examination,] feels grave concern at all of the proposed changes, especially those in Articles three and five of the Order in Council, which so materially affect the rights of neutral commerce. If the proposed rules are *sought to be* put into force and the matter becomes the subject of public discussion in this country, as it undoubtedly will, it is to be [feared] *confidently expected* that it will arouse a spirit of resentment among the American people toward Great Britain, which this Government would extremely regret but which it would be unable to prevent. You will also point out that the enforcement of these rules by the British Government would furnish to those inimicable to Great Britain an opportunity, which they would not be slow to seize, *and which they are already using in our press upon the mere publication of the Order.*

Paragraph. You will further say that the President *earnestly* desires [, if possible,] to avoid a formal protest to those proposed rules and their enforcement and hopes that the British Government will [carefully] *be willing to* consider the advisability of modifying [the objectionable] *these* features of the Order in Council, which possess such latent possibilities. [of disturbing the existing relations between the peoples of the two countries.]

You will impress upon Sir Edward Grey the *President's conviction of the* extreme gravity of the situation and [the] *his* earnest wish [of the President] to avoid *even* causes of irritation and controversy between this Government and the Government of his Majesty.

In presenting the substance of this instruction to Sir Edward Grey you will assure him [that it is done in the most friendly spirit] *of the earnest spirit of friendship in which it is sent. The President is anxious that he should realize that the terms of the Declaration of London represent the limit to which this Gov't could go with the approbation and support of its people.*

Telegraph result of interview as soon as possible.

DOCUMENT 75

"We Are Face to Face with
Something They Are Going to Do. . . ."

Wilson recognized that whereas the British naturally must make the most of their control of the seas they also could not afford to offend the United States. His aim was thus to make certain that, regardless of British pronouncements, the acts of the British did not damage legitimate American trading rights.

These notes by Mr. Lansing are admirable and convincing; but they lead only to debate, and debate with the British Government (which for the time being consists of the War Office and the Admiralty) is at present of no practical avail.

Inconsistencies in the Order and inconsistencies between the Order and Sir Edward Grey's note accompanying it are neither here nor there, as it seems to me; neither is the lack of the ordinary forms of notice of blockade. We are face to face with *something they are going to do,* and they are going to do it no matter what representations we make. We cannot convince them or change them, we can only show them very clearly what we mean to be our own

---

Letter to William Jennings Bryan, March 24, 1915, in *Lansing Papers*, I, 288–289.

attitude and course of action and that we mean to hold them to a strict responsibility for every invasion of our rights as neutrals. In short we must make them understand that the discretion which their officials are vested with must be exercised in such a way that the extraordinary "blockade" they are instituting will *not* in fact violate our rights as neutral traders on the seas.

Take an instance (in the field of argument). It is true that a previous Order in Council adopted all the Declaration of London except the portions defining contraband, as a temporary code of warfare at sea; but that previous Order did not constitute an agreement with any other nation. It was a piece of domestic legislation; and a subsequent Order no doubt repeals it so far as it is inconsistent with it. So *that* line leads nowhere, I fear.

If, then, we speak only to the facts, is not this our right course? Ought we not to say, in effect: You call this a blockade and mean to maintain it as such; but it is obvious that it is unprecedented in almost every respect, but chiefly in this, that it is a blockade of neutral as well as of belligerent coasts and harbours, which no belligerent can claim as a right. We shall expect therefore that the discretion lodged by the Order in Council in the administrative officers and courts of the crown will be exercised to correct what is irregular in this situation and leave the way open to our legitimate trade. If this is not done we shall have to hold you to a strict accountability for every instance of rights violated and injury done; but we interpret Sir Edward Grey's note to mean that this is exactly what will be done.

Note, by the way, the sentence in Page's despatch in which he says that they will heed none of our arguments, but that they will be careful not to offend us in act.

Note, also, that, as a matter of fact, our export trade shows no sign of slackening and that there is little left, by the action of Germany herself (See Gerard's recent despatch and several preceding) for us to trade with Germany in. Our cotton ships bring nothing away on their return voyage.

I hope that Mr. Lansing will be kind enough to try his hand at a note such as I have indicated, and then we can get together (perhaps all three of us?) and put the thing into a shape that will thoroughly hold water (and exclude it, too, as a maritime paper should).

DOCUMENT 76

"The Altogether Indefensible Course. . . ."

Despite his disposition to regard German submarine activity as a more serious violation of American rights than were the British trade restrictions, by 1916 Wilson was thoroughly fed up with the high-handed British treatment of American and other neutral shipping. He was also vexed by the reluctance of Sir Edward Grey, the British Foreign Secretary, to proceed with a plan for United States mediation to bring about an end to the fighting. Wilson's annoyance spilled out in two letters to his close friend and confidant, Colonel House.

I have been giving some very careful thought to your question how we should deal with Sir Edward and his Government at this turning point,—for it really is that.

It seems to me that we should really get down to hard pan.

The situation has altered altogether since you had your conference in London and Paris. The at least temporary removal of the acute German question has concentrated attention here on the altogether indefensible course Great

---

Letter to Edward M. House, May 16, 1916, in Baker, *Wilson, Life and Letters*, VI, 212–213.

Britain is pursuing with regard to trade to and from neutral ports and her quite intolerable interception of mails on the high seas carried by neutral ships. Recently there has been added the great shock opinion in this country has received from the course of the British Government towards some of the Irish rebels.

We are plainly face to face with this alternative, therefore. The United States must either make a decided move for peace (upon some basis that promises to be permanent) or, if she postpones that, must insist to the limit upon her rights of trade and upon such freedom of the seas as inter-national law already justifies her in insisting on as against Great Britain, with the same plain speaking and firmness that she has used against Germany. And the choice must be made immediately. Which does Great Britain prefer? She cannot escape both. To do nothing is now, for us, impossible.

If we move for peace, it will be along these lines 1) Such a settlement with regard to their own immediate interests as the belligerents may be able to agree upon. We have nothing material of any kind to ask for ourselves and are quite aware that we are in no sense parties to the quarrel. Our interest is only in peace and its guarantees; 2) a universal alliance to maintain freedom of the seas and to prevent any war begun either a) contrary to treaty covenants or b) without warning and full inquiry, — a virtual guarantee of territorial integrity and political independence.

It seems to me to be of imperative and pressing importance that Sir Edward should understand all this and that the crisis can not be postponed; and it can be done with the most evident spirit of friendliness through you. Will you not prepare a full cable putting the whole thing plainly to him? We must act, and act at once, in the one direction or the other.

With affectionate messages from us all.

DOCUMENT 77

"Their Intolerable Course"

I am, I must admit, about at the end of my patience with Great Britain and the Allies. This black list business is the last straw. I have told Spring Rice so, and he sees the reasons very clearly. Both he and Jusserand think it a stupid blunder. I am seriously considering asking Congress to authorize me to prohibit loans and restrict exportations to the Allies. It is becoming clear to me that there lies latent in this policy the wish to prevent our merchants getting a foothold in markets which Great Britain has hitherto controlled and all but dominated. Polk and I are compounding a very sharp note. I may feel obliged to make it as sharp and final as the one to Germany on the submarines. What is your own judgment? Can we any longer endure their intolerable course?

D. GERMANY AND THE SUBMARINE

1. A Warning to Germany

DOCUMENT 78

"Strict Accountability"

On February 4, 1915, the Imperial German government announced a submarine blockade of the British Isles. The

---

Letter to Edward M. House, July 23, 1916, in Baker, *Wilson, Life and Letters*, VI, 312.

Instructions to James W. Gerard, February 10, 1915, in *Public Papers*, III, 280–283.

consequent danger to neutral shipping obliged Wilson to formulate a policy with respect to this new and deadly weapon of war. His response to the German announcement virtually ignored the peculiar nature of the submarine, particularly its vulnerability to ramming or surface gunfire from an intended victim. Declining to concede any of the traditional neutral rights, Wilson instructed his ambassador in Berlin, James W. Gerard, to warn Germany that the United States would hold it to strict accountability for the actions of its submarines.

Please address a note immediately to the Imperial German Government to the following effect:

The Government of the United States, having had its attention directed to the proclamation of the German Admiralty issued on the fourth of February, that the waters surrounding Great Britain and Ireland, including the whole of the English Channel, are to be considered as comprised within the seat of war; that all enemy merchant vessels found in those waters after the eighteenth instant will be destroyed, although it may not always be possible to save crews and passengers; and that neutral vessels expose themselves to danger within this zone of war because, in view of the misuse of neutral flags said to have been ordered by the British Government on the thirty-first of January and of the contingencies of maritime warfare, it may not be possible always to exempt neutral vessels from attacks intended to strike enemy ships, feels it to be its duty to call the attention of the Imperial German Government, with sincere respect and the most friendly sentiments but very candidly and earnestly, to the very serious possibilities of the course of action apparently contemplated under that proclamation.

The Government of the United States views those possibilities with such grave concern that it feels it to be its privilege, and indeed its duty in the circumstances, to request the Imperial German Government to consider before action is taken the critical situation in respect of the relations between this country and Germany which might arise were the German naval forces, in carrying out the policy foreshadowed in the Admiralty's proclamation, to destroy any merchant vessel of the United States or cause the death of American citizens.

It is of course not necessary to remind the German Government that the sole right of a belligerent in dealing with neutral vessels on the high seas is limited to visit and search, unless a blockade is proclaimed and effectively maintained, which this Government does not understand to be proposed in this case. To declare or exercise a right to attack and destroy any vessel entering a prescribed area of the high seas without first certainly determining it[s] belligerent nationality and the contraband character of its cargo would be an act so unprecedented in naval warfare that this Government is reluctant to believe that the Imperial Government of Germany in this case contemplates it as possible. The suspicion that enemy ships are using neutral flags improperly can create no just presumption that all ships traversing a prescribed area are subject to the same suspicion. It is to determine exactly such questions that this Government understands the right of visit and search to have been recognized.

This Government has carefully noted the explanatory statement issued by the Imperial German Government at the same time with the proclamation of the German Admiralty, and takes this occasion to remind the Imperial German Government very respectfully that the Government of the United States is open to none of the criticisms for unneutral action to which the German Government believe the governments of certain of other neutral nations have laid themselves open; that the Government of the United States has not consented to or acquiesced in any measures which may have been taken by the other belligerent nations in the present war which operate to restrain neutral trade, but has, on the contrary, taken in all such matters a position which warrants it in holding those governments responsible in the proper way for any untoward effects upon American shipping which the accepted principles of international law do not justify; and that it, therefore, regards itself as free in the present instance to take with a clear conscience and upon accepted principles the position indicated in this note.

If the commanders of German vessels of war should act upon the presumption that the flag of the United States was not being used in good faith and should destroy on the high seas an American vessel or the lives of American citizens, it would be difficult for the Government of the United States to view the act in any other light than as an indefensible violation of neutral rights which it would be very hard indeed to reconcile with the friendly relations now so happily subsisting between the two Governments.

If such a deplorable situation should arise, the Imperial German Government can readily appreciate that the Government of the United States would be constrained to hold the Imperial German Government to a strict accountability for such acts of their naval authorities and to take any steps it might be necessary to take to safeguard American lives and property and to secure to American citizens the full enjoyment of their acknowledged rights on the high seas.

The Government of the United States, in view of these considerations, which it urges with the greatest respect and with the sincere purpose of making sure that no misunderstanding may arise and no circumstance occur that might even cloud the intercourse of the two Governments, expresses the confident hope and expectation that the Imperial German Government can and will give assurance that American citizens and their vessels will not be molested by the naval forces of Germany otherwise than by visit and search, though their vessels may be traversing the sea area delimited in the proclamation of the German Admiralty.

It is added for the information of the Imperial Government that representations have been made to His Britannic Majesty's Government in respect to the unwarranted use of the American flag for the protection of British ships.

2. *The Developing American Policy*

DOCUMENT 79

"On Very High Grounds. . . ."

The sinking of the small British steamer "Falaba" on March 28, 1915, with the resulting death of an American citizen, Leon C. Thrasher, brought a sharp debate within the Wilson administration about its future policy with respect to submarine warfare. One group, led by Secretary of State Bryan, argued that Germany should not be held to a stricter standard of conduct than the Allies, and that to avoid future trouble Americans should be warned not to travel on belligerent ships. It was enough to demand protection for American ships. In opposition, another group, headed by Counselor Lansing, contended that the United States could not yield the right of its citizens to travel in safety on the high seas, and that the sinking of the "Falaba" without provision for the safety of its passengers and crew was a flagrant violation of international law and required proper apology and redress. Partly because he considered the submarine a reprehensible weapon, Wilson inclined to

Letter to William Jennings Bryan, April 22, 1915, in *Lansing Papers*, I, 377–378.

Lansing's view, but at the same time he did not wish a serious clash with the Germans over the death of one American.

Although I have been silent for a long time about the case, I have had it much in my mind, as I have no doubt you have, to work out some practicable course of action with regard to the death of Thrasher; and I have the following to suggest as the outline of a note to the German Government:

(1) State the circumstances, as we have officially received them.

(2) We take it for granted that Germany has had no idea of changing the rules (or, rather, the essential principles) of international law with regard to the safety of non-combatants and of the citizens of neutral countries at sea, however radical the present change in practical conditions of warfare; and that she will, in accordance with her usual frankness in such matters, acknowledge her responsibility in the present instance.

(3) Raise in a very earnest, though of course entirely friendly, way the whole question of the use of submarines against merchant vessels, calling attention circumstantially to the impossibility of observing the safeguards and precautions so long and so clearly recognized as imperative in such matters: the duty of visit and search; the duty, if the vessel proves to belong to an enemy and cannot be put in charge of a prize crew, to secure the safety of the lives of those on board; etc.

(4) On the grounds enter a very moderately worded but none the less solemn and emphatic protest against the whole thing, as contrary to laws based, not on mere interest or convenience, but on humanity, fair play, and a necessary respect for the rights of neutrals.

My idea, as you will see, is to put the whole note on very high grounds,—not on the loss of this single man's life, but on the interests of mankind which are involved and which Germany has always stood for; on the manifest impropriety of a single nation's essaying to alter the understandings of nations; and as all arising out of her mistake in employing an instrument against her enemy's commerce which it is impossible to employ in that use in accordance with any rules that the world is likely to be willing to accept.

3. *The* LUSITANIA *Crisis*

DOCUMENT 80

The First "Lusitania" Note

Wilson had not yet made up his mind how to handle the "Falaba" incident when a much more ominous event occurred—the sinking on May 7, 1915, of the large British passenger liner "Lusitania" with the loss of nearly 1,200 lives, including 124 Americans. Before the "Lusitania" crisis Wilson might have reached some accommodation with the Germans on submarine warfare, but like most Americans he was shocked and outraged by what he regarded as an act of utter barbarity. Reacting deliberately but none the less sternly, on May 13 he instructed Ambassador Gerard to deliver a strongly worded protest, virtually demanding an end to submarine attacks upon unarmed ships.

Please call on the Minister of Foreign Affairs and, after reading to him this communication, leave him with a copy:
In view of recent acts of the German authorities in violation of American rights on the high seas which culminated in the torpedoing and sinking of the British steam-

---

Instructions to James W. Gerard, May 13, 1915, in *Foreign Relations, 1915*, Supplement, *The World War*, pp. 393–396.

ship *Lusitania* on May 7, 1915, by which over 100 American citizens lost their lives, it is clearly wise and desirable that the Government of the United States and the Imperial German Government should come to a clear and full understanding as to the grave situation which has resulted.

The sinking of the British passenger steamer *Falaba* by a German submarine on March 28, through which Leon C. Thrasher, an American citizen was drowned; the attack on April 28 on the American vessel *Cushing* by a German aeroplane; the torpedoing on May 1 of the American vessel *Gulflight* by a German submarine, as a result of which two or more American citizens met their death; and, finally, the torpedoing and sinking of the steamship *Lusitania*, constitute a series of events which the Government of the United States has observed with growing concern, distress, and amazement.

Recalling the humane and enlightened attitude hitherto assumed by the Imperial German Government in matters of international right, and particularly with regard to the freedom of the seas; having learned to recognize the German views and the German influence in the field of international obligation as always engaged upon the side of justice and humanity; and having understood the instructions of the Imperial German Government to its naval commanders to be upon the same plane of humane action prescribed by the naval codes of other nations, the Government of the United States was loath to believe—it can not now bring itself to believe—that these acts, so absolutely contrary to the rules, the practices, and the spirit of modern warfare, could have the countenance or sanction of that great Government. It feels it to be its duty, therefore, to address the Imperial German Government concerning them with the utmost frankness and in the earnest hope that it is not mistaken in expecting action on the part of the

Imperial German Government which will correct the unfortunate impressions which have been created, and vindicate once more the position of that Government with regard to the sacred freedom of the seas.

The Government of the United States has been apprised that the Imperial German Government considered themselves to be obliged by the extraordinary circumstances of the present war and the measures adopted by their adversaries in seeking to cut Germany off from all commerce, to adopt methods of retaliation which go much beyond the ordinary methods of warfare at sea, in the proclamation of a war zone from which they have warned neutral ships to keep away. This Government has already taken occasion to inform the Imperial German Government that it can not admit the adoption of such measures or such a warning of danger to operate as in any degree an abbreviation of the rights of American ship-masters or of American citizens bound on lawful errands as passengers on merchant ships of belligerent nationality; and that it must hold the Imperial German Government to a strict accountability for any infringement of those rights, intentional or incidental. It does not understand the Imperial German Government to question those rights. It assumes, on the contrary, that the Imperial Government accept, as of course, the rule that the lives of non-combatants, whether they be of neutral citizenship or citizens of one of the nations at war, can not lawfully or rightfully be put in jeopardy by the capture or destruction of an unarmed merchantman, and recognize also, as all other nations do, the obligation to take the usual precaution of visit and search to ascertain whether a suspected merchantman is in fact of belligerent nationality or is in fact carrying contraband of war under a neutral flag.

The Government of the United States, therefore, desires to call the attention of the Imperial German Government with the utmost earnestness to the fact that the objection to their present method of attack against the trade of their enemies lies in the practical impossibility of employing submarines in the destruction of commerce without disregarding those rules of fairness, reason, justice, and humanity, which all modern opinion regards as imperative. It is practically impossible for the officers of a submarine to visit a merchantman at sea and examine her papers and cargo. It is practically impossible for them to make a prize of her; and, if they can not put a prize crew on board of her, they can not sink her without leaving her crew and all on board of her to the mercy of the sea in her small boats. These facts it is understood the Imperial German Government frankly admit. We are informed that, in the instances of which we have spoken, time enough for even that poor measure of safety was not given, and in at least two of the cases cited, not so much as a warning was received. Manifestly submarines cannot be used against merchantmen, as the last few weeks have shown, without an inevitable violation of many sacred principles of justice and humanity.

American citizens act within their indisputable rights in taking their ships and in traveling wherever their legitimate business calls them upon the high seas, and exercise those rights in what should be the well-justified confidence that their lives will not be endangered by acts done in clear violation of universally acknowledged international obligations, and certainly in the confidence that their own Government will sustain them in the exercise of their rights.

There was recently published in the newspapers of the United States, I regret to inform the Imperial German Government, a formal warning, purporting to come from the Imperial German Embassy at Washington, addressed to the people of the United States, and stating, in effect, that any citizen of the United States who exercised his right of free travel upon the seas would do so at his peril if his journey should take him within the zone of waters within which the Imperial German Navy was using submarines against the commerce of Great Britain and France, notwithstanding the respectful but very earnest protest of his Government, the Government of the United States. I do not refer to this for the purpose of calling the attention of the Imperial German Government at this time to the surprising irregularity of a communication from the Imperial German Embassy at Washington addressed to the people of the United States through the newspapers, but only for the purpose of pointing out that no warning that an unlawful and inhumane act will be committed can possibly be accepted as an excuse or palliation for that act or as an abatement of the responsibility for its commission.

Long acquainted as this Government has been with the character of the Imperial German Government and with the high principles of equity by which they have in the past been actuated and guided, the Government of the United States can not believe that the commanders of the vessels which committed these acts of lawlessness did so except under a misapprehension of the orders issued by the Imperial German naval authorities. It takes it for granted that, at least within the practical possibilities of every such case, the commanders even of submarines were expected to do nothing that would involve the lives of non-combatants or the safety of neutral ships, even at the cost of failing of their object of capture or destruction. It confidently expects, therefore, that the Imperial German Government will disavow the acts of which the Government of the United States complains, that they will make reparation so far as reparation is possible for injuries which are without measure, and that they will take immediate steps to prevent the recurrence of anything so obviously subversive of the principles of warfare for which the Imperial German Government have in the past so wisely and so firmly contended.

The Government and the people of the United States look to the Imperial German Government for just, prompt, and enlightened action in this vital matter with the greater confidence because the United States and Germany are bound together not only by special ties of friendship but also by the explicit stipulations of the treaty of 1828 between the United States and the Kingdom of Prussia.

Expressions of regret and offers of reparation in case of the destruction of neutral ships sunk by mistake, while they may satisfy international obligations, if no loss of life results, can not justify or excuse a practice, the natural and necessary effect of which is to subject neutral nations and neutral persons to new and immeasureable risks.

The Imperial German Government will not expect the Government of the United States to omit any word or any act necessary to the performance of its sacred duty of maintaining the rights of the United States and its citizens and of safeguarding their free exercise and enjoyment.

DOCUMENT 81

The Right to Travel on Belligerent Ships

Secretary of State Bryan disapproved of the United States protest over the "Lusitania" sinking as unduly severe. Bryan also argued that to avoid further incidents that might lead to war Americans should be warned not to travel on ships of the belligerent nations. Wilson and Lansing, however, believed that the United States should not concede the right of her citizens to travel in safety on any unarmed ship, neutral or belligerent. Submarine attacks without warning and without provision for the safety of crew and passengers were too barbarous and inhumane to accept without protest.

Letter to William Jennings Bryan, May 14, 1915, in Baker, *Wilson, Life and Letters*, V, 341–342.

As to the request to Americans not to take passage on belligerent ships (for I agree with Mr. Lansing that it could be nothing more than a request), my feeling is this: the request is unnecessary, if the object is to save lives, because the danger is already fully known and those who do not refrain because of the danger will not, in all probability, refrain because we request them to do so; and this is not the time to make it, not only for the reason Mr. Lansing suggests, but also because, as I urged this morning, it weakens the effect of our saying to Germany that we mean to support our citizens in the exercise of their right to travel both on our ships and on belligerent. If I thought the notice necessary, or effective, to save lives, the second objection might be waived, but since I do not, I think the second objection ought to prevail.

DOCUMENT 82

German Versus British Violations
of Neutral Rights

Partly because he was responding differently to the British maritime blockade than to the German submarine zone, and in consequence American lives and property were being lost through German but not British action, Wilson felt justified in holding Germany to stricter accountability. The German submarine attacks, he told a dubious Bryan (shortly before the latter resigned on June 8 rather than sign a second strong protest over the "Lusitania" sinking), were much more serious than British trade restrictions because they violated the rights of humanity.

Letter to William Jennings Bryan, June 2, 1915, in *Lansing Papers*, I, 421.

It is interesting and significant how often the German Foreign Office goes over the same ground in different words, and always misses the essential point involved, that England's violation of neutral rights is different from Germany's violation of the rights of humanity.

4. The Break with Germany

DOCUMENT 83

Severing Diplomatic Relations

In the short run Wilson's firm insistence upon the unqualified right to travel on the high seas in safety from submarine attacks was successful. There were several further serious diplomatic clashes with the Imperial German Government, but each time the Germans gave way in the face of stern American protests. In January 1917, however, Germany decided to stake its fate on a resumption of unrestricted submarine warfare regardless of the reaction of the United States. German military leaders were confident that the Allies could be starved into submission before the United States could mobilize its strength, should it decide to enter the war. Wilson had made opposition to unrestricted submarine warfare a cardinal element of American foreign policy, and he therefore had little choice but to retaliate by breaking diplomatic relations.

GENTLEMEN OF THE CONGRESS:

The Imperial German Government on the thirty-first of January announced to this Government and to the governments of other neutral nations that on and after the first

Address to Congress, February 3, 1917, *Public Papers*, IV, 422–26.

day of February, the present month, it would adopt a policy with regard to the use of submarines against all shipping seeking to pass through certain designated areas of
the high seas to which it is clearly my duty to call your
attention.

Let me remind the Congress that on the eighteenth of
April last, in view of the sinking on the twenty-fourth of
March of the cross-channel passenger steamer *Sussex* by a
German submarine, without summons or warning, and the
consequent loss of the lives of several citizens of the
United States who were passengers aboard her, this Gov-
ernment addressed a note to the Imperial German Govern-
ment in which it made the following declaration:

If it is still the purpose of the Imperial Government to prosecute
relentless and indiscriminate warfare against vessels of commerce by the use of submarines without regard to what the
Government of the United States must consider the sacred and
indisputable rules of international law and the universally recognized dictates of humanity, the Government of the United States
is at last forced to the conclusion that there is but one course it
can pursue. Unless the Imperial Government should now immediately declare and effect an abandonment of its present methods
of submarine warfare against passenger and freight-carrying vessels, the Government of the United States can have no choice but
to sever diplomatic relations with the German Empire altogether.

In reply to this declaration the Imperial German Government gave this Government the following assurance:

The German Government is prepared to do its utmost to confine the operations of war for the rest of its duration to the fighting forces of the belligerents, thereby also insuring the freedom
of the seas, a principle upon which the German Government
believes, now as before, to be in agreement with the Government
of the United States.

The German Government, guided by this idea, notifies the
Government of the United States that the German naval forces

have received the following orders: In accordance with the general principles of visit and search and destruction of merchant vessels recognized by international law, such vessels, both within and without the area declared as naval war zone, shall not be sunk without warning and without saving human lives, unless these ships attempt to escape or offer resistance.

"But," it added, "neutrals can not expect that Germany, forced to fight for her existence, shall, for the sake of neutral interest, restrict the use of an effective weapon if her enemy is permitted to continue to apply at will methods of warfare violating the rules of international law. Such a demand would be incompatible with the character of neutrality, and the German Government is convinced that the Government of the United States does not think of making such a demand, knowing that the Government of the United States has repeatedly declared that it is determined to restore the principle of the freedom of the seas, from whatever quarter it has been violated."

To this the Government of the United States replied on the eighth of May, accepting, of course, the assurances given, but adding,

The Government of the United States feels it necessary to state that it takes it for granted that the Imperial German Government does not intend to imply that the maintenance of its newly announced policy is in any way contingent upon the course or result of diplomatic negotiations between the Government of the United States and any other belligerent Government, notwithstanding the fact that certain passages in the Imperial Government's note of the 4th instant might appear to be susceptible of that construction. In order, however, to avoid any possible misunderstanding, the Government of the United States notifies the Imperial Government that it cannot for a moment entertain, much less discuss, a suggestion that respect by German naval authorities for the rights of citizens of the United States upon the high seas should in any way or in the slightest degree be made contingent upon the conduct of any other Government affecting the rights of neutrals and noncombatants. Responsibility in such matters is single, not joint; absolute, not relative.

To this note of the eighth of May the Imperial German Government made no reply.

On the thirty-first of January, the Wednesday of the present week, the German Ambassador handed to the Secretary of State, along with a formal note, a memorandum which contains the following statement:

The Imperial Government, therefore, does not doubt that the Government of the United States will understand the situation thus forced upon Germany by the Entente-Allies' brutal methods of war and by their determination to destroy the Central Powers, and that the Government of the United States will further realize that the now openly disclosed intentions of the Entente-Allies give back to Germany the freedom of action which she reserved in her note addressed to the Government of the United States on May 4, 1916.

Under these circumstances Germany will meet the illegal measures of her enemies by forcibly preventing after February 1, 1917, in a zone around Great Britain, France, Italy, and in the Eastern Mediterranean all navigation, that of neutrals included, from and to England and from and to France, etc., etc. All ships met within the zone will be sunk.

I think that you will agree with me that, in view of this declaration, which suddenly and without prior intimation of any kind deliberately withdraws the solemn assurance given in the Imperial Government's note of the fourth of May, 1916, this Government has no alternative consistent with the dignity and honor of the United States but to take the course which, in its note of the eighteenth of April, 1916, it announced that it would take in the event that the German Government did not declare and effect an abandonment of the methods of submarine warfare which it was then employing and to which it now purposes again to resort.

I have, therefore, directed the Secretary of State to announce to His Excellency the German Ambassador that all diplomatic relations between the United States and the German Empire are severed, and that the American Ambassador at Berlin will immediately be withdrawn; and, in accordance with this decision, to hand to His Excellency his passports.

Notwithstanding this unexpected action of the German Government, this sudden and deeply deplorable renunciation of its assurances, given this Government at one of the most critical moments of tension in the relations of the two governments, I refuse to believe that it is the intention of the German authorities to do in fact what they have warned us they will feel at liberty to do. I cannot bring myself to believe that they will indeed pay no regard to the ancient friendship between their people and our own or to the solemn obligations which have been exchanged between them and destroy American ships and take the lives of American citizens in the wilful prosecution of the ruthless naval programme they have announced their intention to adopt. Only actual overt acts on their part can make me believe it even now.

If this inveterate confidence on my part in the sobriety and prudent foresight of their purpose should unhappily prove unfounded; if American ships and American lives should in fact be sacrificed by their naval commanders in heedless contravention of the just and reasonable understandings of international law and the obvious dictates of humanity, I shall take the liberty of coming again before the Congress, to ask that authority be given me to use any means that may be necessary for the protection of our seamen and our people in the prosecution of their peaceful and legitimate errands on the high seas. I can do nothing less. I take it for granted that all neutral governments will take the same course.

We do not desire any hostile conflict with the Imperial German Government. We are the sincere friends of the German people and earnestly desire to remain at peace with the Government which speaks for them. We shall not believe that they are hostile to us unless and until we are obliged to believe it; and we purpose nothing more than the reasonable defense of the undoubted rights of our people. We wish to serve no selfish ends. We seek merely to stand true alike in thought and in action to the immemorial principles of our people which I sought to express in my address to the Senate only two weeks ago,—seek merely to vindicate our right to liberty and justice and an unmolested life. These are the bases of peace, not war. God grant we may not be challenged to defend them by acts of wilful injustice on the part of the Government of Germany!

DOCUMENT 84

"The Right Is More Precious Than Peace. . . ."

Wilson had not succeeded in curbing the submarine menace through diplomacy; neither was he successful in protecting American shipping by means of an unsatisfactory armed neutrality during March of 1917. On April 2, therefore, he went reluctantly before Congress to request a declaration of war against Germany. Characteristically, he based this choice on moral grounds and stressed the idealistic objectives for which the United States would be fighting.

Address to Congress, April 2, 1917, *Public Papers*, V, 6–16.

I have called the Congress into extraordinary session because there are serious, very serious, choices of policy to be
made, and made immediately, which it was neither right
nor constitutionally permissible that I should assume the
responsibility of making.

On the third of February last I officially laid before you
the extraordinary announcement of the Imperial German
Government that on and after the first day of February it
was its purpose to put aside all restraints of law or of humanity and use its submarines to sink every vessel that
sought to approach either the ports of Great Britain and
Ireland or the western coasts of Europe or any of the ports
controlled by the enemies of Germany within the Mediterranean. That had seemed to be the object of the German
submarine warfare earlier in the war, but since April of last
year the Imperial Government had somewhat restrained
the commanders of its undersea craft in conformity with its
promise then given to us that passenger boats should not
be sunk and that due warning would be given to all other
vessels which its submarines might seek to destroy, when
no resistance was offered or escape attempted, and care
taken that their crews were given at least a fair chance to
save their lives in their open boats. The precautions
taken were meager and haphazard enough, as was proved
in distressing instance after instance in the progress of the
cruel and unmanly business, but a certain degree of restraint was observed. The new policy has swept every
restriction aside. Vessels of every kind, whatever their flag,
their character, their cargo, their destination, their errand,
have been ruthlessly sent to the bottom without warning
and without thought of help or mercy for those on board,
the vessels of friendly neutrals along with those of belligerents. Even hospital ships and ships carrying relief to the
sorely bereaved and stricken people of Belgium, though
the latter were provided with safe conduct through the

proscribed areas by the German Government itself and were distinguished by unmistakable marks of identity, have been sunk with the same reckless lack of compassion or of principle.

I was for a little while unable to believe that such things would in fact be done by any government that had hitherto subscribed to the humane practices of civilized nations. International law had its origin in the attempt to set up some law which would be respected and observed upon the seas, where no nation had right of dominion and where lay the free highways of the world. By painful stage after stage has that law been built up, with meager enough results, indeed, after all was accomplished that could be accomplished, but always with a clear view, at least, of what the heart and conscience of mankind demanded. This minimum of right the German Government has swept aside under the plea of retaliation and necessity and because it had no weapons which it could use at sea except these which it is impossible to employ as it is employing them without throwing to the winds all scruples of humanity or of respect for the understandings that were supposed to underlie the intercourse of the world. I am not now thinking of the loss of property involved, immense and serious as that is, but only of the wanton and wholesale destruction of the lives of non-combatants, men, women, and children, engaged in pursuits which have always, even in the darkest periods of modern history, been deemed innocent and legitimate. Property can be paid for; the lives of peaceful and innocent people cannot be. The present German submarine warfare against commerce is a warfare against mankind.

It is a war against all nations. American ships have been sunk, American lives taken, in ways which it has stirred us very deeply to learn of, but the ships and people of other neutral and friendly nations have been sunk and overwhelmed in the waters in the same way. There has been no discrimination. The challenge is to all mankind. Each nation must decide for itself how it will meet it. The choice we make for ourselves must be made with a moderation of counsel and a temperateness of judgment befitting our character and our motives as a nation. We must put excited feeling away. Our motive will not be revenge or the victorious assertion of the physical might of the nation, but only the vindication of right, of human right, of which we are only a single champion.

When I addressed the Congress on the twenty-sixth of February last I thought that it would suffice to assert our neutral rights with arms, our right to use the seas against unlawful interference, our right to keep our people safe against unlawful violence. But armed neutrality, it now appears, is impracticable. Because submarines are in effect outlaws when used as the German submarines have been used against merchant shipping, it is impossible to defend ships against their attacks as the law of nations has assumed that merchantmen would defend themselves against privateers or cruisers, visible craft giving chase upon the open sea. It is common prudence in such circumstances, grim necessity indeed, to endeavor to destroy them before they have shown their own intention. They must be dealt with upon sight, if dealt with at all. The German Government denies the right of neutrals to use arms at all within the areas of the sea which it has proscribed, even in the defense of rights which no modern publicist has ever before questioned their right to defend. The intimation is conveyed that the armed guards which we have placed on our merchant ships will be treated as beyond the pale of law and subject to be dealt with as pirates would be. Armed neutrality is ineffectual enough at best; in such circumstances and in the face of such pretensions it is worse than ineffectual: it is likely only to produce what it was meant to prevent; it is practically certain to draw us into the war without either the rights or the effectiveness of belligerents. There is one choice we cannot make, we are incapable of making: we will not choose the path of submission and suffer the most sacred rights of our Nation and our people to be ignored or violated. The wrongs against which we now array ouselves are no common wrongs; they cut to the very roots of human life.

With a profound sense of the solemn and even tragical character of the step I am taking and of the grave responsibilities which it involves, but in unhesitating obedience to what I deem my constitutional duty, I advise that the Congress declare the recent course of the Imperial German Government to be in fact nothing less than war against the government and people of the United States; that it formally accept the status of belligerent which has thus been thrust upon it; and that it take immediate steps not only to put the country in a more thorough state of defense but also to exert all its power and employ all its resources to bring the Government of the German Empire to terms and end the war.

What this will involve is clear. It will involve the utmost practicable coöperation in counsel and action with the governments now at war with Germany, and, as incident to that, the extension to those governments of the most liberal financial credits, in order that our resources may so far as possible be added to theirs. It will involve the organization and mobilization of all the material resources of the country to supply the materials of war and serve the incidental needs of the Nation in the most abundant and yet the most economical and efficient way possible. It will involve the immediate full equipment of the navy in all respects but particularly in supplying it with the best means of dealing with the enemy's submarines. It will involve the immediate addition to the armed forces of the

United States already provided for by law in case of war at least five hundred thousand men, who should, in my opinion, be chosen upon the principle of universal liability to service, and also the authorization of subsequent additional increments of equal force so soon as they may be needed and can be handled in training. It will involve also, of course, the granting of adequate credits to the Government, sustained, I hope, so far as they can equitably be sustained by the present generation, by well conceived taxation.

I say sustained so far as may be equitable by taxation because it seems to me that it would be most unwise to base the credits which will now be necessary entirely on money borrowed. It is our duty, I most respectfully urge, to protect our people so far as we may against the very serious hardships and evils which would be likely to arise out of the inflation which would be produced by vast loans.

In carrying out the measures by which these things are to be accomplished we should keep constantly in mind the wisdom of interfering as little as possible in our own preparation and in the equipment of our own military forces with the duty, — for it will be a very practical duty, — of supplying the nations already at war with Germany with the materials which they can obtain only from us or by our assistance. They are in the field and we should help them in every way to be effective there.

I shall take the liberty of suggesting, through the several executive departments of the Government, for the consideration of your committees, measures for the accomplishment of the several objects I have mentioned. I hope that it will be your pleasure to deal with them as having been framed after very careful thought by the branch of the Government upon which the responsibility of conducting the war and safeguarding the Nation will most directly fall.

While we do these things, these deeply momentous things, let us be very clear, and make very clear to all the world what our motives and our objects are. My own thought has not been driven from its habitual and normal course by the unhappy events of the last two months, and I do not believe that the thought of the Nation has been altered or clouded by them. I have exactly the same things in mind now that I had in mind when I addressed the Senate on the twenty-second of January last; the same that I had in mind when I addressed the Congress on the third of February and on the twenty-sixth of February. Our object now, as then, is to vindicate the principles of peace and justice in the life of the world as against selfish and autocratic power and to set up amongst the really free and self-governed peoples of the world such a concert of purpose and of action as will henceforth insure the observance of those principles. Neutrality is no longer feasible or desirable where the peace of the world is involved and the freedom of its peoples, and the menace to that peace and freedom lies in the existence of autocratic governments backed by organized force which is controlled wholly by their will, not by the will of their people. We have seen the last of neutrality in such circumstances. We are at the beginning of an age in which it will be insisted that the same standards of conduct and of responsibility for wrong done shall be observed among nations and their governments that are observed among the individual citizens of civilized states.

We have no quarrel with the German people. We have no feeling towards them but one of sympathy and friendship. It was not upon their impulse that their government acted in entering this war. It was not with their previous knowledge or approval. It was a war determined upon as wars used to be determined upon in the old, unhappy days when peoples were nowhere consulted by their rulers and wars were provoked and waged in the interest of dynasties or of little groups of ambitious men who were accustomed to use their fellow men as pawns and tools. Self-governed nations do not fill their neighbor states with spies or set the course of intrigue to bring about some critical posture of affairs which will give them an opportunity to strike and make conquest. Such designs can be successfully worked out only under cover and where no one has the right to ask questions. Cunningly contrived plans of deception or aggression, carried, it may be, from generation to generation, can be worked out and kept from the light only within the privacy of courts or behind the carefully guarded confidences of a narrow and privileged class. They are happily impossible where public opinion commands and insists upon full information concerning all the nation's affairs.

A steadfast concert for peace can never be maintained except by partnership of democratic nations. No autocratic government could be trusted to keep faith within it or observe its covenants. It must be a league of honor, a partnership of opinion. Intrigue would eat its vitals away; the plottings of inner circles who could plan what they would and render account to no one would be a corruption seated at its very heart. Only free peoples can hold their purpose and their honor steady to a common end and prefer the interests of mankind to any narrow interest of their own.

Does not every American feel that assurance has been added to our hope for the future peace of the world by the wonderful and heartening things that have been happening within the last few weeks in Russia? Russia was known by those who knew it best to have been always in fact democratic at heart, in all the vital habits of her thought, in all the intimate realationships of her people that spoke their natural instinct, their habitual attitude towards life. The autocracy that crowned the summit of her political structure, long as it had stood and terrible as was the reality of its power, was not in fact Russian in origin, character, or purpose; and now it has been shaken off and the great, generous Russian people have been added in all their naïve majesty and might to the forces that are fighting for freedom in the world, for justice, and for peace. Here is a fit partner for a League of Honor.

One of the things that has served to convince us that the Prussian autocracy was not and could never be our friend is that from the very outset of the present war it has filled our unsuspecting communities and even our offices of government with spies and set criminal intrigues everywhere afoot against our national unity of counsel, our peace within and without, our industries and our commerce. Indeed, it is now evident that its spies were here even before the war began; and it is unhappily not a matter of conjecture but a fact proved in our courts of justice that the intrigues which have more than once come perilously near to disturbing the peace and dislocating the industries of the country have been carried on at the instigation, with the support, and even under the personal direction of official agents of the Imperial Government accredited to the Government of the United States. Even in checking these things and trying to extirpate them we have sought to put the most generous interpretation possible upon them because we knew that their source lay not in any hostile feeling or purpose of the German people towards us (who were no doubt as ignorant of them as we ourselves were), but only in the selfish designs of a Government that did what it pleased and told its people nothing. But they have played their part in serving to convince us at last that that Government entertains no real friendship for us and means to act against our peace and security at its convenience. That it means to stir up enemies against us at our very doors the intercepted note to the German Minister at Mexico City is eloquent evidence.

We are accepting this challenge of hostile purpose because we know that in such a Government, following such methods, we can never have a friend; and that in the presence of its organized power, always lying in wait to accomplish we know not what purpose, there can be no assured security for the democratic Governments of the world. We are now about to accept gage of battle with this natural foe to liberty and shall, if necessary, spend the whole force of the Nation to check and nullify its pretensions and its power. We are glad, now that we see the facts with no veil of false pretense about them, to fight thus for the ultimate peace of the world and for the liberation of its peoples, the German peoples included; for the rights of nations great and small and the privilege of men everywhere to choose their way of life and of obedience. The world must be made safe for democracy. Its peace must be planted upon the tested foundations of political liberty. We have no selfish ends to serve. We desire no conquest, no dominion. We seek no indemnities for ourselves, no material compensation for the sacrifices we shall freely make. We are but one of the champions of the rights of mankind. We shall be satisfied when those rights have been made as secure as the faith and the freedom of nations can make them.

Just because we fight without rancor and without selfish object, seeking nothing for ourselves but what we shall wish to share with all free peoples, we shall, I feel confident, conduct our operations as belligerents without passion and ourselves observe with proud punctilio the principles of right and of fair play we profess to be fighting for.

I have said nothing of the Governments allied with the Imperial Government of Germany because they have not made war upon us or challenged us to defend our right and our honor. The Austro-Hungarian Government has, indeed, avowed its unqualified indorsement and acceptance of the reckless and lawless submarine warfare adopted now without disguise by the Imperial German Government, and it has therefore not been possible for this Government to receive Count Tarnowski, the Ambassador recently accredited to this Government by the Imperial and Royal Government of Austria-Hungary; but that Government has not actually engaged in warfare against citizens of the United States on the seas, and I take the liberty, for the present at least, of postponing a discussion of our relations with the authorities at Vienna. We enter this war only where we are clearly forced into it because there are no other means of defending our rights.

It will be all the easier for us to conduct ourselves as belligerents in a high spirit of right and fairness because we act without animus, not in enmity towards a people or with the desire to bring any injury or disadvantage upon them, but only in armed opposition to an irresponsible government which has thrown aside all considerations of humanity and of right and is running amuck. We are, let me say again, the sincere friends of the German people, and shall desire nothing so much as the early reëstablishment of intimate relations of mutual advantage between us,—however hard it may be for them, for the time being, to believe that this is spoken from our hearts. We have borne with their present Government through all these bitter months because of that friendship,—exercising a patience and forbearance which would otherwise have been impossible. We shall, happily, still have an opportunity to prove that friendship in our daily attitude and actions towards the millions of men and women of German birth and native sympathy who live amongst us and share our life, and we shall be proud to prove it towards all who are in fact loyal to their neighbors and to the Government in the hour of test. They are, most of them, as true and loyal Americans as if they had never known any other fealty or allegiance. They will be prompt to stand with us in rebuking and restraining the few who may be of a different mind and purpose. If there should be disloyalty, it will be dealt with with a firm hand of stern repression; but, if it lifts its head at all, it will lift it only here and there and without countenance except from a lawless and malignant few.

It is a distressing and oppressive duty, Gentlemen of the Congress, which I have performed in thus addressing you. There are, it may be, many months of fiery trial and sacrifice ahead of us. It is a fearful thing to lead this great peaceful people into war, into the most terrible and disastrous of all wars, civilization itself seeming to be in the balance. But the right is more precious than peace, and we shall fight for the things which we have always carried nearest our hearts,—for democracy, for the right of those who submit to authority to have a voice in their own Governments, for the rights and liberties of small nations, for a universal dominion of right by such a concert of free peoples as shall bring peace and safety to all nations and make the world itself at last free. To such a task we can dedicate our lives and our fortunes, everything that we are and everything that we have, with the pride of those who know that the day has come when America is privileged to spend her blood and her might for the principles that gave her birth and happiness and the peace which she has treasured. God helping her, she can do no other.

E. PREPAREDNESS

1. Preparedness and Peace

DOCUMENT 85

"We Shall Not Turn America
into a Military Camp"

The outbreak of the war in Europe did not immediately persuade the peace-minded Wilson that American defenses needed to be strengthened. He considered the Navy adequate for present defensive needs and saw little likelihood that American troops would be involved. Consequently, he gave little heed to the emotional demands, by such preparedness advocates as Theodore Roosevelt, that the nation expand its armed forces.

. . . It is said in some quarters that we are not prepared for war. What is meant by being prepared? Is it meant that we are not ready upon brief notice to put a nation in the field, a nation of men trained to arms? Of course we are not ready to do that; and we shall never be in time of peace so long as we retain our present political principles and institutions. And what is it that it is suggested we should be prepared to do? To defend ourselves against attack? We have always found means to do that, and shall find them whenever it is necessary without calling our people away from their necessary tasks to render compulsory military service in times of peace.

Excerpt from annual message to Congress, December 8, 1914, *Public Papers*, III, 223–227.

Allow me to speak with great plainness and directness upon this great matter and to avow my convictions with deep earnestness. I have tried to know what America is, what her people think, what they are, what they most cherish and hold dear. I hope that some of their finer passions are in my own heart,—some of the great conceptions and desires which gave birth to this Government and which have made the voice of this people a voice of peace and hope and liberty among the peoples of the world, and that, speaking my own thoughts, I shall, at least in part, speak theirs also, however faintly and inadequately, upon this vital matter.

We are at peace with all the world. No one who speaks counsel based on fact or drawn from a just and candid interpretation of realities can say that there is reason to fear that from any quarters our independence or the integrity of our territory is threatened. Dread of the power of any other nation we are incapable of. We are not jealous of rivalry in the fields of commerce or of any other peaceful achievement. We mean to live our own lives as we will; but we mean also to let live. We are, indeed, a true friend to all the nations of the world, because we threaten none, covet the possessions of none, desire the overthrow of none. Our friendship can be accepted and is accepted without reservation, because it is offered in a spirit and for a purpose which no one need ever question or suspect. Therein lies our greatness. We are the champions of peace and of concord. And we should be very jealous of this distinction which we have sought to earn. Just now we should be particularly jealous of it, because it is our dearest present hope that this character and reputation may presently, in God's providence, bring us an opportunity such as has seldom been vouchsafed any nation, the opportunity to counsel and obtain peace in the world and reconciliation and a healing settlement of many a matter that has cooled and interrupted the friendship of nations. This is the time above all others when we should wish and resolve to keep our strength by self-possession, our influence by preserving our ancient principles of action.

From the first we have had a clear and settled policy with regard to military establishments. We never have had, and while we retain our present principles and ideals we never shall have, a large standing army. If asked, Are you ready to defend yourself? we reply, Most assuredly, to the utmost; and yet we shall not turn America into a military camp. We will not ask our young men to spend the best years of their lives making soldiers of themselves. There is another sort of energy in us. It will know how to declare itself and make itself effective should occasion arise. And especially when half the world is on fire we shall be careful to make our moral insurance against the spread of the conflagration very definite and certain and adequate indeed.

Let us remind ourselves, therefore, of the only thing we can do or will do. We must depend in every time of national peril, in the future as in the past, not upon a standing army, nor yet upon a reserve army, but upon a citizenry trained and accustomed to arms. It will be right enough, right American policy, based upon our accustomed principles and practices, to provide a system by which every citizen who will volunteer for the training may be made familiar with the use of modern arms, the rudiments of drill and maneuver, and the maintenance and sanitation of camps. We should encourage such training and make it a means of discipline which our young men will learn to value. It is right that we should provide it not only, but that we should make it as attractive as possible, and so induce our young men to undergo it at such times as they can command a little freedom and can seek the physical development they need, for mere health's sake, if for nothing more. Every means by which such things can be stimulated is legitimate, and such a method smacks of true American ideas. It is right, too, that the National Guard of the States should be developed and strengthened by every means which is not inconsistent with our obligations to our own people or with the established policy of our Government. And this, also, not because the time or occasion specially calls for such measures, but because it should be our constant policy to make these provisions for our national peace and safety.

More than this carries with it a reversal of the whole history and character of our polity. More than this, proposed at this time, permit me to say, would mean merely that we had lost our self-possession, that we had been thrown off our balance by a war with which we have nothing to do, whose causes can not touch us, whose very existence affords us opportunities of friendship and disinterested service which should make us ashamed of any thought of hostility or fearful preparation for trouble. This is assuredly the opportunity for which a people and a government like ours were raised up, the opportunity not only to speak but actually to embody and exemplify the counsels of peace and amity and the lasting concord which is based on justice and fair and generous dealing.

A powerful navy we have always regarded as our proper and natural means of defense; and it has always been of defense that we have thought, never of aggression or of conquest. But who shall tell us now what sort of navy to build? We shall take leave to be strong upon the seas, in the future as in the past; and there will be no thought of offense or of provocation in that. Our ships are our natural bulwarks. When will the experts tell us just what kind we should construct—and when will they be right for ten years together, if the relative efficiency of craft of different kinds and uses continues to change as we have seen it change under our very eyes in these last few months? . . .

DOCUMENT 86

"To be Prepared, Not for War,
But Only for Defense. . . ."

The confrontation with Germany over submarine warfare in the summer of 1915 persuaded Wilson to reverse himself and adopt a modest preparedness program. He presented it to the country in a speech in New York on November 4.

. . . In no man's mind, I am sure, is there even raised the question of the wilful use of force on our part against any nation or any people. No matter what military or naval force the United States might develop, statesmen throughout the whole world might rest assured that we were gathering that force, not for attack in any quarter, not for aggression of any kind, not for the satisfaction of any political or international ambition, but merely to make sure of our own security. We have it in mind to be prepared, not for war, but only for defense; and with the thought constantly in our minds that the principles we hold most dear can be achieved by the slow processes of history only in the kindly and wholesome atmosphere of peace, and not by the use of hostile force. The mission of America in the world is essentially a mission of peace and good will among men. She has become the home and asylum of men of all creeds and races. Within her hospitable borders they have found homes and congenial associations and freedom and a wide and cordial welcome, and they have become part of the bone and sinew and spirit of America itself. America has been made up out of the nations of the world and is the friend of the nations of the world.

Excerpt from address to the Manhattan Club, New York, November 4, 1915, *Public Papers*, III, 386–389.

But we feel justified in preparing ourselves to vindicate our right to independent and unmolested action by making the force that is in us ready for assertion.

And we know that we can do this in a way that will be itself an illustration of the American spirit. In accordance with our American traditions we want and shall work for only an army adequate to the constant and legitimate uses of times of international peace. But we do want to feel that there is a great body of citizens who have received at least the most rudimentary and necessary forms of military training; that they will be ready to form themselves into a fighting force at the call of the Nation; and that the Nation has the munitions and supplies with which to equip them without delay should it be necessary to call them into action. We wish to supply them with the training they need, and we think we can do so without calling them at any time too long away from their civilian pursuits.

It is with this idea, with this conception, in mind that the plans have been made which it will be my privilege to lay before the Congress at its next session. That plan calls for only such an increase in the regular Army of the United States as experience has proved to be required for the performance of the necessary duties of the Army in the Philippines, in Hawaii, in Porto Rico, upon the borders of the United States, at the coast fortifications, and at the military posts of the interior. For the rest, it calls for the training within the next three years of a force of 400,000 citizen soldiers to be raised in annual contingents of 133,000, who would be asked to enlist for three years with the colors and three years on furlough, but who during their three years of enlistment with the colors would not be organized as a standing force but would be expected merely to undergo intensive training for a very brief period of each year. Their training would take place in immediate association with the organized units of the regular Army. It would have no touch of the amateur about it, neither would it exact of the volunteers more than they could give in any one year from their civilian pursuits.

And none of this would be done in such a way as in the slightest degree to supersede or subordinate our present serviceable and efficient National Guard. On the contrary, the National Guard itself would be used as part of the instrumentality by which training would be given the citizens who enlisted under the new conditions, and I should hope and expect that the legislation by which all this would be accomplished would put the National Guard itself upon a better and more permanent footing than it has ever been before, giving it not only the recognition which it deserves, but a more definite support from the national government and a more definite connection with the military organization of the nation.

What we all wish to accomplish is that the forces of the Nation should indeed be part of the Nation and not a separate professional force, and the chief cost of the system would not be in the enlistment or in the training of the men, but in the providing of ample equipment in case it should be necessary to call all forces into the field.

Moreover, it has been American policy time out of mind to look to the Navy as the first and chief line of defense. The Navy of the United States is already a very great and efficient force. Not rapidly, but slowly, with careful attention, our naval force has been developed until the Navy of the United States stands recognized as one of the most efficient and notable of the modern time. All that is needed in order to bring it to a point of extraordinary force and efficiency as compared with the other navies of the world is that we should hasten our pace in the policy we have long been pursuing, and that chief of all we should have a definite policy of development, not made from year to year but looking well into the future and planning for a definite consummation. We can and should profit in all that we do by the experience and example that have been made obvious to us by the military and naval events of the actual present. It is not merely a matter of building battleships and cruisers and submarines, but also a matter of making sure that we shall have the adequate equipment of men and munitions and supplies for the vessels we build and intend to build. Part of our problem is the problem of what I may call the mobilization of the resources of the nation at the proper time if it should ever be necessary to mobilize them for national defense. We shall study efficiency and adequate equipment as carefully as we shall study the number and size of our ships, and I believe that the plans already in part made public by the Navy Department are plans which the whole Nation can approve with rational enthusiasm. . . .

2. No Profiteering

DOCUMENT 87

"I Know the Points of Danger. . . ."

Wilson's rather mild preparedness program brought angry charges from peace groups that the President had yielded to the pressures of the militarists and munitions makers, the same interests that had opposed his domestic reforms. He therefore embarked on a speaking tour through the East and Middle West, late in January 1916, to persuade the skeptics that the basis for his program was national need and not private greed.

Excerpt from address at Des Moines, Iowa, February 1, 1916, *Public Papers*, IV, 77–79.

. . . I know that there is a very general impression that influences are at work in this country whose impulse does not come from a thoughtful conviction of danger, but which is said to come from a very thoughtful prospect of profit. I have heard the preposterous statement made that the agitation for preparation for national defense has come chiefly from the men who make armor plate for the ships and munitions for the Army. Why, ladies and gentlemen, do you suppose that all the thoughtful men who are engaged upon this side of this great question are susceptible of being led by influences of that sort? Do you suppose that they are so blind to the manifest opportunities for that sort of profit that they do not know the influences that are abroad and effective in such matters? I have not found the impulse for national defense coming from those sources. I have found it coming from the men with whom I rubbed shoulders on the street and in the factory; I have found it coming from the men who have nothing to do with the making of profits, but who have everything to do with the making of the daily life of this country. And it is from them that I take my inspiration. But I know the points of danger, and from the first, ladies and gentlemen, I have been urging upon Congress — I urged upon Congress before this war began — that the Government of the United States supply itself with the necessary plants to make the armor for the ships and to make the munitions for the guns and the men, and I believe, and confidently predict, that the adoption of measures of that sort will be part of the preparation for national defense; not in order, for it is not necessary, that the Government should make all the armor plate needed for the fleet or all the munitions needed for the men and the guns, but in order that it should make enough to regulate and control the price.

We are not theorists in this matter. We have tried it in one field. The Government is now manufacturing a very considerable proportion of the powder needed for the Navy. The consequence is that it has reduced its price from 53 cents to 36 cents. The point is that it can now get its powder from the private manufacturers of powder at 36 cents, because they know that it can be manufactured for that with a reasonable profit, and that if the Government can not buy it from them, it will make it for itself.

Of course somebody is going to make money out of the things privately manufactured, manufactured by private capital. There are men now in the great belligerent countries making, I daresay, vast sums of money out of the war, but making it perfectly legitimately, and I for one do not stand here to challenge or doubt their patriotism in the matter. America is not going to be held back from any great national enterprise by any great financial interest of any sort, because America, of all places in the world, is alive to things of that sort and knows how to avoid the difficulties which are involved. If there is any thought on the part of those who make armor plate and munitions that they will get extraordinary profit out of preparation for national defense, all I have to say is that they will be sadly disappointed. But these are things which to my mind go without saying, for, ladies and gentlemen, if it is necessary to defend this Nation we are going to defend it no matter who makes money and no matter what it costs.

I have heard some gentleman say, "My constituents do not object to the program, but they do object to the bills that will have to be paid afterwards." I would be very sorry to give that account of any constituency in the United States. I would be very sorry to believe, and I do not believe, that any constituency in the United States will be governed by considerations of that sort. Of course it is going to cost money to prepare for defense, but equally of course the American people are going to pay for it, and pay for it without grumbling. We are not selfishly rich; we are a very rich people, but we can not be rich as a people unless we maintain our character and integrity as a people. Life is not worth anything for us as a nation if the very issues of life for the Nation itself are put in jeopardy by the action which we neglect to take. So I have come out on this errand merely to get into touch with you, my fellow citizens, merely to let you know in temperate words from my own lips that the men who are saying that preparation for national defense is necessary, and immediately necessary, are speaking the sober truth. And I believe that you will credit the statement that no man is in a better position to know that than I am. . . .

3. *Militarism*

DOCUMENT 88

"No Taint of the Spirit of Militarism"

Wilson shared the concern of peace advocates that the expansion of the armed forces might weaken the tradition of civilian leadership in public affairs. He warned the 1916 graduating class at West Point to resist any such spirit of militarism.

. . . You know that the chief thing that is holding many people back from enthusiasm for what is called preparedness is the fear of militarism. I want to say a word to you young gentleman about militarism. You are not militarists because you are military. Militarism does not consist in the existence of an army, not even in the existence of a very

Excerpt from address at the Military Academy, West Point, N.Y., June 13, 1916, *Public Papers*, IV, 203-204.

great army. Militarism is a spirit. It is a point of view. It is a system. It is a purpose. The purpose of militarism is to use armies for aggression. The spirit of militarism is the opposite of the civilian spirit, the citizen spirit. In a country where militarism prevails the military man looks down upon the civilian, regards him as inferior, thinks of him as intended for his, the military man's, support and use; and just so long as America is America that spirit and point of view is impossible with us. There is as yet in this country, so far as I can discover, no taint of the spirit of militarism. You young gentlemen are not preferred in promotion because of the families you belong to. You are not drawn into the Academy because you belong to certain influential circles. You do not come here with a long tradition of military pride back of you.

You are picked out from the citizens of the United States to be that part of the force of the United States which makes its polity safe against interference. You are the part of American citizens who say to those who would interfere, "You must not" and "You shall not." But you are American citizens, and the idea I want to leave with you boys to-day is this: No matter what comes, always remember that first of all you are citizens of the United States before you are officers, and that you are officers because you represent in your particular profession what the citizenship of the United States stands for. There is no danger of militarism if you are genuine Americans, and I for one do not doubt that you are. When you begin to have the militaristic spirit—not the military spirit, that is all right—then begin to doubt whether you are Americans or not.

You know that one thing in which our forefathers took pride was this, that the civil power is superior to the military power in the United States. Once and again the people of the United States have so admired some great military man as to make him President of the United States, when he became commander-in-chief of all the forces of the United States, but he was commander-in-chief because he was President, not because he had been trained to arms, and his authority was civil, not military. I can teach you nothing of military power, but I am instructed by the Constitution to use you for constitutional and patriotic purposes. And that is the only use you care to be put to. That is the only use you ought to care to be put to, because, after all, what is the use in being an American if you do not know what it is? . . .

4. *The Armed-Ship Controversy*

DOCUMENT 89

"No Recourse But to *Armed* Neutrality. . . ."

The resumption of German submarine warfare in February 1917 put Wilson's preparedness program to the test. The program had obviously failed to deter the Germans from this decision. Now, unless the President were meekly to acquiesce in the German action and swallow his stern protests of the preceding two years, he would have to devise some means to protect American ships — or else see them driven from the oceans. Wilson accordingly requested authority from Congress to install Navy guns and gun crews on American vessels sailing in the danger zone.

I have again asked the privilege of addressing you because we are moving through critical times during which it seems to me to be my duty to keep in close touch with the

---

Address to Congress, February 26, 1917, *Public Papers*, IV, 428–432.

Houses of Congress, so that neither counsel nor action shall run at cross purposes between us.

On the third of February I officially informed you of the sudden and unexpected action of the Imperial German Government in declaring its intention to disregard the promises it had made to this Government in April last and undertake immediate submarine operations against all commerce, whether of belligerents or of neutrals, that should seek to approach Great Britain and Ireland, the Atlantic coasts of Europe, or the harbors of the eastern Mediterranean, and to conduct those operations without regard to the established restrictions of international practice, without regard to any considerations of humanity even which might interfere with their object. That policy was forthwith put into practice. It has now been in active execution for nearly four weeks.

Its practical results are not yet fully disclosed. The commerce of other neutral nations is suffering severely, but not, perhaps, very much more severely than it was already suffering before the first of February, when the new policy of the Imperial Government was put into operation. We have asked the co-operation of the other neutral governments to prevent these depredations, but so far none of them has thought it wise to join us in any common course of action. Our own commerce has suffered, is suffering, rather in apprehension than in fact, rather because so many of our ships are timidly keeping to their home ports than because American ships have been sunk.

Two American vessels have been sunk, the *Housatonic* and the *Lyman M. Law*. The case of the *Housatonic*, which was carrying foodstuffs consigned to a London firm, was essentially like the case of the *Fry*, in which, it will be recalled, the German Government admitted its liability for damages, and the lives of the crew, as in the case of the *Fry*, were safeguarded with reasonable care. The case of the *Law*, which was carrying lemon-box staves to Palermo, disclosed a ruthlessness of method which deserves grave condemnation, but was accompanied by no circumstances which might not have been expected at any time in connection with the use of the submarine against merchantmen as the German Government has used it.

In sum, therefore, the situation we find ourselves in with regard to the actual conduct of the German submarine warfare against commerce and its effects upon our own ships and people is substantially the same that it was when I addressed you on the third of February, except for the tying up of our shipping in our own ports because of the unwillingness of our shipowners to risk their vessels at sea without insurance or adequate protection, and the very serious congestion of our commerce which has resulted, a congestion which is growing rapidly more and more serious every day. This in itself might presently accomplish, in effect, what the new German submarine orders were meant to accomplish, so far as we are concerned. We can only say, therefore, that the overt act which I have ventured to hope the German commanders would in fact avoid has not occurred.

But, while this is happily true, it must be admitted that there have been certain additional indications and expressions of purpose on the part of the German press and the German authorities which have increased rather than lessened the impression that, if our ships and our people are spared, it will be because of fortunate circumstances or because the commanders of the German submarines which they may happen to encounter exercise an unexpected discretion and restraint rather than because of the instructions under which those commanders are acting. It would be foolish to deny that the situation is fraught with the gravest possibilities and dangers. No thoughtful man can fail to see that the necessity for definite action may come at any time, if we are in fact, and not in word merely, to defend our elementary rights as a neutral nation. It would be most imprudent to be unprepared.

I cannot in such circumstances be unmindful of the fact that the expiration of the term of the present Congress is immediately at hand, by constitutional limitation; and that it would in all likelihood require an unusual length of time to assemble and organize the Congress which is to succeed it. I feel that I ought, in view of that fact, to obtain from you full and immediate assurance of the authority which I may need at any moment to exercise. No doubt I already possess that authority without special warrant of law, by the plain implication of my constitutional duties and powers; but I prefer, in the present circumstances, not to act upon general implication. I wish to feel that the authority and the power of the Congress are behind me in whatever it may become necessary for me to do. We are jointly the servants of the people and must act together and in their spirit, so far as we can divine and interpret it.

No one doubts what it is our duty to do. We must defend our commerce and the lives of our people in the midst of the present trying circumstances, with discretion but with clear and steadfast purpose. Only the method and the extent remain to be chosen, upon the occasion, if occasion should indeed arise. Since it has unhappily proved impossible to safeguard our neutral rights by diplomatic means against the unwarranted infringements they are suffering at the hands of Germany, there may be no recourse but to *armed* neutrality, which we shall know how to maintain and for which there is abundant American precedent.

It is devoutly to be hoped that it will not be necessary to put armed force anywhere into action. The American people do not desire it, and our desire is not different from theirs. I am sure that they will understand the spirit in which I am now acting, the purpose I hold nearest my heart and would wish to exhibit in everything I do. I am anxious that the people of the nations at war also should understand and not mistrust us. I hope that I need give no further proofs and assurances than I have already given throughout nearly three years of anxious patience that I am the friend of peace and mean to preserve it for America so long as I am able. I am not now proposing or contemplating war or any steps that need lead to it. I merely request that you will accord me by your own vote and definite bestowal the means and the authority to safeguard in practice the right of a great people who are at peace and who are desirous of exercising none but the rights of peace to follow the pursuits of peace in quietness and good will — rights recognized time out of mind by all the civilized nations of the world. No course of my choosing or of theirs will lead to war. War can come only by the wilful acts and aggressions of others.

You will understand why I can make no definite proposals or forecasts of action now and must ask for your supporting authority in the most general terms. The form in which action may become necessary cannot yet be foreseen. I believe that the people will be willing to trust me to act with restraint, with prudence, and in the true spirit of amity and good faith that they have themselves displayed throughout these trying months; and it is in that belief that I request that you will authorize me to supply our merchant ships with defensive arms, should that become necessary, and with the means of using them, and to employ any other instrumentalities or methods that may be necessary and adequate to protect our ships and our people in their legitimate and peaceful pursuits on the seas. I request also that you will grant me at the same time, along with the powers I ask, a sufficient credit to enable me to provide adequate means of protection where they are lacking, including adequate insurance against the present war risks.

I have spoken of our commerce and of the legitimate errands of our people on the seas, but you will not be misled as to my main thought, the thought that lies beneath these phrases and gives them dignity and weight. It is not of material interests merely that we are thinking. It is, rather, of fundamental human rights, chief of all the right of life itself. I am thinking, not only of the rights of Americans to go and come about their proper business by way of the sea, but also of something much deeper, much more fundamental than that. I am thinking of those rights of humanity without which there is no civilization. My theme is of those great principles of compassion and of protection which mankind has sought to throw about human lives, the lives of non-combatants, the lives of men who are peacefully at work keeping the industrial processes of the world quick and vital, the lives of women and children and of those who supply the labour which ministers to their sustenance. We are speaking of no selfish material rights but of rights which our hearts support and whose foundation is that righteous passion for justice upon which all law, all structures alike of family, of state, and of mankind must rest, as upon the ultimate base of our existence and our liberty. I cannot imagine any man with American principles at his heart hesitating to defend these things.

DOCUMENT 90

"A Little Group of Willful Men. . . ."

Congressional approval of Wilson's request to arm American ships was blocked by a small band of progressive Sena-

Statement to the country, March 4, 1917, *Public Papers*, IV, 433–435.

tors in the closing hours of the Sixty-fourth Congress, which expired on March 4. It would be too much to describe their action as a filibuster, for they were not allowed much time to debate an issue of such momentous import. Wilson sternly rebuked their opposition, and he proceeded to arm the ships on his own authority.

The termination of the last session of the Sixty-fourth Congress by constitutional limitation disclosed a situation unparalleled in the history of the country, perhaps unparalleled in the history of any modern Government. In the immediate presence of a crisis fraught with more subtle and far-reaching possibilities of national danger than any other the Government has known within the whole history of its international relations, the Congress has been unable to act either to safeguard the country or to vindicate the elementary rights of its citizens. More than 500 of the 531 members of the two houses were ready and anxious to act; the House of Representatives had acted, by an overwhelming majority; but the Senate was unable to act because a little group of eleven Senators had determined that it should not.

The Senate has no rules by which debate can be limited or brought to an end, no rules by which dilatory tactics of any kind can be prevented. A single member can stand in the way of action, if he have but the physical endurance. The result in this case is a complete paralysis alike of the legislative and of the executive branches of the Government.

This inability of the Senate to act has rendered some of the most necessary legislation of the session impossible at a time when the need of it was most pressing and most evident. The bill which would have permitted such combinations of capital and of organization in the export and import trade of the country as the circumstances of international competition have made imperative—a bill which the business judgment of the whole country approved and demanded—has failed. The opposition of one or two Senators has made it impossible to increase the membership of the Interstate Commerce Commission to give it the altered organization necessary for its efficiency. The Conservation bill, which should have released for immediate use the mineral resources which are still locked up in the public lands, now that their release is more imperatively necessary than ever, and the bill which would have made the unused water power of the country immediately available for industry have both failed, though they have been under consideration throughout the sessions of two Congresses and have been twice passed by the House of Representatives. The appropriations for the army have failed, along with the appropriations for the civil establishment of the Government, the appropriations for the military Academy at West Point and the General Deficiency bill. It has proved impossible to extend the powers of the Shipping Board to meet the special needs of the new situations into which our commerce has been forced or to increase the gold reserve of our national banking system to meet the unusual circumstances of the existing financial situation.

It would not cure the difficulty to call the Sixty-fifth Congress in extraordinary session. The paralysis of the Senate would remain. The purpose and the spirit of action are not lacking now. The Congress is more definitely united in thought and purpose at this moment, I venture to say, than it has been within the memory of any men now in its membership. There is not only the most united patriotic purpose, but the objects members have in view are perfectly clear and definite. But the Senate cannot act unless its leaders can obtain unanimous consent. Its majority is powerless, helpless. In the midst of a crisis of extraordinary peril, when only definite and decided action can make the nation safe or shield it from war itself by the aggression of others, action is impossible.

Although, as a matter of fact, the Nation and the representatives of the Nation stand back of the Executive with unprecedented unanimity and spirit, the impression made abroad will, of course, be that it is not so and that other Governments may act as they please without fear that this Government can do anything at all. We cannot explain. The explanation is incredible. The Senate of the United States is the only legislative body in the world which cannot act when its majority is ready for action. A little group of willful men, representing no opinion but their own, have rendered the great Government of the United States helpless and contemptible.

The remedy? There is but one remedy. The only remedy is that the rules of the Senate shall be so altered that it can act. The country can be relied upon to draw the moral. I believe that the Senate can be relied on to supply the means of action and save the country from disaster.

PART VIII

Mobilization for War

A. MOBILIZING PUBLIC OPINION

DOCUMENT 91

"We Are Not Enemies of the German People. . . ."

Well aware that not all Americans were persuaded of either the desirability or the necessity of entering the war, Wilson launched a massive campaign to educate the nation as to its war aims. One step was the creation of the first significant federal propaganda agency, the Committee on Public Information, headed by a progressive journalist, George Creel. At another level, the President himself sought to arouse public opinion for war service by means of speeches and patriotic statements.

. . . It is plain enough how we were forced into the war. The extraordinary insults and aggressions of the Imperial German Government left us no self-respecting choice but to take up arms in defense of our rights as a free people and of our honor as a sovereign government. The military

---

Excerpts from Flag Day address, Washington, June 14, 1917, *Public Papers*, V, 61–63, 64–65.

masters of Germany denied us the right to be neutral. They filled our unsuspecting communities with vicious spies and conspirators and sought to corrupt the opinion of our people in their own behalf. When they found that they could not do that, their agents diligently spread sedition amongst us and sought to draw our own citizens from their allegiance,—and some of those agents were men connected with the official Embassy of the German Government itself here in our own capital. They sought by violence to destroy our industries and arrest our commerce. They tried to incite Mexico to take up arms against us and to draw Japan into a hostile alliance with her,—and that, not by indirection, but by direct suggestion from the Foreign Office in Berlin. They impudently denied us the use of the high seas and repeatedly executed their threat that they would send to their death any of our people who ventured to approach the coasts of Europe. And many of our own people were corrupted. Men began to look upon their own neighbors with suspicion and to wonder in their hot resentment and surprise whether there was any community in which hostile intrigue did not lurk. What great nation in such circumstances would not have taken up arms? Much as we had desired peace, it was denied us, and not of our own choice. This flag under which we serve would have been dishonored had we withheld our hand.

But that is only part of the story. We know now as clearly as we knew before we were ourselves engaged that we are not the enemies of the German people and that they are not our enemies. They did not originate or desire this hideous war or wish that we should be drawn into it; and we are vaguely conscious that we are fighting their cause, as they will some day see it, as well as our own. They are themselves in the grip of the same sinister power that has now at last stretched its ugly talons out and drawn blood from us. The whole world is at war because the whole world is in the grip of that power and is trying out the great battle which shall determine whether it is to be brought under its mastery or fling itself free.

The war was begun by the military masters of Germany, who proved to be also the masters of Austria-Hungary. These men have never regarded nations as peoples, men, women, and children of like blood and frame as themselves, for whom governments existed and in whom governments had their life. They have regarded them merely as serviceable organizations which they could by force or intrigue bend or corrupt to their own purpose. They have regarded the smaller states, in particular, and the peoples who could be overwhelmed by force, as their natural tools and instruments of domination. Their purpose has long been avowed. The statesmen of other nations, to whom that purpose was incredible, paid little attention; regarded what German professors expounded in their classrooms and German writers set forth to the world as the goal of German policy as rather the dream of minds detached from practical affairs, as preposterous private conceptions of German destiny, than as the actual plans of responsible rulers; but the rulers of Germany themselves knew all the while what concrete plans, what well-advanced intrigues lay back of what the professors and the writers were saying, and were glad to go forward unmolested, filling the thrones of Balkan states with German princes, putting German officers at the service of Turkey to drill her armies and make interest with her government, developing plans of sedition and rebellion in India and Egypt, setting their fires in Persia. The demands made by Austria upon Serbia were a mere single step in a plan which compassed Europe and Asia, from Berlin to Bagdad. They hoped those demands might not arouse Europe, but they meant to press them whether they did or not, for they thought themselves ready for the final issue of arms.

Their plan was to throw a broad belt of German military power and political control across the very center of Europe and beyond the Mediterranean into the heart of Asia; and Austria-Hungary was to be as much their tool and pawn as Serbia or Bulgaria or Turkey or the ponderous states of the East. Austria-Hungary, indeed, was to become part of the central German Empire, absorbed and dominated by the same forces and influences that had originally cemented the German states themselves. The dream had its heart at Berlin. It could have had a heart nowhere else! . . .

The military masters under whom Germany is bleeding see very clearly to what point Fate has brought them. If they fall back or are forced back an inch, their power both abroad and at home will fall to pieces like a house of cards. It is their power at home they are thinking about now more than their power abroad. It is that power which is trembling under their very feet; and deep fear has entered their hearts. They have but one chance to perpetuate their military power or even their controlling political influence. If they can secure peace now with the immense advantages still in their hands which they have up to this point apparently gained, they will have justified themselves before the German people: they will have gained by force what they promised to gain by it: an immense expansion of German power, an immense enlargement of German industrial and commercial opportunities. Their prestige will be secure, and with their prestige their political power. If they fail, their people will thrust them aside; a government accountable to the people themselves will be set up in Germany as it has been in England, in the United States, in France, and in all the great countries of the modern time except Germany. If they succeed they are safe and Germany and the world are undone; if they fail Germany is saved and the world will be at peace. If they succeed,

America will fall within the menace. We and all the rest of the world must remain armed, as they will remain, and must make ready for the next step in their aggression; if they fail, the world may unite for peace and Germany may be of the union. . . .

B. ORGANIZING THE NATION
FOR WAR

1. Selective Service

DOCUMENT 92

"A Team in Which Every Man Shall Play
the Part for Which He Is Best Fitted"

The war-weary Allies quickly appealed for massive American troop reinforcements. Wilson decided to raise these by means of a selective conscription that would insure fairness and the efficient utilization of skilled manpower. Congress quickly passed the necessary legislation, and on May 18, 1917, Wilson announced the date and purpose of the first draft registration.

The power against which we are arrayed has sought to impose its will upon the world by force. To this end it has increased armament until it has changed the face of war. In the sense in which we have been wont to think of ar-

---

Statement accompanying the proclamation for the draft registration, May 18, 1917, *Public Papers*, V, 38–39.

mies there are no armies in this struggle. There are entire nations armed. Thus, the men who remain to till the soil and man the factories are no less a part of the army that is in France than the men beneath the battle flags. It must be so with us. It is not an army that we must shape and train for war; it is a nation. To this end our people must draw close in one compact front against a common foe. But this cannot be if each man pursues a private purpose. All must pursue one purpose. The Nation needs all men; but it needs each man, not in the field that will most pleasure him, but in the endeavor that will best serve the common good. Thus, though a sharpshooter pleases to operate a trip-hammer for the forging of great guns, and an expert machinist desires to march with the flag, the Nation is being served only when the sharpshooter marches and the machinist remains at his levers.

The whole Nation must be a team in which each man shall play the part for which he is best fitted. To this end, Congress has provided that the Nation shall be organized for war by selection and that each man shall be classified for service in the place to which it shall best serve the general good to call him.

The significance of this cannot be overstated. It is a new thing in our history and a landmark in our progress. It is a new manner of accepting and vitalizing our duty to give ourselves with thoughtful devotion to the common purpose of us all. It is in no sense a conscription of the unwilling; it is, rather, selection from a nation which has volunteered in mass. It is no more a choosing of those who shall march with the colors than it is a selection of those who shall serve an equally necessary and devoted purpose in the industries that lie behind the battle line.

The day here named is the time upon which all shall present themselves for assignment to their tasks. It is for that reason destined to be remembered as one of the most conspicuous moments in our history. It is nothing less than the day upon which the manhood of the country shall step forward in one solid rank in defense of the ideals to which this Nation is consecrated. It is important to those ideals no less than to the pride of this generation in manifesting its devotion to them, that there be no gaps in the ranks.

It is essential that the day be approached in thoughtful apprehension of its significance and that we accord to it the honor and the meaning that it deserves. Our industrial need prescribes that it be not made a technical holiday, but the stern sacrifice that is before us, urges that it be carried in all our hearts as a great day of patriotic devotion and obligation when the duty shall lie upon every man, whether he is himself to be registered or not, to see to it that the name of every male person of the designated ages is written on these lists of honor.

2. *Mobilizing Food Supplies*

DOCUMENT 93

"Stimulation and Conservation,

Not Arbitrary Restraint. . . ."

To feed the hungry Allies and meet the vastly expanded needs of American military forces, Wilson established a food-control program under Herbert Hoover, a successful mining engineer who had recently been the director of the Belgian Relief Commission. To buttress Hoover's authority the President asked Congress for sweeping powers over the production and distribution of foodstuffs, fertilizers, fuel, and farm implements. After a lengthy and heated debate, Congress responded with the Lever Act of August 10, 1917,

Statement on the food law, May 19, 1917, *Public Papers*, V, 42–44.

which greatly strengthened Wilson's authority to mobilize the nation's war economy.

It is very desirable, in order to prevent misunderstandings or alarms and to assure coöperation in a vital matter, that the country should understand exactly the scope and purpose of the very great powers which I have thought it necessary in the circumstances to ask the Congress to put in my hands with regard to our food supplies. Those powers are very great indeed, but they are no greater than it has proved necessary to lodge in the other Governments which are conducting this momentous war, and their object is stimulation and conservation, not arbitrary restraint or injurious interference with the normal processes of production. They are intended to benefit and assist the farmer and all those who play a legitimate part in the preparation, distribution, and marketing of foodstuffs.

It is proposed to draw a sharp line of distinction between the normal activities of the Government represented in the Department of Agriculture in reference to food production, conservation, and marketing on the one hand and the emergency activities necessitated by the war in reference to the regulation of food distribution and consumption on the other.

All measures intended directly to extend the normal activities of the Department of Agriculture in reference to the production, conservation, and the marketing of farm crops will be administered as in normal times through that department, and the powers asked for over distribution and consumption, over exports, imports, prices, purchase, and requisition of commodities, storing, and the like which may require regulation during the war will be placed in the hands of a commissioner of food administration appointed by the President and directly responsible to him.

The objects sought to be served by the legislation asked

for are: Full inquiry into the existing available stocks of foodstuffs and into the costs and practices of the various food-producing and distributing trades; the prevention of all unwarranted hoarding of every kind and of the control of foodstuffs by persons who are not in any legitimate sense producers, dealers, or traders; the requisitioning when necessary for the public use of food supplies and of the equipment necessary for handling them properly; the licensing of wholesome and legitimate mixtures and milling percentages; and the prohibition of the unnecessary or wasteful use of foods. Authority is asked also to establish prices, but not in order to limit the profits of the farmers, but only to guarantee to them when necessary a minimum price which will insure them a profit where they are asked to attempt new crops and to secure the consumer against extortion by breaking up corners and attempts at speculation when they occur by fixing temporarily a reasonable price at which middlemen must sell.

I have asked Mr. Herbert Hoover to undertake this all-important task of food administration. He has expressed his willingness to do so on condition that he is to receive no payment for his services and that the whole of the force under him, exclusive of clerical assistance, shall be employed so far as possible upon the same volunteer basis. He has expressed his confidence that this difficult matter of food administration can be successfully accomplished through the voluntary coöperation and direction of legitimate distributors of foodstuffs and with the help of the women of the country.

Although it is absolutely necessary that unquestionable powers shall be placed in my hands in order to insure the success of this administration of the food supplies of the country, I am confident that the exercise of those powers will be necessary only in the few cases where some small and selfish minority proves unwilling to put the Nation's interests above personal advantage and that the whole country will heartily support Mr. Hoover's efforts by supplying the necessary volunteer agencies throughout the country for the intelligent control of food consumption and securing the coöperation of the most capable leaders of the very interests most directly affected, that the exercise of the powers deputed to him will rest very successfully upon the good will and coöperation of the people themselves, and that the ordinary economic machinery of the country will be left substantially undisturbed.

The proposed Food Administration is intended, of course, only to meet a manifest emergency and to continue only while the war lasts. Since it will be composed for the most part of volunteers, there need be no fear of the possibility of a permanent bureaucracy arising out of it. All control of consumption will disappear when the emergency has passed. It is with that object in view that the administration considers it to be of preëminent importance that the existing associations of producers and distributors of foodstuffs should be mobilized and made use of on a volunteer basis. The successful conduct of the projected food administration by such means will be the finest possible demonstration of the willingness, the ability, and the efficiency of democracy, and of its justified reliance upon the freedom of individual initiative. The last thing that any American could contemplate with equanimity would be the introduction of anything resembling Prussian autocracy into the food control in this country.

It is of vital interest and importance to every man who produces food and to every man who takes part in its distribution that these policies thus liberally administered should succeed and succeed altogether. It is only in that way that we can prove it to be absolutely unnecessary to resort to the rigorous and drastic measures which have proved to be necessary in some of the European countries.

3. *Government Operation of the Railroads*

DOCUMENT 94

"A Great National Necessity . . ."

Gradually Wilson moved toward a greater degree of government control over essential economic activities than ever before in the nation's history. By the spring of 1918, for example, he had named Bernard M. Baruch to head a powerful War Industries Board, which had virtually dictatorial authority over much of the economy. Even before this, however, the President had used his powers under the Lever Act to take over the faltering railroad system and place it under unified government management.

I have exercised the powers over the transporation systems of the country which were granted me by the Act of Congress of last August because it has become imperatively necessary for me to so. This is a war of resources no less than of men, perhaps even more than of men, and it is necessary for the complete mobilization of our resources that the transportation systems of the country should be organized and employed under a single authority and a simplified method of coördination which have not proved possible under private management and control. The committee of railway executives who have been coöperating with the Government in this all-important matter have done the utmost that it was possible for them to do; have done it with patriotic zeal and with great ability; but there were difficulties that they could neither escape nor neutralize. Complete unity of administration in the present circumstances involves upon occasion and at many points a serious dislocation of earnings, and the committee was,

Message to Congress, December, 26, 1917, *Public Papers*, V, 147–149.

of course, without power or authority to re-arrange charges or effect proper compensations and adjustments of earnings. Several roads which were willingly and with admirable public spirit accepting the orders of the committee have already suffered from these circumstances and should not be required to suffer further. In mere fairness to them the full authority of the Government must be substituted. The Government itself will thereby gain an immense increase of efficiency in the conduct of the war and of the innumerable activities upon which its successful conduct depends.

The public interest must be first served and, in addition, the financial interests of the Government and the financial interests of the railways must be brought under a common direction. The financial operations of the railways need not then interfere with the borrowings of the Government, and they themselves can be conducted at a greater advantage. Investors in railway securities may rest assured that their rights and interests will be as scrupulously looked after by the Government as they could be by the directors of the several railway systems. Immediately upon the reassembling of Congress I shall recommend that these definite guarantees by given: first, of course, that the railway properties will be maintained during the period of federal control in as good repair and as complete equipment as when taken over by the Government, and, second, that the roads shall receive a net operating income equal in each case to the average net income of the three years preceding June 30, 1917; and I am entirely confident that the Congress will be disposed in this case, as in others, to see that justice is done and full security assured to the owners and creditors of the great systems which the Government must now use under its own direction or else suffer serious embarrassment.

The Secretary of War and I are agreed that, all the circumstances being taken into consideration, the best results can be obtained under the immediate executive direction of the Hon. William G. McAdoo, whose practical experience peculiarly fits him for the service and whose authority as Secretary of the Treasury will enable him to coördinate as no other man could the many financial interests which will be involved and which might, unless systematically directed, suffer very embarrassing entanglements.

The Government of the United States is the only great Government now engaged in the war which has not already assumed control of this sort. It was thought to be in the spirit of American institutions to attempt to do everything that was necessary through private management, and if zeal and ability and patriotic motive could have accomplished the necessary unification of administration, it would certainly have been accomplished; but no zeal or ability could overcome insuperable obstacles, and I have deemed it my duty to recognize that fact in all candor now that it is demonstrated and to use without reserve the great authority reposed in me. A great national necessity dictated the action and I was therefore not at liberty to abstain from it.

4. Heading Off Congressional Interference

DOCUMENT 95

"A Practical Blunder of the Gravest Sort"

Periodically during the war Wilson faced sharp Congressional criticism over the progress of the war effort, and several times he had to contend with attempts to establish a

---

Letter to John Sharp Williams, September 1, 1917, in Baker, *Wilson, Life and Letters*, VII, 251–252.

Congressional committee to investigate and supervise the mobilization programs. The President did not object to normal legislative investigation but, as this letter to a Senator shows, he was determined to resist all efforts by Congress to weaken or divide executive direction of the war effort.

I know what your attitude is towards the proposal to constitute a Congressional Committee to assist in some way in controlling the expenditure of the vast sums of money which Congress has appropriated and is about to appropriate, and I feel sure that you will do your utmost to prevent the creation of any such body, but I am very anxious that my friends in the Senate should all know how serious the matter is. It would constitute a very great added difficulty and burden so far as I am concerned in the administration of the war. The great impediment to an effective control on my part as things stand is that there are so many consultative bodies and so many instrumentalities upon which I must keep my eye at the same time. Fortunately, the instrumentalities which now exist are under my authority. To have another authority put over them or anybody which might be conceived of as exercising an independent authority would be fatal to the unity of the administration and to the very kind of control which the proponents of such a committee have in mind. I have taken the liberty of writing this to you in order that I might have your cooperation, which I know you will generously give, in preventing what would undoubtedly be a practical blunder of the gravest sort.

DOCUMENT 96

"A Direct Vote of Want of Confidence in the Administration"

In beating down one such Congressional threat in the spring of 1918, Wilson used an analogy (in another letter to a Senator) to a parliamentary vote of confidence.

I am sincerely obliged to you for calling my attention to Senate Resolution 241, which in effect proposes to constitute the Military Affairs Committee of the Senate a committee on the conduct of the war.

I deem it my duty to say that I should regard the passage of this resolution as a direct vote of want of confidence in the administration. The purpose which it undoubtedly expresses has been expressed again and again in various forms during the present session, and has always seemed to originate in a rooted distrust of those who are at present in charge of the executive functions of the Government. These executive functions are very clearly understood. They have been defined both by the Constitution and by long experience, and no one can doubt where the responsibility for them lies or what the methods are by which those who are responsible can be held to their duty.

Such activities on the part of a particular committee of the Senate as this resolution would look forward to would constitute nothing less than an attempt to take over the conduct of the war, or at the least so superintend and direct and participate in the executive conduct of it as to

Letter to Thomas S. Martin, May 14, 1918, in *Official Bulletin*, No. 311, May 16, 1918.

interfere in the most serious way with the action of the constituted executive.

I protest most earnestly against the adoption of any such action and shall hope that every Senator who intends to support the present administration in the conduct of the war will vote against it. These are serious times and it is absolutely necessary that the lines should be clearly drawn between friends and opponents.

C. CONTROL OF PROFITEERING

DOCUMENT 97

"Patriotism Leaves Profits Out of the Question"

Sensitive to charges by some progressives that the war would enrich the very interests against which Wilson's domestic reform program had been chiefly directed, the President sought from the first to limit profiteering on war contracts.

MY FELLOW COUNTRYMEN:

The Government is about to attempt to determine the prices at which it will ask you henceforth to furnish various supplies which are necessary for the prosecution of the war and various materials which will be needed in the industries by which the war must be sustained.

We shall, of course, try to determine them justly and to the best advantage of the Nation as a whole; but justice is

Excerpt from address to mine operators and manufacturers, July 12, 1917, *Public Papers*, V, 74–75.

easier to speak of than to arrive at, and there are some considerations which I hope we shall all keep steadily in mind while this particular problem of justice is being worked out. I therefore take the liberty of stating very candidly my own view of the situation and of the principles which should guide both the Government and mine-owners and manufacturers of the country in this difficult matter.

A just price must, of course, be paid for everything the Government buys. By a just price I mean a price which will sustain the industries concerned in a high state of efficiency, provide a living for those who conduct them, enable them to pay good wages, and make possible expansions of their enterprises which will from time to time become necessary as the stupendous undertakings of this great war develop.

We could not wisely or reasonably do less than pay such prices. They are necessary for the maintenance and development of industry; and the maintenance and development of industry are necessary for the great task we have in hand. But I trust that we shall not surround the matter with a mist of sentiment. Facts are our masters now. We ought not to put the acceptance of such prices on the ground of patriotism.

Patriotism has nothing to do with profits in a case like this. Patriotism and profits ought never in the present circumstances to be mentioned together.

It is perfectly proper to discuss profits as a matter of business, with a view to maintaining the integrity of capital and the efficiency of labor in these tragical months when the liberty of free men everywhere and of industry itself trembles in the balance; but it would be absurd to discuss them as a motive for helping to serve and save our country. Patriotism leaves profits out of the question.

In these days of our supreme trial, when we are sending hundreds of thousands of our young men across the seas to serve a great cause, no true man who stays behind to work for them and sustain them by his labor will ask himself what he is personally going to make out of that labor.

No true patriot will permit himself to take toll of their heroism in money or seek to grow rich by the shedding of their blood. He will give as freely and with as unstinted self-sacrifice as they. When they are giving their lives will he not give at least his money? . . .

DOCUMENT 98

"We Are Working at Cross Purposes"

Appeals to patriotism were often not enough to secure reasonable prices. Wilson instructed his associates not to accept exorbitant charges, and throughout the war he kept a wary eye on price policies, intervening on more than one occasion to insist upon a reduction. This letter to the Secretary of War is an example of such intervention.

I am very much distressed about what has been done with regard to agreeing upon a price for coal. The price said to have been agreed upon is clearly too high and I do not think that the government departments would be justified in paying it. It happens to be the particular price upon which charges are at this very time being based by the Department of Justice against the coal dealers.

Letter to Newton D. Baker, June 29, 1917, Baker, *Wilson, Life and Letters*, VII, 136–137.

I am myself personally embarrassed because I had just had conferences with the Federal Trade Commission which made me hopeful that I might be instrumental in bringing about an understanding which would be in every way more fair and reasonable.

I would very much value your counsel upon this matter, and I would appreciate it very much if you and your colleagues of the Council of National Defense would keep me in touch with plans of this sort, because unconsciously we are working at cross purposes.

DOCUMENT 99

"Give Emphasis with Courtesy"

Wilson was equally determined to prevent profiteering by the Allies on charges for shipping and supplies needed by the American forces overseas, though he naturally found this more difficult to control, as this letter to the Secretary of State shows.

You know how much pains we have taken to make arrangements for the purchase of supplies in this country by the Allies on the same terms with our own government and with our civil population. I am sorry to say that the English government has not been equally generous, or perhaps I should say equally successful, in arranging that supplies that this government purchases in England should be purchased upon the same terms upon which sales are made to the British government and to the civil-

---

Letter to Robert Lansing, August 29, 1918, in Baker, *Wilson, Life and Letters*, VIII, 364–365.

ian population of Great Britain. I would be very much obliged to you if you would convey a very earnest intimation to the British government of our hope and expectation that this reciprocal arrangement should be made as promptly and completely as possible. The discriminations I have heard of have disturbed me a good deal, and while I am sure that the men at the top of the government over there would be willing to make a cordial response to such representations, I am equally sure that the traders with whom they are consulting are not equally willing. You will know how to give emphasis with courtesy.

D. CONTROL OF LABOR
DISPUTES IN WARTIME

DOCUMENT 100

"To Strike Against the Award
Is Disloyalty and Dishonor"

Wilson was concerned that the war emergency should not require any substantial sacrifice of the rights and improved conditions won by American workers over the past generation. Maximum production must be achieved, but not at labor's expense. In the spring of 1918, the President created the National War Labor Board to settle labor disputes affecting war production. The Board had no statutory authority,

---

Warning to the Bridgeport strikers, September 13, 1918, Baker, *Wilson, Life and Letters*, VIII, 400–402.

but its rulings were backed by the President's war powers. On several occasions Wilson resorted to these powers to enforce a Board ruling, as when he commandeered the Smith & Wesson Arms plant at Springfield, Massachusetts, because its management refused to accept a Board decision, or when he threatened to draft striking machinists in Bridgeport, Connecticut.

I am in receipt of your resolutions . . . announcing that you have begun a strike against your employers in Bridgeport, Conn. You are members of the Bridgeport branches of the International Union of Machinists. As such, and with the approval of the National officers of your Union, you signed an agreement to submit the questions as to the terms of your employment to the National War Labor Board and to abide [by] the award which . . . might be made.

The members of the Board were not able to reach a unanimous conclusion on all the issues presented, and as provided in its constitution, the questions upon which they did not agree were carried before an arbitrator, the unanimous choice of the members of the Board.

The arbitrator thus chosen has made an award which more than ninety per cent of the workers affected accept. You who constitute less than ten per cent refuse to abide [by] the award although you are the best paid of the whole body of workers affected, and are, therefore, least entitled to press a further increase of wages because of the high cost of living. But, whatever the merits of the issue, it is closed by the award. Your strike against it is a breach of faith calculated to reflect on the sincerity of National organized labor in proclaiming its acceptance of the principles and machinery of the National War Labor Board.

If such disregard of the solemn adjudication of a tribunal

to which both parties submitted their claims be temporized with, agreements become mere scraps of paper. If errors creep into awards, the proper remedy is submission to the award with an application for rehearing to the tribunal. But to strike against the award is disloyalty and dishonor.

The Smith & Wesson Company, of Springfield, Mass., engaged in government work, has refused to accept the mediation of the National War Labor Board and has rules of decision approved by Presidential proclamation. With my consent the War Department has taken over the plant and business of the Company to secure continuity in production and to prevent industrial disturbance.

It is of the highest importance to secure compliance with reasonable rules and procedure for the settlement of industrial disputes. Having exercised a drastic remedy with recalcitrant employers, it is my duty to use means equally well adapted to the end with lawless and faithless employees.

Therefore, I desire that you return to work and abide by the award. If you refuse, each of you will be barred from employment in any war industry in the community in which the strike occurs for a period of one year. During that time the United States Employment Service will decline to obtain employment for you in any war industry elsewhere in the United States, as well as under the War and Navy Departments, the Shipping Board, the Railroad Administration, and all other Government agencies, and the draft boards will be instructed to reject any claim of exemption based on your alleged usefulness on war production.

E. CIVIL LIBERTIES IN WARTIME

1. *Censorship*

DOCUMENT 101

"Doubt Ought Always to Be Resolved in Favor of the Utmost Freedom of Speech"

One of the greatest blots on Wilson's wartime leadership was his failure to restrain emotional and even vigilante patriotism on the part of many Americans, including some members of the administration. The Espionage and Sedition Acts of 1917 and 1918 gave the government dangerously broad authority to punish unpatriotic and subversive activity, including the power to exclude from the mails publications considered dangerous to the war effort. Wilson did not always agree with Postmaster General Albert S. Burleson's often arbitrary judgments, but the President ran hot and cold on the issue of censorship, as the following two letters indicate. In the first, Wilson expressed doubt of the wisdom of Burleson's recent order, ultimately sustained by the courts, denying mailing privileges to the socialist Milwaukee *Leader*.

I am afraid you will be shocked, but I must say that I do not find this hearing very convincing. Some of the things quoted probably cross the line and I have very little doubt that they were all intended to have sinister results, but I must frankly say that I do not think that most of what is

Letter to Albert S. Burleson, October 18, 1917, in Baker, *Wilson, Life and Letters,* VII, 313.

quoted ought to be regarded as unmailable. I have read the hearing with some feeling of misgiving as to the impression that was created upon the representatives of the paper which had been summoned, not because I doubt for a moment the purposes or the intelligence or the careful and conscientious methods of the public officials concerned, but because there is a wide margin of judgment here and I think that doubt ought always to be resolved in favor of the utmost freedom of speech.

It does not appear from the hearing what was done. Was the paper, as they so earnestly urged, given another chance?

DOCUMENT 102

"Scotch a Great Many Snakes"

On the other hand, Wilson was not prepared to tolerate unlimited free speech, as when he urged Attorney General Thomas W. Gregory to prosecute an obscure paper, *The People's Counselor,* for its criticism of the war.

I would very much like you seriously to consider whether publications like the enclosed do not form a sufficient basis for a trial for treason. There are many instances of this sort and one conviction would probably scotch a great many snakes. So far as I can see, an indictment could easily be founded upon such utterances as this.

Letter to Thomas W. Gregory, September 25, 1917, in Baker, *Wilson, Life and Letters*, VII, 283.

2. Mob Action

DOCUMENT 103

"Let Us Show Our Utter Contempt. . . ."

For the most part Wilson chose to overlook the vigilante spirit of many Americans during the war, even though it resulted in wholesale violations of the rights of Negroes, labor radicals, pacifists, and indeed anyone suspected of pro-German feelings. Shortly before the United States entered the war, Wilson had confided to Frank Cobb of the New York *World* his fear that war would make the American people ruthless and intolerant. Yet aside from a vigorous denunciation of lynching in the summer of 1918 (the result of strong pressure from the National Association for the Advancement of Colored People), the President did little to counteract mob spirit either in the country or among some of his overly zealous subordinates.

I take the liberty of addressing you upon a subject which so vitally affects the honor of the Nation and the very character and integrity of our institutions that I trust you will think me justified in speaking very plainly about it.

I allude to the mob spirit which has recently here and there very frequently shown its head amongst us, not in any single region, but in many and widely separated parts of the country. There have been many lynchings, and every one of them has been a blow at the heart of ordered law and humane justice. No man who loves America, no man who really cares for her fame and honor and charac-

Statement to the public, July 26, 1918, *Public Papers*, V, 238–240.

ter, or who is truly loyal to her institutions, can justify mob action while the courts of justice are open and the governments of the States and the Nation are ready and able to do their duty. We are at this very moment fighting lawless passion. Germany has outlawed herself among the nations because she has disregarded the sacred obligations of law and has made lynchers of her armies. Lynchers emulate her disgraceful example. I, for my part, am anxious to see every community in America rise above that level with pride and a fixed resolution which no man or set of men can afford to despise.

We proudly claim to be the champions of democracy. If we really are, in deed and in truth, let us see to it that we do not discredit our own. I say plainly that every American who takes part in the action of a mob or gives it any sort of countenance is no true son of this great democracy, but its betrayer, and does more to discredit her by that single disloyalty to her standards of law and of right than the words of her statesmen or the sacrifices of her heroic boys in the trenches can do to make suffering peoples believe her to be their savior. How shall we commend democracy to the acceptance of other peoples, if we disgrace our own by proving that it is, after all, no protection to the weak? Every mob contributes to German lies about the United States what her most gifted liars cannot improve upon by the way of calumny. They can at least say that such things cannot happen in Germany except in times of revolution, when law is swept away!

I therefore very earnestly and solemnly beg that the governors of all the States, the law officers of every community, and, above all, the men and women of every community in the United States, all who revere America and wish to keep her name without stain or reproach, will coöperate — not passively merely, but actively and watchfully — to make an end of this disgraceful evil. It cannot live where the community does not countenance it.

I have called upon the Nation to put its great energy into this war and it has responded—responded with a spirit and a genius for action that has thrilled the world. I now call upon it, upon its men and women everywhere, to see to it that its laws are kept inviolate, its fame untarnished. Let us show our utter contempt for the things that have made this war hideous among the wars of history by showing how those who love liberty and right and justice and are willing to lay down their lives for them upon foreign fields stand ready also to illustrate to all mankind their loyalty to the things at home which they wish to see established everywhere as a blessing and protection to the peoples who have never known the privileges of liberty and self-government. I can never accept any man as a champion of liberty either for ourselves or for the world who does not reverence and obey the laws of our own beloved land, whose laws we ourselves have made. He has adopted the standards of the enemies of his country, whom he affects to despise.

F. MILITARY STRATEGY

1. *A Separate American Expeditionary Force*

DOCUMENT 104

"A Separate and Distinct Component of the Combined Forces. . . ."

Although he took a keen interest in the military progress of the war, Wilson ordinarily did not interfere in military

---

Instructions to General John J. Pershing, May 26, 1917, in John J. Pershing, *My Experiences in the World War* (New York: Frederick A. Stokes Company, 1931), I, 38–39.

decisions. He preferred to rely on the judgment of the professionals, especially General John J. Pershing, the tough-minded commander of the American Expeditionary Force in France. From the outset both Pershing and Wilson were determined to keep a distinct identity for the A.E.F., and they held steadfastly to this objective in the face of strong pressure from the Allies to merge American troops with French and British forces. Pershing understandably wanted to maintain the integrity of his command, and Wilson recognized that the United States would have more voice in Allied councils if the A.E.F. remained a separate force.

SECRET

FROM: The Secretary of War.

TO: Major General J. J. Pershing, U. S. Army.

SUBJECT: Command, Authority and Duties in Europe.

The President directs me to communicate to you the following:

1. The President designates you to command all the land forces of the United States operating in Continental Europe and in the United Kingdom of Great Britain and Ireland, including any part of the Marine Corps which may be detached for service there with the Army. From your command are excepted the Military Attachés and others of the Army who may be on duty directly with our several embassies.

2. You will proceed with your staff to Europe. Upon arrival in Great Britain, France or any other of the countries at war with the Imperial German Government, you will at once place yourself in communication with the American Embassy and through its agency with the authorities of any country to which the forces of the United States may be sent.

3. You are invested with the authority and duties de-

volved by the laws, regulations, orders and customs of the United States upon the commander of an army in the field in time of war and with the authority and duties in like manner devolved upon department commanders in peace and war, including the special authorities and duties assigned to the commander of the Philippine Department in so far as the same are applicable to the particular circumstances of your command.

4. You will establish, after consultation with the French War Office, all necessary bases, lines of communication, depots, etc., and make all the incidental arrangements essential to active participation at the front.

5. In military operations against the Imperial German Government, you are directed to coöperate with the forces of the other countries employed against that enemy; but in so doing the underlying idea must be kept in view that the forces of the United States are a separate and distinct component of the combined forces, the identity of which must be preserved. This fundamental rule is subject to such minor exceptions in particular circumstances as your judgment may approve. The decision as to when your command, or any of its parts, is ready for action is confided to you, and you will exercise full discretion in determining the matter of coöperation. But, until the forces of the United States are in your judgment sufficiently strong to warrant operations as an independent command, it is understood that you will coöperate as a component of whatever army you may be assigned to by the French Government.

6. You will keep the Department fully advised of all that concerns your command, and will communicate your recommendations freely and directly to the Department. And in general you are vested with all necessary authority to carry on the war vigorously in harmony with the spirit of these instructions and towards a victorious conclusion.

NEWTON D. BAKER.

2. A Bold and Aggressive Naval Policy

DOCUMENT 105

"The Failure of the British Admiralty. . . ."

The heavy shipping losses from German submarine attacks in the early months after the United States entered the war caused Wilson great concern. He had little faith in the ability of the British Admiralty to devise effective strategy to cope with the submarine menace, and he suspected that they were afraid to risk their capital ships. In particular, Wilson was infuriated at the reluctance of the British, as well as some American, admirals to adopt the convoy system. His dissatisfaction with British naval tactics was bluntly expressed in a confidential cable, drafted personally by the President, to Admiral William S. Sims, the commander of American naval forces in Europe, in the summer of 1917.

FOR ADMIRAL SIMS, Confidential from the President:

From the beginning of the war I have been surprised by nothing so much as the failure of the British Admiralty to use Great Britain's great naval superiority in any effective way. In the presence of the present submarine emergency they are helpless to the point of panic. Every plan we suggest they reject for some reason of prudence. In my view this is not a time for prudence but for boldness even at the risk of great losses. In most of your despatches you have very properly advised us of the sort of aid and cooperation desired from us by the Admiralty. The trouble is that their plans and methods do not seem to us effective. I

Instructions to Admiral William S. Sims, July 4, 1917, in Baker, *Wilson, Life and Letters*, VII, 146–147.

would be very much obliged to you if you would report to me, confidentially of course, exactly what the Admiralty have been doing and what they have accomplished and add to the report your own comments and suggestions based upon independent study of the whole situation without regard to the judgments already arrived at on that side of the water. In particular I am not at all satisfied with the conclusions of the Admiralty with regard to the convoying of groups of merchantmen. I do not see how the necessary military supplies and supplies of food and fuel oil are to be delivered at British ports in any other way than under convoy. There will presently not be ships enough or tankers enough and our shipbuilding plans may not begin to yield important results in less than eighteen months. I beg that you will keep these instructions absolutely to yourself and that you will give me such advice as you would give if you were handling an independent navy of your own.

DOCUMENT 106

"We Have Got to Throw Tradition to the Wind"

Wilson's deep interest in the submarine problem, and his readiness to try new and daring countertactics, were revealed in a secret address to the officers of the Atlantic Fleet on August 11, 1917.

. . . Now, the point that is constantly in my mind, gentlemen, is this: This is an unprecedented war and, therefore, it is a war in one sense for amateurs. Nobody ever before

---

Excerpts from address to the officers of the Atlantic Fleet, August 11, 1917, *Public Papers*, V, 83–84, 86–87.

conducted a war like this and therefore nobody can pretend to be a professional in a war like this. Here are two great navies, not to speak of the others associated with us, our own and the British, outnumbering by a very great margin the navy to which we are opposed, and yet casting about for a way in which to use our superiority and our strength, because of the novelty of the instruments used, because of the unprecedented character of the war, because, as I said just now, nobody ever before fought a war like this, in the way that this is being fought at sea—or on land either for that matter. The experienced soldier,—experienced in previous wars,—is a back number so far as his experience is concerned; not so far as his intelligence is concerned. His experience does not count, because he never fought a war as this is being fought, and therefore he is an amateur along with the rest of us. Now, somebody has got to think this war out. Somebody has got to think out the way not only to fight the submarine, but to do something different from what we are doing.

We are hunting hornets all over the farm and letting the nest alone. None of us knows how to go to the nest and crush it, and yet I despair of hunting for hornets all over the sea when I know where the nest is and know that the nest is breeding hornets as fast as I can find them. I am willing for my part, and I know you are willing because I know the stuff you are made of,—I am willing to sacrifice half the navy Great Britain and we together have to crush that nest, because if we crush it, the war is won. I have come here to say that I do not care where it comes from, I do not care whether it comes from the youngest officer or the oldest, but I want the officers of this Navy to have the distinction of saying how this war is going to be won. The Secretary of the Navy and I have just been talking over plans for putting the planning machinery of the Navy at the disposal of the brains of the Navy and not stopping to ask what rank that brains has, because, as I have said before and want to repeat, so far as experience in this kind of war is concerned we are all of the same rank. I am not saying that I do not expect the Admirals to tell us what to do, but I am saying that I want the youngest and most modest youngster in the service to tell us what we ought to do if he knows what it is. I am willing to make any sacrifice for that. I mean any sacrifice of time or anything else. I am ready to put myself at the disposal of any officer in the Navy who thinks he knows how to run this war. I will not undertake to tell you whether he does or not, because I know I cannot, but I will undertake to put him in communication with those who can find out whether his idea will work or not. I have the authority to do that and I will do it with the greatest pleasure. . . .

We have got to throw tradition to the wind. As I have said, gentlemen, I take it for granted that nothing that I say here will be repeated and therefore I am going to say this: Every time we have suggested anything to the British Admiralty the reply has come back that virtually amounted to this, that it had never been done that way, and I felt like saying, "Well, nothing was ever done so systematically as nothing is being done now. Therefore, I should like to see something unusual happen, something that was never done before; and inasmuch as the things that are being done to you were never done before, don't you think it is worth while to try something that was never done before against those who are doing them to you." There is no other way to win, and the whole principle of this war is the kind of thing that ought to hearten and stimulate America. America has always boasted that she could find men to do anything. She is the prize amateur nation of the world. Germany is the prize professional nation of the world. Now, when it comes to doing new things and doing them well, I will back the amateur against the professional every time, because the professional does it out of the book and the amateur does it with his eyes open upon a new world and with a new set of circumstances. He knows so little about it that he is fool enough to try the right thing. The men that do not know the danger are the rashest men, and I have several times ventured to make this suggestion to the men about me in both arms of the service: Please leave out of your vocabulary altogether the word "prudent." Do not stop to think about what is prudent for a moment. Do the thing that is audacious to the utmost point of risk and daring, because that is exactly the thing that the other side does not understand, and you will win by the audacity of method when you cannot win by circumspection and prudence. I think that there are willing ears to hear this in the American Navy and the American Army because that is the kind of folks we are. We get tired of the old ways and covet the new ones. . . .

PART IX

Toward a Peaceful World Order

A. EARLY PEACE EFFORTS

DOCUMENT 107

"To Use Our Utmost Moral Force. . . ."

In addition to guarding neutral rights, from the beginning
of the war Wilson hoped to be the means to bring about an
end to the senseless slaughter. In 1915 and again in 1916 he
sent his trusted adviser, Colonel Edward M. House, to
Europe to sound out the belligerent governments as to
the possibility of a negotiated peace. Wilson's instructions
to House on the second mission outlined the sort of peace
settlement he hoped to secure, and included an ambiguous
pledge to use American moral force against whichever side
might prove reluctant to come to the conference table. It
should be noted that German-American relations were tense
at this time over the submarine issue, and Wilson and House
assumed that the Allies, with whom they were on better
terms, would be more receptive to American mediation. As
it turned out, neither side was yet ready to give up the hope
of all-out victory and accept a negotiated stalemate.

You ask for instructions as to what attitude and tone you
are to take at the several capitals. I feel that you do not

Letter to Edward M. House, December 24, 1915, in Baker, *Wilson, Life
and Letters*, VI, 138.

need any. Your own letters (for example, this one in which you report your conversation with Bernstorff) exactly echo my own views and purposes. I agree with you that we have nothing to do with local settlements,—territorial questions, indemnities, and the like,—but are concerned only in the future peace of the world and the guarantees to be given for that. The only possible guarantees, that is, the only guarantees that any rational man could accept, are (a) military and naval disarmament and (b) a league of nations to secure each nation against aggression and maintain the absolute freedom of the seas. If either party to the present war will let us say to the other that they are willing to discuss peace on such terms, it will clearly be our duty to use our utmost moral force to oblige the other to parley, and I do not see how they could stand in the opinion of the world if they refused.

DOCUMENT 108

"A Peace That Will Win the Approval

of Mankind. . . ."

The continued reluctance of the belligerents to accept United States mediation for a negotiated settlement vexed but did not entirely discourage Wilson. A month after his re-election in 1916, he dispatched a note to the various belligerent governments asking them to state their war aims. When nothing came of these secret negotiations, the President outlined to the world his concept of a proper peace settlement, in a remarkable address to the Senate on January 22, 1917. Nine days later the Germans gave their answer—resumption of unrestricted submarine warfare.

Address to the Senate, January 22, 1917, *Public Papers*, IV, 407–414.

GENTLEMEN OF THE SENATE:

On the eighteenth of December last I addressed an identic note to the governments of the nations now at war requesting them to state, more definitely than they had yet been stated by either group of belligerents, the terms upon which they would deem it possible to make peace. I spoke on behalf of humanity and of the rights of all neutral nations like our own, many of whose most vital interests the war puts in constant jeopardy. The Central Powers united in a reply which stated merely that they were ready to meet their antagonists in conference to discuss terms of peace. The Entente Powers have replied much more definitely and have stated, in general terms, indeed, but with sufficient definiteness to imply details, the arrangements, guarantees, and acts of reparation which they deem to be the indispensable conditions of a satisfactory settlement. We are that much nearer a definite discussion of the peace which shall end the present war. We are that much nearer the discussion of the international concert which must thereafter hold the world at peace. In every discussion of the peace that must end this war it is taken for granted that that peace must be followed by some definite concert of power which will make it virtually impossible that any such catastrophe should ever overwhelm us again. Every lover of mankind, every sane and thoughtful man must take that for granted.

I have sought this opportunity to address you because I thought that I owed it to you, as the counsel associated with me in the final determination of our international obligations, to disclose to you without reserve the thought and purpose that have been taking form in my mind in regard to the duty of our Government in the days to come when it will be necessary to lay afresh and upon a new plan the foundations of peace among the nations.

It is inconceivable that the people of the United States

should play no part in that great enterprise. To take part in such a service will be the opportunity for which they have sought to prepare themselves by the very principles and purposes of their polity and the approved practices of their Government ever since the days when they set up a new nation in the high and honorable hope that it might in all that it was and did show mankind the way to liberty. They cannot in honor withhold the service to which they are now about to be challenged. They do not wish to withhold it. But they owe it to themselves and to the other nations of the world to state the conditions under which they will feel free to render it.

That service is nothing less than this, to add their authority and their power to the authority and force of other nations to guarantee peace and justice throughout the world. Such a settlement cannot now be long postponed. It is right that before it comes this Government should frankly formulate the conditions upon which it would feel justified in asking our people to approve its formal and solemn adherence to a League for Peace. I am here to attempt to state those conditions.

The present war must first be ended; but we owe it to candor and to a just regard for the opinion of mankind to say that, so far as our participation in guarantees of future peace is concerned, it makes a great deal of difference in what way and upon what terms it is ended. The treaties and agreements which bring it to an end must embody terms which will create a peace that is worth guaranteeing and preserving, a peace that will win the approval of mankind, not merely a peace that will serve the several interests and immediate aims of the nations engaged. We shall have no voice in determining what those terms shall be, but we shall, I feel sure, have a voice in determining whether they shall be made lasting or not by the guarantees of a universal covenant, and our judgment upon what is fundamental and essential as a condition precedent to permanency should be spoken now, not afterwards when it may be too late.

No covenant of co-operative peace that does not include the peoples of the New World can suffice to keep the future safe against war; and yet there is only one sort of peace that the peoples of America could join in guaranteeing. The elements of that peace must be elements that engage the confidence and satisfy the principles of the American governments, elements consistent with their political faith and with the practical convictions which the peoples of America have once for all embraced and undertaken to defend.

I do not mean to say that any American government would throw any obstacle in the way of any terms of peace the governments now at war might agree upon, or seek to upset them when made, whatever they might be. I only take it for granted that mere terms of peace between the belligerents will not satisfy even the belligerents themselves. Mere agreements may not make peace secure. It will be absolutely necessary that a force be created as a guarantor of the permanency of the settlement so much greater than the force of any nation now engaged or any alliance hitherto formed or projected that no nation, no probable combination of nations could face or withstand it. If the peace presently to be made is to endure, it must be a peace made secure by the organized major force of mankind.

The terms of the immediate peace agreed upon will determine whether it is a peace for which such a guarantee can be secured. The question upon which the whole future peace and policy of the world depends is this: Is the present war a struggle for a just and secure peace, or only for a new balance of power? If it be only a struggle for a new balance of power, who will guarantee, who can guarantee the stable equilibrium of the new arrangement? Only a tranquil Europe can be a stable Europe. There must be, not a balance of power, but a community of power; not organized rivalries, but an organized common peace.

Fortunately we have received very explicit assurances on this point. The statesmen of both of the groups of nations now arrayed against one another have said, in terms that could not be misinterpreted, that it was no part of the purpose they had in mind to crush their antagonists. But the implications of these assurances may not be equally clear to all—may not be the same on both sides of the water. I think it will be serviceable if I attempt to set forth what we understand them to be.

They imply, first of all, that it must be a peace without victory. It is not pleasant to say this. I beg that I may be permitted to put my own interpretation upon it and that it may be understood that no other interpretation was in my thought. I am seeking only to face realities and to face them without soft concealments. Victory would mean peace forced upon the loser, a victor's terms imposed upon the vanquished. It would be accepted in humiliation, under duress, at an intolerable sacrifice, and would leave a sting, a resentment, a bitter memory upon which terms of peace would rest, not permanently, but only as upon quicksand. Only a peace between equals can last. Only a peace the very principle of which is equality and a common participation in a common benefit. The right state of mind, the right feeling between nations, is as necessary for a lasting peace as is the just settlement of vexed questions of territory or of racial and national allegiance.

The equality of nations upon which peace must be founded if it is to last must be an equality of rights; the guarantees exchanged must neither recognize nor imply a difference between big nations and small, between those that are powerful and those that are weak. Right must be based upon the common strength, not upon the individual strength, of the nations upon whose concert peace will depend. Equality of territory or of resources there of course cannot be; nor any other sort of equality not gained in the ordinary peaceful and legitimate development of the peoples themselves. But no one asks or expects anything more than an equality of rights. Mankind is looking now for freedom of life, not for equipoises of power.

And there is a deeper thing involved than even equality of right among organized nations. No peace can last, or ought to last, which does not recognize and accept the principle that governments derive all their just powers from the consent of the governed, and that no right anywhere exists to hand peoples about from sovereignty to sovereignty as if they were property. I take it for granted, for instance, if I may venture upon a single example, that statesmen everywhere are agreed that there should be a united, independent, and autonomous Poland, and that henceforth inviolable security of life, of worship, and of industrial and social development should be guaranteed to all peoples who have lived hitherto under the power of governments devoted to a faith and purpose hostile to their own.

I speak of this, not because of any desire to exalt an abstract political principle which has always been held very dear by those who have sought to build up liberty in America, but for the same reason that I have spoken of the other conditions of peace which seem to me clearly indispensable — because I wish frankly to uncover realities. Any peace which does not recognize and accept this principle will inevitably be upset. It will not rest upon the affections or the convictions of mankind. The ferment of spirit of whole populations will fight subtly and constantly against it, and all the world will sympathize. The world can be at peace only if its life is stable, and there can be no stability where the will is in rebellion, where there is not tranquillity of spirit and a sense of justice, of freedom, and of right.

So far as practicable, moreover, every great people now struggling towards a full development of its resources and of its powers should be assured a direct outlet to the great highways of the sea. Where this cannot be done by the cession of territory, it can no doubt be done by the neutralization of direct rights of way under the general guarantee which will assure the peace itself. With a right comity of arrangement no nation need be shut away from free access to the open paths of the world's commerce.

And the paths of the sea must alike in law and in fact be free. The freedom of the seas is the *sine qua non* of peace, equality, and co-operation. No doubt a somewhat radical reconsideration of many of the rules of international practice hitherto thought to be established may be necessary in order to make the seas indeed free and common in practically all circumstances for the use of mankind, but the motive for such changes is convincing and compelling. There can be no trust or intimacy between the peoples of the world without them. The free, constant, unthreatened intercourse of nations is an essential part of the process of peace and of development. It need not be difficult either to define or to secure the freedom of the seas if the governments of the world sincerely desire to come to an agreement concerning it.

It is a problem closely connected with the limitation of naval armaments and the co-operation of the navies of the world in keeping the seas at once free and safe. And the question of limiting naval armaments opens the wider and perhaps more difficult question of the limitation of armies and of all programs of military preparation. Difficult and delicate as these questions are, they must be faced with the utmost candor and decided in a spirit of real accommodation if peace is to come with healing in its wings, and come to stay. Peace cannot be had without concession and sacrifice. There can be no sense of safety and equality among the nations if great preponderating armaments are henceforth to continue here and there to be built up and maintained. The statesmen of the world must plan for peace and nations must adjust and accommodate their policy to it as they have planned for war and made ready for pitiless contest and rivalry. The question of armaments, whether on land or sea, is the most immediately and intensely practical question connected with the future fortunes of nations and of mankind.

I have spoken upon these great matters without reserve and with the utmost explicitness because it has seemed to me to be necessary if the world's yearning desire for peace was anywhere to find free voice and utterance. Perhaps I am the only person in high authority amongst all the peoples of the world who is at liberty to speak and hold nothing back. I am speaking as an individual, and yet I am speaking also, of course, as the responsible head of a great government, and I feel confident that I have said what the people of the United States would wish me to say. May I not add that I hope and believe that I am in effect speaking for liberals and friends of humanity in every nation and of every program of liberty? I would fain believe that I am speaking for the silent mass of mankind everywhere who have as yet had no place or opportunity to speak their real hearts out concerning the death and ruin they see to have come already upon the persons and the homes they hold most dear.

And in holding out the expectation that the people and Government of the United States will join the other civilized nations of the world in guaranteeing the permanence of peace upon such terms as I have named I speak with the greater boldness and confidence because it is clear to every man who can think that there is in this promise no breach in either our traditions or our policy as a nation, but a fulfilment, rather, of all that we have professed or striven for.

I am proposing, as it were, that the nations should with one accord adopt the doctrine of President Monroe as the doctrine of the world: that no nation should seek to extend its polity over any other nation or people, but that every people should be left free to determine its own polity, its own way of development, unhindered, unthreatened, unafraid, the little along with the great and powerful.

I am proposing that all nations henceforth avoid entangling alliances which would draw them into competitions of power; catch them in a net of intrigue and selfish rivalry, and disturb their own affairs with influences intruded from without. There is no entangling alliance in a concert of power. When all unite to act in the same sense and with the same purpose all act in the common interest and are free to live their own lives under a common protection.

I am proposing government by the consent of the governed; that freedom of the seas which in international conference after conference representatives of the United States have urged with the eloquence of those who are the convinced disciples of liberty; and that moderation of armaments which makes of armies and navies a power for order merely, not an instrument of aggression or of selfish violence.

These are American principles, American policies. We could stand for no others. And they are also the principles and policies of forward looking men and women everywhere, of every modern nation, of every enlightened community. They are the principles of mankind and must prevail.

B. THE DEVELOPMENT OF THE LEAGUE

OF NATIONS CONCEPT

DOCUMENT 109

Pan-American Unity

In his instructions to Colonel House late in December 1915, before the latter's second European mission (See Document 107), Wilson indicated his acceptance of the idea that the peace settlement should be enforced by a general association of nations. During the ensuing months he continued to develop and ultimately to popularize the idea of a League of Nations, a concept also being promoted by other American and some British publicists. Wilson's first public support for the idea came in a proposal for an association of American states to guarantee the security of the Americas. He made the proposal in an address to the Pan American Scientific Congress on January 6, 1916.

. . . I have been told a very interesting fact—I hope it is true—that while this Congress has been discussing science, it has been, in spite of itself, led into the feeling that behind the science there was some inference with regard to politics, and that if the Americans were to be united in thought they must in some degree sympathetically be united in action. What these statesmen, who have been conferring from month to month in Washington, have come to realize, is that back of the community of material interest there is a community of political interest.

Excerpt from address to the Pan American Scientific Congress, Washington, D.C., January 6, 1916., *Public Papers,* III, 442–445.

I hope I can make clear to you in what sense I use these words. I do not mean a mere partnership in the things that are expedient. I mean what I was trying to indicate a few moments ago, that you cannot separate politics from these things, that you cannot have real intercourse of any kind amidst political jealousies, which is only another way of saying that you cannot commune unless you are friends, and that friendship is based upon your political relations with each other perhaps more than upon any other kind of relationship between nations. If nations are politically suspicious of one another, all their intercourse is embarrassed. That is the reason, I take it, if it be true, as I hope it is, that your thoughts even during this Congress, though the questions you are called upon to consider are apparently to foreign politics, have again and again been drawn back to the political inferences. The object of American statesmanship on the two continents is to see to it that American friendship is founded on a rock.

The Monroe Doctrine was proclaimed by the United States on her own authority. It always has been maintained and always will be maintained upon her own responsibility. But the Monroe Doctrine demanded merely that European Governments should not attempt to extend their political systems to this side of the Atlantic. It did not disclose the use which the United States intended to make of her power on this side of the Atlantic. It was a hand held up in warning, but there was no promise in it of what America was going to do with the implied and partial protectorate which she apparently was trying to set up on this side of the water; and I believe you will sustain me in the statement that it has been fears and suspicions on this score which have hitherto prevented the greater intimacy and confidence and trust between the Americas. The States of America have not been certain what the United States would do with her power. That doubt must be removed. And latterly there has been a very frank interchange of views between the authorities in Washington and those who represented the other States of this hemisphere, an interchange of views charming and hopeful, because based upon an increasingly sure appreciation of the spirit in which they were undertaken. These gentlemen have seen that if America is to come into her own, into her legitimate own, in a world of peace and order, she must establish the foundations of amity so that no one will hereafter doubt them.

I hope and I believe that this can be accomplished. These conferences have enabled me to foresee how it will be accomplished. It will be accomplished in the first place, by the States of America uniting in guaranteeing to each other absolutely political independence and territorial integrity. In the second place, and as a necessary corollary to that, guaranteeing the agreement to settle all pending boundary disputes as soon as possible and by amicable process; by agreeing that all disputes among themselves, should they unhappily arise, will be handled by patient, impartial investigation, and settled by arbitration; and the agreement necessary to the peace of the Americas, that no State of either continent will permit revolutionary expeditions against another State to be fitted out on its territory, and that they will prohibit the exportation of the munitions of war for the purpose of supplying revolutionists against neighboring Governments.

You see what our thought is, gentlemen, not only the international peace of America but the domestic peace of America. If American States are constantly in ferment, if any of them are constantly in ferment, there will be a standing threat to their relations with one another. It is just as much to our interest to assist each other to the orderly processes within our own borders as it is to orderly processes in our controversies with one another. These are very practical suggestions which have sprung up in the minds of thoughtful men, and I, for my part, believe that they are going to lead the way to something that America has prayed for for many a generation. For they are based, in the first place, so far as the stronger States are concerned, upon the handsome principle of self-restraint and respect for the rights of everybody. They are based upon the principles of absolute political equality among the States, equality of right, not equality of indulgence. They are based, in short, upon the solid eternal foundations of justice and humanity. No man can turn away from these things without turning away from the hope of the world. These are things, ladies and gentlemen, for which the world has hoped and waited with prayerful heart. God grant that it may be granted to America to lift this light on high for the illumination of the world.

DOCUMENT 110

"The United States Is Willing

to Become a Partner . . ."

Within a short time Wilson was prepared to pledge publicly that the United States would join any feasible organization of nations to preserve peace and provide collective security.

When the invitation to be here to-night came to me, I was glad to accept it—not because it offered me an opportunity to discuss the programme of the League—that you will, I am sure, not expect of me—but because the desire of the

---

Address to the League to Enforce Peace, Washington, D.C., May 27, 1916, *Public Papers*, IV, 184–188.

whole world now turns eagerly, more and more eagerly, towards the hope of peace, and there is just reason why we should take our part in counsel upon this great theme. It is right that I, as spokesman of our Government, should attempt to give expression to what I believe to be the thought and purpose of the people of the United States in this vital matter.

This great war that broke so suddenly upon the world two years ago, and which has swept within its flame so great a part of the civilized world, has affected us very profoundly, and we are not only at liberty, it is perhaps our duty, to speak very frankly of it and of the great interests of civilization which it affects.

With its causes and its objects we are not concerned. The obscure fountains from which its stupendous flood has burst forth we are not interested to search for or explore. But so great a flood, spread far and wide to every quarter of the globe, has of necessity engulfed many a fair province of right that lies very near to us. Our own rights as a Nation, the liberties, the privileges, and the property of our people have been profoundly affected. We are not mere disconnected lookers-on. The longer the war lasts, the more deeply do we become concerned that it should be brought to an end and the world be permitted to resume its normal life and course again. And when it does come to an end we shall be as much concerned as the nations at war to see peace assume an aspect of permanence, give promise of days from which the anxiety of uncertainty shall be lifted, bring some assurance that peace and war shall always hereafter be reckoned part of the common interest of mankind. We are participants, whether we would or not, in the life of the world. The interests of all nations are our own also. We are partners with the rest. What affects mankind is inevitably our affair as well as the affair of the nations of Europe and of Asia.

One observation on the causes of the present war we are
at liberty to make, and to make it may throw some light
forward upon the future, as well as backward upon the
past. It is plain that this war could have come only as it
did, suddenly and out of secret counsels, without warning
to the world, without discussion, without any of the deliberate movements of counsel with which it would seem
natural to approach so stupendous a contest. It is probable
that if it had been foreseen just what would happen, just
what al'iances would be formed, just what forces arrayed
agains' one another, those who brought the great contest
on would have been glad to substitute conference for
force. If we ourselves had been afforded some opportunity
to apprise the belligerents of the attitude which it would
be our duty to take, of the policies and practices against
which we would feel bound to use all our moral and economic strength, and in certain circumstances even our
physical strength also, our own contribution to the counsel
which might have averted the struggle would have been
considered worth weighing and regarding.

And the lesson which the shock of being taken by surprise in a matter so deeply vital to all the nations of the
world has made poignantly clear is, that the peace of the
world must henceforth depend upon a new and more
wholesome diplomacy. Only when the great nations of the
world have reached some sort of agreement as to what they
hold to be fundamental to their common interest, and as to
some feasible method of acting in concert when any nation
or group of nations seeks to disturb those fundamental
things, can we feel that civilization is at last in a way of
justifying its existence and claiming to be finally established. It is clear that nations must in the future be governed by the same high code of honor that we demand of
individuals.

We must, indeed, in the very same breath with which

we avow this conviction admit that we have ourselves upon occasion in the past been offenders against the law of diplomacy which we thus forecast; but our conviction is not the less clear, but rather the more clear, on that account. If this war has accomplished nothing else for the benefit of the world, it has at least disclosed a great moral necessity and set forward the thinking of the statesmen of the world by a whole age. Repeated utterances of the leading statesmen of most of the great nations now engaged in war have made it plain that their thought has come to this, that the principle of public right must henceforth take precedence over the individual interests of particular nations, and that the nations of the world must in some way band themselves together to see that that right prevails as against any sort of selfish aggression; that henceforth alliance must not be set up against alliance, understanding against understanding, but that there must be a common agreement for a common object, and that at the heart of that common object must lie the inviolable rights of peoples and of mankind. The nations of the world have become each other's neighbors. It is to their interest that they should understand each other. In order that they may understand each other, it is imperative that they should agree to co-operate in a common cause, and that they should so act that the guiding principle of that common cause shall be even-handed and impartial justice.

This is undoubtedly the thought of America. This is what we ourselves will say when there comes proper occasion to say it. In the dealings of nations with one another arbitrary force must be rejected and we must move forward to the thought of the modern world, the thought of which peace is the very atmosphere. That thought constitutes a chief part of the passionate conviction of America.

We believe these fundamental things: First, that every people has a right to choose the sovereignty under which they shall live. Like other nations, we have ourselves no doubt once and again offended against that principle when for a little while controlled by selfish passion as our franker historians have been honorable enough to admit; but it has become more and more our rule of life and action. Second, that the small states of the world have a right to enjoy the same respect for their sovereignty and for their territorial integrity that great and powerful nations expect and insist upon. And, third, that the world has a right to be free from every disturbance of its peace that has its origin in aggression and disregard of the rights of peoples and nations.

So sincerely do we believe in these things that I am sure that I speak the mind and wish of the people of America when I say that the United States is willing to become a partner in any feasible association of nations formed in order to realize these objects and make them secure against violation.

There is nothing that the United States wants for itself that any other nation has. We are willing, on the contrary, to limit ourselves along with them to a prescribed course of duty and respect for the rights of others which will check any selfish passion of our own, as it will check any aggressive impulse of theirs.

If it should ever be our privilege to suggest or initiate a movement for peace among the nations now at war, I am sure that the people of the United States would wish their Government to move along these lines: First, such a settlement with regard to their own immediate interests as the belligerents may agree upon. We have nothing material of any kind to ask for ourselves, and are quite aware that we are in no sense or degree parties to the present quarrel. Our interest is only in peace and its future guarantees. Second, an universal association of the nations to maintain the inviolate security of the highway of the seas for the common and unhindered use of all the nations of the world, and to prevent any war begun either contrary to treaty covenants or without warning and full submission of the causes to the opinion of the world — a virtual guarantee of territorial integrity and political independence.

But I did not come here, let me repeat, to discuss a programme. I came only to avow a creed and give expression to the confidence I feel that the world is even now upon the eve of a great consummation, when some common force will be brought into existence which shall safeguard right as the first and most fundamental interest of all peoples and all governments, when coercion shall be summoned not to the service of political ambition or selfish hostility, but to the service of a common order, a common justice, and a common peace. God grant that the dawn of that day of frank dealing and of settled peace, concord, and co-operation may be near at hand!

DOCUMENT 111

"Why begin at the impossible end . . . ?"

Once Wilson had adopted the League of Nations concept as an indispensable part of his peace program, he was determined to play the major role in shaping the League's structure and functions. He had little patience with those who proposed elaborate and — to his mind — impractical organizational schemes, for he believed the League must begin modestly and grow slowly if it were to endure. Wilson expressed these views forcibly in a letter to Colonel House in March 1918, shortly before House was to confer with a group of prominent pro-League Republicans.

Letter to Edward M. House, March 22, 1918, in Baker, *Wilson, Life and Letters*, VIII, 43–44.

Yes, indeed, I think your lunch with Taft, Lowell, and Root is most wise and should be most helpful, if they have any sense among them—which I sometimes seriously doubt.

My own conviction, as you know, is that the administrative *constitution* of the League must *grow* and not be made; that we must *begin* with solemn covenants, covering mutual guarantees of political independence and territorial integrity (if the final territorial agreements of the peace conference are fair and satisfactory and *ought* to be perpetuated), but that the method of carrying those mutual pledges out should be left to develop of itself, case by case. Any attempt to begin by putting executive authority in the hands of any particular group of powers would be to sow a harvest of jealousy and distrust which would spring up at once and choke the whole thing. To take one thing, and only one, but quite sufficient in itself: The United States Senate would never ratify any treaty which put the force of the United States at the disposal of any such group or body. Why begin at the impossible end when there is a possible end and it is feasible to plant a system which will slowly but surely ripen into fruition?

C. WAR AIMS

DOCUMENT 112

The Eradication of German Militarism

While urging the American people to wage war relentlessly, Wilson at the same time began to prepare them for a peace

Excerpts from address to Congress, December 4, 1917, *Public Papers*, V, 128–134, 138–139.

settlement based on justice and magnanimity. In particular, he differentiated between the enemy peoples and their leaders, as when he asked Congress to declare war on Austria-Hungary in December 1917.

. . . I shall not go back to debate the causes of the war. The intolerable wrongs done and planned against us by the sinister masters of Germany have long since become too grossly obvious and odious to every true American to need to be rehearsed. But I shall ask you to consider again and with a very grave scrutiny our objectives and the measures by which we mean to attain them; for the purpose of discussion here in this place is action, and our action must move straight towards definite ends. Our object is, of course, to win the war; and we shall not slacken or suffer ourselves to be diverted until it is won. But it is worth while asking and answering the question, When shall we consider the war won?

From one point of view it is not necessary to broach this fundamental matter. I do not doubt that the American people know what the war is about and what sort of an outcome they will regard as a realization of their purpose in it. As a nation we are united in spirit and intention. I pay little heed to those who tell me otherwise. I hear the voices of dissent,—who does not? I hear the criticism and the clamor of the noisily thoughtless and troublesome. I also see men here and there fling themselves in impotent disloyalty against the calm, indomitable power of the Nation. I hear men debate peace who understand neither its nature nor the way in which we may attain it with uplifted eyes and unbroken spirits. But I know that none of these speaks for the Nation. They do not touch the heart of anything. They may safely be left to strut their uneasy hour and be forgotten.

But from another point of view I believe that it is necessary to say plainly what we here at the seat of action consider the war to be for and what part we mean to play in the settlement of its searching issues. We are the spokesmen of the American people and they have a right to know whether their purpose is ours. They desire peace by the overcoming of evil, by the defeat once for all of the sinister forces that interrupt peace and render it impossible, and they wish to know how closely our thought runs with theirs and what action we propose. They are impatient with those who desire peace by any sort of compromise,—deeply and indignantly impatient,—but they will be equally impatient with us if we do not make it plain to them what our objectives are and what we are planning for in seeking to make conquest of peace by arms.

I believe that I speak for them when I say two things: First, that this intolerable Thing of which the masters of Germany have shown us the ugly face, this menace of combined intrigue and force which we now see so clearly as the German power, a Thing without conscience or honor or capacity for covenanted peace, must be crushed and, if it be not utterly brought to an end, at least shut out from the friendly intercourse of the nations; and, second, that when this Thing and its power are indeed defeated and the time comes that we can discuss peace,—when the German people have spokesmen whose word we can believe and when those spokesmen are ready in the name of their people to accept the common judgment of the nations as to what shall henceforth be the bases of law and of covenant for the life of the world,—we shall be willing and glad to pay the full price for peace, and pay it ungrudgingly. We know what that price will be. It will be full, impartial justice,—justice done at every point and to every nation that the final settlement must affect, our enemies as well as our friends.

You catch, with me, the voices of humanity that are in the air. They grow daily more audible, more articulate, more persuasive, and they come from the hearts of men everywhere. They insist that the war shall not end in vindictive action of any kind; that no nation or people shall be robbed or punished because the irresponsible rulers of a single country have themselves done deep and abominable wrong. It is this thought that has been expressed in the formula "No annexations, no contributions, no punitive indemnities." Just because this crude formula expresses the instinctive judgment as to right of plain men everywhere it has been made diligent use of by the masters of German intrigue to lead the people of Russia astray — and the people of every other country their agents could reach, in order that a premature peace might be brought about before autocracy has been taught its final and convincing lesson, and the people of the world put in control of their own destinies.

But the fact that a wrong use has been made of a just idea is no reason why a right use should not be made of it. It ought to be brought under the patronage of its real friends. Let it be said again that autocracy must first be shown the utter futility of its claims to power or leadership in the modern world. It is impossible to apply any standard of justice so long as such forces are unchecked and undefeated as the present masters of Germany command. Not until that has been done can Right be set up as arbiter and peace-maker among the nations. But when that has been done, — as, God willing, it assuredly will be, — we shall at last be free to do an unprecedented thing, and this is the time to avow our purpose to do it. We shall be free to base peace on generosity and justice, to the exclusion of all selfish claims to advantage even on the part of the victors.

Let there be no misunderstanding. Our present and immediate task is to win the war, and nothing shall turn us aside from it until it is accomplished. Every power and resource we possess, whether of men, of money, or of materials, is being devoted and will continue to be devoted to that purpose until it is achieved. Those who desire to bring peace about before that purpose is achieved I counsel to carry their advice elsewhere. We will not entertain it. We shall regard the war as won only when the German people say to us, through properly accredited representatives, that they are ready to agree to a settlement based upon justice and the reparation of the wrongs their rulers have done. They have done a wrong to Belgium which must be repaired. They have established a power over other lands and peoples than their own,—over the great Empire of Austria-Hungary, over hitherto free Balkan states, over Turkey, and within Asia,—which must be relinquished.

Germany's success by skill, by industry, by knowledge, by enterprise we did not grudge or oppose, but admired, rather. She had built up for herself a real empire of trade and influence, secured by the peace of the world. We were content to abide the rivalries of manufacture, science, and commerce that were involved for us in her success and stand or fall as we had or did not have the brains and the initiative to surpass her. But at the moment when she had conspicuously won her triumphs of peace she threw them away, to establish in their stead what the world will no longer permit to be established, military and political domination by arms, by which to oust where she could not excel the rivals she most feared and hated. The peace we make must remedy that wrong. It must deliver the once fair lands and happy peoples of Belgium and northern France from the Prussian conquest and the Prussian menace, but it must also deliver the peoples of Austria-Hungary, the peoples of the Balkans, and the peoples of Turkey, alike in Europe and in Asia, from the impudent and alien dominion of the Prussian military and commercial autocracy.

We owe it, however, to ourselves to say that we do not wish in any way to impair or to re-arrange the Austro-Hungarian Empire. It is no affair of ours what they do with their own life, either industrially or politically. We do not purpose or desire to dictate to them in any way. We only desire to see that their affairs are left in their own hands, in all matters, great or small. We shall hope to secure for the peoples of the Balkan peninsula and for the people of the Turkish Empire the right and opportunity to make their own lives safe, their own fortunes secure against oppression or injustice and from the dictation of foreign courts or parties.

And our attitude and purpose with regard to Germany herself are of a like kind. We intend no wrong against the German Empire, no interference with her internal affairs. We should deem either the one or the other absolutely unjustifiable, absolutely contrary to the principles we have professed to live by and to hold most sacred throughout our life as a nation.

The people of Germany are being told by the men whom they now permit to deceive them and to act as their masters that they are fighting for the very life and existence of their Empire, a war of desperate self-defense against deliberate aggression. Nothing could be more grossly or wantonly false, and we must seek by the utmost openness and candor as to our real aims to convince them of its falseness. We are in fact fighting for their emancipation from fear, along with our own,—from the fear as well as from the fact of unjust attack by neighbors or rivals or schemers after world empire. No one is threatening the existence or the independence or the peaceful enterprise of the German Empire.

The worst that can happen to the detriment of the German people is this, that if they should still, after the war is over, continue to be obliged to live under ambitious and intriguing masters interested to disturb the peace of the world, men or classes of men whom the other peoples of the world could not trust, it might be impossible to admit them to the partnership of nations which must henceforth guarantee the world's peace. That partnership must be a partnership of peoples, not a mere partnership of governments. It might be impossible, also, in such untoward circumstances to admit Germany to the free economic intercourse which must inevitably spring out of the other partnerships of a real peace. But there would be no aggression in that; and such a situation, inevitable because of distrust, would in the very nature of things sooner or later cure itself, by processes which would assuredly set in.

The wrongs, the very deep wrongs, committed in this war will have to be righted. That of course. But they cannot and must not be righted by the commission of similar wrongs against Germany and her allies. The world will not permit the commission of similar wrongs as a means of reparation and settlement. Statesmen must by this time have learned that the opinion of the world is everywhere wide awake and fully comprehends the issues involved. No representative of any self-governed nation will dare disregard it by attempting any such covenants of selfishness and compromise as were entered into at the Congress of Vienna. The thought of the plain people here and everywhere throughout the world, the people who enjoy no privilege and have very simple and unsophisticated standards of right and wrong, is the air all governments must henceforth breathe if they would live. It is in the full disclosing light of that thought that all policies must be conceived and executed in this midday hour of the world's life. German rulers have been able to upset the peace of the world only because the German people were not suffered under their tutelage to share the comradeship of the other peoples of the world either in thought or in purpose. They were allowed to have no opinion of their own which might be set up as a rule of conduct for those who exercised authority over them. But the congress that concludes this war will feel the full strength of the tides that run now in the hearts and conscience of free men everywhere. Its conclusions will run with those tides. . . .

It is because it is for us a war of high, disinterested purpose, in which all the free peoples of the world are banded together for the vindication of right, a war for the preservation of our Nation and of all that it has held dear of principle and of purpose, that we feel ourselves doubly constrained to propose for its outcome only that which is righteous and of irreproachable intention, for our foes as well as for our friends. The cause being just and holy, the settlement must be of like motive and quality. For this we can fight, but for nothing less noble or less worthy of our traditions. For this cause we entered the war and for this cause will we battle until the last gun is fired.

I have spoken plainly because this seems to me the time when it is most necessary to speak plainly, in order that all the world may know that even in the heat and ardor of the struggle and when our whole thought is of carrying the war through to its end we have not forgotten any ideal or principle for which the name of America has been held in honor among the nations and for which it has been our glory to contend in the great generations that went before us. A supreme moment of history has come. The eyes of the people have been opened and they see. The hand of God is laid upon the nations. He will show them favor, I devoutly believe, only if they rise to the clear heights of His own justice and mercy.

DOCUMENT 113

"Impartial Justice in Every Item
of the Settlement. . . ."

Increasingly, Wilson came to see himself as the spokesman of mankind in the struggle to secure a just and lasting peace.

. . . The war has lasted more than four years and the whole world has been drawn into it. The common will of mankind has been substituted for the particular purposes of individual states. Individual statesmen may have started the conflict, but neither they nor their opponents can stop it as they please. It has become a peoples' war, and peoples of all sorts and races, of every degree of power and variety of fortune, are involved in its sweeping processes of change and settlement. We came into it when its character had become fully defined and it was plain that no nation could stand apart or be indifferent to its outcome. Its challenge drove to the heart of everything we cared for and lived for. The voice of the war had become clear and gripped our hearts. Our brothers from many lands, as well as our own murdered dead under the sea, were calling to us, and we responded, fiercely and of course.

The air was clear about us. We saw things in their full, convincing proportions as they were; and we have seen them with steady eyes and unchanging comprehension ever since. We accepted the issues of the war as facts, not as any group of men either here or elsewhere had defined them, and we can accept no outcome which does not squarely meet and settle them. Those issues are these:

Excerpt from address opening the Fourth Liberty Loan, New York, September 27, 1918, *Public Papers*, V, 254–258.

Shall the military power of any nation or group of nations be suffered to determine the fortunes of peoples over whom they have no right to rule except the right of force?

Shall strong nations be free to wrong weak nations and make them subject to their purpose and interest?

Shall peoples be ruled and dominated, even in their own internal affairs, by arbitrary and irresponsible force or by their own will and choice?

Shall there be a common standard of right and privilege for all peoples and nations or shall the strong do as they will and the weak suffer without redress?

Shall the assertion of right be haphazard and by casual alliance or shall there be a common concert to oblige the observance of common rights?

No man, no group of men, chose these to be the issues of the struggle. They *are* the issues of it; and they must be settled,—by no arrangement or compromise or adjustment of interests, but definitely and once for all and with a full and unequivocal acceptance of the principle that the interest of the weakest is as sacred as the interest of the strongest.

This is what we mean when we speak of a permanent peace, if we speak sincerely, intelligently, and with a real knowledge and comprehension of the matter we deal with.

We are all agreed that there can be no peace obtained by any kind of bargain or compromise with the governments of the Central Empires, because we have dealt with them already and have seen them deal with other governments that were parties to this struggle, at Brest-Litovsk and Bucharest. They have convinced us that they are without honor and do not intend justice. They observe no covenants, accept no principle but force and their own interest. We cannot "come to terms" with them. They have made it impossible. The German people must by this time be fully aware that we cannot accept the word of those who forced this war upon us. We do not think the same thoughts or speak the same language of agreement.

It is of capital importance that we should also be explicitly agreed that no peace shall be obtained by any kind of compromise or abatement of the principles we have avowed as the principles for which we are fighting. There should exist no doubt about that. I am, therefore, going to take the liberty of speaking with the utmost frankness about the practical implications that are involved in it.

If it be in deed and in truth the common object of the Governments associated against Germany and of the nations whom they govern, as I believe it to be, to achieve by the coming settlements a secure and lasting peace, it will be necessary that all who sit down at the peace table shall come ready and willing to pay the price, the only price, that will procure it; and ready and willing, also, to create in some virile fashion the only instrumentality by which it can be made certain that the agreements of the peace will be honored and fulfilled.

That price is impartial justice in every item of the settlement, no matter whose interest is crossed; and not only impartial justice, but also the satisfaction of the several peoples whose fortunes are dealt with. That indispensable instrumentality is a League of Nations formed under covenants that will be efficacious. Without such an instrumentality, by which the peace of the world can be guaranteed, peace will rest in part upon the word of outlaws and only upon that word. For Germany will have to redeem her character, not by what happens at the peace table, but by what follows.

And, as I see it, the constitution of that League of Nations and the clear definition of its objects must be a part, is in a sense the most essential part, of the peace settlement itself. It cannot be formed now. If formed now, it would be merely a new alliance confined to the nations associated against a common enemy. It is not likely that it could be formed after the settlement. It is necessary to guarantee the peace; and the peace cannot be guaranteed as an afterthought. The reason, to speak in plain terms again, why it must be guaranteed is that there will be parties to the peace whose promises have proved untrustworthy, and means must be found in connection with the peace settlement itself to remove that source of insecurity. It would be folly to leave the guarantee to the subsequent voluntary action of the Governments we have seen destroy Russia and deceive Rumania.

But these general terms do not disclose the whole matter. Some details are needed to make them sound less like a thesis and more like a practical program. These, then, are some of the particulars, and I state them with the greater confidence because I can state them authoritatively as representing this Government's interpretation of its own duty with regard to peace.

First, the impartial justice meted out must involve no discrimination between those to whom we wish to be just and those to whom we do not wish to be just. It must be a justice that plays no favorites and knows no standard but the equal rights of the several peoples concerned;

Second, no special or separate interest of any single nation or any group of nations can be made the basis of any part of the settlement which is not consistent with the common interest of all;

Third, there can be no leagues or alliances or special covenants and understandings within the general and common family of the League of Nations.

Fourth, and more specifically, there can be no special, selfish economic combinations within the League and no employment of any form of economic boycott or exclusion except as the power of economic penalty by exclusion from the markets of the world may be vested in the League of Nations itself as a means of discipline and control.

Fifth, all international agreements and treaties of every kind must be made known in their entirety to the rest of the world.

Special alliances and economic rivalries and hostilities have been the prolific source in the modern world of the plans and passions that produce war. It would be an insincere as well as insecure peace that did not exclude them in definite and binding terms.

The confidence with which I venture to speak for our people in these matters does not spring from our traditions merely and the well-known principles of international action which we have always professed and followed. In the same sentence in which I say that the United States will enter into no special arrangements or understandings with particular nations let me say also that the United States is prepared to assume its full share of responsibility for the maintenance of the common covenants and understandings upon which peace must henceforth rest. We still read Washington's immortal warning against "entangling alliances" with full comprehension and an answering purpose. But only special and limited alliances entangle; and we recognize and accept the duty of a new day in which we are permitted to hope for a general alliance which will avoid entanglements and clear the air of the world for common understandings and the maintenance of common rights.

DOCUMENT 114

"Nobody Has a Right to Get Anything
Out of This War . . ."

Although Wilson declared that the United States was not fighting for any selfish motives, he did little to ascertain

Excerpt from confidential address to 20 correspondents of foreign newspapers, April 18, 1918, in Baker, *Wilson, Life and Letters*, VIII, 80.

what the war aims of his Allies were or to head off any that might run counter to his objective of an impartial peace settlement. He was confident that the people of the world would sustain him, and perhaps for this reason he went out of his way to explain his idealistic goal to a group of foreign news-correspondents in April 1918.

. . . That speech I made on Saturday I hope was correctly understood. We are fighting, as I understand it, for justice to everybody and are ready to stop just as soon as justice to everybody is everybody's programme. . . . I would be ashamed to use the knock-down and drag-out language; that is not the language of liberty, that is the language of braggadocio. For my part, I have no desire to march triumphantly into Berlin. If they oblige us to march triumphantly into Berlin, then we will do it if it takes twenty years. But the world will come to its senses some day, no matter how mad some parts of it may be now, and this is my feeling, that we ought when the thing is over to be able to look back upon a course which had no element in it which we need be ashamed of. So it is so difficult in any kind of a speech, this kind or any other, to express two things that seem to be going in opposite directions that I wasn't sure that I had succeeded in expressing them on Saturday—the sincere willingness to discuss peace whenever the proposals are themselves sincere and yet at the same time the determination never to discuss it until the basis laid down for the discussion is justice. By that I mean justice to everybody. Nobody has the right to get anything out of this war, because we are fighting for peace if we mean what we say, for permanent peace. No injustice furnishes a basis for permanent peace. If you leave a rankling sense of injustice anywhere, it will not only produce a running sore presently which will result in trouble and probably war, but it ought to produce war somewhere. . . .

DOCUMENT 115

The Fourteen Points

By all odds the most important statement of Wilson's war aims was made in his celebrated address to Congress on January 8, 1918, outlining the Fourteen Points of his peace program.

Once more, as repeatedly before, the spokesmen of the Central Empires have indicated their desire to discuss the objects of the war and the possible bases of a general peace. Parleys have been in progress at Brest-Litovsk between representatives of the Central Powers to which the attention of all the belligerents has been invited for the purpose of ascertaining whether it may be possible to extend these parleys into a general conference with regard to terms of peace and settlement. The Russian representatives presented not only a perfectly definite statement of the principles upon which they would be willing to conclude peace but also an equally definite program of the concrete application of those principles. The representatives of the Central Powers, on their part, presented an outline of settlement which, if much less definite, seemed susceptible of liberal interpretation until their specific program of practical terms was added. That program proposed no concessions at all either to the sovereignty of Russia or to the preferences of the populations with whose fortunes it dealt, but meant, in a word, that the Central Empires were to keep every foot of territory their armed forces had occupied, — every province, every city, every point of vantage, — as a permanent addition to their territories and their power. It is a reasonable conjecture that the

Address to Congress, January 8, 1918, *Public Papers*, V, 155–162.

general principles of settlement which they at first suggested originated with the more liberal statesmen of Germany and Austria, the men who have begun to feel the
force of their own peoples' thought and purpose, while the
concrete terms of actual settlement came from the military
leaders who have no thought but to keep what they have
got. The negotiations have been broken off. The Russian
representatives were sincere and in earnest. They cannot
entertain such proposals of conquest and domination.

The whole incident is full of significance. It is also full
of perplexity. With whom are the Russian representatives
dealing? For whom are the representatives of the Central
Empires speaking? Are they speaking for the majorities of
their respective parliaments or for the minority parties,
that military and imperialistic minority which has so far
dominated their whole policy and controlled the affairs of
Turkey and of the Balkan states which have felt obliged to
become their associates in this war? The Russian representatives have insisted, very justly, very wisely, and in
the true spirit of modern democracy, that the conferences
they have been holding with the Teutonic and Turkish
statesmen should be held within open, not closed, doors,
and all the world has been audience, as was desired. To
whom have we been listening, then? To those who speak
the spirit and intention of the Resolutions of the German
Reichstag of the ninth of July last, the spirit and intention
of the liberal leaders and parties of Germany, or to those
who resist and defy that spirit and intention and insist
upon conquest and subjugation? Or are we listening, in
fact, to both, unreconciled and in open and hopeless con-
tradiction? These are very serious and pregnant questions.
Upon the answer to them depends the peace of the world.

But, whatever the results of the parleys at Brest-Litovsk,
whatever the confusions of counsel and of purpose in the
utterances of the spokesmen of the Central Empires, they

have again attempted to acquaint the world with their objects in the war and have again challenged their adversaries to say what their objects are and what sort of settlement they would deem just and satisfactory. There is no good reason why that challenge should not be responded to, and responded to with the utmost candor. We did not wait for it. Not once, but again and again, we have laid our whole thought and purpose before the world, not in general terms only, but each time with sufficient definition to make it clear what sort of definitive terms of settlement must necessarily spring out of them. Within the last week Mr. Lloyd George has spoken with admirable candor and in admirable spirit for the people and Government of Great Britain. There is no confusion of counsel among the adversaries of the Central Powers, no uncertainty of principle, no vagueness of detail. The only secrecy of counsel, the only lack of fearless frankness, the only failure to make definite statement of the objects of the war, lies with Germany and her Allies. The issues of life and death hang upon these definitions. No statesman who has the least conception of his responsibility ought for a moment to permit himself to continue this tragical and appalling outpouring of blood and treasure unless he is sure beyond a peradventure that the objects of the vital sacrifice are part and parcel of the very life of Society and that the people for whom he speaks think them right and imperative as he does.

There is, moreover, a voice calling for these definitions of principle and of purpose which is, it seems to me, more thrilling and more compelling than any of the many moving voices with which the troubled air of the world is filled. It is the voice of the Russian people. They are prostrate and all but helpless, it would seem, before the grim power of Germany, which has hitherto known no relenting and no pity. Their power, apparently, is shattered. And yet their soul is not subservient. They will not yield either in principle or in action. Their conception of what is right, of what it is humane and honorable for them to accept, has been stated with a frankness, a largeness of view, a generosity of spirit, and a universal human sympathy which must challenge the admiration of every friend of mankind; and they have refused to compound their ideals or desert others that they themselves may be safe. They call to us to say what it is that we desire, in what, if in anything, our purpose and our spirit differ from theirs; and I believe that the people of the United States would wish me to respond, with utter simplicity and frankness. Whether their present leaders believe it or not, it is our heartfelt desire and hope that some way may be opened whereby we may be privileged to assist the people of Russia to attain their utmost hope of liberty and ordered peace.

It will be our wish and purpose that the processes of peace, when they are begun, shall be absolutely open and that they shall involve and permit henceforth no secret understandings of any kind. The day of conquest and aggrandizement is gone by; so is also the day of secret covenants entered into in the interest of particular governments and likely at some unlooked-for moment to upset the peace of the world. It is this happy fact, now clear to the view of every public man whose thoughts do not still linger in an age that is dead and gone, which makes it possible for every nation whose purposes are consistent with justice and the peace of the world to avow now or at any other time the objects it has in view.

We entered this war because violations of right had occurred which touched us to the quick and made the life of our own people impossible unless they were corrected and the world secured once for all against their recurrence. What we demand in this war, therefore, is nothing peculiar to ourselves. It is that the world be made fit and safe to live in; and particularly that it be made safe for every peace-loving nation which, like our own, wishes to live its own life, determine its own institutions, be assured of justice and fair dealing by the other peoples of the world as against force and selfish aggression. All the peoples of the world are in effect partners in this interest, and for our own part we see very clearly that unless justice be done to others it will not be done to us. The program of the world's peace, therefore, is our program; and that program, the only possible program, as we see it, is this:

I. Open covenants of peace, openly arrived at, after which there shall be no private international understandings of any kind but diplomacy shall proceed always frankly and in the public view.

II. Absolute freedom of navigation upon the seas, outside territorial waters, alike in peace and in war, except as the seas may be closed in whole or in part by international action for the enforcement of international covenants.

III. The removal, so far as possible, of all economic barriers and the establishment of an equality of trade conditions among all the nations consenting to the peace and associating themselves for its maintenance.

IV. Adequate guarantees given and taken that national armaments will be reduced to the lowest point consistent with domestic safety.

V. A free, open-minded, and absolutely impartial adjustment of all colonial claims, based upon a strict observance of the principle that in determining all such questions of sovereignty the interests of the populations concerned must have equal weight with the equitable claims of the government whose title is to be determined.

VI. The evacuation of all Russian territory and such a settlement of all questions affecting Russia as will secure the best and freest coöperation of the other nations of the world in obtaining for her an unhampered and unembarrassed opportunity for the independent determination of her own political development and national policy and assure her of a sincere welcome into the society of free nations under institutions of her own choosing; and, more than a welcome, assistance also of every kind that she may need and may herself desire. The treatment accorded Russia by her sister nations in the months to come will be the acid test of their good will, of their comprehension of her needs as distinguished from their own interests, and of their intelligent and unselfish sympathy.

VII. Belgium, the whole world will agree, must be evacuated and restored, without any attempt to limit the sovereignty which she enjoys in common with all other free nations. No other single act will serve as this will serve to restore confidence among the nations in the laws which they have themselves set and determined for the government of their relations with one another. Without this healing act the whole structure and validity of international law is forever impaired.

VIII. All French territory should be freed and the invaded portions restored, and the wrong done to France by P. ussia in 1871 in the matter of Alsace-Lorraine, which has unsettled the peace of the world for nearly fifty years, should be righted, in order that peace may once more be made secure in the interest of all.

IX. A readjustment of the frontiers of Italy should be effected along clearly recognizable lines of nationality.

X. The peoples of Austria-Hungary, whose place among the nations we wish to see safeguarded and assured, should be accorded the freest opportunity of autonomous development.

XI. Rumania, Serbia, and Montenegro should be evacuated; occupied territories restored; Serbia accorded free and secure access to the sea; and the relations of the several Balkan states to one another determined by friendly counsel along historically established lines of allegiance and nationality; and international guarantees of the political and economic independence and territorial integrity of the several Balkan states should be entered into.

XII. The Turkish portions of the present Ottoman Empire should be assured a secure sovereignty, but the other nationalities which are now under Turkish rule should be assured an undoubted security of life and an absolutely unmolested opportunity of autonomous development, and the Dardanelles should be permanently opened as a free passage to the ships and commerce of all nations under international guarantees.

XIII. An independent Polish state should be erected which should include the territories inhabited by indisputably Polish populations, which should be assured a free and secure access to the sea, and whose political and economic independence and territorial integrity should be guaranteed by international covenant.

XIV. A general association of nations must be formed under specific covenants for the purpose of affording mutual guarantees of political independence and territorial integrity to great and small states alike.

In regard to these essential rectifications of wrong and assertions of right we feel ourselves to be intimate partners of all the governments and peoples associated together against the Imperialists. We cannot be separated in interest or divided in purpose. We stand together until the end.

For such arrangements and covenants we are willing to fight and to continue to fight until they are achieved; but only because we wish the right to prevail and desire a just and stable peace such as can be secured only by removing the chief provocations to war, which this program does remove. We have no jealousy of German greatness, and there is nothing in this program that impairs it. We grudge her no achievement or distinction of learning or of pacific enterprise such as have made her record very bright and very enviable. We do not wish to injure her or to block in any way her legitimate influence or power. We do not wish to fight her either with arms or with hostile arrangements of trade if she is willing to associate herself with us and the other peace-loving nations of the world in covenants of justice and law and fair dealing. We wish her only to accept a place of equality among the peoples of the world,—the new world in which we now live,—instead of a place of mastery.

Neither do we presume to suggest to her any alteration or modification of her institutions. But it is necessary, we must frankly say, and necessary as a preliminary to any intelligent dealings with her on our part, that we should know whom her spokesmen speak for when they speak to us, whether for the Reichstag majority or for the military party and the men whose creed is imperial domination.

We have spoken now, surely, in terms too concrete to admit of any further doubt or question. An evident principle runs through the whole program I have outlined. It is the principle of justice to all peoples and nationalities, and their right to live on equal terms of liberty and safety with one another, whether they be strong or weak. Unless this principle be made its foundation no part of the structure of international justice can stand. The people of the United States could act upon no other principle; and to the vindication of this principle they are ready to devote their lives, their honor, and everything that they possess. The moral climax of this the culminating and final war for human liberty has come, and they are ready to put their own strength, their own highest purpose, their own integrity and devotion to the test.

DOCUMENT 116

The Four Supplementary Points

Wilson subsequently elaborated on his Fourteen Points, notably in an address at Mount Vernon on July 4, 1918. The capstone of his program remained a League of Nations to insure peace and collective security for all nations, large and small.

GENTLEMEN OF THE DIPLOMATIC CORPS AND MY FELLOW CITIZENS:

I am happy to draw apart with you to this quiet place of old counsel in order to speak a little of the meaning of this day of our Nation's independence. The place seems very still and remote. It is as serene and untouched by the hurry of the world as it was in those great days long ago when General Washington was here and held leisurely conference with the men who were to be associated with him in the creation of a nation. From these gentle slopes they looked out upon the world and saw it whole, saw it with the light of the future upon it, saw it with modern eyes that turned away from a past which men of liberated spirits could no longer endure. It is for that reason that we cannot feel, even here, in the immediate presence of this sacred tomb, that this is a place of death. It was a place of achievement. A great promise that was meant for all mankind was here given plan and reality. The associations by which we are here surrounded are the inspiriting associations of that noble death which is only a glorious consummation. From this green hillside we also ought to be able to see with comprehending eyes the world that lies about

---

Address at Mount Vernon, Va., July 4, 1918, *Public Papers*, V, 231–235.

us and should conceive anew the purposes that must set men free.

It is significant,—significant of their own character and purpose and of the influences they were setting afoot,— that Washington and his associates, like the barons at Runnymede, spoke and acted, not for a class, but for a people. It has been left for us to see to it that it shall be understood that they spoke and acted, not for a single people only, but for all mankind. They were thinking, not of themselves and of the material interests which centered in the little groups of landholders and merchants and men of affairs with whom they were accustomed to act, in Virginia and the colonies to the north and south of her, but of a people which wished to be done with classes and special interests and the authority of men whom they had not themselves chosen to rule over them. They entertained no private purpose, desired no peculiar privilege. They were consciously planning that men of every class should be free and America a place to which men out of every nation might resort who wished to share with them the rights and privileges of free men. And we take our cue from them,— do we not? We intend what they intended. We here in America believe our participation in this present war to be only the fruitage of what they planted. Our case differs from theirs only in this, that it is our inestimable privilege to concert with men out of every nation what shall make not only the liberties of America secure but the liberties of every other people as well. We are happy in the thought that we are permitted to do what they would have done had they been in our place. There must now be settled once for all what was settled for America in the great age upon whose inspiration we draw to-day. This is surely a fitting place from which calmly to look out upon our task, that we may fortify our spirits for its accomplishment. And this is the appropriate place from which to avow, alike to the friends who look on and to the friends with whom we have the happiness to be associated in action, the faith and purpose with which we act.

This, then, is our conception of the great struggle in which we are engaged. The plot is written plain upon every scene and every act of the supreme tragedy. On the one hand stand the peoples of the world,—not only the peoples actually engaged, but many others also who suffer under mastery but cannot act; peoples of many races and in every part of the world,—the people of stricken Russia still, among the rest, though they are for the moment unorganized and helpless. Opposed to them, masters of many armies, stand an isolated, friendless group of governments who speak no common purpose but only selfish ambitions of their own by which none can profit but themselves, and whose peoples are fuel in their hands; governments which fear their people and yet are for the time their sovereign lords, making every choice for them and disposing of their lives and fortunes as they will, as well as of the lives and fortunes of every people who fall under their power,—governments clothed with the strange trappings and the primitive authority of an age that is altogether alien and hostile to our own. The Past and the Present are in deadly grapple and the peoples of the world are being done to death between them.

There can be but one issue. The settlement must be final. There can be no compromise. No halfway decision would be tolerable. No halfway decision is conceivable. These are the ends for which the associated peoples of the world are fighting and which must be conceded them before there can be peace:

I. The destruction of every arbitrary power anywhere that can separately, secretly, and of its single choice disturb the peace of the world; or, if it cannot be presently destroyed, at the least its reduction to virtual impotence.

II. The settlement of every question, whether of territory, of sovereignty, of economic arrangement, or of political relationship, upon the basis of the free acceptance of that settlement by the people immediately concerned, and not upon the basis of the material interest or advantage of any other nation or people which may desire a different settlement for the sake of its own exterior influence or mastery.

III. The consent of all nations to be governed in their conduct towards each other by the same principles of honor and of respect for the common law of civilized society that govern the individual citizens of all modern states in their relations with one another; to the end that all promises and covenants may be sacredly observed, no private plots or conspiracies hatched, no selfish injuries wrought with impunity, and a mutual trust established upon the handsome foundation of a mutual respect for right.

IV. The establishment of an organization of peace which shall make it certain that the combined power of free nations will check every invasion of right and serve to make peace and justice the more secure by affording a definite tribunal of opinion to which all must submit and by which every international readjustment that cannot be amicably agreed upon by the peoples directly concerned shall be sanctioned.

These great objects can be put into a single sentence. What we seek is the reign of law, based upon the consent of the governed and sustained by the organized opinion of mankind.

These great ends cannot be achieved by debating and seeking to reconcile and accommodate what statesmen may wish, with their projects for balances of power and of national 'opportunity. They can be realized only by the determination of what the thinking peoples of the world desire, with their longing hope for justice and for social freedom and opportunity.

I can fancy that the air of this place carries the accents of such principles with a peculiar kindness. Here were started forces which the great nation against which they were primarily directed at first regarded as a revolt against its rightful authority but which it has long since seen to have been a step in the liberation of its own people as well as of the people of the United States; and I stand here now to speak, — speak proudly and with confident hope, — of the spread of this revolt, this liberation, to the great stage of the world itself! The blinded rulers of Prussia have roused forces they knew little of, — forces which, once roused, can never be crushed to earth again; for they have at their heart an inspiration and a purpose which are deathless and of the very stuff of triumph!

DOCUMENT 117

Announcing the Armistice

The President played a major role in the delicate negotiations with the Germans and the Allies, leading to an armistice on November 11, 1918, that was based upon general acceptance of his Fourteen Points. Although Wilson's announcement of the armistice expressed confidence that America's war objectives had been won, privately he realized that he still faced the more difficult task of translating his Fourteen Points into a workable peace settlement.

Statement to the public, November 11, 1918, *Public Papers*, V, 293.

MY FELLOW COUNTRYMEN:
  The armistice was signed this morning. Everything for which America fought has been accomplished. It will now be our fortunate duty to assist by example, by sober, friendly counsel and by material aid in the establishment of just democracy throughout the world.

D. MAKING THE PEACE SETTLEMENT

DOCUMENT 118

"I Am Ready to Repudiate
Any Selfish Programme Openly. . . ."

By the time of the armistice Wilson was suspicious of the selfish war aims of his Allies and was prepared to use public opinion and, if necessary, economic pressure to force them to stand by their commitments to his idealistic peace program. He bluntly expressed his attitude in a cable to his special emissary in Europe, Colonel House, late in October 1918.

3. Can be no real difficulty about peace terms and interpretation of fourteen points if the Entente statesmen will be perfectly frank with us and have no selfish aims of their own which would in any case alienate us from them altogether. It is the fourteen points that Germany has accepted. England cannot dispense with our friendship in the fu-

---

Cable to Edward M. House, *ca.* October 29, 1918, in *Foreign Relations, Supplement, The Paris Peace Conference* (Washington, D.C.: Government Printing Office, 1942), I, 285.

ture and the other Allies cannot without our assistance get their rights as against England. If it is the purpose of the Allied statesmen to nullify my influence force the purpose boldly to the surface and let me speak of it to all the world as I shall. League of nations underlies freedom of the seas and every other part of peace programme so far as I am concerned. I am ready to repudiate any selfish programme openly, but assume that the Allies cannot honorably turn the present discussions into a peace conference without me. Please do not use wireless.

DOCUMENT 119

A Determination to Lead the Peace Conference

Convinced that only his leadership and actual presence at the peace conference could secure the adoption of his peace program, Wilson was determined to head the American delegation and personally take part in the drafting of the peace treaty. He had no patience with advice from Colonel House that the Allies were something less than enthusiastic over this decision.

Your 107 upsets every plan we had made. I infer that French and English leaders desire to exclude me from the Conference for fear I might there lead the weaker nations against them. If I were to come to the seat of the Conference and remain outside I would be merely the centre of a sort of sublimated lobby. All weak parties would resort to me and there would be exactly the same jealousy that was excited by the Germans addressing themselves exclusively to me. I play the same part in our government that the

---

Cable to Edward M. House, November 16, 1918, in *Foreign Relations, Supplement, The Paris Peace Conference,* I, 134–135.

prime ministers play in theirs. The fact that I am head of the state is of no practical consequence. No point of dignity must prevent our obtaining the results we have set our hearts upon and must have. It is universally expected and generally desired here that I should attend the conference, but I believe that no one would wish me to sit by and try to steer from the outside. I am thrown into complete confusion by the change of programme. The programme proposed for me by Clemenceau, George, Reading, and the rest seems to me a way of pocketing me. I hope you will be very shy of their advice and give me your own independent judgment after reconsideration.

DOCUMENT 120

Wilson's First Draft of the Covenant

of the League of Nations

To Wilson, the heart of the peace treaty would be the League of Nations, which would provide the machinery to enforce the settlement as well as to rectify any mistakes made by the conference. The President, always interested in the problems of constitution-making, labored throughout the summer of 1918 on a draft of the Covenant (his word) for the proposed international organization. When he departed for Paris in December he took with him his first draft of the Covenant. It included a qualified guarantee of the independence and territorial integrity of member nations (Article 3, ultimately Article 10), as well as authority for member states to apply various sanctions, including force to any nation commencing hostilities against another (Article 7, ultimately Article 16).

Ray Stannard Baker, *Woodrow Wilson and World Settlement* (Garden City, N.Y.: Doubleday, Page & Company, 1922), III, 88–93.

COVENANT.
Preamble.

In order to secure peace, security, and orderly government by the prescription of open and honorable relations between nations, by the firm establishment of the understandings of international law as the actual rule of conduct among governments, and by the maintenance of justice and a scrupulous respect of all treaty obligations in the dealings of all organized peoples with one another, the Powers signatory to this covenant and agreement jointly and severally adopt this constitution of the League of Nations.

Article I. — The action of the Signatory Powers under the terms of this agreement shall be effected through the instrumentality of a Body of Delegates which shall consist of the ambassadors and ministers of the contracting Powers accredited to H[olland] and the Minister for Foreign Affairs of H[olland]. The meetings of the Body of Delegates shall be held at the seat of government of H[olland] and the Minister for Foreign Affairs of H[olland] shall be the presiding officer of the Body.

Whenever the Delegates deem it necessary or advisable, they may meet temporarily at the seat of government of B[elgium] or of S[witzerland], in which case the Ambassador or Minister to H[olland] of the country in which the meeting is held shall be the presiding officer *pro tempore.*

Article II. — The Body of Delegates shall regulate their own procedure and shall have power to appoint such committees as they may deem necessary to inquire into and report upon any matters which lie within the field of their action.

They shall organize a Secretariat to act as their ministerial agency, and the expense of the maintenance of the Secretariat shall be borne as they may prescribe.

In all matters covered by this Article the Body of Delegates may decide by a majority vote of the whole Body.

Article III. — The Contracting Powers unite in guaranteeing to each other political independence and territorial integrity; but it is understood between them that such territorial readjustments, if any, as may in the future become necessary by reason of changes in present racial conditions and aspirations or present social and political relationships, pursuant to the principle of self-determination, and also such territorial readjustments as may in the judgment of three-fourths of the Delegates be demanded by the welfare and manifest interest of the peoples concerned, may be effected, if agreeable to those peoples; and that territorial changes may in equity involve material compensation. The Contracting Powers accept without reservation the principle that the peace of the world is superior in importance to every question of political jurisdiction or boundary.

Article IV. — (H. 21.)[1] The Contracting Powers recognize the principle that the establishment and maintenance of peace will require the reduction of national armaments to the lowest point consistent with domestic safety and the enforcement by common action of international obligations; and the Delegates are directed to formulate at once plans by which such a reduction may be brought about. The plan so formulated shall be binding when, and only when, unanimously approved by the Governments signatory to this Covenant.

The Contracting Powers further agree that munitions and implements of war shall not be manufactured by private enterprise or for private profit, and that there shall be full and frank publicity as to all national armaments and military or naval programmes.

Article V. — The Contracting Powers agree that all

---

[1] In this document the numbers in parentheses refer to ideas expressed in various articles of a draft of a proposed covenant prepared by Colonel Edward M. House for Wilson, July 16, 1918. [ed.]

disputes arising between or among them of whatever nature, which shall not be satisfactorily settled by diplomacy, shall be referred for arbitration to three arbitrators, one of the three to be selected by each of the parties to the dispute, when there are but two such parties, and the third by the two thus selected. When there are more than two parties to the dispute, one arbitrator shall be named by each of the several parties and the arbitrators thus named shall add to their number others of their own choice, the number thus added to be limited to the number which will suffice to give a deciding voice to the arbitrators thus added in case of a tie vote among the arbitrators chosen by the contending parties. In case the arbitrators chosen by the contending parties cannot agree upon an additional arbitrator or arbitrators, the additional arbitrator or arbitrators shall be chosen by the Body of Delegates.

On the appeal of a party to the dispute the decision of the arbitrators may be set aside by a vote of three-fourths of the Delegates, in case the decision of the arbitrators was unanimous, or by a vote of two-thirds of the Delegates in case the decision of the arbitrators was not unanimous, but unless thus set aside shall be finally binding and conclusive.

When any decision of arbitrators shall have been thus set aside the dispute shall again be submitted to arbitrators chosen as heretofore provided, none of whom shall, however, have previously acted as arbitrators in the dispute in question, and the decision of the arbitrators rendered in this second arbitration shall be finally binding and conclusive without right of appeal.

ARTICLE VI.—(H. 14.) Any power which the Body of Delegates shall declare to have failed to submit any dispute to arbitration under the terms of Article V of this Covenant or to have refused or failed to carry out any decision of such arbitration shall thereupon lose and be deprived of all rights of commerce and intercourse with any of the Contracting Powers.

ARTICLE VII.—If any Power shall declare war or begin hostilities, or take any hostile step short of war, against another Power before submitting the dispute involved to arbitrators as herein provided, or shall declare war or begin hostilities, or take any hostile step short of war, in regard to any dispute which has been decided adversely to it by arbitrators chosen and empowered as herein provided, the Contracting Powers hereby bind themselves not only to cease all commerce and intercourse with that Power but also to unite in blockading and closing the frontiers of that power to commerce or intercourse with any part of the world and to use any force that may be necessary to accomplish that object.

ARTICLE VIII.—(H. 5, 7, 8.) Any war or threat of war, whether immediately affecting any of the Contracting Powers or not, is hereby declared a matter of concern to the League of Nations and to all the Powers signatory hereto, and those Powers hereby reserve the right to take any action that may be deemed wise and effectual to safeguard the peace of nations.

The Delegates shall meet in the interest of peace whenever war is rumoured or threatened, and also whenever the Delegate of any Power shall inform the Delegates that a meeting and conference in the interest of peace is advisable.

The Delegates may also meet at such other times and upon such other occasions as they shall from time to time deem best and determine.

ARTICLE IX.—(H. 16, 17.) In the event of a dispute arising between one of the Contracting Powers and a Power not a party to this Covenant, the Contracting Power involved hereby binds itself to endeavour to obtain the submission of the dispute to judicial decision or to arbitration. If the other Power will not agree to submit the dispute to judicial decision or to arbitration, the Contracting Power shall bring the matter to the attention of the Body of Delegates. The Delegates shall in such case, in the name of the League of Nations, invite the Power not a party to this Covenant to become *ad hoc* a party and to submit its case to judicial decision or to arbitration, and if that Power consents it is hereby agreed that the provisions hereinbefore contained and applicable to the submission of disputes to arbitration shall be in all respects applicable to the dispute both in favour of and against such Power as if it were a party to this Covenant.

In case the Power not a party to this Covenant shall accept the invitation of the Delegates to become *ad hoc* a party, it shall be the duty of the Delegates immediately to institute an inquiry into the circumstances and merits of the dispute involved and to recommend such joint action by the Contracting Powers as may seem best and most effectual in the circumstances disclosed.

ARTICLE X. — (H. 18.) If hostilities should be begun or any hostile action taken against the Contracting Power by the Power not a party to this Covenant before a decision of the dispute by arbitrators or before investigation, report, and recommendation by the Delegates in regard to the dispute, or contrary to such recommendation, the Contracting Powers shall thereupon cease all commerce and communication with that Power and shall also unite in blockading and closing the frontiers of that Power to all commerce or intercourse with any part of the world, employing jointly any force that may be necessary to accomplish that object. The Contracting Powers shall also unite in coming to the assistance of the Contracting Power against which hostile action has been taken, combining their armed forces in its behalf.

ARTICLE XI. — (H. 19.) In case of a dispute between

states not parties to this Covenant, any Contracting Power may bring the matter to the attention of the Delegates, who shall thereupon tender the good offices of the League of Nations with a view to the peaceable settlement of the dispute.

If one of the states, a party to the dispute, shall offer and agree to submit its interests and cause of action wholly to the control and decision of the League of Nations, that state shall *ad hoc* be deemed a Contracting Power. If no one of the states, parties to the dispute, shall so offer and agree, the Delegates shall of their own motion take such action and make such recommendation to their governments as will prevent hostilities and result in the settlement of the dispute.

ARTICLE XII.—(H. 22.) Any Power not a party to this Covenant may apply to the Body of Delegates for leave to become a party. If the Delegates shall regard the granting thereof as likely to promote the peace, order, and security of the World, they may act favourably on the application, and their favourable action shall operate to constitute the Power so applying in all respects a full signatory party to this Covenant.

ARTICLE XIII.—(H. 23.) The Contracting Powers severally agree that the present Covenant and Convention is accepted as abrogating all treaty obligations *inter se* which are inconsistent with the terms hereof, and solemnly engage that they will not enter into any engagements inconsistent with the terms hereof.

In case any of the Powers signatory hereto or subsequently admitted to the League of Nations shall, before becoming a party to this covenant, have undertaken any treaty obligations which are inconsistent with the terms of this Covenant, it shall be the duty of such Power to take immediate steps to procure its release from such obligations.

DOCUMENT 121

"A Living Thing Is Born . . ."

At Paris, Wilson won from the leaders of the major powers reluctant assent that the League of Nations should be an integral part of the peace treaty. The President chaired the fourteen-member League of Nations Commission, which drafted a revised Covenant based substantially on his ideas. Appropriately, it was Wilson who presented the Covenant to a plenary session of the delegates on February 14, explaining its purposes in one of the memorable speeches of the conference.

I have the honor and as I esteem it the very great privilege of reporting in the name of the commission constituted by this conference on the formulation of a plan for the league of nations. I am happy to say that it is a unanimous report, a unanimous report from the representatives of fourteen nations—the United States, Great Britain, France, Italy, Japan, Belgium, Brazil, China, Czecho-Slovakia, Greece, Poland, Portugal, Rumania, and Serbia. I think it will be serviceable and interesting if I, with your permission, read the document as the only report we have to make. . . .

It gives me pleasure to add to this formal reading of the result of our labors that the character of the discussion which occurred at the sittings of the commission was not only of the most constructive but of the most encouraging sort. It was obvious throughout our discussions that, although there were subjects upon which there were individual differences of judgment, with regard to the method by which our objects should be obtained, there was prac-

---

Address to the Third Plenary Session of the Peace Conference, February 14, 1919, *Public Papers*, V, 413, 423–429.

tically at no point any serious difference of opinion or motive as to the objects which we were seeking. Indeed, while these debates were not made the opportunity for the expression of enthusiasms and sentiments, I think the other members of the commission will agree with me that there was an undertone of high resolve and of enthusiasm for the thing we were trying to do, which was heartening throughout every meeting; because we felt that in a way this conference had intrusted to us the expression of one of its highest and most important purposes, to see to it that the concord of the world in the future with regard to the objects of justice should not be subject to doubt or uncertainty; that the coöperation of the great body of nations should be assured from the first in the maintenance of peace upon the terms of honor and of the strict regard for international obligation. The compulsion of that task was constantly upon us, and at no point was there shown the slightest desire to do anything but suggest the best means to accomplish that great object. There is very great significance, therefore, in the fact that the result was reached unanimously. Fourteen nations were represented, among them all of those powers which for convenience we have called the great powers, and among the rest a representation of the greatest variety of circumstance and interest. So that I think we are justified in saying that it was a representative group of the members of this great conference. The significance of the result, therefore, has that deepest of all meanings, the union of wills in a common purpose, a union of wills, which cannot be resisted, and which I dare say no nation will run the risk of attempting to resist.

Now, as to the character of the document. While it has consumed some time to read this document, I think you will see at once that it is, after all, very simple, and in nothing so simple as in the structure which it suggests for the League of Nations—a body of delegates, an executive council, and a permanent secretariat. When it came to the question of determining the character of the representation in the body of delegates, we were all aware of a feeling which is current throughout the world. Inasmuch as I am stating it in the presence of official representatives of the various Governments here present, including myself, I may say that there is a universal feeling that the world cannot rest satisfied with merely official guidance. There reached us through many channels the feeling that if the deliberative body of the League was merely to be a body of officials representing the various Governments, the peoples of the world would not be sure that some of the mistakes which preoccupied officials had admittedly made might not be repeated. It was impossible to conceive a method or an assembly so large and various as to be really representative of the great body of the peoples of the world, because, as I roughly reckon it, we represent as we sit around this table more than twelve hundred million people. You cannot have a representative assembly of twelve hundred million people, but if you leave it to each Government to have, if it pleases, one or two or three representatives, though only a single vote, it may vary its representation from time to time, not only but it may origin-ate the choice of its several representatives, if it should have several in different ways. Therefore, we thought that this was a proper and a very prudent concession to the practically universal opinion of plain men everywhere that they wanted the door left open to a variety of representation instead of being confined to a single official body with which they might or might not find themselves in sympathy.

And you will notice that this body has unlimited rights of discussion — I mean of discussion of anything that falls within the field of international relationship — and that it is specially agreed that war or international misunderstand-ings or anything that may lead to friction and trouble is everybody's business, because it may affect the peace of the world. And in order to safeguard the popular power so far as we could of this representative body it is provided, you will notice, that when a subject is submitted, not to arbitration, but to discussion by the executive council, it can upon the initiative of either one of the parties to the dispute be drawn out of the executive council onto the larger forum of the general body of delegates, because throughout this instrument we are depending primarily and chiefly upon one great force, and that is the moral force of the public opinion of the world — the cleansing and clarifying and compelling influences of publicity — so that intrigues can no longer have their coverts, so that designs that are sinister can at any time be drawn into the open, so that those things that are destroyed by the light may be properly destroyed by the overwhelming light of the universal expression of the condemnation of the world.

Armed force is in the background in this program, but it *is* in the background, and if the moral force of the world will not suffice, the physical force of the world shall. But that is the last resort, because this is intended as a constitution of peace, not as a league of war.

The simplicity of the document seems to me to be one of its chief virtues, because, speaking for myself, I was unable to forsee the variety of circumstances with which this League would have to deal. I was unable, therefore, to plan all the machinery that might be necessary to meet differing and unexpected contingencies. Therefore, I should say of this document that it is not a straitjacket, but a vehicle of life. A living thing is born, and we must see to it that the clothes we put upon it do not hamper it — a vehicle of power, but a vehicle in which power may be varied at the discretion of those who exercise it and in accordance with the changing circumstances of the time. And yet, while it is elastic, while it is general in its terms, it is definite in the one thing that we were called upon to make definite. It is a definite guarantee of peace. It is a definite guarantee by word against aggression. It is a definite guarantee against the things which have just come near bringing the whole structure of civilization into ruin. Its purposes do not for a moment lie vague. Its purposes are declared and its powers made unmistakable.

It is not in contemplation that this should be merely a League to secure the peace of the world. It is a League which can be used for coöperation in any international matter. That is the significance of the provision introduced concerning labor. There are many ameliorations of labor conditions which can be effected by conference and discussion. I anticipate that there will be a very great usefulness in the bureau of labor which it is contemplated shall be set up by the League. While men and women and children who work have been in the background through long ages, and sometimes seemed to be forgotten, while Governments have had their watchful and suspicious eyes upon the maneuvers of one another, while the thought of statesmen has been about structural action and the large transactions of commerce and of finance, now, if I may believe the picture which I see, there comes into the foreground the great body of the laboring people of the world, the men and women and children upon whom the great burden of sustaining the world must from day to day fall, whether we wish it to do so or not; people who go to bed tired and wake up without the stimulation of lively hope. These people will be drawn into the field of international consultation and help, and will be among the wards of the combined Governments of the world. There is, I take leave to say, a very great step in advance in the mere conception of that.

Then, as you will notice, there is an imperative article concerning the publicity of all international agreements.

Henceforth no member of the League can claim any agreement valid which it has not registered with the secretary general, in whose office, of course, it will be subject to the examination of anybody representing a member of the League. And the duty is laid upon the secretary general to publish every document of that sort at the earliest possible time. I suppose most persons who have not been conversant with the business of foreign offices do not realize how many hundreds of these agreements are made in a single year, and how difficult it might be to publish the more unimportant of them immediately—how uninteresting it would be to most of the world to publish them immediately—but even they must be published just so soon as it is possible for the secretary general to publish them.

Then there is a feature about this covenant which to my mind is one of the greatest and most satisfactory advances that has been made. We are done with annexations of helpless people, meant in some instances by some powers to be used merely for exploitation. We recognize in the most solemn manner that the helpless and undeveloped peoples of the world, being in that condition, put an obligation upon us to look after their interests primarily before we use them for our interest; and that in all cases of this sort hereafter it shall be the duty of the League to see that the nations who are assigned as the tutors and advisers and directors of those peoples shall look to their interest and to their development before they look to the interests and material desires of the mandatory nation itself. There has been no greater advance than this, gentlemen. If you look back upon the history of the world you will see how helpless peoples have too often been a prey to powers that had no conscience in the matter. It has been one of the many distressing revelations of recent years that the great power which has just been happily defeated put intolerable burdens and injustices upon the helpless people of some of the colonies which it annexed to itself; that its interest was rather their extermination than their development; that the desire was to possess their land for European purposes, and not to enjoy their confidence in order [that] mankind might be lifted in those places to the next higher level. Now, the world, expressing its conscience in law, says there is an end of that. Our consciences shall be applied to this thing. States will be picked out which have already shown that they can exercise a conscience in this matter, and under their tutelage the helpless peoples of the world will come into a new light and into a new hope.

So I think I can say of this document that it is at one and the same time a practical document and a humane document. There is a pulse of sympathy in it. There is a compulsion of conscience throughout it. It is practical, and yet it is intended to purify, to rectify, to elevate. And I want to say that, so far as my observation instructs me, this is in one sense a belated document. I believe that the conscience of the world has long been prepared to express itself in some such way. We are not just now discovering our sympathy for these people and our interest in them. We are simply expressing it, for it has long been felt, and in the administration of the affairs of more than one of the great States represented here—so far as I know, of all the great States that are represented here—that humane impulse has already expressed itself in their dealings with their colonies whose peoples were yet at a low stage of civilization. We have had many instances of colonies lifted into the sphere of complete self-government. This is not the discovery of a principle. It is the universal application of a principle. It is the agreement of the great nations which have tried to live by these standards in their separate administrations to unite in seeing that their common force and their common thought and intelligence are lent to this great and humane enterprise. I think it is an occasion, therefore, for the most profound satisfaction that this humane decision should have been reached in a matter for which the world has long been waiting and until a very recent period thought that it was still too early to hope.

Many terrible things have come out of this war, gentlemen, but some very beautiful things have come out of it. Wrong has been defeated, but the rest of the world has been more conscious than it ever was before of the majesty of right. People that were suspicious of one another can now live as friends and comrades in a single family, and desire to do so. The miasma of distrust, of intrigue, is cleared away. Men are looking eye to eye and saying, "We are brothers and have a common purpose. We did not realize it before, but now we do realize it, and this is our covenant of fraternity and of friendship."

DOCUMENT 122

Final Text of the League Covenant

To head off criticism already building up against the League in some quarters in the United States, Wilson, at the urging of William Howard Taft and several other prominent pro-League Republicans, persuaded the conference during April to adopt certain changes in the Covenant. From the standpoint of American desires, the most important of these revisions was the addition of a new Article 21, specifically declaring that nothing in the Covenant invalidated "regional understandings like the Monroe Doctrine." Other amendments designed to allay American fears included a provision under which members could withdraw from the League (Article 1), reserved domestic questions from League jurisdiction (Article 15), and made optional

Baker, *Wilson and World Settlement*, III, 175–187.

the acceptance of a League mandated territory (Article 22). Wilson believed the final text of the Covenant, as it appeared in the Versailles Treaty, adequately protected all legitimate American interests.

THE COVENANT OF THE LEAGUE OF NATIONS.

THE HIGH CONTRACTING PARTIES,

In order to promote international coöperation and to achieve international peace and security

> by the acceptance of obligations not to resort to war,
>
> by the prescription of open, just and honourable relations between nations,
>
> by the firm establishment of the understandings of international law as the actual rule of conduct among Governments, and
>
> by the maintenance of justice and a scrupulous respect for all treaty obligations in the dealings of organised peoples with one another,

Agree to this Covenant of the League of Nations.

ARTICLE 1.—The original Members of the League of Nations shall be those of the Signatories which are named in the Annex to this Covenant and also such of those other States named in the Annex as shall accede without reservation to this Covenant. Such accession shall be effected by a Declaration deposited with the Secretariat within two months of the coming into force of the Covenant. Notice thereof shall be sent to all other Members of the League.

Any fully self-governing State, Dominion or Colony not named in the Annex may become a Member of the League if its admission is agreed to by two-thirds of the Assembly, provided that it shall give effective guarantees of its sincere intention to observe its international obligations, and shall accept such regulations as may be prescribed by the League in regard to its military, naval, and air forces and armaments.

Any Member of the League may, after two years' notice of its intention so to do, withdraw from the League, provided that all its international obligations and all its obligations under this Covenant shall have been fulfilled at the time of its withdrawal.

ARTICLE 2. — The action of the League under this Covenant shall be effected through the instrumentality of an Assembly and of a Council, with a permanent Secretariat.

ARTICLE 3. — The Assembly shall consist of Representatives of the Members of the League.

The Assembly shall meet at stated intervals and from time to time as occasion may require at the Seat of the League or at such other place as may be decided upon.

The Assembly may deal at its meetings with any matter within the sphere of action of the League or affecting the peace of the world.

At meetings of the Assembly each Member of the League shall have one vote, and may have not more than three Representatives.

ARTICLE 4. — The Council shall consist of Representatives of the Principal Allied and Associated Powers, together with Representatives of four other Members of the League. These four Members of the League shall be selected by the Assembly from time to time in its discretion. Until the appointment of the Representatives of the four Members of the League first selected by the Assembly, Representatives of Belgium, Brazil, Spain, and Greece shall be members of the Council.

With the approval of the majority of the Assembly, the Council may name additional Members of the League whose Representatives shall always be members of the Council; the Council with like approval may increase the number of Members of the League to be selected by the Assembly for representation on the Council.

The Council shall meet from time to time as occasion

may require, and at least once a year, at the Seat of the League, or at such other place as may be decided upon.

The Council may deal at its meetings with any matter within the sphere of action of the League or affecting the peace of the world.

Any Member of the League not represented on the Council shall be invited to send a Representative to sit as a member at any meeting of the Council during the consideration of matters specially affecting the interests of that Member of the League.

At meetings of the Council, each Member of the League represented on the Council shall have one vote, and may have not more than one Representative.

ARTICLE 5.—Except where otherwise expressly provided in this Covenant or by the terms of the present Treaty, decisions at any meeting of the Assembly or of the Council shall require the agreement of all the Members of the League represented by the meeting.

All matters of procedure at meetings of the Assembly or of the Council, including the appointment of Committees to investigate particular matters, shall be regulated by the Assembly or by the Council and may be decided by a majority of the Members of the League represented at the meeting.

The first meeting of the Assembly and the first meeting of the Council shall be summoned by the President of the United States of America.

ARTICLE 6.—The permanent Secretariat shall be established at the Seat of the League. The Secretariat shall comprise a Secretary General and such secretaries and staff as may be required.

The first Secretary General shall be the person named in the Annex; thereafter the Secretary General shall be appointed by the Council with the approval of the majority of the Assembly.

The secretaries and staff of the Secretariat shall be appointed by the Secretary General with the approval of the Council.

The Secretary General shall act in that capacity at all meetings of the Assembly and of the Council.

The expenses of the Secretariat shall be borne by the Members of the League in accordance with the apportionment of the expenses of the International Bureau of the Universal Postal Union.

ARTICLE 7. — The Seat of the League is established at Geneva.

The Council may at any time decide that the Seat of the League shall be established elsewhere.

All positions under or in connection with the League, including the Secretariat, shall be open equally to men and women.

Representatives of the Members of the League and officials of the League when engaged on the business of the League shall enjoy diplomatic privileges and immunities.

The buildings and other property occupied by the League or its officials or by Representatives attending its meetings shall be inviolable.

ARTICLE 8. — The Members of the League recognise that the maintenance of peace requires the reduction of national armaments to the lowest point consistent with national safety and the enforcement by common action of international obligations.

The Council, taking account of the geographical situation and circumstances of each State, shall formulate plans for such reduction for the consideration and action of the several Governments.

Such plans shall be subject to reconsideration and revision at least every ten years.

After these plans shall have been adopted by the several Governments, the limits of armaments therein fixed shall not be exceeded without the concurrence of the Council.

The Members of the League agree that the manufacture by private enterprise of munitions and implements of war is open to grave objections. The Council shall advise how the evil effects attendant upon such manufacture can be prevented, due regard being had to the necessities of those Members of the League which are not able to manufacture the munitions and implements of war necessary for their safety.

The Members of the League undertake to interchange full and frank information as to the scale of their armaments, their military, naval and air programmes and the condition of such of their industries as are adaptable to war-like purposes.

ARTICLE 9. — A permanent Commission shall be constituted to advise the Council on the execution of the provisions of Articles 1 and 8 and on military, naval, and air questions generally.

ARTICLE 10. — The Members of the League undertake to respect and preserve as against external aggression the territorial integrity and existing political independence of all Members of the League. In case of any such aggression or in case of any threat or danger of such aggression the Council shall advise upon the means by which this obligation shall be fulfilled.

ARTICLE 11. — Any war or threat of war, whether immediately affecting any of the Members of the League or not, is hereby declared a matter of concern to the whole League, and the League shall take any action that may be deemed wise and effectual to safeguard the peace of nations. In case any such emergency should arise the Secretary General shall on the request of any Member of the League forthwith summon a meeting of the Council.

It is also declared to be the friendly right of each Member of the League to bring to the attention of the Assembly or of the Council any circumstance whatever affecting international relations which threatens to disturb international peace or the good understanding between nations upon which peace depends.

ARTICLE 12. — The Members of the League agree that if there should arise between them any dispute likely to lead to a rupture, they will submit the matter either to arbitration or to inquiry by the Council, and they agree in no case to resort to war until three months after the award by the arbitrators or the report by the Council.

In any case under this Article the award of the arbitrators shall be made within a reasonable time, and the report of the Council shall be made within six months after the submission of the dispute.

ARTICLE 13. — The Members of the League agree that whenever any dispute shall arise between them which they recognise to be suitable for submission to arbitration and which cannot be satisfactorily settled by diplomacy, they will submit the whole subject-matter to arbitration.

Disputes as to the interpretation of a treaty, as to any question of international law, as to the existence of any fact which if established would constitute a breach of any international obligation, or as to the extent and nature of the reparation to be made for any such breach, are declared to be among those which are generally suitable for submission to arbitration.

For the consideration of any such dispute the court of arbitration to which the case is referred shall be the court agreed on by the parties to the dispute or stipulated in any convention existing between them.

The Members of the League agree that they will carry out in full good faith any award that may be rendered, and that they will not resort to war against a Member of the League which complies therewith. In the event of any failure to carry out such an award, the Council shall propose what steps should be taken to give effect thereto.

ARTICLE 14. — The Council shall formulate and submit to the Members of the League for adoption plans for the establishment of a Permanent Court of International Justice. The Court shall be competent to hear and determine any dispute of an international character which the parties thereto submit to it. The Court may also give an advisory opinion upon any dispute or question referred to it by the Council or by the Assembly.

ARTICLE 15. — If there should arise between Members of the League any dispute likely to lead to a rupture, which is not submitted to arbitration in accordance with Article 13, the Members of the League agree that they will submit the matter to the Council. Any party to the dispute may effect such submission by giving notice of the existence of the dispute to the Secretary General, who will make all necessary arrangements for a full investigation and consideration thereof.

For this purpose the parties to the dispute will communicate to the Secretary General, as promptly as possible, statements of their case with all the relevant facts and papers, and the Council may forthwith direct the publication thereof.

The Council shall endeavour to effect a settlement of the dispute, and if such efforts are successful, a statement shall be made public giving such facts and explanations regarding the dispute and the terms of settlement thereof as the Council may deem appropriate.

If the dispute is not thus settled, the Council either unanimously or by a majority vote shall make and publish a report containing a statement of the facts of the dispute and the recommendations which are deemed just and proper in regard thereto.

Any Member of the League represented on the Council may make public a statement of the facts of the dispute and of its conclusions regarding the same.

If a report by the Council is unanimously agreed to by the Members thereof other than the Representatives of one or more of the parties to the dispute, the Members of the League agree that they will not go to war with any party to the dispute which complies with the recommendations of the report.

If the Council fails to reach a report which is unanimously agreed to by the Members thereof, other than the representatives of one or more of the parties to the dispute, the Members of the League reserve to themselves the right to take such action as they shall consider necessary for the maintenance of right and justice.

If the dispute between the parties is claimed by one of them, and is found by the Council, to arise out of a matter which by international law is solely within the domestic jurisdiction of that party, the Council shall so report, and shall make no recommendation as to its settlement.

The Council may in any case under this Article refer the dispute to the Assembly. The dispute shall be so referred at the request of either party to the dispute, provided that such request be made within fourteen days after the submission of the dispute to the Council.

In any case referred to the Assembly, all the provisions of this Article and of Article 12 relating to the action and powers of the Council shall apply to the action and powers of the Assembly, provided that a report made by the Assembly, if concurred in by the Representatives of those Members of the League represented on the Council and of a majority of the other Members of the League, exclusive in each case of the Representatives of the parties to the dispute, shall have the same force as a report by the Council concurred in by all the members thereof other than the Representatives of one or more of the parties to the dispute.

ARTICLE 16. — Should any Member of the League resort

to war in disregard of its covenants under Articles 12, 13 or 15, it shall *ipso facto* be deemed to have committed an act of war against all other Members of the League, which hereby undertake immediately to subject it to the severance of all trade or financial relations, the prohibition of all intercourse between their nationals and the nationals of the covenant-breaking State, and the prevention of all financial, commercial or personal intercourse between the nationals of the covenant-breaking State and the nationals of any other State, whether a Member of the League or not.

It shall be the duty of the Council in such case to recommend to the several Governments concerned what effective military, naval or air force the Members of the League shall severally contribute to the armed forces to be used to protect the covenants of the League.

The Members of the League agree, further, that they will mutually support one another in the financial and economic measures which are taken under this article, in order to minimise the loss and inconvenience resulting from the above measures, and that they will mutually support one another in resisting any special measures aimed at one of their number by the covenant-breaking State, and that they will take the necessary steps to afford passage through their territory to the forces of any of the Members of the League which are coöperating to protect the covenants of the League.

Any member of the League which has violated any covenant of the League may be declared to be no longer a Member of the League by a vote of the Council concurred in by the Representatives of all the other Members of the League represented thereon.

ARTICLE 17. — In the event of a dispute between a Member of the League and a State which is not a Member of the League, or between States not Members of the

League, the State or States not Members of the League shall be invited to accept the obligations of membership in the League for the purposes of such dispute, upon such conditions as the Council may deem just. If such invitation is accepted, the provisions of Articles 12 to 16 inclusive shall be applied with such modifications as may be deemed necessary by the Council.

Upon such invitation being given the Council shall immediately institute an inquiry into the circumstances of the dispute and recommend such action as may seem best and most effectual in the circumstances.

If a State so invited shall refuse to accept the obligations of membership in the League for the purposes of such dispute, and shall resort to war against a Member of the League, the provisions of Article 16 shall be applicable as against the State taking such action.

If both parties to the dispute when so invited refuse to accept the obligations of membership in the League for the purposes of such dispute, the Council may take such measures and make such recommendations as will prevent hostilities and will result in the settlement of the dispute.

ARTICLE 18. — Every treaty or international engagement entered into hereafter by any Member of the League shall be forthwith registered with the Secretariat and shall as soon as possible be published by it. No such treaty or international engagement shall be binding until so registered.

ARTICLE 19. — The Assembly may from time to time advise the reconsideration by Members of the League of treaties which have become inapplicable and the consideration of international conditions whose continuance might endanger the peace of the world.

ARTICLE 20. — The Members of the League severally agree that this Covenant is accepted as abrogating all obligations or understandings *inter se* which are inconsistent with the terms thereof, and solemnly undertake that they will not hereafter enter into any engagements inconsistent with the terms thereof.

In case any Member of the League shall, before becoming a Member of the League, have undertaken any obligations inconsistent with the terms of this Covenant, it shall be the duty of such Member to take immediate steps to procure its release from such obligations.

ARTICLE 21.—Nothing in this Covenant shall be deemed to affect the validity of international engagements, such as treaties of arbitration or regional understandings like the Monroe Doctrine, for securing the maintenance of peace.

ARTICLE 22.—To those colonies and territories which as a consequence of the late war have ceased to be under the sovereignty of the States which formerly governed them and which are inhabited by peoples not yet able to stand by themselves under the strenuous conditions of the modern world, there should be applied the principle that the well-being and development of such peoples form a sacred trust of civilisation and that securities for the performance of this trust should be embodied in this Covenant.

The best method of giving practical effect to this principle is that the tutelage of such peoples should be entrusted to advanced nations who by reason of their resources, their experience or their geographical position can best undertake this responsibility, and who are willing to accept it, and that this tutelage should be exercised by them as Mandatories on behalf of the League.

The character of the mandate must differ according to the stage of the development of the people, the geographical situation of the territory, its economic conditions, and other similar circumstances.

Certain communities formerly belonging to the Turkish Empire have reached a stage of development where their existence as independent nations can be provisionally recognised subject to the rendering of administrative advice and assistance by a Mandatory until such time as they are able to stand alone. The wishes of these communities must be a principal consideration in the selection of the Mandatory.

Other peoples, especially those of Central Africa, are at such a stage that the Mandatory must be responsible for the administration of the territory under conditions which will guarantee freedom of conscience and religion, subject only to the maintenance of public order and morals, the prohibition of abuses such as the slave trade, the arms traffic and the liquor traffic, and the prevention of the establishment of fortifications or military and naval bases and of military training of the natives for other than police purposes and the defence of territory, and will also secure equal opportunities for the trade and commerce of other Members of the League.

There are territories, such as South-West Africa and certain of the South Pacific Islands, which, owing to the sparseness of their population, or their small size, or their remoteness from the centres of civilisation, or their geographical contiguity to the territory of the Mandatory, and other circumstances, can be best administered under the laws of the Mandatory as integral portions of its territory subject to the safeguards above mentioned in the interests of the indigenous population.

In every case of mandate, the Mandatory shall render to the Council an annual report in reference to the territory committed to its charge.

The degree of authority, control, or administration to be exercised by the Mandatory shall, if not previously agreed upon by the Members of the League, be explicitly defined in each case by the Council.

A permanent Commission shall be constituted to receive and examine the annual reports of the Mandatories and to advise the Council on all matters relating to the observance of the mandates.

ARTICLE 23. — Subject to and in accordance with the

provisions of international conventions existing or hereafter to be agreed upon, the Members of the League:

(a) will endeavour to secure and maintain fair and humane conditions of labour for men, women, and children, both in their own countries and in all countries to which their commercial and industrial relations extend, and for that purpose will establish and maintain the necessary international organizations;

(b) undertake to secure just treatment of the native inhabitants of territories under their control;

(c) will entrust the League with the general supervision over the execution of agreements with regard to the traffic in women and children, and the traffic in opium and other dangerous drugs;

(d) will entrust the League with the general supervision of the trade in arms and ammunition with the countries in which the control of this traffic is necessary in the common interest;

(e) will make provision to secure and maintain freedom of communications and of transit and equitable treatment for the commerce of all Members of the League. In this connection, the special necessities of the regions devastated during the war of 1914–1918 shall be borne in mind;

(f) will endeavour to take steps in matters of international concern for the prevention and control of disease.

ARTICLE 24.—There shall be placed under the direction of the League all international bureaux already established by general treaties if the parties to such treaties consent. All such international bureaux and all commissions for the regulation of matters of international interest hereafter constituted shall be placed under the direction of the League.

In all matters of international interest which are regulated by general conventions but which are not placed under the control of international bureaux or commissions, the Secretariat of the League shall, subject to the consent of the Council and if desired by the parties, collect and distribute all relevant information and shall render any other assistance which may be necessary or desirable.

The Council may include as part of the expenses of the Secretariat the expenses of any bureau or commission which is placed under the direction of the League.

ARTICLE 25. — The Members of the League agree to encourage and promote the establishment and coöperation of duly authorised voluntary national Red Cross organisations having as purposes the improvement of health, the prevention of disease and the mitigation of suffering throughout the world.

ARTICLE 26. — Amendments to this Covenant will take effect when ratified by the Members of the League whose Representatives compose the Council and by a majority of the Members of the League whose Representatives compose the Assembly.

No such amendment shall bind any Member of the League which signifies its dissent therefrom, but in that case it shall cease to be a Member of the League.

DOCUMENT 123

An Optimistic Appraisal of the Peace Settlement

Because he so fervently believed the League of Nations to be the most important element of the peace settlement, Wilson was willing to compromise on some other matters in order to win acceptance of the League. He reasoned that the League would make it possible to rectify any bad blun-

Letter to George D. Herron, April 28, 1919, in Algie M. Simons MSS, State Historical Society of Wisconsin.

ders of the conference once wartime passions and hatreds had died down. Thus, he accepted some agreements that violated the spirit of his Fourteen Points — Japan's claims to Shantung, the transfer of German-speaking Austrians to Italy, reparations, and the war-guilt clause. Still, it was due to Wilson's vigilance that the treaty in its final form was nearer to the Fourteen Points than most men, including his major colleagues at the conference, had thought possible at the start, and he was inclined to feel satisfied with his labors.

I am sorry that you are so deeply discouraged about the work of the conference. It is undoubtedly true that many of the results arrived at are far from ideal, but I think that on the whole we have been able to keep tolerably close to the lines laid down at the outset, and I am confirmed in this opinion by the judgment of many conscientious men about me, by whose conscience as well as by my own I try to be guided. The treaty which ends so terrible a war must unavoidably seem harsh towards the outlaw who started the war, but when the details are read and understood I believe that that impression will be largely removed. Perhaps my judgment is affected by the consciousness that results are so much better than at one time I feared, that they now seem to me better than they are.

DOCUMENT 124

"It Is Much More Than a Treaty of Peace. . . ."

In the beautiful *Galerie des Glaces* at Versailles on June 28 the various delegations to the peace conference, including

---

Cable to the American people upon the signing of the Versailles Treaty, June 28, 1919, *Public Papers*, V, 523–524.

now the unhappy Germans, affixed their signatures to the finished treaty. The work of six arduous months was done. Wilson promptly dispatched a cable to the American people summarizing the meaning of the event, and departed gratefully for home.

The treaty of peace has been signed. If it is ratified and acted upon in full and sincere execution of its terms it will furnish the charter for a new order of affairs in the world. It is a severe treaty in the duties and penalties it imposes upon Germany, but it is severe only because great wrongs done by Germany are to be righted and repaired; it imposes nothing that Germany cannot do; and she can regain her rightful standing in the world by the prompt and honorable fulfillment of its terms. And it is much more than a treaty of peace with Germany. It liberates great peoples who have never before been able to find the way to liberty. It ends once for all, an old and intolerable order under which small groups of selfish men could use the peoples of great empires to serve their own ambition for power and dominion. It associates the free Governments of the world in a permanent league in which they are pledged to use their united power to maintain peace by maintaining right and justice. It makes international law a reality supported by imperative sanctions. It does away with the right of conquest and rejects the policy of annexation and substitutes a new order under which backward nations—populations which have not yet come to political consciousness and peoples who are ready for independence but not yet quite prepared to dispense with protection and guidance—shall no more be subjected to the domination and exploitation of a stronger nation, but shall be put under the friendly direction and afforded the helpful assistance of governments which undertake to be responsible to the opinion of mankind in the execution of their task by accepting the direction of the League of Nations. It recognizes the inalienable rights of nationality; the rights of minorities and the sanctity of religious belief and practice. It lays the basis for conventions which shall free the commercial intercourse of the world from unjust and vexatious restrictions and for every sort of international coöperation that will serve to cleanse the life of the world and facilitate its common action in beneficent service of every kind. It furnishes guarantees such as were never given or even contemplated before for the fair treatment of all who labor at the daily tasks of the world. It is for this reason that I have spoken of it as a great charter for a new order of affairs. There is ground here for deep satisfaction, universal reassurance, and confident hope.

PART X

The Politics of Peacemaking

A. SEEDS OF PARTISANSHIP

DOCUMENT 125

The Appeal for a Democratic Congress

With the signing of the peace treaty, Wilson faced the most important battle of his political career—winning the consent of the Senate to his handiwork. Always a strong believer in party government, he had—with some difficulty—restrained his partisan impulses during the war, and he had brought some Republicans into war posts in his administration. But he distrusted most of the Republican leaders in Congress, and he had continued to rely on his normally secure Democratic majority there. Shortly before the Congressional elections of 1918, Wilson unwisely yielded to the pleas of worried Democrats and called upon the country to return a Democratic Congress. He compounded the blunder, moreover, by declaring that a Republican victory would be looked upon abroad as a repudiation of his leadership. It was a dangerous and needless gamble—one that Wilson lost when the Republicans won narrow control of both Houses of Congress.

Statement to the country, October 25, 1918, *Public Papers*, V, 286–288.

MY FELLOW COUNTRYMEN, — The Congressional elections are at hand. They occur in the most critical period our country has ever faced or is likely to face in our time. If you have approved of my leadership and wish me to continue to be your unembarrassed spokesman in affairs at home and abroad, I earnestly beg that you will express yourselves unmistakably to that effect by returning a Democratic majority to both the Senate and the House of Representatives. I am your servant and will accept your judgment without cavil, but my power to administer the great trust assigned me by the Constitution would be seriously impaired should your judgment be adverse, and I must frankly tell you so because so many critical issues depend upon your verdict. No scruple of taste must in grim times like these be allowed to stand in the way of speaking the plain truth.

I have no thought of suggesting that any political party is paramount in matters of patriotism. I feel too keenly the sacrifices which have been made in this war by all our citizens, irrespective of party affiliations, to harbor such an idea. I mean only that the difficulties and delicacies of our present task are of a sort that makes it imperatively necessary that the Nation should give its undivided support to the Government under a unified leadership, and that a Republican Congress would divide the leadership.

The leaders of the minority in the present Congress have unquestionably been pro war, but they have been anti-administration. At almost every turn, since we entered the war they have sought to take the choice of policy and the conduct of the war out of my hands and put it under the control of instrumentalities of their own choosing. This is no time either for divided counsel or for divided leadership. Unity of command is as necessary now in civil action as it is upon the field of battle. If the control of the House and Senate should be taken away from the party now in power an opposing majority could assume control of legislation and oblige all action to be taken amidst contest and obstruction.

The return of a Republican majority to either House of the Congress would, moreover, certainly be interpreted on the other side of the water as a repudiation of my leadership. Spokesmen of the Republican Party are urging you to elect a Republican Congress in order to back up and support the President, but even if they should in this way impose upon some credulous voters on this side of the water, they would impose on no one on the other side. It is well understood there as well as here that the Republican leaders desire not so much to support the President as to control him. The peoples of the allied countries with whom we are associated against Germany are quite familiar with the significance of elections. They would find it very difficult to believe that the voters of the United States had chosen to support their President by electing to the Congress a majority controlled by those who are not in fact in sympathy with the attitude and action of the administration.

I need not tell you, my fellow countrymen, that I am asking your support not for my own sake or for the sake of a political party, but for the sake of the Nation itself, in order that its inward unity of purpose may be evident to all the world. In ordinary times I would not feel at liberty to make such an appeal to you. In ordinary times divided counsels can be endured without permanent hurt to the country. But these are not ordinary times. If in these critical days it is your wish to sustain me with undivided minds, I beg that you will say so in a way which it will not be possible to misunderstand either here at home or among our associates on the other side of the sea. I submit my difficulties and my hopes to you.

B. DETERIORATING
RELATIONS WITH THE SENATE

DOCUMENT 126

A Half-Hearted Gesture at Bipartisanship

Wilson was well aware that in the new Sixty-sixth Congress
the Republicans would control the Senate by a margin of
two votes, with his old enemy, Henry Cabot Lodge, serving
as Senate majority leader and chairman of the crucial Foreign Relations Committee. The President was confident,
however, that Lodge and other Republican critics could do
little more than snipe ineffectually at the peace settlement.
Wilson nevertheless made a gesture at bipartisanship on
the day he presented the League Covenant to the peace
conference; he cabled an invitation to the members of the
Senate Foreign Relations Committee to meet with him to
discuss the Covenant upon his return to the United States
for a brief business trip the following week.

Last night the committee of the conference charged with
the duty of drafting a constitution for a League of Nations
concluded its work and this afternoon before leaving for
the United States it is to be my privilege and duty to read
to a plenary session of the conference the text of the 26
articles agreed upon by the committee.

The committee which drafted these articles was fairly
representative of the world. Besides the representatives of
the United States, Great Britain, France, Italy, and Japan,
representatives of Belgium, Serbia, China, Greece, Rumania, Czecho-Slovakia, Poland, Brazil, Portugal, actively

---

Cable to the Senate Foreign Relations Committee, February 14, 1919,
Public Papers, V, 412.

participated in the debates and assisted materially in the drafting of this constitution. Each article was passed only after the most careful examination by each member of the committee. There is a good and sufficient reason for the phraseology and substance of each article. I request that I be permitted to go over with you article by article the constitution before this part of the work of the conference is made the subject of debate of Congress. With this in view I request that you dine with me at the White House as soon after I arrive in the United States as my engagements permit.

DOCUMENT 127

"Those Who Stand in the Way

Are Overwhelmed"

On his short trip back to the United States in late February, Wilson discovered that his Republican opponents were shrewdly working to undercut his influence and the popular appeal of his League of Nations. His White House dinner for Congressional leaders made few converts, despite his earnest explanation of the Covenant. And Republicans successfully blocked action on appropriation bills in the outgoing Sixty-fifth Congress, so that the President would be forced to call Congress into special session months ahead of schedule, thus giving his Republican adversaries a forum from which to criticize him. On March 4, the day before Wilson was to return to Paris, Senator Lodge read a Round Robin pronunciamento into the *Congressional Record*. Signed by thirty-nine Senators or Senators-elect,

Excerpts from address at the Metropolitan Opera House, New York, March 4, 1919, *Public Papers*, V, 444–448, 449–451.

six more than necessary to defeat a treaty, the statement declared the Covenant unacceptable in its present form. That night, in a speech at the Metropolitan Opera House in New York, Wilson gratefully accepted the support of former President Taft but struck back hard at his critics. He warned them that he intended to tie the League of Nations inextricably to the peace settlement, so that his opponents would have no choice but to accept or reject the entire package.

I accept the intimation of the air just played. I will not come back "'til it's over, over there." And yet I pray God in the interests of peace of the world that that may be soon.

The first thing that I am going to tell the people on the other side of the water is that an overwhelming majority of the American people is in favor of the League of Nations. I know that that is true. I have had unmistakable intimations of it from all parts of the country, and the voice rings true in every case. I account myself fortunate to speak here under the unusual circumstances of this evening. I am happy to associate myself with Mr. Taft in this great cause. He has displayed an elevation of view and devotion to public duty which is beyond praise.

And I am the more happy because this means that this is not a party issue. No party has a right to appropriate this issue and no party will in the long run dare oppose it.

We have listened to so clear and admirable an exposition of many of the main features of the proposed covenant of the League of Nations that it is perhaps not necessary for me to discuss in any particular way the contents of the document. I will seek rather to give you its setting. I do not know when I have been more impressed than by the conferences of the commission set up by the conference of peace to draw up the covenant for a League of Nations. The representatives of fourteen nations sat around that board—not young men, not men inexperienced in the affairs of their own countries, not men inexperienced in the politics of the world—and the inspiring influence of every meeting was the concurrence of purpose on the part of all those men to come to an agreement and an effective working agreement with regard to this league of the civilized world.

There was a conviction in the whole impulse; there was conviction of more than one sort; there was the conviction that this thing ought to be done; and there was also the conviction that not a man there would venture to go home and say that he had not tried to do it.

Mr. Taft has set a picture for you of what failure of this great purpose would mean. We have been hearing for all these weary months that this agony of war has lasted of the sinister purpose of the Central Empires and we have made maps of the course that they meant their conquests to take. Where did the lines of that map lie, of that central line that we used to call from Bremen to Bagdad? They lay through these very regions to which Mr. Taft has called your attention, but they lay then through a united empire. The Austro-Hungarian Empire, whose integrity Germany was bound to respect as her ally, lay in the path of that line of conquest; the Turkish Empire, whose interests she professed to make her own, lay in the direct path that she intended to tread. And now what has happened? The Austro-Hungarian Empire has gone to pieces and the Turkish Empire has disappeared, and the nations that effected that great result—for it was the result of liberation—are now responsible as the trustees of the assets of those great nations. You not only would have weak nations lying in this path, but you would have nations in which that old poisonous seed of intrigue could be planted with the certainty that the crop would be abundant, and one of the things that the League of Nations is intended to watch is the course of intrigue. Intrigue cannot stand publicity, and if the League of Nations were nothing but a great debating society it would kill intrigue.

It is one of the agreements of this covenant that it is the friendly right of every nation a member of the League to call attention to anything that it thinks will disturb the peace of the world, no matter where that thing is occurring. There is no subject that may touch the peace of the world which is exempt from inquiry and discussion, and I think everybody here present will agree with me that Germany would never have gone to war if she had permitted the world to discuss the aggression upon Serbia for a single week. The British Foreign Office pleaded that there might be a day or two delay so that representatives of the nations of Europe could get together and discuss the possibilities of a settlement. Germany did not dare permit a day's discussion. You know what happened. So soon as the world realized that an outlaw was at large the nations began, one by one, to draw together against her. We know for certainty that if Germany had thought for a moment that Great Britain would go in with France and Russia she never would have undertaken the enterprise, and the League of Nations is meant as notice to all outlaw nations that not only Great Britain but the United States and the rest of the world will go in to check enterprises of that sort. And so the League of Nations is nothing more nor less than the covenant that the world will always maintain the standards which it has now vindicated by some of the most precious blood every spilt.

The liberated peoples of the Austro-Hungarian Empire and of the Turkish Empire call out to us for this thing. It has not arisen in the councils of statesmen. Europe is a bit sick at heart at this very moment because it sees that the statesmen have had no vision and that the only vision has been the vision of the people. Those who suffer see. Those against whom wrong is wrought know how desirable is the right of the righteous. Nations that have long been under the heel of Austria, that have long cowered before the German, that have long suffered the indescribable agonies of being governed by the Turk, have called out to the world generation after generation for justice, liberation, and succor, and no cabinet in the world has heard them. Private organizations, pitying hearts, philanthropic men and women, have poured out their treasure in order to relieve these sufferings, but no nation has said to the nations responsible, "You must stop; this thing is intolerable and we will not permit it." And the vision has been with the people. My friends, I wish you would reflect upon this proposition; the vision as to what is necessary for great reforms has seldom come from the top in the nations of the world. It has come from the need and aspiration and self-assertion of great bodies of men who meant to be free. And I can explain some of the criticisms which have been leveled against this great enterprise only by the supposition that men who utter the criticisms have never felt the great pulse of the heart of the world.

And I am amazed—not alarmed but amazed—that there should be in some quarters such a comprehensive ignorance of the state of the world. These gentlemen do not know what the mind of men is just now. Everybody else does. I do not know where they have been closeted, I do not know by what influences they have been blinded, but I do know they have been separated from the general currents of the thought of mankind.

And I want to utter this solemn warning, not in the way of a threat; the forces of the world do not threaten, they operate. The great tides of the world do not give notice that they are going to rise and run; they rise in their majesty and overwhelming might, and those who stand in the way are overwhelmed. Now the heart of the world is awake and the heart of the world must be satisfied. Do not let yourselves suppose for a moment that uneasiness in the populations of Europe is due entirely to economic causes or economic motives; something very much deeper underlies it all than that. They see that their Governments have never been able to defend them against intrigue or aggression, and that there is no force of foresight or of prudence in any modern cabinet to stop war. And therefore they say, "There must be some fundamental cause for this," and the fundamental cause they are beginning to perceive to be that nations have stood singly or in little jealous groups against each other, fostering prejudice, increasing the danger of war rather than concerting measures to prevent it; and that if there is right in the world, if there is justice in the world, there is no reason why nations should be divided in support of justice. . . .

There is another thing which I think the critics of this covenant have not observed. They not only have not observed the temper of the world but they have not even observed the temper of those splendid boys in khaki that they sent across the seas. I have had the proud consciousness of the reflected glory of those boys because the Constitution made me their commander-in-chief, and they have taught me some lessons. When we went into the war we went into it on the basis of declarations which it was my privilege to utter because I believed them to be an interpretation of the purpose and thought of the people of the United States.

And those boys went over there with the feeling that they were sacredly bound to the realization of those ideals; that they were not only going over there to beat Germany; they were not going over there merely with resentment in their hearts against a particular outlaw nation; but that they were crossing those 3,000 miles of sea in order to show to Europe that the United States, when it became necessary, would go anywhere where the rights of mankind were threatened. They would not sit still in the trenches. They would not be restrained by the prudence of experienced continental commanders. They thought they had come over there to do a particular thing, and they were going to do it and do it at once. And just as soon as that rush of spirit as well as the rush of body came in contact with the lines of the enemy they began to break, and they continued to break until the end. They continued to break, my fellow citizens, not merely because of the physical force of those lusty youngsters but because of the irresistible spiritual force of the armies of the United States. It was that that they felt. It was that that awed them. It was that that made them feel if these youngsters ever got a foothold they could never be dislodged, and that therefore every foot of ground that they won was permanently won for the liberty of mankind.

And do you suppose that, having felt that crusading spirit of these youngsters who went over there not to glorify America but to serve their fellow men, I am going to permit myself for one moment to slacken in my effort to be worthy of them and of their cause? What I said at the opening I said with a deeper meaning than perhaps you have caught; I do not mean to come back until it's over over there, and it must not be over until the nations of the world are assured of the permanency of peace.

Gentlemen on this side of the water would be very much profited by getting into communication with some gentlemen on the other side of the water. We sometimes think, my fellow citizens, that the experienced statesmen of European nations are an unusually hardheaded set of men, by which we generally mean, although we do not admit it, they are a bit cynical; they say "This is a practical world," by which you always mean that it is not an ideal world; that they do not believe things can be settled upon an ideal basis. Well, I never came into intimate contact with them before, but if they used to be that way they are not that way now. They have been subdued, if that was once their temper, by the awful significance of recent events and the awful importance of what is to ensue, and there is not one of them with whom I have come in contact who does not feel he cannot in conscience return to his people from Paris unless he has done his utmost to do something more than attach his name to a treaty of peace. Every man in that conference knows the treaty of peace in itself will be inoperative, as Mr. Taft has said, without this constant support and energy of a great organization such as is supplied by the League of Nations.

And men who, when I first went over there, were skeptical of the possibility of forming a league of nations, admitted that if we could but form it it would be an invaluable instrumentality through which to secure the operation of the various parts of the treaty; and when that treaty comes back gentlemen on this side will find the Covenant not only in it, but so many threads of the treaty tied to the covenant that you cannot dissect the covenant from the treaty without destroying the whole vital structure. The structure of peace will not be vital without the League of Nations, and no man is going to bring back a cadaver with him.

I must say that I have been puzzled by some of the criticisms — not by the criticisms themselves — I can understand them perfectly even when there was no foundation for them — but by the fact of the criticism. I cannot imagine how these gentlemen can live and not live in the atmosphere of the world. I cannot imagine how they can live and not be in contact with the events of their times, and I particularly cannot imagine how they can be Americans and set up a doctrine of careful selfishness thought out to the last detail. I have heard no counsel of generosity in their criticism. I have heard no constructive suggestion. I have heard nothing except, "Will it not be dangerous to us to help the world?" It would be fatal to us not to help it. . . .

DOCUMENT 128

"Dare We Reject It and Break the Heart of the World?"

Wilson's address presenting the peace treaty to the Senate on July 10, 1919, was an eloquent plea for American leadership to make the League of Nations an effective instrument for peace and security. It was also a plea to his countrymen to recognize that isolationism was no longer a valid foreign policy.

. . . That there should be a League of Nations to steady the counsels and maintain the peaceful understandings of the world, to make, not treaties alone, but the accepted principles of international law as well, the actual rule of conduct among the governments of the world, had been one of the agreements accepted from the first as the basis of peace with the Central Powers. The statesmen of all the belligerent countries were agreed that such a league must be created to sustain the settlements that were to be effected. But at first I think there was a feeling among some of them that, while it must be attempted, the formation of such a league was perhaps a counsel of perfection which practical men, long experienced in the world of affairs, must agree to very cautiously and with many misgivings. It

Excerpts from address to the Senate, July 10, 1919, *Public Papers*, V, 545–549, 551–552.

was only as the difficult work of arranging an all but universal adjustment of the world's affairs advanced from day to day from one stage of conference to another that it became evident to them that what they were seeking would be little more than something written upon paper, to be interpreted and applied by such methods as the chances of politics might make available if they did not provide a means of common counsel which all were obliged to accept, a common authority whose decisions would be recognized as decisions which all must respect.

And so the most practical, the most skeptical among them turned more and more to the League as the authority through which international action was to be secured, the authority without which, as they had come to see it, it would be difficult to give assured effect either to this treaty or to any other international understanding upon which they were to depend for the maintenance of peace. The fact that the Covenant of the League was the first substantive part of the treaty to be worked out and agreed upon, while all else was in solution, helped to make the formulation of the rest easier. The Conference was, after all, not to be ephemeral. The concert of nations was to continue, under a definite Covenant which had been agreed upon and which all were convinced was workable. They could go forward with confidence to make arrangements intended to be permanent. The most practical of the conferees were at last the most ready to refer to the League of Nations the superintendence of all interests which did not admit of immediate determination, of all administrative problems which were to require a continuing oversight. What had seemed a counsel of perfection had come to seem a plain counsel of necessity. The League of Nations was the practical statesman's hope of success in many of the most difficult things he was attempting.

And it had validated itself in the thought of every member of the Conference as something much bigger, much greater every way, than a mere instrument for carrying out the provisions of a particular treaty. It was universally recognized that all the peoples of the world demanded of the Conference that it should create such a continuing concert of free nations as would make wars of aggression and spoliation such as this that has just ended forever impossible. A cry had gone out from every home in every stricken land from which sons and brothers and fathers had gone forth to the great sacrifice that such a sacrifice should never again be exacted. It was manifest why it had been exacted. It had been exacted because one nation desired dominion and other nations had known no means of defense except armaments and alliances. War had lain at the heart of every arrangement of the Europe,—of every arrangement of the world,—that preceded the war. Restive peoples had been told that fleets and armies, which they toiled to sustain, meant peace; and they now knew that they had been lied to: that fleets and armies had been maintained to promote national ambitions and meant war. They knew that no old policy meant anything else but force, force,—always force. And they knew that it was intolerable. Every true heart in the world, and every enlightened judgment demanded that, at whatever cost of independent action, every government that took thought for its people or for justice or for ordered freedom should lend itself to a new purpose and utterly destroy the old order of international politics. Statesmen might see difficulties, but the people could see none and could brook no denial. A war in which they had been bled white to beat the terror that lay concealed in every Balance of Power must not end in a mere victory of arms and a new balance. The monster that had resorted to arms must be put in

chains that could not be broken. The united power of free
nations must put a stop to aggression, and the world must
be given peace. If there was not the will or the intelligence to accomplish that now, there must be another and a
final war and the world must be swept clean of every
power that could renew the terror. The League of Nations
was not merely an instrument to adjust and remedy old
wrongs under a new treaty of peace; it was the only hope
for mankind. Again and again had the demon of war been
cast out of the house of the peoples and the house swept
clean by a treaty of peace; only to prepare a time when he
would enter in again with spirits worse than himself. The
house must now be given a tenant who could hold it
against all such. Convenient, indeed indispensable, as
statesmen found the newly planned League of Nations to
be for the execution of present plans of peace and reparation, they saw it in a new aspect before their work was
finished. They saw it as the main object of the peace, as
the only thing that could complete it or make it worth
while. They saw it as the hope of the world, and that hope
they did not dare to disappoint. Shall we or any other free
people hesitate to accept this great duty? Dare we reject it
and break the heart of the world?

And so the result of the Conference of Peace, so far as
Germany is concerned, stands complete. The difficulties
encountered were very many. Sometimes they seemed
insuperable. It was impossible to accommodate the interests of so great a body of nations,—interests which directly or indirectly affected almost every nation in the
world,—without many minor compromises. The treaty, as a
result, is not exactly what we would have written. It is
probably not what any one of the national delegations
would have written. But results were worked out which on
the whole bear test. I think that it will be found that the
compromises which were accepted as inevitable nowhere

cut to the heart of any principle. The work of the Conference squares, as a whole, with the principles agreed upon as the basis of the peace as well as with the practical possibilities of the international situations which had to be faced and dealt with as facts. . . .

. . . Our isolation was ended twenty years ago; and now fear of us is ended also, our counsel and association sought after and desired. There can be no question of our ceasing to be a world power. The only question is whether we can refuse the moral leadership that is offered us, whether we shall accept or reject the confidence of the world.

The war and the Conference of Peace now sitting in Paris seem to me to have answered that question. Our participation in the war established our position among the nations and nothing but our own mistaken action can alter it. It was not an accident or a matter of sudden choice that we are no longer isolated and devoted to a policy which has only our own interest and advantage for its object. It was our duty to go in, if we were indeed the champions of liberty and of right. We answered to the call of duty in a way so spirited, so utterly without thought of what we spent of blood or treasure, so effective, so worthy of the admiration of true men everywhere, so wrought out of the stuff of all that was heroic, that the whole world saw at last, in the flesh, in noble action, a great ideal asserted and vindicated, by a Nation they had deemed material and now found to be compact of the spiritual forces that must free men of every nation from every unworthy bondage. It is thus that a new rôle and a new responsibility have come to this great Nation that we honor and which we would all wish to lift to yet higher levels of service and achievement.

The stage is set, the destiny disclosed. It has come about by no plan of our conceiving, but by the hand of God who led us into this way. We cannot turn back. We can only go forward, with lifted eyes and freshened spirit, to follow the vision. It was of this that we dreamed at our birth. America shall in truth show the way. The light streams upon the path ahead, and nowhere else.

DOCUMENT 129

"I Am Unable to Understand
Why Such Doubts Should Be Entertained"

During July and August, while the Senate Foreign Relations Committee under Lodge's astute leadership held protracted hearings to mobilize opposition to the treaty, Wilson conferred with wavering Senators, seeking to reassure them that American interests were adequately protected. Patiently he explained the various concessions he had secured to meet American concerns about the Covenant. On August 19 he invited the members of the Foreign Relations Committee to the White House for a discussion of the treaty; even if the discussion changed no votes on either side, it at least enabled the President to summarize his views as to the meaning of those parts of the Covenant under heaviest criticism.

. . . Nothing, I am led to believe, stands in the way of ratification of the treaty except certain doubts with regard to the meaning and implication of certain articles of the Covenant of the League of Nations; and I must frankly say that I am unable to understand why such doubts should be entertained. You will recall that when I had the pleasure of a conference with your committee and with the committee of the House of Representatives on Foreign Affairs

---

Excerpt from statement to the Senate Foreign Relations Committee, August 19, 1919, *Public Papers,* V, 576–580.

at the White House in March last the questions now most frequently asked about the League of Nations were all canvassed with a view to their immediate clarification. The Covenant of the League was then in its first draft and subject to revision. It was pointed out that no express recognition was given to the Monroe Doctrine; that it was not expressly provided that the League should have no authority to act or to express a judgment on matters of domestic policy; that the right to withdraw from the League was not expressly recognized; and that the constitutional right of the Congress to determine all questions of peace and war was not sufficiently safeguarded. On my return to Paris all these matters were taken up again by the Commission on the League of Nations and every suggestion of the United States was accepted.

The views of the United States with regard to the questions I have mentioned had, in fact, already been accepted by the Commission and there was supposed to be nothing inconsistent with them in the draft of the Covenant first adopted—the draft which was the subject of our discussion in March—but no objection was made to saying explicitly in the text what all had supposed to be implicit in it. There was absolutely no doubt as to the meaning of any one of the resulting provisions of the Covenant in the minds of those who participated in drafting them, and I respectfully submit that there is nothing vague or doubtful in their wording.

The Monroe Doctrine is expressly mentioned as an understanding which is in no way to be impaired or interfered with by anything contained in the Covenant and the expression "regional understandings like the Monroe Doctrine" was used, not because any one of the conferees thought there was any comparable agreement anywhere else in existence or in contemplation, but only because it was thought best to avoid the appearance of dealing in such a document with the policy of a single nation. Absolutely nothing is concealed in the phrase.

With regard to domestic questions Article 16 of the Covenant expressly provides that, if in case of any dispute arising between members of the League the matter involved is claimed by one of the parties "and is found by the council to arise out of a matter which by international law is solely within the domestic jurisdiction of that party, the council shall so report, and shall make no recommendation as to its settlement." The United States was by no means the only Government interested in the explicit adoption of this provision, and there is no doubt in the mind of any authoritative student of international law that such matters as immigration, tariffs, and naturalization are incontestably domestic questions with which no international body could deal without express authority to do so. No enumeration of domestic questions was undertaken because to undertake it, even by sample, would have involved the danger of seeming to exclude those not mentioned.

The right of any sovereign State to withdraw had been taken for granted, but no objection was made to making it explicit. Indeed, so soon as the views expressed at the White House conference were laid before the commission it was at once conceded that it was best not to leave the answer to so important a question to inference. No proposal was made to set up any tribunal to pass judgment upon the question whether a withdrawing nation had in fact fulfilled "all its international obligations and all its obligations under the Covenant." It was recognized that that question must be left to be resolved by the conscience of the nation proposing to withdraw; and I must say that it did not seem to me worth while to propose that the article be made more explicit, because I knew that the United

States would never itself propose to withdraw from the League if its conscience was not entirely clear as to the fulfillment of all its international obligations. It has never failed to fulfill them and never will.

Article X is in no respect of doubtful meaning when read in the light of the Covenant as a whole. The council of the League can only "advise upon" the means by which the obligations of that great article are to be given effect to. Unless the United States is a party to the policy or action in question, her own affirmative vote in the council is necessary before any advice can be given, for a unanimous vote of the council is required. If she is a party, the trouble is hers anyhow. And the unanimous vote of the council is only advice in any case. Each Government is free to reject it if it pleases. Nothing could have been made more clear to the conference than the right of our Congress under our Constitution to exercise its independent judgment in all matters of peace and war. No attempt was made to question or limit that right. The United States will, indeed, undertake under Article X to "respect and preserve as against external aggression the territorial integrity and existing political independence of all members of the League," and that engagement constitutes a very grave and solemn moral obligation. But it is a moral, not a legal, obligation, and leaves our Congress absolutely free to put its own interpretation upon it in all cases that call for action. It is binding in conscience only, not in law.

Article X seems to me to constitute the very backbone of the whole Covenant. Without it the League would be hardly more than an influential debating society.

It has several times been suggested, in public debate and in private conference, that interpretations of the sense in which the United States accepts the engagements of the Covenant should be embodied in the instrument of ratification. There can be no reasonable objection to such interpretations accompanying the act of ratification provided they do not form a part of the formal ratification itself. Most of the interpretations which have been suggested to me embody what seems to me the plain meaning of the instrument itself. But if such interpretations should constitute a part of the formal resolution of ratification, long delays would be the inevitable consequence, inasmuch as all the many Governments concerned would have to accept, in effect, the language of the Senate as the language of the treaty before ratification would be complete. The assent of the German Assembly at Weimar would have to be obtained, among the rest, and I must frankly say that I could only with the greatest reluctance approach that Assembly for permission to read the treaty as we understand it and as those who framed it quite certainly understood it. If the United States were to qualify the document in any way, moreover, I am confident from what I know of the many conferences and debates which accompanied the formulation of the treaty that our example would immediately be followed in many quarters, in some instances with very serious reservations, and that the meaning and operative force of the treaty would presently be clouded from one end of its clauses to the other.

Pardon me, Mr. Chairman, if I have been entirely unreserved and plain-spoken in speaking of the great matters we all have so much at heart. If excuse is needed, I trust that the critical situation of affairs may serve as my justification. The issues that manifestly hang upon the conclusions of the Senate with regard to peace and upon the time of its action are so grave and so clearly insusceptible of being thrust on one side or postponed that I have felt it necessary in the public interest to make this urgent plea, and to make it as simply and as unreservedly as possible. . . .

C. THE APPEAL TO THE COUNTRY

Concluding that he could not reason with his partisan critics, and unwilling to accept reservations that he believed would cripple the League, early in September Wilson embarked upon a speaking tour through the Middle West and West to win popular support for the peace treaty. He was confident that if the people understood what was at stake they would not permit the Senate to scuttle his noble dream. In his speeches Wilson eloquently pleaded for acceptance of the League and stressed the folly of rejecting this instrument of peace, however inadequate and imperfect.

DOCUMENT 130

At Billings, Montana, September 11, 1919

. . . The fundamental principle of this treaty is a principle never acknowledged before, a principle which had its birth and has had its growth in this country, that the countries of the world belong to the people who live in them, and that they have a right to determine their own destiny and their own form of government and their own policy, and that no body of statesmen, sitting anywhere, no matter whether they represent the overwhelming physical force of the world or not, has the right to assign any great people to a sovereignty under which it does not care to live. This is the great treaty which is being debated. This is the treaty which is being examined with a microscope. This is the treaty which is being pulled about and about which

Public Papers, VI, 105 – 106, 109.

suggestions are made as to changes of phraseology. Why, my friends, are you going to be so nearsighted as to look that way at a great charter of human liberty? The thing is impossible. You cannot have any other treaty, because you can never get together again the elements that agreed to this treaty. You cannot do it by dealing with separate governments. You cannot assemble the forces again that were back of it. You cannot bring the agreement upon which it rests into force again. It was the laborious work of many, many months of the most intimate conference. It has very, very few compromises in it and is, most of it, laid down in straight lines according to American specifications. The choice is either to accept this treaty or play a lone hand. What does that mean? To play a lone hand means that we must always be ready to play by ourselves. That means that we must always be armed, that we must always be ready to mobilize the man strength and the manufacturing resources of the country; it means that we must continue to live under not diminishing but increasing taxes; it means that we shall devote our thought and the organization of our Government to being strong enough to beat any nation in the world. An absolute reversal of all the ideal of American history. If you are going to play a lone hand, the hand that you play must be upon the handle of the sword. You cannot play a lone hand and do your civil business except with the other hand — one hand incidental for the business of peace, the other hand constantly for the assertion of force. It is either this treaty or a lone hand, and the lone hand must have a weapon in it. The weapon must be all the young men of the country trained to arms, and the business of the country must pay the piper, must pay for the whole armament, the arms and the men. That is the choice. Do you suppose, my fellow citizens, that any nation is going to stand for that? We are not the only people who are sick of war. We are not the only people who have made up our minds that our Government must devote its attention to peace and to justice and to right. The people all over the world have made up their minds as to that. We need peace more than we ever needed it before. We need ordered peace, calm peace, settled peace, assured peace—for what have we to do? We have to re-regulate the fortunes of men. We have to reconstruct the machinery of civilization. I use the words deliberately—we have to reconstruct the machinery of civilization. . . .

Suppose that you were feeling that there was a danger of a general conflagration in your part of the country; I mean a literal fire. Which would you rather have, no insurance at all or 10 per cent insurance? Don't you think some insurance is better than none at all? Put the security obtained by this treaty at its minimum, and it is a great deal better than no security at all, and without it there is no security at all, and no man can be sure what his business will be from month to month, or what his life will be from year to year. The leisureliness of some debates creates the impression on my mind that some men think there is leisure. There is no leisure in the world, my fellow citizens, with regard to the reform of the conditions under which men live. There is no time for any talk, but get down to the business of what we are going to do. . . .

DOCUMENT 131

At Helena, Montana, September 11, 1919

. . . We fought Germany in order that there should be a world fit to live in. The world is not fit to live in, my fellow citizens, if any great government is in a position to do what the German Government did—secretly plot a war and be-

---

gin it with the whole strength of its people, without so much as consulting its own people. A great war cannot begin with public deliberation. A great war can begin only by private plot, because the peoples of this world are not asleep, as they used to be. The German people is a great educated people. All the thoughtful men in Germany, so far as I have been able to learn, who were following peaceful pursuits — the bankers and the merchants and the manufacturers — deemed it folly to go into that war. They said so then and they have said so since, but they were not consulted. The masters of Germany were the general military staff; it was these men who nearly brought a complete cataclysm upon civilization itself. It stands to reason that if we permit anything of that sort to happen again we are recreant to the men we sent across the seas to fight this war. We are deliberately guilty then of preparing a situation which will inevitably lead to what? What shall I call it? The final war? Alas, my fellow citizens, it might be the final arrest, though I pray only the temporary arrest, of civilization itself; and America has, if I may take the liberty of saying so, a greater interest in the prevention of that war than any other nation. America is less exhausted by the recent war than the other belligerents; she is not exhausted at all. America has paid for the war that has gone by less heavily, in proportion to her wealth, than the other nations. America still has free capital enough for its own industries and for the industries of the other countries that have to build their industries anew. The next war would have to be paid for in American blood and American money. The nation of all nations that is most interested to prevent the recurrence of what has already happened is the nation which would assuredly have to bear the brunt of that great catastrophe — either have to bear it or stop where we are. Who is going to check the growth of this Nation? Who is going to check the accumulation of physical power by this Nation — if you choose to put it in that form? Who is going to reduce the natural resources of this country? Who is going to change the circumstance that we largely feed the rest of the world? Who is going to change the circumstance that many of our resources are unique and indispensable? America is going to grow more and more powerful; and the more powerful she is the more inevitable it is that she should be trustee for the peace of the world. . . .

DOCUMENT 132

At San Francisco, California, September 17, 1919

. . . I want you to realize, my fellow countrymen, that those Americans who are opposing this plan of the League of Nations offer no substitute. They offer nothing that they pretend will accomplish the same object. On the contrary, they are apparently willing to go back to that old and evil order which prevailed before this war began and which furnished a ready and fertile soil for those seeds of envy which sprung up like dragon's teeth out of the bloody soil of Europe. They are ready to go back to that old and ugly plan of armed nations, of alliances, of watchful jealousies, of rabid antagonisms, of purposes concealed, running by the subtle channels of intrigue through the veins of people who do not dream what poison is being injected into their systems. They are willing to have the United States stand alone, withdraw from the concert of nations; and what does that mean, my fellow citizens? It means that we shall arm as Germany was armed, that we shall submit our young men to the kind of constant military service that the young men of Germany were subjected to. It means that we shall pay not lighter but heavier taxes. It means that we shall trade in a world in which we are suspected and watched and disliked, instead of in a world which is now ready to trust us, ready to follow our leadership, ready to receive our traders, along with our political representatives as friends, as men who are welcome, as men who bring goods and ideas for which the world is ready and for which the world has been waiting. That is the alternative which they offer. . . .

DOCUMENT 133

At San Francisco, California, September 18, 1919

. . . In order that we may not forget, I brought with me the figures as to what this war meant to the world. This is a body of business men, and you will understand these figures. They are too big for the imagination of men who do not handle big things. Here is the cost of the war in money, exclusive of what we loaned one another.: Great Britain and her dominions, $38,000,000,000; France, $26,000,000,000; the United States, $22,000,000,000 (this is the direct cost of our operations); Russia, $18,000,000,000; Italy, $13,000,000,000; and the total, including Belgium, Japan, and other countries, $123,000,000,000. This is what it cost the Central Powers: Germany, $39,000,000,000, the biggest single item; Austria-Hungary, $21,000,000,000; Turkey and Bulgaria, $3,000,000,000; a total of $63,000,000,000, and a grand total of direct war costs of $186,000,000,000 — almost the capital of the world. The expenditures of the United States were at the rate of $1,000,000 an hour for two years, including nighttime with daytime. The battle deaths during the war were as follows: Russia lost in dead 1,700,000 men, poor Russia, that got nothing but terror and despair out of it

Public Papers, VI, 261–262.

all; Germany, 1,600,000; France, 1,385,000; Great Britain, 900,000; Austria, 800,000; Italy, 364,000; the United States, 50,300 dead. The total for all the belligerents, 7,450,200 men—just about seven and a half million killed because we could not have arbitration and discussion, because the world had never had the courage to propose the conciliatory methods which some of us are now doubting whether we ought to accept or not. The totals for wounded are not obtainable except our own. Our own wounded were 230,000, excluding those who were killed. The total of all battle deaths in all the wars of the world from the year 1793 to 1914 was something under 6,000,000 men, so that about a million and a half more men were killed in this war than in all the wars of something more than 100 preceding years. We really cannot realize that. Those of us who lost sons or brothers can realize it. We know what it meant. The women who have little children crowding about their knees know what it means; they know that the world has hitherto been devoted to brutal methods of settlement, and that every time a war occurs it is the flower of the manhood that is destroyed; that it is not so much the present generation as the next generation that goes maimed off the stage or is laid away in obscure graves upon some battlefield; and that great nations are impaired in their vitality for two generations together and all their life embittered by a method of settlement for which we could find, and have now found, a substitute.

My fellow citizens, I believe in Divine Providence. If I did not, I would go crazy. If I thought the direction of the disordered affairs of this world depended upon our finite intelligence, I should not know how to reason my way to sanity, and I do not believe that there is any body of men, however they concert their power or their influence, that can defeat this great enterprise, which is the enterprise of divine mercy and peace and good will.

DOCUMENT 134

The End of the Line

One of Wilson's longest and most effective speeches on his western tour was delivered to a great crowd at Pueblo, Colorado, on September 25. It was also his last major speech, for that night en route to Wichita he collapsed and his doctor canceled the remainder of the tour. A week later, at the White House, the President suffered a crippling stroke that effectively ended his leadership of the fight to save the treaty. Wilson's Pueblo speech, because of its importance, is given here in its entirety.

MR. CHAIRMAN AND FELLOW COUNTRYMEN:

It is with a great deal of genuine pleasure that I find myself in Pueblo, and I feel it a compliment that I should be permitted to be the first speaker in this beautiful hall. One of the advantages of this hall, as I look about, is that you are not too far away from me, because there is nothing so reassuring to men who are trying to express the public sentiment as getting into real personal contact with their fellow citizens. I have gained a renewed impression as I have crossed the continent this time of the homogeneity of this great people to whom we belong. They come from many stocks, but they are all of one kind. They come from many origins, but they are all shot through with the same principles and desire the same righteous and honest things. I have received a more inspiring impression this time of the public opinion of the United States than it was ever my privilege to receive before.

The chief pleasure of my trip has been that it has nothing to do with my personal fortunes, that it has nothing to do with my personal reputation, that it has nothing to do

Public Papers, VI, 399–416.

with anything except great principles uttered by Americans of all sorts and of all parties which we are now trying to realize at this crisis of the affairs of the world. But there have been unpleasant impressions as well as pleasant impressions, my fellow citizens, as I have crossed the continent. I have perceived more and more that men have been busy creating an absolutely false impression of what the treaty of peace and the Covenant of the League of Nations contain and mean. I find, moreover, that there is an organized propaganda against the League of Nations and against the treaty proceeding from exactly the same sources that the organized propaganda proceeded from which threatened this country here and there with disloyalty, and I want to say — I cannot say too often — any man who carries a hyphen about with him carries a dagger that he is ready to plunge into the vitals of this Republic whenever he gets ready. If I can catch any man with a hyphen in this great contest I will know that I have got an enemy of the Republic. My fellow citizens, it is only certain bodies of foreign sympathies, certain bodies of sympathy with foreign nations that are organized against this great document which the American representatives have brought back from Paris. Therefore, in order to clear away the mists, in order to remove the impressions, in order to check the falsehoods that have clustered around this great subject, I want to tell you a few very simple things about the treaty and the Covenant.

Do not think of this treaty of peace as merely a settlement with Germany. It is that. It is a very severe settlement with Germany, but there is not anything in it that she did not earn. Indeed, she earned more than she can ever be able to pay for, and the punishment exacted of her is not a punishment greater than she can bear, and it is absolutely necessary in order that no other nation may ever plot such a thing against humanity and civilization. But the treaty is so much more than that. It is not merely a settlement with Germany; it is a readjustment of those great injustices which underlie the whole structure of European and Asiatic society. This is only the first of several treaties. They are all constructed upon the same plan. The Austrian treaty follows the same lines. The treaty with Hungary follows the same lines. The treaty with Bulgaria follows the same lines. The treaty with Turkey, when it is formulated, will follow the same lines. What are those lines? They are based upon the purpose to see that every government dealt with in this great settlement is put in the hands of the people and taken out of the hands of coteries and of sovereigns who had no right to rule over the people. It is a people's treaty, that accomplishes by a great sweep of practical justice the liberation of men who never could have liberated themselves, and the power of the most powerful nations has been devoted not to their aggrandizement but to the liberation of people whom they could have put under their control if they had chosen to do so. Not one foot of territory is demanded by the conquerors, not one single item of submission to their authority is demanded by them. The men who sat around that table in Paris knew that the time had come when the people were no longer going to consent to live under masters, but were going to live the lives that they chose themselves, to live under such governments as they chose themselves to erect. That is the fundamental principle of this great settlement.

And we did not stop with that. We added a great international charter for the rights of labor. Reject this treaty, impair it, and this is the consequence to the laboring men of the world, that there is no international tribunal which can bring the moral judgments of the world to bear upon the great labor questions of the day. What we need to do with regard to the labor questions of the day, my fellow countrymen, is to lift them into the light, is to lift them out of the haze and distraction of passion, of hostility, not [out?]

into the calm spaces where men look at things without passion. The more men you get into a great discussion the more you exclude passion. Just so soon as the calm judgment of the world is directed upon the question of justice to labor, labor is going to have a forum such as it never was supplied with before, and men everywhere are going to see that the problem of labor is nothing more nor less than the problem of the elevation of humanity. We must see that all the questions which have disturbed the world, all the questions which have eaten into the confidence of men toward their governments, all the questions which have disturbed the processes of industry, shall be brought out where men of all points of view, men of all attitudes of mind, men of all kinds of experience, may contribute their part to the settlement of the great questions which we must settle and cannot ignore.

At the front of this great treaty is put the Covenant of the League of Nations. It will also be at the front of the Austrian treaty and the Hungarian treaty and the Bulgarian treaty and the treaty with Turkey. Every one of them will contain the Covenant of the League of Nations, because you cannot work any of them without the Covenant of the League of Nations. Unless you get the united, concerted purpose and power of the great Governments of the world behind this settlement, it will fall down like a house of cards. There is only one power to put behind the liberation of mankind, and that is the power of mankind. It is the power of the united moral forces of the world, and in the Covenant of the League of Nations the moral forces of the world are mobilized. For what purpose? Reflect, my fellow citizens, that the membership of this great League is going to include all the great fighting nations of the world, as well as the weak ones. It is not for the present going to include Germany, but for the time being Germany is not a great fighting country. All the nations that have power that can be mobilized are going to be members of this League, including the United States. And what do they unite for? They enter into a solemn promise to one another that they will never use their power against one another for aggression; that they never will impair the territorial integrity of a neighbor; that they never will interfere with the political independence of a neighbor; that they will abide by the principle that great populations are entitled to determine their own destiny and that they will not interfere with that destiny; and that no matter what differences arise amongst them they will never resort to war without first having done one or other of two things—either submitted the matter of controversy to arbitration, in which case they agree to abide by the result without question, or submitted it to the consideration of the council of the League of Nations, laying before that council all the documents, all the facts, agreeing that the council can publish the documents and the facts to the whole world, agreeing that there shall be six months allowed for the mature consideration of those facts by the council, and agreeing that at the expiration of the six months, even if they are not then ready to accept the advice of the council with regard to the settlement of the dispute, they will still not go to war for another three months. In other words, they consent, no matter what happens, to submit every matter of difference between them to the judgment of mankind, and just so certainly as they do that, my fellow citizens, war will be in the far background, war will be pushed out of that foreground of terror in which it has kept the world for generation after generation, and men will know that there will be a calm time of deliberate counsel. The most dangerous thing for a bad cause is to expose it to the opinion of the world. The most certain way that you can prove that a man is mistaken is by letting all his neighbors know what he thinks, by letting all his neighbors discuss what he thinks, and if he is in the wrong you will notice that he will stay at home, he will not walk on the street. He will be afraid of the eyes of his neighbors. He will be afraid of their judgment of his character. He will know that his cause is lost unless he can sustain it by the arguments of right and of justice. The same law that applies to individuals applies to nations.

But, you say, "We have heard that we might be at a disadvantage in the League of Nations." Well, whoever told you that either was deliberately falsifying or he had not read the Covenant of the League of Nations. I leave him the choice. I want to give you a very simple account of the organization of the League of Nations and let you judge for yourselves. It is a very simple organization. The power of the League, or rather the activities of the League, lie in two bodies. There is the council, which consists of one representative from each of the principal allied and associated powers—that is to say, the United States, Great Britain, France, Italy, and Japan, along with four other representatives of smaller powers chosen out of the general body of the membership of the League. The council is the source of every active policy of the League, and no active policy of the League can be adopted without a unanimous vote of the council. That is explicitly stated in the Covenant itself. Does it not evidently follow that the League of Nations can adopt no policy whatever without the consent of the United States? The affirmative vote of the representative of the United States is necessary in every case. Now, you have heard of six votes belonging to the British Empire. Those six votes are not in the council. They are in the assembly, and the interesting thing is that the assembly does not vote. I must qualify that statement a little, but essentially it is absolutely true. In every matter in which the assembly is given a voice, and there are only four or five, its vote does not count unless concurred in by the representatives of all the nations represented on the council, so that there is no validity to any vote of the assembly unless in that vote also the representative of the United States concurs. That one vote of the United States is as big as the six votes of the British Empire. I am not jealous for advantage, my fellow citizens, but I think that is a perfectly safe situation. There is no validity in a vote, either by the council or the assembly, in which we do not concur. So much for the statements about the six votes of the British Empire.

Look at it in another aspect. The assembly is the talking body. The assembly was created in order that anybody that purposed anything wrong should be subjected to the awkward circumstance that everybody could talk about it. This is the great assembly in which all the things that are likely to disturb the peace of the world or the good understanding between nations are to be exposed to the general view, and I want to ask you if you think it was unjust, unjust to the United States, that speaking parts should be assigned to the several portions of the British Empire? Do you think it unjust that there should be some spokesman in debate for that fine little stout Republic down in the Pacific, New Zealand? Do you think it was unjust that Australia should be allowed to stand up and take part in the debate — Australia, from which we have learned some of the most useful progressive policies of modern time, a little nation only five million in a great continent, but counting for several times five in its activities and in its interest in liberal reform? Do you think it unjust that the little Republic down in South Africa, whose gallant resistance to being subjected to any outside authority at all we admired for so many months and whose fortunes we followed with such interest, should have a speaking part? Great Britain obliged South Africa to submit to her sovereignty, but she immediately after that felt that it was convenient and right to hand the whole self-government of that colony over to the very men whom she had beaten. The representatives of South Africa in Paris were two of the most distinguished generals of the Boer Army, two of the realest men I ever met, two men that could talk sober counsel and wise advice, along with the best statesmen in Europe. To exclude General Botha and General Smuts from the right to stand up in the parliament of the world and say something concerning the affairs of mankind would be absurd. And what about Canada? Is not Canada a good neighbor? I ask you, Is not Canada more likely to agree with the United States than with Great Britain? Canada has a speaking part. And then, for the first time in the history of the world, that great voiceless multitude, that throng hundreds of millions strong in India, has a voice, and I want to testify that some of the wisest and most dignified figures in the peace conference at Paris came from India, men who seemed to carry in their minds an older wisdom than the rest of us had, whose traditions ran back into so many of the unhappy fortunes of mankind that they seemed very useful counselors as to how some ray of hope and some prospect of happiness could be opened to its people. I for my part have no jealousy whatever of those five speaking parts in the assembly. Those speaking parts cannot translate themselves into five votes that can in any matter override the voice and purpose of the United States.

Let us sweep aside all this language of jealousy. Let us be big enough to know the facts and to welcome the facts, because the facts are based upon the principle that America has always fought for, namely, the equality of self-governing peoples, whether they were big or little—not counting men, but counting rights, not counting representation, but counting the purpose of that representation. When you hear an opinion quoted you do not count the number of persons who hold it; you ask, "Who said that?" You weigh opinions, you do not count them, and the beauty of all democracies is that every voice can be heard, every voice can have its effect, every voice can contribute to the general judgment that is finally arrived at. That is the object of democracy. Let us accept what America has always fought for, and accept it with pride that America showed the way and made the proposal. I do not mean that America made the proposal in this particular instance; I mean that the principle was an American principle, proposed by America.

When you come to the heart of the Covenant, my fellow citizens, you will find it in Article X, and I am very much interested to know that the other things have been blown away like bubbles. There is nothing in the other contentions with regard to the League of Nations, but there is something in Article X that you ought to realize and ought to accept or reject. Article X is the heart of the whole matter. What is Article X? I never am certain that I can from memory give a literal repetition of its language, but I am sure that I can give an exact interpretation of its meaning. Article X provides that every member of the League covenants to respect and preserve the territorial integrity and existing political independence of every other member of the League as against external aggression. Not against internal disturbance. There was not a man at that table who did not admit the sacredness of the right of self-determination, the sacredness of the right of any body of people to say that they would not continue to live under the Government they were then living under, and under Article XI of the Covenant they are given a place to say whether they will live under it or not. For following Article X is Article XI, which makes it the right of any member of the League at any time to call attention to anything, anywhere, that is likely to disturb the peace of the world or the good understanding between nations upon which the peace of the world depends. I want to give you an illustration of what that would mean.

You have heard a great deal—something that was true and a great deal that was false—about that provision of the treaty which hands over to Japan the rights which Germany enjoyed in the Province of Shantung in China. In the first place, Germany did not enjoy any rights there that other nations had not already claimed. For my part, my judgment, my moral judgment, is against the whole set of concessions. They were all of them unjust to China, they ought never to have been exacted, they were all exacted by duress, from a great body of thoughtful and ancient and helpless people. There never was any right in any of them. Thank God, America never asked for any, never dreamed of asking for any. But when Germany got this concession in 1898, the Government of the United States made no protest whatever. That was not because the Government of the United States was not in the hands of high-minded and conscientious men. It was. William McKinley was President and John Hay was Secretary of State—as safe hands to leave the honor of the United States in as any that you can cite. They made no protest because the state of international law at that time was that it was none of their business unless they could show that the interests of the United States were affected, and the only thing that they could show with regard to the interests of the United States was that Germany might close the doors of Shantung Province against the trade of the United States. They, therefore, demanded and obtained promises that we could continue to sell merchandise in Shantung. Immediately following that concession to Germany there was a concession to Russia of the same sort, of Port Arthur, and Port Arthur was handed over subsequently to Japan on the very territory of the United States. Don't you remember that when Russia and Japan got into war with one another the war was brought to a conclusion by a treaty written at Portsmouth, N. H., and in that treaty without the slightest intimation from any authoritative sources in America that the Government of the United States had any objection, Port Arthur, Chinese territory, was turned over to Japan? I want you distinctly to understand that there is no thought of criticism in my mind. I am expounding to you a state of international law. Now, read Articles X and XI. You will see that international law is revolutionized by putting morals into it. Article X says that no member of the League, and that includes all these nations that have demanded these things unjustly of China, shall impair the territorial integrity or the political independence of any other member of the League. China is going to be a member of the League. Article XI says that any member of the League can call attention to anything that is likely to disturb the peace of the world or the good understanding between nations, and China is for the first time in the history of mankind afforded a standing before the jury of the world. I, for my part, have a profound sympathy for China, and I am proud to have taken part in an arrangement which promises the protection of the world to the rights of China. The whole atmosphere of the world is changed by a thing like that, my fellow citizens. The whole international practice of the world is revolutionized.

But you will say, "What is the second sentence of Article X? That is what gives very disturbing thoughts." The second sentence is that the council of the League shall advise what steps, if any, are necessary to carry out the guarantee of the first sentence, namely, that the members will respect and preserve the territorial integrity and political independence of the other members. I do not know any other meaning for the word "advise" except "advise." The council advises, and it cannot advise without the vote of the United States. Why gentlemen should fear that the Congress of the United States would be advised to do something that it did not want to do I frankly cannot imagine, because they cannot even be advised to do anything unless their own representative has participated in the advice. It may be that that will impair somewhat the vigor of the League, but, nevertheless, the fact is so, that we are not obliged to take any advice except our own, which to any man who wants to go his own course is a very satisfactory state of affairs. Every man regards his own advice as best, and I dare say every man mixes his own advice with some thought of his own interest. Whether we use it wisely or unwisely, we can use the vote of the United States to make impossible drawing the United States into any enterprise that she does not care to be drawn into.

Yet Article X strikes at the taproot of war. Article X is a statement that the very things that have always been sought in imperialistic wars are henceforth forgone by every ambitious nation in the world. I would have felt very lonely, my fellow countrymen, and I would have felt very much disturbed if, sitting at the peace table in Paris, I had supposed that I was expounding my own ideas. Whether you believe it or not, I know the relative size of my own ideas; I know how they stand related in bulk and proportion to the moral judgments of my fellow countrymen, and I proposed nothing whatever at the peace table at Paris that I had not sufficiently certain knowledge embodied the moral judgment of the citizens of the United States. I had gone over there with, so to say, explicit instructions. Don't you remember that we laid down fourteen points which should contain the principles of the settlement? They were not my points. In every one of them I was conscientiously trying to read the thought of the people of the United States, and after I uttered those points I had every assurance given me that could be given me that they did speak the moral judgment of the United States and not my single judgment. Then when it came to that critical period just a little less than a year ago, when it was evident that the war was coming to its critical end, all the nations engaged in the war accepted those fourteen principles explicitly as the basis of the armistice and the basis of the peace. In those circumstances I crossed the ocean under bond to my own people and to the other governments with which I was dealing. The whole specification of the method of settlement was written down and accepted beforehand, and we were architects building on those specifications. It reassures me and fortifies my position to find how before I went over men whose judgment the United States has often trusted were of exactly the same opinion that I went abroad to express. Here is something I want to read from Theodore Roosevelt:

"The one effective move for obtaining peace is by an agreement among all the great powers in which each should pledge itself not only to abide by the decisions of a common tribunal but to back its decisions by force. The great civilized nations should combine by solemn agreement in a great world league for the peace of righteousness; a court should be established. A changed and amplified Hague court would meet the requirements, composed of representatives from each nation, whose representatives are sworn to act as judges in each case and not in a representative capacity." Now there is Article X. He goes on and says this: "The nations should agree on certain rights that should not be questioned, such as territorial integrity, their right to deal with their domestic affairs, and with such matters as whom they should admit to citizenship. All such [should?] guarantee each of their number in possession of these rights."

Now, the other specification is in the Covenant. The Covenant in another portion guarantees to the members the independent control of their domestic questions. There is not a leg for these gentlemen to stand on when they say that the interests of the United States are not safeguarded in the very points where we are most sensitive. You do not need to be told again that the Covenant expressly says that nothing in this Covenant shall be construed as affecting the validity of the Monroe Doctrine, for example. You could not be more explicit than that. And every point of interest is covered, partly for one very interesting reason. This is not the first time that the Foreign Relations Committee of the Senate of the United States has read and considered this Covenant. I brought it to this country in March last in a tentative, provisional form, in practically the form that it now has, with the exception of certain additions which I shall mention immediately. I asked the Foreign Relations Committees of both Houses to come to the White House and we spent a long evening in the frankest discussion of every portion that they wished to discuss. They made certain specific suggestions as to what should be contained in this document when it was to be revised. I carried those suggestions to Paris, and every one of them was adopted. What more could I have done? What more could have been obtained? The very matters upon which these gentlemen were most concerned were, the right of withdrawal, which is now expressly stated; the safeguarding of the Monroe Doctrine, which is now accomplished; the exclusion from action by the League of domestic questions, which is now accomplished. All along the line, every suggestion of the United States was adopted after the Covenant had been drawn up in its first form and had been published for the criticism of the world. There is a very true sense in which I can say this is a tested American document.

I am dwelling upon these points, my fellow citizens, in spite of the fact that I dare say to most of you they are perfectly well known, because in order to meet the present situation we have got to know what we are dealing with. We are not dealing with the kind of document which this is represented by some gentlemen to be; and inasmuch as we are dealing with a document simon-pure in respect of the very principles we have professed and lived up to, we have got to do one or other of two things—we have got to adopt it or reject it. There is no middle course. You cannot go in on a special-privilege basis of your own. I take it that you are too proud to ask to be exempted from responsibilities which the other members of the League will carry. We go in upon equal terms or we do not go in at all; and if we do not go in, my fellow citizens, think of the tragedy of that result—the only sufficient guarantee to the peace of the world withheld! Ourselves drawn apart with that dangerous pride which means that we shall be ready to take care of ourselves, and that means that we shall maintain great standing armies and an irresistible navy; that means we shall have the organization of a military nation; that means we shall have a general staff, with the kind of power that the general staff of Germany had; to mobilize this great manhood of the Nation when it pleases, all the energy of our young men drawn into the thought and preparation for war. What of our pledges to the men that lie dead in France? We said that they went over there not to prove the prowess of America or her readiness for another war but to see to it that there never was such a war again. It always seems to make it difficult for me to say anything, my fellow citizens, when I think of my clients in this case. My clients are the children; my clients are the next generation. They do not know what promises and bonds I undertook when I ordered the armies of the United States to the soil of France, but I know, and I intend to redeem my pledges to the children; they shall not be sent upon a similar errand.

Again and again, my fellow citizens, mothers who lost their sons in France have come to me and, taking my hand, have shed tears upon it not only, but they have added, "God bless you, Mr. President!" Why, my fellow citizens, should they pray God to bless me? I advised the Congress of the United States to create the situation that led to the death of their sons. I ordered their sons oversea. I consented to their sons being put in the most difficult parts of the battle line, where death was certain, as in the impenetrable difficulties of the forest of Argonne. Why should they weep upon my hand and call down the blessings of God upon me? Because they believe that their boys died for something that vastly transcends any of the immediate and palpable objects of the war. They believe, and they rightly believe, that their sons saved the liberty of the world. They believe that wrapped up with the liberty of the world is the continuous protection of that liberty by the concerted powers of all civilized people. They believe that this sacrifice was made in order that other sons should not be called upon for a similar gift—the gift of life, the gift of all that died—and if we did not see this thing through, if we fulfilled the dearest present wish of Germany and now dissociated ourselves from those alongside whom we fought in the war, would not something of the halo go away from the gun over the mantelpiece, or the sword? Would not the old uniform lose something of its significance? These men were crusaders. They were not going forth to prove the might of the United States. They were going forth to prove the might of justice and right, and all the world accepted them as crusaders, and their transcendent achievement has made all the world believe in America as it believes in no other nation organized in the modern world. There seems to me to stand between us and the rejection or qualification of this treaty the serried ranks of those boys in khaki, not only these boys who came home, but those dear ghosts that still deploy upon the fields of France.

My friends, on last Decoration Day I went to a beautiful hillside near Paris, where was located the cemetery of Suresnes, a cemetery given over to the burial of the American dead. Behind me on the slopes was rank upon rank of living American soldiers, and lying before me upon the levels of the plain was rank upon rank of departed American soldiers. Right by the side of the stand where I spoke there was a little group of French women who had adopted those graves, had made themselves mothers of those dear ghosts by putting flowers every day upon those graves, taking them as their own sons, their own beloved, because they had died in the same cause—France was free and the world was free because America had come! I wish some men in public life who are now opposing the settlement for which these men died could visit such a spot as that. I wish that the thought that comes out of those graves could penetrate their consciousness. I wish that they could feel the moral obligation that rests upon us not to go back on those boys, but to see the thing through, to see it through to the end and make good their redemption of the world. For nothing less depends upon this decision, nothing less than the liberation and salvation of the world.

You will say, "Is the League an absolute guarantee against war?" No; I do not know any absolute guarantee against the errors of human judgment or the violence of human passion, but I tell you this: With a cooling space of nine months for human passion, not much of it will keep hot. I had a couple of friends who were in the habit of losing their tempers, and when they lost their tempers they were in the habit of using very unparliamentary language. Some of their friends induced them to make a promise that they never would swear inside the town limits. When the impulse next came upon them, they took a streetcar to go out of town to swear, and by the time they got out of town they did not want to swear. They came back convinced that they were just what they were, a couple of unspeakable fools, and the habit of getting angry and of swearing suffered great inroads upon it by that experience. Now, illustrating the great by the small, that is true of the passions of nations. It is true of the passions of men however you combine them. Give them space to cool off. I ask you this: If it is not an absolute insurance against war, do you want no insurance at all? Do you want nothing? Do you want not only no probability that war will not recur, but the probability that it will recur? The arrangements of justice do not stand of themselves, my fellow citizens. The arrangements of this treaty are jŭst, but they need the support of the combined power of the great nations of the world. And they will have that support. Now that the mists of this great question have cleared away, I believe that men will see the truth, eye to eye and face to face. There is one thing that the American people always rise to and extend their hand to, and that is the truth of justice and of liberty and of peace. We have accepted that truth and we are going to be led by it, and it is going to lead us, and through us the world, out into pastures of quietness and peace such as the world never dreamed of before.

D. THE SENATE BATTLE
OVER RESERVATIONS

DOCUMENT 135

"The Door Will Probably Then Be Open. . . ."

While Wilson, isolated and out of touch with political realities, slowly recovered from his narrow brush with death,

---

Letter to Gilbert M. Hitchcock, in *Congressional Record*, LVIII (November 19, 1919), 8768.

Senator Lodge carefully mobilized the anti-treaty forces. Whether Lodge hoped to reject the treaty completely is not clear, but he was determined to attach to it a series of Republican reservations clarifying the treaty—and particularly the Covenant—with respect to American interests. Wilson believed that these reservations were unnecessary, and in a few cases positively harmful, and that they represented simply a partisan attempt to embarrass his administration. Recalling the enthusiasm of the crowds on his western tour, he could not bring himself to believe that the Senate would dare reject the treaty. On November 18, the day before the Senate was to vote on the treaty, he instructed his minority leader in the Senate, Gilbert M. Hitchcock of Nebraska, to stand firm against the Lodge reservations —or, indeed, against any compromise with the more mild reservationists.

You were good enough to bring me word that the Democratic Senators supporting the treaty expected to hold a conference before the final vote on the Lodge resolution of ratification and that they would be glad to receive a word of counsel from me.

I should hesitate to offer it in any detail, but I assume that the Senators only desire my judgment upon the all-important question of the final vote on the resolution containing the many reservations by Senator Lodge. On that I can not hesitate, for, in my opinion, the resolution in that form does not provide for ratification but, rather, for the nullification of the treaty. I sincerely hope that the friends and supporters of the treaty will vote against the Lodge resolution of ratification.

I understand that the door will probably then be open for a genuine resolution of ratification.

I trust that all true friends of the treaty will refuse to support the Lodge resolution.

DOCUMENT 136

"Personally, I Do Not Accept the Action of the Senate . . . as the Decision of the Nation"

Ailing and isolated, and angry over the rebuff by the Senate, which had rejected the treaty by a party-line vote on November 19, Wilson continued to resist compromise. He was convinced that his enemies were not interested in any compromise he could accept. For a time the President toyed with a fantastic scheme to submit the issue to the country by demanding the resignation of those Senators who had opposed the treaty and having them seek immediate re-election on the basis of their record. If an anti-treaty majority should then be returned, Wilson would resign at once, leaving the way open for the accession to the Presidency of a Republican Secretary of State. His advisers talked him out of this impractical resort to parliamentary government. Wilson, however, continued to believe that the best hope for the treaty lay in submitting the issue to the electorate, and in an uncompromising letter dispatched to the Democratic Jackson Day dinner on January 8, 1920, he suggested making the 1920 national elections "a great and solemn referendum" on the issue.

It is with the keenest regret that I find that I am to be deprived of the pleasure and privilege of joining you and the other loyal Democrats who are to assemble to-night to celebrate Jackson Day and renew their vows of fidelity to the great principles of our party, the principles which must

---

Letter to Homer S. Cummings, January 8, 1920, *Public Papers*, VI, 453–456.

now fulfill the hopes not only of our own people but of the world.

The United States enjoyed the spiritual leadership of the world until the Senate of the United States failed to ratify the treaty by which the belligerent nations sought to effect the settlements for which they had fought throughout the war.

It is inconceivable that at this supreme crisis and final turning point in the international relations of the whole world, when the results of the Great War are by no means determined and are still questionable and dependent upon events which no man can foresee or count upon, the United States should withdraw from the concert of progressive and enlightened nations by which Germany was defeated, and all similar Governments (if the world be so unhappy as to contain any) warned of the consequences of any attempt at a like iniquity, and yet that is the effect of the course which the United States has taken with regard to the Treaty of Versailles.

Germany is beaten, but we are still at war with her and the old stage is reset for a repetition of the old plot. It is now ready for a resumption of the old offensive and defensive alliances which made settled peace impossible. It is now open again to every sort of intrigue.

The old spies are free to resume their former abominable activities. They are again at liberty to make it impossible for Governments to be sure what mischief is being worked among their own people, what internal disorders are being fomented.

Without the Covenant of the League of Nations there may be as many secret treaties as ever, to destroy the confidence of Governments in each other, and their validity cannot be questioned.

None of the objects we professed to be fighting for has been secured, or can be made certain of, without this Nation's ratification of the treaty and its entry into the Covenant. This Nation entered the Great War to vindicate its own rights and to protect and preserve free government. It went into the war to see it through to the end, and the end has not yet come. It went into the war to make an end of militarism, to furnish guarantees to weak nations, and to make a just and lasting peace. It entered it with noble enthusiasm. Five of the leading belligerents have accepted the treaty and formal ratifications soon will be exchanged. The question is whether this country will enter and enter whole-heartedly. If it does not do so, the United States and Germany will play a lone hand in the world.

The maintenance of the peace of the world and the effective execution of the treaty depend upon the whole-hearted participation of the United States. I am not stating it as a matter of power. The point is that the United States is the only Nation which has sufficient moral force with the rest of the world to guarantee the substitution of discussion for war. If we keep out of this agreement, if we do not give our guarantees, then another attempt will be made to crush the new nations of Europe.

I do not believe that this is what the people of this country wish or will be satisfied with. Personally, I do not accept the action of the Senate of the United States as the decision of the Nation.

I have asserted from the first that the overwhelming majority of the people of this country desire the ratification of the treaty, and my impression to that effect has recently been confirmed by the unmistakable evidences of public opinion given during my visit to seventeen of the States.

I have endeavored to make it plain that if the Senate wishes to say what the undoubted meaning of the League is I shall have no objection. There can be no reasonable objection to interpretations accompanying the act of ratification itself. But when the treaty is acted upon, I must know whether it means that we have ratified or rejected it.

We cannot rewrite this treaty. We must take it without changes which alter its meaning, or leave it, and then, after the rest of the world has signed it, we must face the unthinkable task of making another and separate treaty with Germany.

But no mere assertions with regard to the wish and opinion of the country are credited. If there is any doubt as to what the people of the country think on this vital matter, the clear and single way out is to submit it for determination at the next election to the voters of the Nation, to give the next election the form of a great and solemn referendum, a referendum as to the part the United States is to play in completing the settlements of the war and in the prevention in the future of such outrages as Germany attempted to perpetrate.

We have no more moral right to refuse now to take part in the execution and administration of these settlements than we had to refuse to take part in the fighting of the last few weeks of the war which brought victory and made it possible to dictate to Germany what the settlements should be. Our fidelity to our associates in the war is in question and the whole future of mankind. It will be heartening to the whole world to know the attitude and purpose of the people of the United States.

I spoke just now of the spiritual leadership of the United States, thinking of international affairs. But there is another spiritual leadership which is open to us and which we can assume.

The world has been made safe for democracy, but democracy has not been finally vindicated. All sorts of crimes are being committed in its name, all sorts of preposterous perversions of its doctrines and practices are being attempted.

This, in my judgment, is to be the great privilege of the democracy of the United States, to show that it can lead the way in the solution of the great social and industrial problems of our time, and lead the way to a happy, settled order of life as well as to political liberty. The program for this achievement we must attempt to formulate, and in carrying it out we shall do more than can be done in any other way to sweep out of existence the tyrannous and arbitrary forms of power which are now masquerading under the name of popular government.

Whenever we look back to Andrew Jackson we should draw fresh inspiration from his character and example. His mind grasped with such a splendid definiteness and firmness the principles of national authority and national action. He was so indomitable in his purpose to give reality to the principles of the Government, that this is a very fortunate time to recall his career and to renew our vows of faithfulness to the principles and the pure practices of democracy.

I rejoice to join you in this renewal of faith and purpose. I hope that the whole evening may be of the happiest results as regards the fortunes of our party and the Nation.

DOCUMENT 137

"I Realize That Negative Criticism Is Not All That Is Called For. . ."

Wilson's Jackson Day letter was regarded by many as more uncompromising than he probably intended. Even some Democrats objected privately (and William Jennings Bryan objected publicly) to the President's implied suggestion of

---

Letter to Gilbert M. Hitchcock, January 26, 1920, *Public Papers*, VI, 460–461.

deferring further action on the treaty until after the 1920 elections. When Wilson learned from his minority leader, Senator Hitchcock, that negotiations were under way to find a possible compromise, he responded with a letter agreeing to several innocuous interpretive reservations but refusing any reservation with respect to the crucial Article 10, which he considered the heart of the Covenant. The compromise negotiations collapsed in the face of Wilson's unyielding attitude and—even more important—the bitter opposition of Republican irreconcilables.

I have greatly appreciated your thoughtful kindness in keeping me informed concerning the conferences you and some of your colleagues have had with spokesmen of the Republican Party concerning the possibility of ratification of the treaty of peace, and send this line in special appreciative acknowledgment of your letter of the twenty-second. I return the clipping you were kind enough to enclose.

To the substance of it I, of course, adhere. I am bound to. Like yourself I am solemnly sworn to obey and maintain the Constitution of the United States. But I think the form of it very unfortunate. Any reservation or resolution stating that "The United States assumes no obligation under such and such an Article unless or except" would, I am sure, chill our relationship with the nations with which we expect to be associated in the great enterprise of maintaining the world's peace.

That association must in any case, my dear Senator, involve very serious and far-reaching implications of honor and duty which I am sure we shall never in fact be desirous of ignoring. It is the more important not to create the impression that we are trying to escape obligations.

But I realize that negative criticism is not all that is called for in so serious a matter. I am happy to be able to add, therefore, that I have once more gone over the reservations proposed by yourself, the copy of which I return herewith, and am glad to say that I can accept them as they stand.

I have never seen the slightest reason to doubt the good faith of our associates in the war, nor ever had the slightest reason to fear that any nation would seek to enlarge our obligations under the Covenant of the League of Nations, or seek to commit us to lines of action which, under our Constitution, only the Congress of the United States can in the last analysis decide.

May I suggest that with regard to the possible withdrawal of the United States it would be wise to give to the President the right to act upon a resolution of Congress in the matter of withdrawal? In other words, it would seem to be permissible and advisable that any resolution giving notice of withdrawal should be a joint rather than a concurrent resolution.

I doubt whether the President can be deprived of his veto power under the Constitution, even with his own consent. The use of a joint resolution would permit the President, who is, of course, charged by the Constitution with the conduct of foreign policy, to merely exercise a voice in saying whether so important a step as withdrawal from the League of Nations should be accomplished by a majority or by a two-thirds vote.

The Constitution itself providing that the legislative body was to be consulted in treaty-making and having prescribed a two-thirds vote in such cases, it seems to me that there should be no unnecessary departure from the method there indicated.

I see no objection to a frank statement that the United States can accept a mandate with regard to any territory under Article XIII, Part 1, or any other provision of the treaty of peace, only by the direct authority and action of the Congress of the United States.

I hope, my dear Senator, that you will never hesitate to call upon me for any assistance that I can render in this or any other public matter.

DOCUMENT 138

The Final Senate Vote

Strong pressure from pro-League forces around the country forced Senate leaders to agree to a reconsideration of the treaty. Shortly before the second vote on March 19, Wilson snuffed out the last hope for ratification with a ringing appeal to his followers to stand fast against both the "nullifiers" and the "mild-nullifiers." He thus killed any lingering impulse for compromise on the part of mild-reservationist Republicans.

I understand that one or two of your colleagues do me the honor of desiring to know what my views are with reference to Article X of the League of Nations and the effect upon the League of the adoption of certain reservations to that article. I welcome the opportunity to throw any light I can upon a subject which has become so singularly beclouded by misapprehensions and misinterpretations of every kind.

There is no escaping the moral obligations which are expressed in positive terms in this article of the Covenant. We won a moral victory over Germany, far greater even than the military victory won on the field of battle, because the opinion of the whole world swung to our support and

Letter to Gilbert M. Hitchcock, March 8, 1920, in *Chronology of Woodrow Wilson*, comp. John R. Bolling (New York: Frederick A. Stokes Company, 1927), 332–338.

the support of the nations associated with us in the great struggle. It did so because of our common profession and promise that we meant to establish an organization of peace, which should make it certain that the combined power of free nations would check every invasion of right, and serve to make peace and justice the more secure by affording a definite tribunal of opinion to which all must submit and by which every international readjustment that cannot be amicably agreed upon by the people directly concerned shall be sanctioned.

This promise and assurance were written into the preliminaries of the armistice and into the preliminaries of the peace itself and constitute one of the most sacred obligations ever assumed by any nation or body of nations. It is unthinkable that America should set the example of ignoring such a solemn moral engagement.

For myself, I feel that I could not look the soldiers of our gallant armies in the face again if I did not do everything in my power to remove every obstacle that lies in the way of the adoption of this particular article of the Covenant, because we made these pledges to them as well as to the rest of the world, and it was to this cause they deemed themselves devoted in a spirit of crusaders. I should be forever unfaithful to them if I did not do my utmost to fulfill the high purpose for which they fought.

I think, my dear Senator, we can dismiss from our minds the idea that it is necessary to stipulate in connection with Article X the constitutional methods we should use in fulfilling our obligations under it. We gain nothing by such stipulations and secure nothing which is not already secured. It was understood as a matter of course at the conference in Paris that whatever obligations any Government assumed or whatever duties it understood under the treaty would of course have to be fulfilled by its usual and established constitutional methods of action.

Once or twice in meetings of the conference, when the treaty was under consideration, "reservations" were made to that effect by the representatives of individual powers, and those "reservations" were invariably received in the way in which men who have met for business and not for talk always receive acts of scrupulous supererogation — listened to with indifferent silence, as such men listen to what is a matter of course and was not necessary to say.

There can be no objection to explaining again what our constitutional method is and that our Congress alone can declare or determine the causes or occasions for war, and that it alone can authorize the use of the armed forces of the United States on land or on the sea. But to make such a declaration would certainly be a work of supererogation.

I am sorry to say that the reservations that have come under my notice are almost without exception not interpretations of the articles to which it is proposed to attach them but in effect virtual nullifications of those articles.

Any reservation which seeks to deprive the League of Nations of the force of Article X cuts at the heart and life of the Covenant itself. Any League of Nations which does not guarantee as a matter of incontestable right the political independence and integrity of each of its members might be hardly more than a futile scrap of paper, as ineffective in operation as the agreement between Belgium and Germany which the Germans violated in 1914.

Article X, as written into the Treaty of Versailles, represents the renunciation by Great Britain and Japan, which before the war had begun to find so many interests in common in the Pacific; by France, by Italy, by all the great fighting powers of the world of the old pretensions of political conquest and territorial aggrandizement. It is a new doctrine in the world's affairs and must be recognized or there is no secure basis for the peace which the whole world so desperately needs.

If Article X is not adopted and acted upon, the Governments which reject it will, I think, be guilty of bad faith to their people, whom they induced to make the infinite sacrifices of the war by the pledge that they would be fighting to redeem the world from the old order of force and aggression. They will be acting also in bad faith to the opinion of the world at large, to which they appealed for support in a concerted stand against the aggressions and pretensions of Germany.

If we were to reject Article X, or so to weaken it as to take its full force out of it, it would mark us as desiring to return to the old world of jealous rivalry and misunderstandings from which our gallant soldiers have rescued us and would leave us without any vision or new conception of justice and peace. We would have learned no lesson from the war, but gained only the regret that it had involved us in its maelstrom of suffering. If America has awakened, as the rest of the world has, to the vision of a new day in which the mistakes of the past are to be corrected, it will welcome the opportunity to share the responsibilities of Article X.

It must not be forgotten, Senator, that the article constitutes a renunciation of all ambition on the part of powerful nations with whom we were associated in the war. It is by no means certain that without this article any such renunciation will take place. Militaristic ambitions and imperialistic policies are by no means dead, even in counsels of the nations whom we most trust and with whom we most desire to be associated in the tasks of peace.

Throughout the sessions of the conference in Paris it was evident that a militaristic party, under the most influential leadership, was seeking to gain ascendancy in the counsels of France. They were defeated then, but are in control now. The chief arguments advanced in Paris in support of the Italian claims on the Adriatic were strategic arguments; that is to say, military arguments, which had at their back the thought of naval supremacy in that sea. For my own part I am as intolerant of imperialistic designs on the part of other nations as I was of such designs on the part of Germany.

The choice is between two ideals; on the one hand, the ideal of democracy, which represents the rights of free peoples everywhere to govern themselves, and, on the other hand, the ideal of imperialism, which seeks to dominate by force and unjust power, an ideal which is by no means dead and which is earnestly held in many quarters still.

Every imperialistic influence in Europe was hostile to the embodiment of Article X, in the Covenant of the League of Nations, and its defeat now would mark the complete consummation of their efforts to nullify the treaty. I hold the doctrine of Article X, as the essence of Americanism. We cannot repudiate it or weaken it without at the same time repudiating our own principles.

The imperialist wants no League of Nations, but if, in response to the universal cry of the masses everywhere, there is to be one, he is interested to secure one suited to his own purposes, one that will permit him to continue the historic game of pawns and peoples — the juggling of provinces, the old balance of power, and the inevitable wars attendant upon these things.

The reservation proposed would perpetuate the old order. Does anyone really want to see the old game played again? Can any one really venture to take part in reviving the old order? The enemies of a League of Nations have by every true instinct centered their efforts against Article X, for it is undoubtedly the foundation of the whole structure. It is the bulwark, and the only bulwark, of the rising democracy of the world against the forces of imperialism and reaction.

Either we should enter the League fearlessly, accepting the responsibility and not fearing the rôle of leadership, which we now enjoy, contributing our efforts toward establishing a just and permanent peace, or we should retire as gracefully as possible from the great concert of powers by which the world was saved. For my own part, I am not willing to trust to the counsel of diplomats the working out of any salvation of the world from the things which it has suffered.

I believe that when the full significance of this great question has been generally apprehended, obstacles will seem insignificant before the opportunity, a great and glorious opportunity, to contribute our overwhelming moral and material force to the establishment of an international régime in which our own ideals of justice and right may be made to prevail and the nations of the world be allowed a peaceful development under conditions of order and safety hitherto impossible.

I need not say, Senator, that I have given a great deal of thought to the whole matter of reservations proposed in connection with the ratification of the treaty and particularly that portion of the treaty which contains the Covenant of the League of Nations, and I have been struck by the fact that practically every so-called reservation was in effect a rather sweeping nullification of the terms of the treaty itself.

I hear of reservationists and mild-reservationists, but I cannot understand the difference between a nullifier and a mild-nullifier. Our responsibility as a nation in this turning point of history is an overwhelming one, and if I had the opportunity, I would beg everyone concerned to consider the matter in the light of what it is possible to accomplish for humanity, rather than in the light of special national interest.

If I have been truly informed concerning the desire of some of your colleagues to know my views in this matter, I would be very glad if you should show this letter to them.

E. THE 1920 ELECTIONS

DOCUMENT 139

"This Election Is to Be
a Genuine National Referendum"

The Senate's second rejection of the Versailles Treaty effectively killed Wilson's dream of American leadership to make the League of Nations a vital instrument of peace. Yet the President's stubbornness and strong partisanship were partly responsible for the debacle. Wilson continued to hope that the 1920 Presidential election would be a referendum on the treaty, and late in the campaign he appealed to the voters to use their ballots to endorse the League of Nations.

The issues of the present campaign are of such tremendous importance, of such far-reaching significance for the influence of the country and the development of its future relations, and I have necessarily had so much to do with their development, that I am sure you will think it natural and proper that I should address to you a few words concerning them.

Everyone who sincerely believes in government by the people must rejoice at the turn affairs have taken in regard to this campaign. This election is to be a genuine national referendum. The determination of a great policy upon which the influence and authority of the United States in the world must depend is not to be left to groups of politi-

---

Appeal to the country, October 3, 1920, *Public Papers*, VI, 503–505.

cians of either party, but is to be referred to the people themselves for a sovereign mandate to their representatives. They are to instruct their own Government what they wish done.

The chief question that is put to you is, of course: Do you want your country's honor vindicated and the Treaty of Versailles ratified? Do you in particular approve of the League of Nations as organized and empowered in that treaty? And do you wish to see the United States play its responsible part in it?

You have been grossly misled with regard to the treaty, and particularly with regard to the proposed character of the League of Nations, by those who have assumed the serious responsibility of opposing it. They have gone so far that those who have spent their lives, as I have spent my life, in familiarizing themselves with the history and traditions and policies of the Nation, must stand amazed at the gross ignorance and impudent audacity which have led them to attempt to invent an "Americanism" of their own, which has no foundation whatever in any of the authentic traditions of the Government.

Americanism, as they conceive it, reverses the whole process of the last few tragical years. It would substitute America for Prussia in the policy of isolation and defiant segregation. Their conception of the dignity of the Nation and its interest is that we should stand apart and watch for opportunities to advance our own interests, involve ourselves in no responsibility for the maintenance of the right in the world or for the continued vindication of any of the things for which we entered the war to fight.

The conception of the great creators of the Government was absolutely opposite to this. They thought of America as the light of the world as created to lead the world in the assertion of the rights of peoples and the rights of free nations; as destined to set a responsible example to all the world of what free Government is and can do for the maintenance of right standards, both national and international.

This light the opponents of the League would quench. They would relegate the United States to a subordinate rôle in the affairs of the world.

Why should we be afraid of responsibilities which we are qualified to sustain and which the whole of our history has constituted a promise to the world we would sustain!

This is the most momentous issue that has ever been presented to the people of the United States, and I do not doubt that the hope of the whole world will be verified by an absolute assertion by the voters of the country of the determination of the United States to live up to all the great expectations which they created by entering the war and enabling the other great nations of the world to bring it to a victorious conclusion, to the confusion of Prussianism and everything that arises out of Prussianism. Surely we shall not fail to keep the promise sealed in the death and sacrifice of our incomparable soldiers, sailors and marines who await our verdict beneath the sod of France.

Those who do not care to tell you the truth about the League of Nations tell you that Article X of the Covenant of the League would make it possible for other nations to lead us into war, whether we will it by our own independent judgment or not. This is absolutely false. There is nothing in the Covenant which in the least interferes with or impairs the rights of Congress to declare war or not declare war, according to its own independent judgment, as our Constitution provides.

Those who drew the Covenant of the League were careful that it should contain nothing which interfered with or impaired the constitutional arrangements of any of the great nations which are to constitute its members. They would have been amazed and indignant at the things that are now being ignorantly said about this great and sincere document.

The whole world will wait for your verdict in November as it would wait for an intimation of what its future is to be.

F. THE SIGNIFICANCE
OF ARMISTICE DAY

DOCUMENT 140

"The Opportunity to Retrieve the Past. . . ."

The overwhelming victory of Republican Warren G. Harding in the 1920 Presidential election revealed how wrong Wilson had been in his hope that the people would rally to his League of Nations. The election was no referendum; the issues were too many and too confused. Wilson retired quietly to his Washington home, still confident that one day the American people would awaken to their responsibilities of world leadership. On the evening of November 10, 1923, his strength ebbing, he spoke briefly from his home to the largest radio audience yet assembled. It was his last public address, for within three months he was dead.

The anniversary of Armistice Day should stir us to great exaltation of spirit because of the proud recollection that it was our day, a day above those early days of that never-to-be-forgotten November which lifted the world to the high levels of vision and achievement upon which the great war for democracy and right was fought and won, although the stimulating memories of that happy triumph

Radio address, November 10, 1923, *Public Papers*, VI, 540–541.

are forever marred and embittered for us by the shameful fact that when the victory was won—won, be it remembered, chiefly by the indomitable spirit and ungrudging sacrifices of our own incomparable soldiers—we turned our backs upon our associates and refused to bear any responsible part in the administration of peace, or the firm and permanent establishment of the results of the war—won at so terrible a cost of life and treasure—and withdrew into a sullen and selfish isolation, which is deeply ignoble because manifestly cowardly and dishonorable.

This must always be a source of deep mortification to us and we shall inevitably be forced by the moral obligations of freedom and honor to retrieve that fatal error and assume once more the rôle of courage, self-respect, and helpfulness which every true American must wish to regard as our natural part in the affairs of the world.

That we should have thus done a great wrong to civilization at one of the most critical turning points in the history of the world is the more to be deplored because every anxious year that has followed has made the exceeding need for such service as we might have rendered more and more pressing as demoralizing circumstances which we might have controlled have gone from bad to worse.

And now, as if to furnish a sort of sinister climax, France and Italy between them have made waste paper of the Treaty of Versailles, and the whole field of international relationship is in perilous confusion.

The affairs of the world can be set straight only by the firmest and most determined exhibition of the will to lead and make right prevail.

Happily, the present situation in the world of affairs affords us the opportunity to retrieve the past and to render to mankind the inestimable service of proving that there is at least one great and powerful nation which can turn away from programs of self-interest and devote itself to practicing and establishing the highest ideals of disinterested service and the consistent standards of conscience and of right.

The only way in which we can worthily give proof of our appreciation of the high significance of Armistice Day is by resolving to put self-interest away and once more formulate and act upon the highest ideals and purposes of international policy.

Thus, and only thus, can we return to the true traditions of America.

Index

553